5.95
03/
07

International acclaim for Flora Fraser's

Beloved Emma

"Excellent reading. . . . There can be little left to say after a biography of this length and thoroughness."
— *The Sunday Telegraph*

"[A] fine biography. . . . This highly readable work becomes the standard life." — *Library Journal*

"Fraser is to be heartily congratulated in telling an entirely fascinating story in which all her characters come vividly, and sometimes pitiably, to life." — *Country Life*

"A beautifully written, absorbing account."
— *The Times Educational Supplement*

"Thoroughly researched. . . . A colorful picture of the late 1700s and early 1800s."
— *The Sunday Telegram* (Worcester, MA)

ALSO BY FLORA FRASER

The Unruly Queen

FLORA FRASER

Beloved Emma

Flora Fraser is the author of a biography of Queen
Caroline, *The Unruly Queen*, and a forthcoming book
on the daughters of George III. She lives in London
with her husband and three children.

26 Apr. 1765 – 15 Jan. 1815

Beloved Emma

The Life of Emma, Lady Hamilton

FLORA FRASER

ANCHOR BOOKS
A Division of Random House, Inc.
New York

FIRST ANCHOR BOOKS EDITION, FEBRUARY 2004

Copyright © 1986 by Flora Fraser

All rights reserved under International and Pan-American Copyright Conventions.
Published in the United States by Anchor Books, a division of Random House, Inc.,
New York. Originally published in Great Britain in slightly different form under the title
Emma, Lady Hamilton by Weidenfeld and Nicolson, London, in 1986. Subsequently
published in hardcover in the United States in slightly different form under the same title
by Alfred A. Knopf, a division of Random House, Inc., New York, in 1987. This edition,
under its current title, was originally published in Great Britain by John Murray
(Publishers), a division of Hodder Headline, London, in 2003.

Anchor Books and colophon are registered trademarks of Random House, Inc.

The Library of Congress has cataloged the Knopf edition as follows:
Fraser, Flora.
Emma, Lady Hamilton / Flora Fraser.—1st American ed.
p.   cm.
Includes index and bibliography.
ISBN 0-394-53053-5
1. Hamilton, Emma, Lady, 1761?–1815.   2. Nelson, Horatio Nelson, Viscount,
1758–1805—Relations with women.   3. Hamilton, William, Sir, 1730–1803—Marriage.
4. British—Italy—Naples—History—18th century.   5. Ambassadors' spouses—Great
Britain—Biography.   6. Mistresses—Great Britain—Biography.
DA483.H3 F34 1987
941.07'3'0924—dc19   86-020947

Anchor ISBN: 1-4000-7514-9

Author photograph © Porter Gifford Photography

www.anchorbooks.com

Printed in the United States of America
10   9   8   7   6   5   4   3   2   1

For Stella, Simon and Tommy

Contents

Illustrations

Author's Note

1983

Twenty years have passed since I first went, fresh out of university and newly married, to the Wirral and to Naples and to Norfolk to research Emma Hamilton's life. I published *Beloved Emma*, the result of my findings there and elsewhere, in 1986, and I welcome this new edition as an opportunity to look over – with occasional amusement but with great fondness – this, my first biography. I have not altered, except to make minor corrections, a text that I wrote slowly, painfully and exuberantly so long ago. While I might not today pepper my text with so many Latin phrases and classical allusions, I was very pleased with them at the time. I paid less attention then than I might do now to Emma's poignant relics of Lord Nelson – especially his pigtail cut off for her at his request. My acknowledgements, still deeply felt, to those who helped me are couched in more formal terms than are in common use today. I hope that new readers will overlook these weaknesses and enjoy what I believe is still a credible account of a remarkable woman's extraordinary life.

Stories about Emma and Nelson come and go, of course, as the power of this couple's romantic association over the public mind ebbs and flows. A large early-nineteenth-century anchor brooch bearing the initials H and N was sold at Sotheby's, on Trafalgar Day 2002, for over £100,000, on the presumption that it was a gift from Nelson to Emma. Of more certain provenance – and acquired for the nation at that sale, also for over £100,000, by the National Maritime Museum – is a remarkable cache of letters from Fanny Nelson, the most interesting of them written between 1798 and 1801. They spell out this modest gentlewoman's desperate fears and mortifications as her husband, the Hero of the Nile, first dallies in Italy with the Hamiltons, and then, returning to England, spurns her.

'Tell me honestly if you think silence is the best way sometimes to answer harsh and severe letters undeserved,' Lady Nelson writes to her husband's man of business, Alexander Davison, on 2 March 1801 after Lord Nelson has rejected in no uncertain terms her offer to come and nurse his inflamed eyes. At her side, instead, wringing his hands and saying, 'My Horace was always a good boy – but he is gone a little out of the straight road,' is Nelson's ailing father, the Reverend Edmund.

These letters of Fanny's, full of domestic worries and inventories of plate and cutlery as she moves about the country, hoping against hope to set up permanent home in a good town house with her husband, make uncomfortable reading.

But *Beloved Emma* is Emma's story. And a letter from her to Alexander Davison, from this same sale, written after Nelson's death and during her days of poverty, shows her magnificent, grandiloquent and high-spirited as ever:

> He that I loved more than life, he is gone. Why then should I live or wish to live? I lived but for him. All now is a dreary prospect before me. I never lamented the loss of a kingdom (for I was Queen of Naples) for seven years; nor one sigh ever escaped me for the loss I sustained when I fell from such an height of greatness and happiness at Naples to misery and wretchedness – But all I could have sustained with firmness but the loss of Nelson. Under this dreadful weight of most wretched misery that I suffer, I feel and hope that I shall not be long after him.

Recovering herself even as she writes, and after a side-swipe at both Nelson's brother and Fanny, Emma cheers up: 'The poor old Duke [the elderly Duke of Queensberry, from whom she hoped for a legacy] has sent ten times today and wrote a most affectionate letter to me. I suppose your company are gone. Did you remember me to Sir Evan Nepean [another possible source of financial aid]?'

There has been much to relish but nothing in these letters or elsewhere to change the opinion of Emma that I formed when I was researching and writing her life, and that you will find in the following chapters of *Beloved Emma*. (From my point of view, the most interesting biographical detail to emerge – again from the Davison papers – since I wrote my book has been that a Mary Cornish 'lived servant with her ladyship, and was present at her death'.)

The other characters in Emma's story have, however, attracted attention since. For students of Romney as a romantic artist I would recommend Alex Kidson's exhibition catalogue, *George Romney* 1734–1802 (National Portrait Gallery, 2002). The exhibition and catalogue *Vases and Volcanoes: Sir William Hamilton and His Collection* by Ian Jenkins and Kim Sloan (British Museum, 1996) have added substantially to our understanding of Emma's husband and his world, as has *Fields of Fire: A Life of Sir William Hamilton* by David Constantine (2001). And mention should be made of an unusual comer into the field of Hamiltonian and Nelsonian studies, Susan Sontag's *The Volcano Lover* (1992).

Since I wrote *Beloved Emma*, Nelson has been enjoying something of a renaissance, especially as we now sail towards the bicentenary of the Battle of Trafalgar on 21 October 1805. As part of a decade of publishing leading towards this anniversary, the naval historian Colin White, who has just published *The Nelson Encyclopaedia* (2002), will in due course publish all Nelson's letters not published in Nicolas's nineteenth-century *Letters and Despatches*. With that exciting project in mind, and courtesy of Mr White and the National Maritime Museum, here is one of the unpublished letters he has unearthed in that museum library from Nelson to Emma, written on board the *Victory* on 16 March 1805:

> The ship is just parting and I take the last moment to renew my assurances to my dearest beloved Emma of my eternal love, affection and adoration, you are ever with me in my soul your resemblance is never absent from my mind, and my own dearest Emma I hope very soon that I shall embrace the substantial part of you instead of the ideal That will I am sure give us both real pleasure and exquisite happiness, longing as I do to be with you yet I am sure under the circumstances in which I am placed you would be the first to say, my Nelson try and get at those French fellows and come home with glory to your own Emma, or if they will not come out then come home for a short time and arrange your affairs which have long been neglected, don't I say, my own love, you would say. Only continue to love me as affectionately as I do you and we must then be the happiest couple in the world.

Curiously enough, while Romney, Sir William and Nelson have been the subject of enquiry and speculation, biography and exhibitions, Emma herself has not attracted, since I wrote her biography, the attention of those engaged in celebrating the lives of women of achievement. Indeed, in recent years, with the growth of interest in Nelson and even in Sir William Hamilton, there has been a tendency to revert to Victorian values, and dismiss her as a 'mere mistress'. But when the actress Harriet Walter read some of Emma's letters at the National Portrait Gallery in the summer of 2002, Emma's personality and character came alive in Miss Walter's phrasing, and this was no 'mere mistress' speaking. I hope that anyone who reads *Beloved Emma* will bear in mind that in Emma's own estimation we are dealing with a Queen of Naples – at least!

Flora Fraser
London 2003

Acknowledgements

In writing this book, I have been inspired and encouraged by books and conversations and pictures and places – in particular, Naples. To Dott. Carlo Knight and to Barone Francesco Leporano di Acton, connoisseurs of the city, I am indebted. The late Dott. Salvatore Loschiavo and Donna Maria Rosaria Capece Minutolo are among many others I must also thank for their help. If of nobody and nothing else, special mention must be made of Sir Harold Acton and his masterly evocation of the eighteenth-century city, *The Bourbons of Naples*.

Venturing into Nelson territory in England, I have been helped enormously by Mrs Lily MacCarthy and by Mr Michael Nash, editor of the *Nelson Dispatch*. Mr and Mrs James Teacher have been most kind in granting me access to the d'Avigdor Goldsmid Papers; Mollie Hardwick, herself a distinguished biographer of Emma Hamilton, and Philippa Lewis, have generously allowed me use of their invaluable research material; and Jane Flower of Phillips has made available to me an unpublished typescript of great value.

In my own researches, the British Library and its staff have been indispensable. The London Library, the Royal Commission on Historical Manuscripts, Quality Court, the Library of the National Maritime Museum, Greenwich, and the Biblioteca Nazionale, Naples, have all been most helpful. Dr Robert Guy and Dr Carlos Picón introduced me to ancient art. Charlotte Gere of the National Art Collections Fund Review, Professor Francis Haskell, of the Department of History of Art, Oxford, Alan Rubin of the Pelham Galleries, and Clive Wainwright of the Victoria and Albert Museum, have all provided most stimulating advice.

I would like to thank, in particular, my brother Orlando Fraser for his tireless researches, Sig.ra Laura Chanter, Nicola Cousins, Nicola Dahrendorf and Konrad Loewenstein. Others who have been extremely kind with their time and knowledge are: Giancarlo Alisio, Raffaele Amati, Lieutenant-Commander Charles Addis, Sir Philip Antrobus, Celia Ayres, Lady Silvia Combe, Erica Davies, the Earl Cawdor, John Eyre and Brian Bloomfield, previous and present Administrators of the National Trust at Uppark, Herr Joachim Fest, Sig. Stefano Fiorentini, the Hon. Mrs Simon Fraser, Professor Robert Ireland, Lowell Libson,

Philip Lloyd-Bostock, Candida Melly, Napier Miles, Franco Miraco, William and Gaia Mostyn-Owen, Sig.ra A. Natale, Diane Nash, Sig. and Sig.ra Ruberto, the Hon. Jacob Rothschild, Mrs James de Rothschild, Nicholas Ward-Jackson, Sarah Wimbush, Maurice Woolf, and many more.

To Richard Bates, Leonora Clarke, Maria Ellis and Monica Green, I owe an immense debt of gratitude for putting my manuscript into type. Elizabeth Burke and John Gross are due thanks for their early work on this book, as are Peter James for his intelligent copy-editing and Douglas Matthews for the index. I would also like to thank Anne McDermid for her superb professional advice. John Curtis and, especially, Linden Lawson of Weidenfeld & Nicolson have been incisive and encouraging editors; to Robert Gottlieb of Knopf Inc. for his powers of suggestion and for his constant watch over this book I am eternally grateful.

Finally I would like to thank my mother, Antonia Fraser, and my grandmother, Elizabeth Longford, for introducing me to the methods of historical research. Their example, and an enjoyable collaboration on other work with my father, Hugh Fraser, led to this book. To my husband, Robert Powell-Jones, I dedicate it.

Flora Fraser
London 1986

It has been a pleasure and a challenge to prepare this new edition of *Beloved Emma* for John Murray and Anchor Books, and I would like to thank for their advice, support and encouragement: Leonora Clarke, Lizzie Dipple, Antonia Fraser, Robert Gottlieb, Peter James, Lowell Libson, Jonathan Lloyd, Sonny Mehta, Michael Nash, Roland Philipps, John Siciliano, Peter Soros, Wendy Wasserstein and Colin White. I am grateful to Jean and Jay Kislak, Christopher Hanson-Abbott and the National Maritime Museum for permission to read and quote from letters they have recently acquired. And I would like to thank Martyn Downer, Peter Beale and Henry Wyndham for their kindness in arranging for me to read those letters after the Alexander Davison sale at Sotheby's last autumn. The text of the main body of the book is as published in 1986, bar corrections I made originally in a 1994 Papermac edition.

Flora Fraser
London 2003

Beloved Emma

CHAPTER ONE

From Hawarden to Sir Harry

Emma Hamilton began life as Emy Lyon on 26 April. That, at least, is the date she always celebrated as her birthday. As no record of her birth survives, the year of her birth is not known for sure, but her parents, Henry and Mary Lyon, were married on 11 June 1764. Emy was baptized on 12 May 1765. It seems reasonable to assume she was born in the year of her baptism.

She was born in Ness, near Denhall, on the windy Wirral Peninsula in Cheshire, overlooking the Dee estuary. The parish of Neston was described in 1809 as one of the most miserable townships on the Peninsula, a collection of hovels inhabited only by colliers. The pit at Denhall had been opened in 1750, and Henry Lyon was identified on Emy's baptismal certificate as smith 'of Ness'. Probably he worked in connection with the pit.

A tall building, known as Swan Cottage, still stands on a bank at Denhall. From the uppermost rooms, there is a fine view across the wide estuary to the northern coast of Wales. No hovel, by reason of its commanding height it was later used as a shipping beacon. However, it is reputed to have been the smith's house at this date. At the back of the house is a plaque inscribed 'I.L. S.L. 1724', so there may have been Lyons living here before Henry. In this house we may see Emma Hamilton's birthplace.

Of Henry Lyon little is known. As he signed his marriage certificate with a cross, the illiterate's mark, we may safely dismiss more romantic tales which sprang up in the Victorian times. Emma Hamilton's great-grandson believed Henry was the estranged son of a nobleman, beating out his anger against his sire on the anvil.

Henry died from unknown causes and was buried on 21 June, being named then as smith 'of Denhall', barely two months after his daughter's birth. We need linger no further in squalid Denhall. Tradition has it that his widow immediately took her infant across the estuary to Hawarden in Wales, where her parents lived.

Mary Lyon's parents, Mr and Mrs Kidd, lived in a small 'cruck' cottage, distinguished from the other thatched and whitewashed dwellings in the village by a set of red sandstone steps. Mary had at least one brother, William, and three sisters, who were to become the Mrs

Moore, Connor and Reynolds. Possibly, when Mary brought her baby, there were one or two of these still living at home.

The Steps, as the house was known, lay at the end of an old lane which ran down under the park wall of Broad Lane Hall, on the opposite side of the road to the Glynne Arms. Sir John Glynne was owner of the estate, which, in later years, as Hawarden Castle, was to be Prime Minister Gladstone's country home. Many of the villagers worked for Sir John in some capacity or other. There was a variety of industry practised in Hawarden – cheese-making, arable farming, coal mining. Mrs Kidd had a carrier's business and took produce from the Hall, together with sacks of coal from the works, to sell in Chester market.

Sarah Kidd was a formidable lady. In the 1890s a story was still remembered in which robbers were said to have attempted to steal the proceeds of her sales at Chester. They lay in wait on the road leading back from Chester along the southern side of the Dee estuary. Mrs Kidd, stout in defence of the contents of her loose pocket, belaboured them with her whip with such ferocity that they fled.

The Kidd men played second fiddle to the women of the family. Emma's grandfather was allotted in his wife's enterprise only the part of taking her proceeds up to the Hall. Otherwise he guarded sheep on Saltney marshes, a sodden stretch of land to the east of the village. It is said he used to dig a deep hole and stand in it, firing an ancient shotgun at marauding dogs who ventured near his flocks.

Of Emma as a child we know little. In the 1890s the local historian Hilda Gamlin could discover only the tradition that Emma had stood by a donkey on the Chester road and offered handfuls of coal for sale. Whether this was a scheme of her grandmother's or of her own devising, it is the only instance in her life where Emma showed any financial grasp.

Other ancestral memories of Emma being a sweet young girl, and very generous always, ring true. She spoke of herself as of having been 'wild and thoughtless' as a child. In a household where those who could work did so – with the exception of William, who declared himself, surprisingly, 'never brought up to work' – Emma probably enjoyed a degree of healthy neglect. There is comfort in Mary Wollstonecraft's words: 'Most women who have acted like rational creatures, or shown any vigour of intellect, have accidentally been allowed to run wild.'

With this liberty of action, in Emma's case, went a less satisfactory neglect of her education. She was to say later that her education only began when she was seventeen. She was not wholly illiterate before this date, however. Where she got her scanty education is not known. Stories that Mary Lyon was mistress or sempstress to Lord Halifax, that he paid for Emma's education till he remarried when the girl was twelve, founder under the fact that there was no Lord Halifax at this date. (Sir John Glynne did remarry when Emma was about twelve.) We do not anyway know for certain that Emma's mother was living in Hawarden during her daughter's childhood. Emma always spoke of her grandmother with great affection, saying that 'my grandmother always gave me her last shilling'. Quite possibly it was her grandmother who brought her up, and wielded such authority as existed over her.

When she was still young, Emma was placed as under-nursemaid in the Thomas family. Mr Honoratus Leigh Thomas was a successful surgeon, who lived in Hawarden and practised in Chester. He was partner to Dr Sutton, celebrated for his inoculations against smallpox. The rapacious disease attacked one in six of the population each year. Possibly the credit for Emma's fresh, wild-rose complexion should go to Dr Thomas and his preventative measures.

Mrs Thomas was deeply respected in the village. She was a Boydell by birth, which meant rather more then than now. Throughout the eighteenth century, the Boydells were land agents to the Glynnes. There were two sons and four daughters, all under the age of seventeen, when Emma was employed here. A drawing of the house gives a good idea of the decent, mildly prosperous family its gables, wings and neat borders housed. A sketch of Emma from this date survives. The eldest Miss Thomas was the artist. The exquisite conformation of eye-socket and nose which was later to excite such attention can be seen here before maturity brought chiselled Greek perfection. Probably Emma began work here some time after her twelfth birthday in 1777.

Emma's mother, we are told, went to London once she had seen her daughter established at the Thomases. She then found a post for Emma in the capital and ordered Emma to join her. Emma was so distressed at leaving the Thomases that she could only be persuaded to go on condition she return soon on a visit. She duly did return, but, such had been the heady influence of London life, she roistered till deep into the night with some youths at Wepre Fair, and her visit ended abruptly.

Of her post in London there is firm evidence. In 1791, when she had just made a marriage that intrigued all Society, Emma was to stare 'rapt' at an actress on the stage of the Drury Lane Theatre. An enquirer was told that the actress in question, Mrs Jane Powell, had been 'under-housemaid' in Dr Richard Budd's house at Chatham Place, Blackfriars, at the same time that Lady Hamilton had been nursery-maid there. Dr Pettigrew, Nelson's 1849 biographer, attempted in an appendix to set out the truth of Emma's early life, and confirmed this. He had known Budd, a physician at St Bartholomew's Hospital, at the time and could vouch for the employ.[1] Emma herself, in so emphatically acknowledging her ties with Jane Powell, seems to have been at pains to stress her employment with the Budds as an honourable episode in her past, perhaps one she wished remembered in lieu of later, less innocent positions held. The dates of her employment in Chatham Place must fall between 1777 and 1778, Emma then being twelve or thirteen.

An incident concerning Emma and Jane Powell as young employees of Dr Budd is recounted which bears a suspicious likeness to the story of Emma's lapse from good behaviour at Hawarden. The two girls, the story goes, stole off to Cocksheath Camp. Setting up as ballad singers, they acquired two young admirers with whom they dallied away the evening hours. One of these youths, we are told, was James Perry, later celebrated editor of the *Morning Chronicle* and, incidentally, to become a good friend of Lady Hamilton. The girls, finding their admirers becoming a trifle pressing in their advances, gave them the slip. Young Perry and friend, standing disconsolate on London Bridge, were still further put out to hear taunting cries from the river beneath them and see the two hoydens skim beneath their noses down the Thames on a wherry. The girls were dismissed from the Budd household when they came in at dawn.

This and the Hawarden stories are so similar that there is, of course, every reason to suspect the truth of one or both. Yet fairs and venues of outdoor gaiety, in Emma's day, were a popular and cheap form of entertainment for the poorer classes. Spectacles and crowds, not to mention admiration, always did have a most deleterious effect on Emma's sense of moderation. It is quite possible that both incidents did occur. If not, the inventors of both tales showed a shrewd appreciation of what Emma would have enjoyed, aged twelve or thirteen.

Emma probably worked next for the Linley family. Thomas Linley, father of the family, had the direction of the Bath Assembly Room concerts from the mid-1760s, and to those concerts and to his celebrated 'Attic Entertainments' came Boyce, Giardini, J. C. Bach, and many other musical luminaries. The jewel that drew in the crowds was the eldest Linley daughter, Elizabeth, who looked like an angel and sang like one, too.[2]

She and her younger sister, Maria, sang at Royal Command performances and were mobbed outside the London theatres when they visited the capital in 1772. Elizabeth then married Richard Brinsley Sheridan, son of her father's great friends, and, with his refusal to allow his wife to sing in public, Maria, an able but less divinely beautiful singer, proved less of a draw.

In 1776, Mr Linley bought with his son-in-law the major shareholding in the Drury Lane Theatre from Garrick, who was retiring. In 1777, Linley and his wife took the decision to move to London, he to take over the musical direction of the theatre, she to manage the wardrobe and, with Elizabeth, the accounts. They may well have been influenced in their decision by a desire to prevent their erratic son-in-law from spending all the proceeds of the theatre's success.

By the summer of 1778, the Linleys were in London at an elegant house in Norfolk Street, off the Strand. In August, they heard there the tragic news that their composer son, Thomas, had drowned after a boat had capsized on the Duke of Ancaster's lake. It is about now that Emma is said to have joined their household as maidservant, being thirteen years old. The story that she did so hangs on the *Reminiscences* of one Henry Angelo, a writer who, admittedly, had a tendency to dress 'Truth severe with fairy Fiction'. In the account he gives of Emma's stay at the Linleys', however, there is some reason to accept his word. His father, Domenico Angelo, riding and fencing master to the Royal Family and other lesser mortals, and his mother were intimate friends of the Linleys and Sheridans.

It is interesting that, at an impressionable age, Emma should have worked in this musical household. The singers of the Linley and (William) Jackson 'school' were noted for their 'peculiar pathos and sweetness of expression', qualities noted in Emma's own later singing and theatrical performances. Emma's penchant for the theatre and the company of singers and actresses, not to mention her 'theatrical' manner, may have had its roots in this early brush with Drury Lane.

Emma worked as maidservant to Mrs Linley when the lady was mistress at Drury Lane 'Theatre', Angelo says. 'The actresses would often insist on having certain dresses for their characters, and Emma was usually employed on those occasions as the means of communication between them and Mrs Linley.' Emma would bring the actresses' requests to Mrs Linley in her private box at the theatre. 'Very frequently, when Mrs Linley was in an ill humour, Emma was sent back with no favourable answer.' Mrs Linley was, in fact, an absolute dragon for a balanced book, and saw no reason why Lady Macbeth's costume should not serve Portia very well. Sarah Siddons was one of very few to triumph over her thrift and play Lady Macbeth in a glorious gold-cloth dress. Emma must have had some uneasy moments as Mrs Linley's ambassador.

In December 1778, according to Angelo, further disaster struck the gifted family. Samuel, the Linleys' second son, arrived in Norfolk Street desperately ill, from a fever he had contracted as a midshipman. Mrs Linley told Mrs Angelo that Emma attended Samuel assiduously 'up to the last moment of his decease'. On his death, Mrs Linley said, Emma 'was so attached to her son, and her affliction made such an impression on her mind, that no entreaties could prevail on her to remain, not even a day'. This history has been dismissed as sounding like housemaids' fiction. Yet Emma was always soft-hearted to an extreme and to see an eighteen-year-old boy – and a Byronically handsome boy – waste away to death under her nursing cannot have been other than a traumatic experience. At thirteen, the exhaustion of nursing and the shock of his death could well have conspired to send her, unthinking, from the scene of these sufferings. Samuel Linley was buried on 21 December 1778; Angelo tells us he was a pall-bearer with Sheridan and Tickell.

Angelo notes that it was some few days after Samuel's funeral that his feelings were 'powerfully excited by the figure of a young woman, meanly attired, in the attitude of dejection, leaning against the post' at the corner of New Compton Street, in Soho. He approached her and spoke to her, but she would not answer. Seeing an acquaintance approaching, and perhaps remembering he was newly married and ought not to be seen talking to 'girls of the town', Angelo asked the girl to be there at eight that evening. 'With a deep drawn sigh, she replied, "Yes".' He was punctual; so was she, but she was hardly more forthcoming. She only sighed and said her name was Emma. She added that she had not eaten all that day – 'the truth of which she proved by the voracious manner in which she devoured some biscuits I ordered to be placed before her'. Angelo, perhaps from sheer curiosity, perhaps in hopes of some better return for his biscuits than those endless sighs, arranged to meet same time, same place, next evening. He failed to keep the appointment and feared her lost.

Happily, he soon saw her again, no longer wearing her rags, but dressed in 'all the grandeur of fashion' and 'with a countenance beaming with pleasure'. She was walking with two 'élégantes' among other 'beaux and belles' in Kensington Gardens. Angelo says he was surprised, but she 'immediately relieved me by saying she lived at Mrs Kelly's, Arlington Street'. This lady was a procuress, or 'madame', as we would say now. Then she was known as an 'abbess' – her girls being the nunnery. 'For some short time after I frequently saw her in the abbess's carriage,' says Angelo.

According to the anonymous 1815 *Memoirs of Lady Hamilton*, Emma worked as maid to a 'lady of fortune'. Perhaps she did begin at Mrs Kelly's as a domestic but she is unlikely to have remained one for long.

If Angelo's story is true, it was no domestic who sauntered through Kensington Gardens, and was taken about in her mistress's carriage. Angelo is very insistent that Emma did live with Mrs Kelly, and he says her departure from that house occasioned an 'on-dit', which means her presence there must have been known to others besides himself.

William Hickey describes one evening in London some twelve months after Emma may have gone to Mrs Kelly's. He and his brother went to dine with the 'useful, if not respectable, Madam Kelly, at Arlington Street, who upon my entrance saluted me with a volley of abuse . . .' Hickey had introduced a rogue to the house who had 'bilked every girl in the family' and owed Madam Kelly over a hundred pounds for suppers and wines. 'In the evening we attended three of her chickens in the old beldam's coach, to Turnham Green, to drink tea at the Pack Horse, and treat the misses to a swing, there being a capital one fixed up in the garden.'[3]

If Emma did in 1779 form part of Mrs Kelly's 'family', this charming vignette of Hickey's gives a good idea of how her time there would have been occupied. Mrs Kelly's girls were available for picnics, visits to Ranelagh and Vauxhall Gardens, and for the hours following. Her extreme youth cannot be said to tell against the possibility. One of Hickey's 'nun' friends was procured when she was twelve.

In 1802, at a time when he knew Emma, the Prince of Wales was to tell the painter Mme Vigée-Le Brun that he had been struck, years before, by the beauty of a girl at the door of a fruiterer's. This girl, whom he remembered as wearing wooden shoes and meanly clad, he later recognized in the person of Lady Hamilton. The 1815 *Memoirs* only mention that Emma worked for a tradesman in St James's Market.

The garrulous Prince did not see fit to sully Vigée-Le Brun's ears with another story about Emma – the tale that she lost her virginity to a great friend of his, one Rear-Admiral Jack Willet-Payne. The 1815 *Memoirs* relate that Emma went to Willet-Payne, then a captain, in the early years of the American War, to beg that a cousin of hers, who had been press-ganged, should be released. Payne granted her request, he became her suitor, and 'she soon became the mistress of her new admirer'.

There was, in Emma's lifetime a rumour, as hotly denied by her friends as it was credited by others, that she had posed as a Goddess of Health, transparently draped, in an extraordinary establishment called the Temple of Aesculapius, or Health. The proprietor of this fanum which had its being in the late summer of 1779 in the Royal Terrace, Adelphi, was a Dr James Graham from Edinburgh. He had obtained tremendous encomia from Georgiana Duchess of Devonshire among others, when he had treated them earlier in the year with electricity at Aix-la-Chapelle. Experiments to discover the properties and potential of electricity were all the rage in these years. Graham did very well to emphasize its benefits to bodily health – another preoccupation of the time. By 1779, all fashionable London was flocking to pay a crown's admittance and enter the doors which gigantic footmen flanked. The gentlemen strode in boldly, the ladies were masked and slipped in discreetly past the array of discarded crutches and medicaments with which Graham strewed the front hall as practical proof of his healing powers.[4] At a time when Cagliostro and Mesmer exerted their unholy fascination, Graham's Temple became exceedingly popular.

There was no harm in the Doctor. By day, his Temple was open to all who were infirm, disabled or merely elderly. A certain Frederick Reynolds, whose home backed on to the Temple, says the queues of mendicants waiting for free issue of Imperial pills or Nervous Aethereal Balsam or Electrical Aether were a hindrance to passers-by.[5] The richer evening visitors had to pay for such supplies as they desired. A 'Celestial Bed' with gilt dragons and the inscription '*Dolorifica res est si quis homo dives nullum habet domi suae successorem*' (It is a sad thing if a rich man has no heir to his property) was available for childless couples to roll around in for £50 a night. Most came to attend the highfalutin lectures on longevity, sterility and procreation which constituted the evening's entertainment. The heavy burden of sexual innuendo these lectures carried, and the windows of the hall painted with portraits of Hygeia and associated deities, hardly made much impact on Polite Society's greedy appetite for novelty. Horace Walpole called Graham a dull mountebank. Standing by Graham, however, as he delivered his lectures, were several lovelies dressed in their Grecian drapery.

Emma could have been the 'warbling chorister' who sang off-stage, or she could have played a classical maiden in 1779 or 1780 at the Adelphi Temple. She cannot have been the Goddess of Health, for Graham only presented this deity in 1781. By that date Emma was elsewhere. Furthermore, we are told that she was 'gigantic' – which Emma at this date was not – and Frederick Reynolds says that the Goddess died in mid-career. The author of the 1815 *Memoirs* is very certain that she did pose at the Temple, saying that a person 'of the very highest literary reputation' told him 'the whole history' in 1791. Angelo is very sure Emma did not appear there. It is just possible that visitors to the Temple remembered Romney's window-painting of Hygeia, which was depicted with all the classical attributes of that goddess, namely heavy drapery, staff and bowl. Perhaps they were confused, having heard of Graham's Goddess of Health at the later Temple and seeing Romney's later 'fancy' pictures of Emma in classical attire, into thinking Emma had played the Goddess.

The other story about Emma in these mysterious years, which is associated with the above tale, relates that she modelled naked for artists and even for the Royal Academicians' life classes. Angelo enquired into this and found that the only Academician still living in 1830 who could have gazed on Emma's charms denied the story. That same Academician, James Northcote, is reported by another to have said that only prostitutes past their prime would consent to model naked for the life classes. They were reluctant models, one always arriving and departing in a mask, another saying it was 'unnatural'. The rumour about Emma probably arose retrospectively out of a brilliant cartoon by Rowlandson in 1791. It shows Lady Hamilton performing her famous Attitudes naked on a model's stage with a host of prurient old men looking on. Rowlandson would have been delighted that his satirical view for the Attitudes gave rise to the *Memoirs* story that she had indeed been a life model.

Angelo says Emma 'suddenly disappeared [from Mrs Kelly's] and the on-dit at the time was, that Sir Harry Fetherstonhaugh had taken her from there under his protection'. Now we pass from rumour to fact. Emma made the acquaintance of a lively young baronet, Sir Harry Fetherstonhaugh, and he took her to Up Park, or Uppark, his elegant Dutch mansion on the South Downs in Sussex. Tradition has it that she was installed in a pretty house, Rosemary Cottage, in South Harting, the village at the foot of the hill leading to the mansion. As Sir Harry's mother was living at Uppark at this time, tradition is almost certainly correct.

Emma was here as Sir Harry's 'cottager' by the hot summer of 1781, when she was sixteen. In a letter written ten years later, Emma was to refer to her early life. She wrote: 'Oh, my dear friend, for a time I own through distress my virtue was vanquished, but my sense of virtue was not overcome.' If Emma's virtue, as seems probable, was already vanquished when she encountered Sir Harry, financial distress was certainly vanquished under rich Sir Harry's protection.

Uppark was quite unlike anything Emma had known. Sir Harry's father, Matthew, had furnished the house in style. The large saloon was a most magnificent room, rich in gilt and plasterwork. There was a fine staircase, good Continental furniture. Above all, there were superb views from the house over the open Downs – on a fine day, to the distant English Channel.

Of the young baronet who owned this jewel of a property we have an entertaining glimpse, when he was making a second tour of the

Continent in 1776. (Only a year before, the historian Edward Gibbon, referring to Sir Harry's inheritance on his father's death in 1774, had written: 'Sir Harry is very civil and good humoured. But from the unavoidable temper of youth, I fear he will cost many a tear to Lady F [his mother]. She consults everybody, but has neither authority nor plan.')[6] Sir Harry certainly cost quite a few tears to Dr John Moore, who was escorting the young Duke of Hamilton on an educative tour of Switzerland and Italy in 1776. The good divine had encouraged his charge to bathe in Lake Geneva in September (to the amazement of the natives), dine with professors of natural history, and eschew the expensive habit of sending messages 'on horseback'. At Naples, unfortunately, the Duke fell in with Sir Harry. Forgoing the artistic and archaeological treasures of the city, together they went off to the remoter game reserves of the Kingdom. Sir William Hamilton, the Duke's kinsman, and English Minister at Naples, supplemented their rough fare, sending presents of pâté and ginger. When the two, 'inseparable', as Moore sniffed, left Naples for Rome, Sir William had further works of charity to perform. He had to offer £300 to a lady for a scrape the Duke or Sir Harry had got into.

In Rome Sir Harry was very much taken with Lady Cowper's sister, Miss Gower. 'As Sir H. is not a man to control any Inclination that he can gratify, I dare say he will yield to his present penchent. Proposals will be made, and he has an Estate of Seven or Eight thousand pounds a year, so it is not *absolutely impossible* but the affair may be arranged.' Moore hoped the Duke of Hamilton's mother would 'forgive this Tittle Tattle'. In a further verse of this restrained hymn of hate against the tempter who had undone all Moore's good work, in matters aesthetic, spiritual and monetary, we are given a summing up of Sir Harry's character. 'He is good natured, formal, effeminate, and obliging, without violent Passions or Ambition, a negative character who will Rather be acted upon than act for himself.' To this we might add the physical description gleaned from his portraits, and particularly from the one painted by Pompeo Batoni when he was in Rome in 1776: he was distinctly dolichocephalic, with a friendly cast to small features in his long face, had sandy hair, and was of a certain languid length. He would not have changed much by the time Emma met him. Moore's final exasperated reference to Sir Harry is as follows. He wrote from Florence on 1 June to the Duke's mother. They had intended to leave the day before, but Sir Harry had written to say he would be in Florence on the first. So the Duke had decided to wait for his friend, 'who I suppose will accompany us all the way to Paris'.[7]

It was on this trip that Sir Harry bought some of the exquisite French furniture with which he supplemented his father's original furnishings at Uppark. However, such an 'eye' was unlikely to redeem his other excesses, and his style of life was not one to appeal to the older generation. From Oxford on, despite being a rich man, he was always in financial difficulties. These were not matters to bother persons of his own age, and the weaknesses and hedonistic vacuity which his elders deplored found favour among his contemporaries. For Emma, aged fifteen or sixteen, and impressionable all her life, his allure was strong.

Chief among the dissipations on offer at Uppark were the private race meetings which Sir Harry held on the Downs. It is said that Emma rode in these events, having become a dare-devil horsewoman under Sir Harry's tuition. She was certainly an accomplished horsewoman later in Naples, and used to have horses sent over from Lord Pembroke's stables in England. As there was no opportunity for her to learn in the interval between her leaving Uppark and going to Naples, there seems no reason to doubt the tradition that Sir Harry taught her. The *Memoirs* say she 'obtained great applause on account of her equestrian powers, sitting on her horse with uncommon elegance, and rivalling in speed the boldest of her acquaintances'.

Tradition relates that Emma, or Emily Hart, as she was calling herself at the end of her liaison with Sir Harry, danced naked on the dining-room table at Uppark – presumably in further pursuit of the admiration of Sir Harry's friends. This exhibition may account for the *Memoirs* remark that 'her real character was known, and despised, even by those who were under the necessity of obeying her commands,' when she was 'nominal mistress' of the 'noble mansion'. As we have seen, it is questionable whether Emma lived in the house. Probably Emma came up the steep hill in the evenings, when his mother had retired. Perhaps she danced naked in the white and gold saloon.

Another who sauntered down to Rosemary Cottage was the Honourable Charles Greville, second son of the Earl of Warwick. Whether or not he became a lover of Emma's then, he arranged for her to make a surreptitious visit to London, some time before June 1781. They seem to have then prosecuted a desultory affair, unbeknownst to Sir Harry, through the summer and early autumn of that year. A letter from Emma to Greville and his reply of January 1782 constitute almost our only source for the dramatic events of 1781.

In the correspondence Greville scolds Emma for some sort of sexual peccadillo on her first visit to him in London, and for some other casual sexual encounter, in words which suggest he saw himself as an 'official' lover, like Sir Harry. Greville talks of Emma's 'faults and bad conduct to Sir H. and myself'. From the letter, it is clear, though, that Greville was well aware that he who paid the piper had the girl at his call. He could only expect a small share of Emma's favour while Sir Harry kept her. Though plainly very attracted to Emma, Greville seems to have been satisfied with a smaller share and was probably wise to be so. Emma preferred glamorous, rich Sir Harry to Greville.

Why was Emma running about with Greville, and acquiring other 'connexions' and 'engagements' when Sir Harry and his fortune were at her disposal? The short answer is that they were not there for long. Greville's letter makes it clear that Sir Harry had tired of Emma, and that she then gave him up as lost. The *Memoirs* corroborate this. In the autumn of 1781, they say, Sir Harry brought Emma to London, and deposited her in private lodgings. He then went off – presumably to the Fetherstonhaugh town house in Whitehall – and proceeded to neglect her. According to the *Memoirs*, Emma took the opportunity of a rare visit from Sir Harry to quarrel. Emma's temper probably rode high with the insult to her pride, and Sir Harry broke with her for good.

The *Memoirs* say that 'the variety of scenes through which this daughter of vicissitude passed, after experiencing that treachery which most commonly follows the sacrifice of virgin innocence', are best not detailed. Greville later refers with distaste to the time 'when you were last in Town'. He dwells on her 'giddiness and disipation'. Immediately after her dismissal by Sir Harry, she was promiscuous. She slept with those who could afford her what the *Memoirs* call 'guilty support', or, in plain language, money for food and lodging. She was 'in reall distress'.

To compound her troubles, Emma discovered she was pregnant, and she believed Sir Harry to be the father. The child was conceived in June or July 1781. It was born before 12 March the next year.

In the late autumn she confided her troubles to Greville. He seems to have advised her to track down Sir Harry. An indefatigable hunting man, Sir Harry was in Leicestershire at this point, and to Leicestershire Emma went, armed with a bundle of envelopes ready franked by Greville, so she could inform him of progress. Greville recounts that Sir Harry, far from taking pity on her, hardly gave her enough money to get to her friends, to whom she then travelled. Emma then wrote seven letters to Sir Harry from these friends' home at Chester. All went unanswered. She wrote to Greville, detailing her woes. He wrote back. Then they wrote again. By the time Emma writes the letter set out below, which was received on 10 January 1782, an agreement has been reached that she is to be taken under Charles Greville's protection.

Emma's letter has been often quoted to show how desperate she was. It is rather an emotional letter of thanks to her saviour who is about to pull her from the slough of despond. At sixteen, to be pregnant and thrown over by a rich lover, to feel that her friends in Cheshire had looked coldly on her, to be afraid to tell her mother – it was a sorry time.

Now Greville had altered all. In this letter, Emma was informing Greville that her hopes of Sir Harry were finally at an end. She was at his disposal, and needed the coach fare to get to him. The fact that she encloses a copy of her baptismal entry on Greville's request shows that negotiations were well advanced.

January 1782

Yesterday did I receive your kind let^r. It put me in some spirits for believe me I am allmost distracktid, I have never hard from Sir H. and he is not at Lechster now, I am sure, what shall I dow, good God what shall I dow, I have wrote 7 letters and no anser, I cant come to town for want of mony, I have not a farthing to bless myself with and I think my frenda looks cooly on me, I think so. O G what shall I dow what shall I dow. O how your letter affected me wen you wished me happiness. O G that I was in your posesion as I was in Sir H. What a happy girl would I have been, girl indead, or what else am I but a girl in distress, in reall distress, for Gods sake G. write the minet you get this and only tell me what I ham to dow, derect some whay. I am allmos mad. O for Gods sake tell me what is to become on me. O dear Grevell write to me. Write to me G. Adue and believe yours for ever
        Emily Hart

Dont tell my mother what distress I am in and dow afford me some comfort. My age was got out of the Reggister and I have sent it to My Dear Charles. Once more Adue, once more adue. O you dear friend.

Notice that Emy Lyon has become Emily Hart. On the copy of the baptismal entry, 'Emy Lyon' is altered to 'Emyly' – Emily was perhaps deemed a more sophisticated name than Emy by Greville. Miss Lyon, on returning pregnant to her childhood home, presumably invented a husband, and became 'Mrs Hart'. The name was perhaps suggested by South Harting, the village of Uppark.

CHAPTER TWO

You will live very retired

Charles Greville answered Emma's letter the same day he received it. Just as Emma dissembled a little in her letter, so he did in his. He writes at first as if Emma, six months pregnant, had a wide choice of willing protectors on whom she might call, and offers his own protection as something of a last resort. He then immediately details the conditions on which he could be prevailed on to offer that protection, and on which its continuation could be ensured. Then he details the plan he has drawn up for Emma's confinement, gives instructions for the proper use of the money he encloses, and ends by reiterating his demand that Emma write to Sir Harry and formally terminate their lapsed liaison. In effect, this is a letter of contract, which sets out the conditions and terms under which he agrees to maintain Emma and her child. Naturally, it rehearses a great deal that has been gone over in less formal interchanges. It is evident, from Greville's casual phrase 'if you mean to have my protection . . .', that he had offered it to Emma in a previous letter, and that she had dallied, hoping for word from Sir Harry. Then, with 'O G, that I was in your posesion', she accepted his offer firmly.

Greville kept a copy of his letter, no doubt in case either party (i.e. Emma) should at any point betray the terms of the agreement. This copy, which was among Greville's papers at his death, was presumably kept ready at hand throughout Emma's liaison with Greville to be brandished, like the Mosaic Laws, should she do Greville wrong. When he wrote to his uncle, Sir William Hamilton, in later years of the sentiments he 'ever impressed on her mind', that their liaison was to be of a 'limited experiment', this letter is probably what he was referring to:

My dear Emily,

I do not make apologies for Sir H's behaviour to you & altho I advised you to deserve his esteem by your good conduct, I own I never expected better from him, it was your duty to deserve good treatment, & it gave me great concern to see you imprudent the first time you came to G: from the country, & as the same conduct was repeated when you was last in town, I began to despair of your happiness, to prove to you that I do not accuse you falsly I only mention 5 guineas, & half a guinea for coach, but my Emily, as you seem quite miserable now, I do not mean to give you uneasiness, but comfort, & tell you that I will forget your faults & bad conduct to Sir H. & to myself & will not repent my good humor, if I shall find that you have learnt by experience to value yourself & endeavor to preserve your Friends by good conduct & affection.

I will now answer your last letter. You tell me you think your Friends look cooly on you, it is therefore time to leave them, but it is necessary for you to decide some points *before* you come to Town.

You are sensible that for the three next months your situation will not admit of a giddy life if you had wished it, & would therefore be imprudent to come & hunt after new connexion, or try to regain the one you gave up as lost, after you have told me that Sir H. gave you barely money to get to your friends, & has never answer'd one letter since, & neither provides for you, nor takes any notice of you; it might appear laughing at you, to advise you to make Sir H. more kind & attentive. I do not think a great deal of time should be lost, as I have never seen a woman clever enough to keep a man who was tired of her, but it is a great deal more for me to *advise you* never to see him again, & to write only to inform him of your determination. You must, however do the one or the other.

You may easily see my Dearest Emily, why it is absolutely necessary for this point to be completely settled *before* I can move one step. If you love Sir H. you should not give him up & if you continue with him, it would be ridiculous in me to take care of his girl, who is better able to maintain her, but besides this my Emily, I would not be troubled with your connexions (excepting your mother) & with Sir H. friends for the universe.

My advice then is to take a steady resolution, try whatever you please & if Sir H will continue your friend, or if you prefer any other friend, do not be your own enymy, & at last if everything fails, if you mean to have my protection I must *first* know from you that *you are clear of every connexion,* & that *you will never take them again without my consent.* I shall then be free to dry up the tears of my lovely Emily & to give her comfort, if you do not forfeit my esteem perhaps my Emily may be happy. You know I have been so, by avoiding the vexation which so frequently arises from ingratitude & caprices, nothing but your letter & your distress could incline me to alter my system, but remember I never will give up my peace, nor continue my connexion one moment after my confidence is again betray'd.

If you should come to town free from all engagements & take my advice, you will live very retired, *till* you are brought to bed. You should part with your maid, & take another *name*, by degrees I would get you a new set of acquaintance, & by keeping your own secret, & nobody about you having it in their power to betray you, I may expect to see you respected & admired. Thus far relates to yourself, as to the child, Sir H. may be informed of circumstances which may reasonably make him doubt & it is not worth while to make it a subject of altercation, its mother shall obtain its kindness from me & it shall never want.

I enclose you some money, do not throw it away, you may send some presents when you arrive in Town, but do not be on the road without some money to *spare*, in case you should be fatigued & wish to take your time: I will send Sophy anything she wishes for, give her a good many kisses & a thousand to my dearest Emily. God bless you my dearest lovely girl, take your determination soon & let me hear from you. Once more Adieu my D. Emily.

Some few days after 10 January 1782, Emma received that letter, the posts luckily being speedy at that time. Sometime before 12 March 1782, when she sat to the artist George Romney, she had her child. It was a daughter and she was named Emma. No record of her birth has ever been found. It is possible Emma disobeyed Greville's advice in this matter and remained in the Chester area throughout her pregnancy. She certainly deposited 'little Emma', as she called her daughter, with her grandmother, Mrs Kidd, at Hawarden. The child was living there in 1784, and was probably placed there soon after her birth. Emma's mother appears again now, joining Emma in the house Greville took near the Edgware Road in London by early March 1782, and was not to depart from her side again till her own death.

Leaving Emma ensconced in her new home, and perhaps reflecting on what a comparatively happy turn events had taken when all seemed set for disaster, we turn to discover what we can of her benefactor.

The Honourable Charles Francis Greville was born on 12 May 1749, the second son of Lord Brooke, created Earl of Warwick in 1759. Charles's mother was born Elizabeth Hamilton, daughter of Lord Archibald Hamilton and so granddaughter of the third Duke of that name. When Charles was thirteen, in 1763, Sir Joshua Reynolds painted him, and the portrait is good evidence that Greville was as old before his years physically as he was in character. The picture could as well be of a young man of nineteen as a boy of thirteen. Perhaps Charles's maturity was of help to him when ructions developed between his parents. They ended in 1765 with the Countess being refused admittance to the family town house in Hill Street, Mayfair, and she married General Robert Clark.[1] Her break with her husband made her all the closer to her Hamilton relations. She was a Hamilton twice over. Her mother, Lady Archibald Hamilton, had been a daughter of the sixth Earl of Abercorn, head of another branch of this close-knit family. Charles was brought up on close terms with a host of Hamilton, Cathcart and Stormont cousins. It was a family looked on kindly by George III, moreover – in despite of, or perhaps because of, a long liaison between his father, Frederick Prince of Wales, and Lady Archibald, Charles's grandmother. So, though Sir Harry was infinitely richer, Greville was by far the better-connected.

In 1769, aged twenty, Charles was in Naples, where he struck up a friendship with a most distinguished member of the clan. His uncle, William Hamilton, had been Envoy Extraordinary since 1764, and Minister Plenipotentiary also since 1768, to the Kingdom of the Two Sicilies. Though uncle and nephew were twenty years apart in age, they were united by a common interest in antiquities and in collecting that multitude of artefacts that went under the name of virtu. Curiosities of the Roman period, sixteenth- and seventeenth-century paintings, geological specimens, Greek vases − all were grist to the virtu man's mill, though Greville and his uncle each had his special field. A correspondence between them, which began on Charles's departure from Naples and was to run a course of thirty years, gives a good indication both of Greville's character and of the tastes and ambitions which were to preoccupy him all his life.

From Rome, Charles writes: 'I am running about the antiquities from 9 to 11 with Byers [James Byres, antiquarian and purveyor of the arts to the English in Rome] and from 11 to 2 with Miss A [probably Angelica Kauffmann, the painter].' He asks his uncle to procure him some Greek vases, 'if you can pick up any . . . of which you have duplicates', with the proviso that they be 'well conserved', few and 'elegant'. Greville shows here a casual disregard for his uncle's special field ('duplicate' Greek vases do not exist), which was later equalled by his uncle's lack of interest in his own specialist collection of minerals. Each found the other's lack of interest incomprehensible − at best irritating, inexcusable when a prime piece slipped through the one's hands through the other's dilatory failure to secure it.

Charles seems to have loathed every aspect of Neapolitan life except the antiquities and the volcanic minerals. Not even the charms of the celebrated courtesan Mme Tschudi could do anything to reconcile Charles to the enchanted city which hung above the Bay. Urbane, clerical Rome was more to his taste. He wrote of Mme Tschudi, from Vienna, 'I have since been contented with worse, but she contrived to make me perfectly disgusted with her.'

Greville's penchant for 'girls of the town' was a striking note in his otherwise fastidious personality. He seems to have taken advantage of the licence tacitly granted to the English abroad to indulge his taste everywhere on this tour. Sir William makes a sly reference to Greville's activities in Venice: 'I can conceive that a gondola with a fine woman in it must seem a most luxurious conveyance for a young man in his prime.'

Back in England, Charles continued to pursue his twin interests. He writes of a visit to Almack's, the fashionable assembly rooms, in

1773: 'Triste au dernier point. Only three of four girls of the town there.' In the same year, with the eminent natural historian Joseph Banks, whose most recent exploits had been his journey on Captain Cook's *Endeavour* and a trip to see the eruption of Hecla in Iceland, he went off on a tamer trip to Amsterdam. Banks and Greville were both interested in buying cabinets, as collections were then called, of minerals. This interest in mineralogy, perhaps begun by contact with Banks, was to become the ruling passion in Greville's life. The Trustees of the British Museum were to write of his collection: 'the series of crystallized Rubies, Sapphires, Emeralds, Topazes, Rubelites, Diamonds, and precious Stones in general, far surpass any that are known . . . to them in the different European collections.'[2]

Greville's collection, which he found 'only interesting if considered in a philosophical connection', was an expensive hobby. And Greville was not rich. In 1774 he was negotiating to buy an important collection of German minerals for £600, when his income for that year was one hundred pounds short of that. In later years he bought yet more expensively, though his income remained the same. He kept the bailiffs from the door by acting as agent in sales of paintings and of virtu to his friends.

Sir William Hamilton in 1772 left an important Correggio with Greville, in the hopes he could find a buyer for it. In 1773, Greville was advising the Russian Minister on what to buy for his Imperial master. In the same year, he was commissioning a relatively unknown artist, George Romney, to pick up masterpieces for him in Italy. He furnished him with letters, too, to Sir William, Sir Horace Mann and others, peremptorily directing them to take those pictures off their walls of which Romney felt Greville would like copies – all with a view to future sales.

In July 1773, the Earl of Warwick died, and left his second son only £100 with which to buy a mourning ring. The yearly allowance of £200 he had made Charles during his lifetime ceased. Charles had made efforts to reconcile his father and his elder brother, efforts which had been successful to his own cost. Though he had hopes that the new Earl would come forward with a promised £5,000, these hopes do not seem to have been realized. Charles was left with only £500 a year from a maternal inheritance, for the rest of his life. He attempted to redress his position, taking over his brother's place on the Board of Trade and assuming one of the two seats for Warwick in the Commons. The meagre emolument he received could not substantially mitigate the severe blow of his virtual disinheritance. He wrote to his uncle, 'as the greater part of my life will be from hand to mouth, I shall never be able to settle in a family way; very few chances there are of my being made miserable by such a negative, but such is the perverseness of manhood, may be I may be the more eager about it.'

In the next few years, he was busy building up his collection of minerals. In return for sending his uncle hogsheads of English porter from Warwick, he was offered pictures by Caracci, Parmigianino and Albani at modest prices. After he expressed a preference for Cambiaso, Sir William gave him a 'hairy Magdalen' by that artist. He toyed with an idea of going to make his fortune in America, where many of his relations were administrators.

In 1778, fulfilling his own prediction of 1773, Greville wrote to his uncle: 'Of all the chateaux I ever built, none ever lasted so long as that of my wish to settle.' Having given the matter much thought over the years since his father's death, he had come to the sensible decision that he must settle for a rich wife. With most peculiar logic, his first step √ in this enterprise was to beggar himself further by building a mansion in Portman Square. This was a newly fashionable part of London, where houses had been going up since 1760. He told Sir William, who remonstrated with him, that the house was a form of double speculation. It would create the impression, for his future unspecified bride's family, that he was a man of substance. Once the heiress had been caught, and her fortune made his, he could sell the house at a profit and pay back the huge sum he had borrowed to finance the venture. A more hare-brained scheme has rarely been conceived.

The scheme came to nothing. Greville had a mysterious heiress in mind in 1778 who would bring him a dowry of £20,000. 'I am so well with Granby, Ly. [wife of the heir to the Dukedom of Rutland], the Duchess, & Ly. B. C. that I think they have a real friendship for me.' The difficulty came with Charles's reluctance to press his suit to the point of popping the question. He said he was afraid to ask, and 'have a short No'. He excused his lack of verve with the remark, 'I shall be a Fabius, slow and sure,' but faint heart never won fair lady. Two years later he was still unwed. Moreover, his house in Portman Square, where he was living and 'which is much talked of, through my placing my collection and statues there', was still unsold. His double speculation had turned out badly.

Possibly out of pride, Greville always displayed the most extra-ordinary optimism when it was least justified. Sir William wrote to offer dampening advice, presumably in answer to burblings of other heiresses and possible buyers for the house. 'Don't marry a rich Devil,' he said, and 'sell off your house or it will be a millstone round your neck.' In October 1780, Charles moved out of his house, on getting a job at the Admiralty, which brought with it rent-free accommodation in the King's Mews. Still, his house was unsold, and remained so, 'on my hands', till 1784.

Now he concentrated again on the tried and tested method of supplementing his income – dealing in art. In 1781, he was putting together a collection of some fifty inscribed gems, scarabs and ring bezels, for Alderman Boydell to engrave and publish in a book with examples from Lord Percy's collection of the same. The purpose of such books of prints was not far off that of a Christie's or Sotheby's sales catalogue. Involved in such abstruse work, Greville spent his time with possible clients for his wares and with fellow members of the Royal Society, the British Museum, the Societies of Dilettanti and Antiquaries, and the Royal Horticultural. Not surprisingly, as these fellow members were rather older than he, he wrote to his uncle that he felt 'a little lonely in my virtuous life'.

It was a letter from Sir William, being a tedious catalogue of all the thousands of wild beasts he had shot with His Sicilian Majesty, which occasioned this plaintive remark. It had some foundation. Greville's closest friend among his cousins was Charles Cathcart, who has been described by Walter Sichel as playing Pylades to Greville's Orestes (not a very flattering comparison as the Greek tragedians' Pylades is a non-speaking part). Cathcart, a colonel, was abroad with his regiment that year, 1781, and Greville felt bereft. To find his uncle, on whom he counted for rational, informed conversation, rattling off lists of deer, boar and wolves slaughtered seemed a betrayal of all that he valued. 'Surely you cannot be dead to virtue,' he pleaded – ironically enough. His uncle, in these years, was building up the collection of Greek vases which form the basis of the Department of Greek and Roman Antiquities at the British Museum.

Such was the man, short on friends, long on schemes, who invited Emma to live with him and be his love on 10 January 1782. The first information we have of her new life with Greville is that she sat to George Romney on 12 March, at eleven o'clock.[3] So the painter's Day Book tells us. Greville did not take on the financial support of a girl, her mother and her child, from humane feelings alone. His rich wife had not materialized. Still, he wished to settle, have a home and all the domestic comfort his bachelor lodgings could not afford him. That was among his calculations in offering Emma his protection. More importantly, he had the idea that he could commission from his friend Romney a series of pictures of Emma as a 'speculation'. Greville was to write after he and Emma had parted, referring to payments for pictures of Emma, that he wished he could have completed all his plans. The terms in which Greville spoke of Emma, as 'a modern piece of virtu', ridiculous man, also suggest that he saw his protection of her, as he did all his buys of virtu, as an investment. Letters from Greville to Romney in 1786, after Emma's departure, make it clear he had paid for few of Romney's pictures of Emma. Most of them had remained, after they were finished, in Romney's studio – presumably to tempt visitors into offering for them. If the 'scheme' that Romney should paint Emma for Greville's profit was in Greville's mind when he offered to take on Emma and her dependants, his offer becomes less puzzling.

Emma headed her letters, 'Edgware Road'. In 1782 this was a rough road, bordered by fields. It led up from the public gallows and grandstands at Tyburn Tree, past the village of Paddington and out to Harrow. But the whole expanse of open country between Tyburn Tree and Paddington was designated Edgware Road. Any of the few houses on the road to Paddington, or any of the houses surrounding Paddington Green, would have suited Greville's desire for respectable seclusion.

Sir William, having visited the house in 1784, referred to Emma as 'The Fair Tea-Maker of Edgware Row'. This properly described a short row of houses at the beginnings of the Edgware Road, near the modern Marble Arch, on the east side. Angelo says Emma gave her address as 'the Paddington Road, No. 14, Oxford Street'. That description would fit a house in the row described. Romney, on one occasion in 1784, made an exception to his rule of painting his sitters at his house in Cavendish Square, and notes in his Day Book, 'Mrs Hart, 10 [i.e. in the morning] Edgware Road'.

Greville, in 1788, bought a house on Paddington Green, in which he lived until his death. Some have mistaken this for the house he hired for Emma in 1782. The earlier house was large enough to accommodate, besides Emma, her mother and two maids. There was space enough for Greville, in 1784, to have his 'own set of apartments'. The house had also later to accommodate his collection of minerals, his paintings and statues and his other pieces of virtu, after the Portman Square house was sold in 1784. There was, as shown by payments in account books that survive for the period from October 1784 to February 1785, a gardener. Greville perhaps here, as in his later house, grew botanical specimens for the Horticultural Society. Alternatively, the gardener may have been digging vegetable beds. The surviving account books, which may have been the only ones kept, give an impression that the household was managed with economy but supplied with all the genteel comforts. Greville reckoned life there was supported on £100 a year. In fact, projecting the sums we know spent, it was more like three hundred, more than half the income Greville could depend on. Possibly at the outset, in 1782, a tighter rein was kept on the expenditure.

So the odd household, consisting of an aesthete, a gay, reprobate girl and a sensible countrywoman, settled down. According to the Reverend John Romney, the painter's son, Emma confided to George Romney a story of an altercation which took place early on in her life with Greville. It was more of a clash of personalities than anything else, but it had a decisive effect on life in Edgware Row. The *Memoirs* tell the story, too, differing only from John Romney in point of detail. Greville took Emma off to Ranelagh Gardens, 'then the favourite theatre of gaiety and gallantry', as the *Memoirs* say. Emma attracted such attention 'with her form and agility' that she got carried away, and, 'to increase the applause with which she had been flattered, she gave the company some delightful specimens of her unrivalled powers both in musical expression and flexibility of action'. The passers-by adored her song-and-dance, and applauded her ecstatically. Thrilling to their praise, she redoubled her efforts to 'renewed peals of applause'. At that point Greville dragged her away. He had taken her to Ranelagh to give her a little harmless amusement, and 'to dazzle beholders by her beauty', not to 'please fools' with that beauty for the sake of their casual admiration. No doubt, at home, the copy Greville had taken of his January letter to Emma was produced, phrases in it sorrowfully pointed out, a lecture, in the manner of Mr Casaubon, delivered. The liaison seemed destined to founder, from Emma's failure to 'respect Greville's sentiments'. But, on this occasion keeping her temper, Emma went upstairs and, the *Memoirs* say, she exchanged her finery for a cottage dress, returning to announce her intention to relieve him for ever of her presence. Romney said that it was the dress of a lady's maid which she put on, in which she 'ever after appeared, and never again went to any public place'.[4]

Romney's version of the story receives some support from Angelo, who says he met her about this time dressed and behaving rather more like a religieuse than the kept woman she was. He says he met her 'in Rathbone Place . . . (. . . in the deepest mourning habiliments), walking with a solemn pace'. Having told him her address, she said 'at present she owed her ease and affluence to the F. G. [which we must take to denote Greville] and that both honour and gratitude forbade her to meet me [Angelo] again'. A lady's maid's dress might easily have been mistaken for deep mourning. This chastened Emma was surely encountered after the Ranelagh episode and her consequent moral reform.

The Reverend John Romney says Emma dressed always in her penitential maid's outfit while she was with Greville. Large sums were paid to a dressmaker, a Mrs Hackwood, in 1784 and 1785. If she was employed only to make these uniforms they were of shot silk. It is quite likely, though, that Emma continued to wear the outfit for some time after she first adopted it. Then, perhaps, as with so many of her impulsive projects for self-abasement, the novelty wore off. What is certain is that, in all the four years of Emma's liaison with Greville, this Ranelagh episode stands out as the only occasion on which Emma seems to have acted impulsively. Every other account of these years shows her obeying Greville's wish that she should lead a retired life. She anticipated his wishes and chose friends 'in a line of prudence & plainness', as Greville writes to his uncle, 'which, tho' I might have wished for, I could not have proposed to confine her'. Not a thought did Emma have in these years but to win Greville's approval, and, at all costs, prevent a recurrence of his disapproval which she found so dreadful. There were to be quarrels in the future, but, with Emma doing her utmost to ensure that they were not occasioned by her conduct, none was to be as shattering as the quarrel sparked by the Ranelagh episode.

After an occasion on which Greville and Emma had had words, in 1784, Emma wrote to him: 'you have made me unhappy by scolding me; how can you ... when you know it breaks my heart to be scolded, & speacily by Greville?' Her efforts to please Greville, a most demanding critic, and to suppress her natural inclination for excitement encouraged in her a rather nervous disposition, in constant dread of Greville's disapproval, always longing for his praise. When his weighty disapproval fell on her for some trifling fault, she was prone to be affected physically by the 'scolding'. A history of rashes which took her to doctors and off to sea-bathing establishments may well have been nervous in origin. Still, Emma forgot all scoldings when Greville was pleased to be pleased with her. The tedium of her secluded existence, and the limited diversions allowed to her, being magazines, music (she seems to have had lessons) and sittings to Romney, came with time to seem a full and varied life.

Greville understood Emma's character all too well, and played on it to his advantage. He knew perfectly well that she was capable of more than running a cosy home for him. In fact, he wrote to his uncle in 1785 that she was 'capable of anything grand, masculine or feminine'. Nevertheless, recognizing that 'there is a degree of nature in her, that she has the same pleasure in a retired & confined life as in a more extensive one', he saw no reason to 'make a parade of her, or a sacrifice of [his] amusements or business'. His seclusion of Emma was not totally a selfish act. He told her, and probably believed, that, by 'being totally clear from all the society and habits of kept women, creditable & quiet people' would respect her, and her reputation would be recovered. This sounds odd, because of course Emma was as much a kept woman now as she had been at Uppark. However, since Greville did not live constantly in Edgware Row, but spent some time at his Portman Square house, Emma's neighbourhood acquaintances would think her a lady of independent means, Edgware Row her own house, and Greville just a gentleman caller.

It is unlikely Emma's lady friends were so deceived. In fact, they may well have thought that Greville's brother, Colonel 'Wellbred' Robert, and friends like Cathcart, Heneage Legge and Richard Cumberland, whom Greville occasionally invited to the house, were enjoying Emma's favours too. The evenings on which these bachelor parties took place were red-letter days in Emma's life, when she could sparkle to a larger audience than just Greville and her mother.

Emma's mother, Mrs Lyon, mysteriously became Mrs Cadogan at some point during her time in Paddington – as mysteriously as her daughter had become Mrs Hart. The Reverend John Romney tells us that Mrs Cadogan always escorted Emma to his father's painting-room, and that they always travelled the short distance by hackney carriage. In fact, the entries in Emma's account books for coach fare do not always square with the dates in Romney's Day Books on which she sat to him. The painter's son's purpose in making these categorical statements was to deny a rumour originating in the *Memoirs* that Emma had been his father's mistress. So he stressed the immense respectability of the circumstances in which the sittings had taken place. Mrs Cadogan was probably not present at each of the three hundred and more sittings.

George Romney had few other interests in life than his painting. Born in 1734 in the north, he had a sketchy education. In 1762 he abandoned his wife and children and moved to London. Having studied the great artists' work there, he went on that visit to Italy where Greville acted as his patron. Inspired by the Italian painters, and by Raphael above all, he returned to London. He set up in Cavendish Square, and was immediately patronized by the nobility. Lord Chancellor Thurlow declared in 1781: 'Reynolds and Romney divide the Town; I am of the Romney faction.' So it was to a celebrated artist that Emma sat in March 1782.

Romney, though untutored in Latin and Greek, felt a strong attraction to classical subjects. One of the first paintings he did of Emma was that vital depiction of Circe advancing with arm upraised, perhaps magicking Odysseus' shipmates into swine. But the first picture of all, for which sketches were begun on 13 April 1782, was that now known as *Lady Hamilton as Nature*. John Romney writes that Emma was first brought 'by the Honourable Charles Greville to sit for a three-quarters portrait. It was that beautiful one, so full of *naivete*, in which she is represented with a little spaniel lap-dog under her arm.' One wonders whether that dog was Emma's own, a thoughtful present from Greville, perhaps, to replace the infant which had by then been sent away.

Emma sat to Romney thirteen more times in 1782 after her first visit to Cavendish Square, the last appointment being on 3 August. What time was not given to *Nature*, was devoted to *Circe*. The poet William Hayley, in his *Life* of Romney, says he had a letter from a friend in 1782, 'describing the very powerful impression made by this picture [*Circe*] on a party who then surveyed it'. The picture was still in Romney's painting-room in 1787, for Mrs Knowles, a Quaker lady who worked needlework portraits, saw it there then and declared, 'What a number of bad, indifferent, moderate, good and very good pictures must the hand paint ere it attains the sublimity of that figure!' This picture is so arresting, the colours so vivid even now, it is difficult to imagine that Greville preferred to see it excite visitors to Cavendish Square rather than possess it himself. As he did on another occasion, Greville reserved the painting for himself and then left it at Romney's till he was able to pay. In this case, he never did pay. *Circe* was destined to remain among Romney's many rolls of canvas till his death. The picture was never quite completed, which may have made Greville hesitate to pay for it. There was a small matter of wild beasts, with which Romney had intended to surround the enchantress. Gilpin was to do them, but never did. A surgeon who bought the picture cheaply at a sale following Romney's death took it upon himself to paint in a leopard on Circe's left, and two wolves on her right. The leopard has since been painted out; the wolves remain.

From this picture, from a beautiful preliminary painting of Circe's head, and from *Nature*, a fair description can be given of Emma's appearance when she first lived at Edgware Row. Huge, violet eyes were dominant under long, heavily marked eyebrows in a short oval face. Her nose was long, without much bridge to it, but sat delicately enough above an exquisitely indented upper lip. Emma's mouth was quite extraordinarily admired in her lifetime, and was the component of her beauty which most elicited comparisons with Greek sculpture. Her short expanse of forehead and softly moulded, small chin fostered the classical illusion, while her flawless complexion induced thoughts of marble in those who preferred statuary to life. Romney's innumerable sketches of Emma about this time show, however, that she had a whole range of expressions which, while they always exhibited a certain sweetness, had nothing to do with the pensive airs she thought appropriate when she posed as Circe or Ariadne or other antique personages.

Her figure at seventeen was not as striking a feature of her appearance as it was to be some six or seven years later. She was tall and well proportioned, her small head with its magnificent, thick load of auburn hair set off by square shoulders and a powerful bosom. Her waist in the *Circe* picture, however, is only moderately neat, and the draperies look to conceal quite heavy hips and limbs. Emma, at this date, was evidently beautiful, but she was not yet at the height of her attraction. Greville for instance told his uncle later that, when Emma first came to him, he considered himself an 'over-match' for her.

Nature, Circe, and the head for *Circe*, are the only paintings of Emma by Romney we can be sure were painted in this first series of sittings in 1782. He made a great number of drawings of her both now and when she sat again to him over a period from December 1783 to March 1786. These drawings are in pencil, gone over with pen and brush, often with a brown wash. Though some are in sketchbooks marked, for instance, 'January–June 84', others are on loose sheets of blue paper and undated. The drawings featuring Emma range from rough likenesses, probably jotted down while she was at rest between poses, to elaborate designs and compositions, intended for later transference to canvas.

One set of designs we can assign to the 1782 period on stylistic grounds. These are designs for a composition of Medea slaying her children. Romney had been interested in this part of the Argonaut epic since his days in Rome. He produced a cartoon for a painting of Medea in about 1778 or 1779 – after the classicist Dr Potter had sent him the appropriate translated extract from Euripides' *Medea*. In 1781, Romney went so far as to read the whole of Potter's translation of the play, when it was published that year. At any rate, his name was on the subscribers' list. When Emma appeared in his painting-room the following year, he recognized, Hayley says, that she had 'such expressive powers, as could furnish to a historical painter, an inspiring model for the various characters, either delicate, or sublime, that he might have occasion to represent'. Romney's sketches of Emma as Medea slaying her children are in quite a different mould to his commissioned portraits, which can suggest the chocolate box. There can be little doubt that these designs, four in all, date from this time.

Romney may also have begun, at this date, designs for a large-scale historical painting, in which Emma features as *Thetis Pleading with Achilles Before the Walls of Troy*. No designs have ever been discovered for this exceptional work. Stylistically the picture resembles *The Ghost of Darius* and *The Dream of Atossa*, on which he was working shortly before 1782. Like all Romney's historical paintings, this was painted for his own pleasure, and never left his studio. Working the designs up to a state where the composition might be committed to canvas was hard work to him. He probably painted the canvas over a period of years, doing only the designs at this date.

Romney worked on these designs for *Medea* and *Thetis* in the evenings; after dining simply at four, he would walk out into the countryside with his sketch-book. Romney probably made only a rough sketch of Emma in some suitable attitude in the morning and then worked from memory. As Hayley says, he 'delighted in sketching scenes from fancy'. Unfortunately, 'he did not equally love the less amusing labor, by which a figure rapidly invented must be slowly ripened into an accurate perfection of form'. The *Medea* designs are among hundreds which Romney never committed to canvas.

The sittings came to a temporary halt on 3 August 1783. Not until 1784 was Romney to paint again Emma's features – which Hayley likened to the language of Shakespeare in their power to express 'all the gradations of every passion, with a most fascinating truth'. If Romney missed Emma, her attendance at Cavendish Square had been a welcome break from her domestic round at Edgware Row.

Richard Cumberland has described Romney's style of conversation. When he was:

> in company with his intimates . . . he would give vent to the effusions of his fancy, and harangue in the most animated manner upon the subject of his art, with a sublimity of idea, and a peculiarity of expressive language, that was entirely his own; and in which education or reading had no share. These sallies of natural genius, clothed in natural eloquence, were perfectly original, very highly edifying, and entertaining in the extreme. They were uttered in a hurried accent, an elevated tone, and very commonly accompanied with tears, to which he was by constitution prone.

The mild-faced, stocky painter, from whom these torrents issued, may well have seemed a sage to the girl thirty years his junior. Emma was a natural pupil. Romney probably told her, as she sat there, of the theories of theatrical realism which his friend, the actor Henderson, was at this date expounding to him. Henderson, Sheridan and their cronies now were eager to express the weaknesses and emotions, and the 'human condition', of the characters they played. Emma definitely took heed of Henderson's theories, as her expression in the *Medea* designs, for example, shows. She must have been distressed to give up this exciting whirl of classical legend and wildly expressed ideas about art.

She probably did not know, when she left Cavendish Square on 3

August, that there was to be any more than a month's interval till
they next met. Romney went to stay with his friend William Hayley
in Kent. Greville went, as was his custom, to Warwick Castle in the
month of August. Emma and her mother may have gone to Hawarden
to see Mrs Kidd and 'little Emma', while he was away. Later, in 1784,
Emma tells Greville that she loves her two-year-old daughter, and
'when she comes & looks in my face & calls me "mother", endead
I then truly am a mother, for all the mother's feelings rise at once, &
tels me I am or ought to be a mother'. This sounds as though she had,
at some earlier point, probably in August 1782, felt exactly the opposite
about the child, and was astonished by these new feelings.

Why the sittings did not resume with painter's and patron's return
to London in October cannot be known. There was no jealousy of
Romney on Greville's part. Greville liked other men to admire Emma
in vain. In fact, he mentions to his uncle, with pride, their offers of
marriage and other proposals made to her. He had inculcated in Emma
such a strong 'desire for prudence', or habit of monogamy, that she was
never to be tempted from it for nearly twenty years.

The sittings may have lapsed because Greville was in financial difficulties. In 1781, he wrote to his uncle, 'I have gone on a little in the midst
of poverty in virtu,' and again, 'I go on, more bit by virtu than ever,
consequently I buy but very little.' He may have thought himself poor
then, but matters swiftly worsened. On 20 March 1782, Lord North, the
Prime Minister who had appointed Greville to the Board of Admiralty,
was driven to resign. The Opposition had successfully won support from
all sides of the House for motions condemning the continuation of the
American War. George III wrote to North on 27 March: 'At last the
fatal day is come, when the misfortunes of the times . . . have drove
me to, of changing the Ministry, and a more general removal of other
persons than I believe, was ever known before. I have fought to the last
for individuals, but the number I have saved, except my Bedchamber,
is incredibly few.' Greville was not among those saved. At the very
time when he was busy assuming the support of Emma, her mother
and child, his 'philosophy, patience, and resolution', as his uncle put
it, were thus put to a severe trial. He was particularly cheerful, as he
tended to be when real trouble faced him. He moved out of King's
Mews, back into Portman Square. And he said he gave up all his luxuries
– a carriage and some horses – as easily as he had taken them up.

Sir William's view, expressed in May 1782, that he dared say it
would not be long before Greville was 'in' again, was optimistic.
Greville declined to 'go in' with the ministry Lord Shelburne formed
following Rockingham's death in July 1782. He explained that he

did not 'like precipitately to join any set', though the members of Shelburne's administration suited his political colour perfectly – once Charles James Fox and his coterie had resigned. He waited. He had a disastrous tendency, in these years of coalition governments, to hang back when he should have advanced, and to withdraw when he should have hung on. He wrote in this same letter to his uncle that he was 'enmeshed in politics', but, in reality, he never engaged, except on behalf of others. He truly declared himself to be 'an excellent jobber for a friend'. He used his good political connections and his abilities as a 'character' judge to others' advantage, never to his own. He had a more distinct vision of the ignominious fall than of the glorious leap.

The winter months of 1782 went by, and still no opportunity seemed right for Greville to 'go in' with the Government. The 'handouts' which Greville made periodically to Emma, and with which she maintained the household, became less generous. Greville was naturally parsimonious. No doubt he made Emma feel that every one of her expenditures this winter brought him nearer to ruin. Her reference, in 1791, to her time with Greville being 'years of poverty and distress' may have been less of an exaggeration that at first it seems. In 1784, she was deeply apologetic about some few shillings she had been constrained to spend. With her capacity for self-denial, Emma may well have been the one to suggest that her sittings to Romney should halt.

Romney charged at this time twenty guineas for a three-quarter-length portrait (the popular size), eighty for a full-length, and forty for a half-length. So for *Nature* and the *Circe*, Greville would have to pay at some point one hundred guineas. He may well have been reluctant to initiate further payments. He prided himself on his 'credit and punctuality in money matters', which, he told his uncle in 1789, gave him 'the air of a rich man', although he was then 'at my worst'. Fine words. In fact, he paid only for *Nature* (in 1788), and never for the unfinished *Circe*.

There was only one glimmer of hope for Greville in the sea of financial worries that faced him, now he was maintaining Emma on £500 a year. Sir William's wife, Lady Hamilton, died at a country villa outside Naples from a *febbre biliare*, or bilious fever, in August 1782. Charles wrote to Sir William, when he heard the news in September, to express the shock he felt at 'the unexpected news of your loss'. In fact, the news cannot have been very unexpected. Poor Lady Hamilton had survived a serious crisis in her health, never good, in 1781. In April 1782, she had been so ill that she had penned letters to Sir William specifically for him to read after her death, and he had written sorrowfully to Greville of her 'tattered constitution'. Nor did

Greville feel so much shocked as anxious. Horace Walpole, writing to Sir Horace Mann in Florence, mentions the matter which concerned Greville. 'I hope', wrote Walpole, 'as she was a good fortune in land, that Sir William loses nothing by her death.'[5] Catherine Hamilton possessed estates in Pembrokeshire and other parts of Wales which brought in £8,000 a year. She left the lands, for which Sir William had originally married her, to her adored husband, as all expected. As Sir William's favourite nephew, Greville stood a fair chance of inheriting these Welsh estates himself, in due course.

While Greville was thinking of plans by which he could somehow capitalize on these expectations in his uncle's lifetime, what of Emma? She was pursuing her attempts to rectify the 'little or no education' which, she told a correspondent in 1802, she had had till she was seventeen. She was running the household to Greville's exacting standards on a shoe-string, and trying to be in all things 'what Greville pleases'. Her letters of 1784, in which she reflected on the past two years at Edgware Row, provide a clear picture of her trials and joys.

She had only 'one happiness in view', she wrote then, and that was to 'manege myself & try to be like Greville'. Emma was an immensely flattering companion. Her spirit of competition and her tendency to deride her own qualities led her to try and acquire others' characters. She also attempted to follow them in all their pursuits. This led to trouble with Greville. He wished Edgware Row to be a haven where he might 'read wright or set still' in his own apartments, as Emma put it. He wished Emma to provide an 'agreeable' home, 'without disturbing him' in any pursuits he wished to follow. For Emma his arrival at the house was a moment of high excitement in her life, a moment to which she might well have looked forward for days. She no doubt pestered him, as he saw it, with displays of affection while he was busy at his desk, interrupted his work with chatter and questions. He, tired from the dissipations of town life, rebuffed her demonstrations of affection, answered her questions shortly. Her expectations disappointed, her hurt feelings and hurt pride led her to anger. The 'eveness and steadiness of temper', the 'amiable goodness' Emma tells us, with which Greville met her outbursts, may be imagined.

He knew very well that Emma, once having 'tried [him] to the utmost', would then become miserably penitent, and desperately grateful for his magnanimous forgiveness of her 'little temper'. He could then impress on her the importance of his doings in town which kept him away from her, the importance to him of a noiseless home, free of disturbances such as conversation. Emma, still breathing *mea culpa*, would agree in everything with him. 'I have allways thought you right in the end when I have come to reason,' she wrote, speaking of her 'past follies'. Greville wrote to his uncle of Emma, 'I have made her conduct suitable to my retired stile by leading her by good humour and confidence.' Again he writes: 'I have never known any one led so completely by good nature, & I believe she would die before she yielded to ill-treatment.' As we have seen, there was a good deal of sadism in his 'good nature'.

Greville was, on the whole, pleased with Emma's efforts to improve herself, which pleased her in turn. In 1786, she told him her principal worry at the thought of being parted from him was that she 'should neither profit by [Greville's] conversation nor improve in any degree'. Even Emma, who was always insecure of Greville's feelings for her, felt confident enough in 1784 to declare 'there as been some little pleasure as well as pain'. Their sexual relationship was certainly satisfactory. Greville, that fastidious critic of women, wrote in 1785, 'she is the only woman I have ever slept with without having ever had any of my senses offended, & a cleanlier, sweeter bedfellow does not exist'.

Greville says Emma had a certain amount of vanity, and was pleased to discover her looks improved by her sober life. Whatever the difficulties involved in pleasing Greville, she would not have given him up for the King himself. She was painfully in love with him when he heard in early 1783 that his uncle was coming home on leave. Sir William Hamilton meant to bury his wife's embalmed body and to look into the management of his newly acquired estates in Wales.

CHAPTER THREE

Endead I then truly am a mother

The death of Lady Hamilton had dealt the English Minister a blow which, as he wrote both to his sister, the Dowager Countess of Warwick, and to a niece, Mary Hamilton, all his philosophy could not sustain. Though he knew the vanity of regrets, he told Mary Hamilton, he could not help indulging himself in them every moment. He had depended on his wife for twenty-four years, since their marriage in 1758, to make his home comfortable and his hours there a quiet delight. Now he found the traces of her industrious personality, 'a chair, a table, a pianoforte', insupportable. He told his sister in October that he felt 'quite unhinged by the cruel separation'. Sir William attempted to 'drive away thought as much as I can' through the autumn and winter following her death with a 'savage' programme of hunting and fishing expeditions with the King of Naples. He passed his evenings with the Queen and the Princess Royal, unwilling to remain at home. 'What is a home', he remarked, speaking again in 1785 of his 'desolate' situation, 'without a bosom friend and companion?'

When young William Hamilton married plain, rich Miss Barlow ('somewhat against my inclination', as he confided to Greville), he did not foresee what an agreeable wife she was to make him. It had proved a remarkably happy union, in large part because Catherine Hamilton allowed Sir William to ride rough-shod over her wishes. 'Her passion for him . . . was as lively to the last moment of her life as it was when she first knew him' – so Sir William's nieces Lady Stormont and Mary Hamilton agreed in 1784. 'She had no object in life but him & only regretted dying because she left him behind.'

Catherine Hamilton took a dislike to the Court of King Ferdinand and Queen Maria Carolina on arrival in Naples in 1764. Writing to a relation to invite her to stay in 1768 she said that she 'need not fear any of the Italian ceremonies and nonsense with us. We enter as little as we can into their stupid Assemblys.' And she later described the Court as 'the most extraordinary Court in Europe, – so full of Spanish etiquette at times; then no etiquette at all'. She never changed her opinion, and declared herself in 1777, on a visit to England, as 'thoroughly unwilling to go [back to Naples] . . . I am a bad Courtier.'

She offended the Duchess of Beaufort, who visited the Kingdom in 1772, by saying she had never heard of her. The Duchess then declared, '*Ce n'est pas surprenant qu'une petite Bourgeoise ne me connoît pas.*' As a result, Lady Mary Coke cancelled her own plans to visit Naples. She was not going there 'to be treated impertinently by Lady Hamilton'.[1] Catherine probably did well to make only rare sorties into Court and diplomatic life. Her preferred form of entertainment was giving concerts, at which all the best musicians, herself included, performed.

Sir William adored the life. He had been bred at the English Court, and he found the oddities of the Bourbon Court most entertaining. 'It is highly proper when one has an office to perform the duties of it with the utmost exactness,' was his view. Leaving Catherine to live 'the life of a hermit', he followed the passionate hunter King Ferdinand up hill, down dale, in pursuit of game. He stood by and encouraged while Ferdinand sported among the *lazzaroni*, the beggar population of Naples he loved. He thought that the King could have contended at the ancient Olympic games with success. The Queen, who had all the interest in statecraft and foreign policy her spouse lacked, was similarly fond of the English Minister. Sir William could be all things to all men, and he courted her as assiduously, in his urbane way, as he did her husband, for she directed the affairs of the country. He could say in 1775 that he had 'long been Le Doyen du Corps Diplomatique', a position more rightfully, at a Bourbon Court, that of the Spanish or French Minister.

Catherine hoped one day to settle in her native Wales. Sir William's thoughts were fixed on promotion. He was supremely happy in Naples. Still, as he wrote to Greville in 1775, 'I think it right to endeavour at getting to the head of one's profession.' He wanted to become an ambassador, not remain an envoy to a minor court. If he felt that Catherine did not help him by her reluctance to make a show at Court, he never said so.

They were happiest together in their charming villa at Portici, where they went when the Court removed annually to the Palace there. Catherine adored the quiet. She spent happy hours playing her instruments, the pianoforte and the harpsichord, in a music-room which was 'vis-à-vis' to Vesuvius. Catherine, always animated when talking about her beloved music, described to Mary Hamilton in 1778 how the volcano 'now & then treats me with an explosion while I am playing, the other night there was the finest "Girandole" of red hot Stones you can imagine, it made an amazing report but we played on, as you would, if you had heard a pop-gun in the street – See what custom does.' Sir William, on this occasion, had joined her at her instrument with his violin. All too often, he was out all day taking 'great & almost constant exercise' with the King and only came home to drink tea before going off to the Palace to play a lottery game called Biribis with the King and Queen. 'How tedious are the hours I pass in the absence of my beloved,' she wrote in a soliloquy in April 1782. How tedious, and, it is tempting to add, how many. William only discovered the extent of her loneliness and isolation when he found the soliloquy and two letters addressed to him in her workbox following her death. 'No one but those who have felt it can know the miserable anxiety of an undivided love,' she wrote in one of her impassioned revelations of her soul. 'When he is present, every object has a different appearance, when he is absent how lonely, how isolated I feel.'

Her attempts to 'seek peace in company' generally made her only more 'uneasy'. In 1780 she made a friend, a cousin of her husband's, who could afford her some kind of peace while Sir William was occupied. By this date, Catherine had become severely religious. Indeed, her earnest wish at her death was that William, a professed free-thinker, should give up his 'dissipated life' and attend to 'those great truths in comparison of which all is folly'. Twenty-year-old William Beckford, future author of *Vathek* and a confirmed exhibitionist, found he had a dark, brooding side in common with Catherine Hamilton, and a love of the pianoforte. Combining the two, he wrote, 'we indulge our imaginations at home [while Sir William hunted] and play strange dreams upon the pianoforte and talk in a melancholy visionary style which would . . . fill you with pleasing sadness.'[2] Catherine had a real understanding of music. Dr Burney was much indebted to her for information on Sicilian music when he visited Naples in 1770 to research his *History of Music*. She played before the young Mozart. What Beckford prized above all in Catherine, however, was this. 'I can venture expressing to you all my wayward thoughts, can murmur – can even weep in your company.' Catherine's companionable qualities were what her husband also valued. Sad, then, that it should have been young Beckford who took her 'weak, tottering frame' for drives in the delightfully verdant King's Boschetto. It was Beckford who had the benefit of her informed conversation in the last days of her life in 1782.

Lady Hamilton's other favourite was Dr Drummond, a noted English doctor, who had retired to Naples in the 1770s. Drummond 'does not act as a physician here, but is happy to assist his countrymen on all occasions', Sir William informed a friend. He was, to all intents and purposes, Lady Hamilton's personal physician. The nature of the illness that plagued her all her life is not clear. Horace Walpole described her in 1764 as 'dying of an asthma', and the Marchese di Gallo,

Neapolitan Minister to the French Court, confirmed that she was '*un poco astmatica*'. Sir William refers to her 'too frequent and severe sufferings', and Greville to her 'weak frame'. The resignation with which Catherine announced to her husband, 'My cold has turned into a cough,' suggests that such occurrences were all too frequent. Perhaps the 'miserable anxiety' of her love for Sir William preyed on her nerves and resulted in physical debility. Dr Drummond calmed those nerves just as Beckford did. Catherine was looking forward to the tonic of his presence at the Portici villa when he was thrown from a horse on his way from Naples. He died of his injuries on 13 August 1782. The loss of this treasured companion is said to have contributed to her end. She died on the twenty-fifth of that month.

In February 1783, Sir William applied to Lord Grantham, the Foreign Secretary, for leave. He drew attention to 'the heavy loss' he had sustained the preceding August. He also wished to settle his affairs in England after five years' absence. He was unhappy about the steward of the Welsh estates. He intended to 'put my affairs in Wales on another footing'. At the same time, he would carry out Catherine's wish that she should be buried in Slebech in the county of Pembrokeshire. In her workbox letters she had also entreated him 'not to suffer me to be shut up after I am dead till it is absolutely necessary' and to 'remember the promise you have made me that your bones should lie by mine when God shall please to call you'.

Another project he had in mind was the sale of a painting by Correggio, and of a number of pieces of antiquity. He was £4,000 in debt to James Byres, among other dealers in virtu. Hopes of selling the Correggio to the Grand Duke of Russia had not been realized.

Among the antiquities he hoped to sell was a Roman glass vase which he had bought from Byres recently for a thousand pounds. Sir William believed it to be one of the finest 'monuments of antiquity'. The translucent cobalt vessel was adorned with a mythological frieze in milky white glass. Debt persuaded him to bring the vase with him to England in 1783. He had heard that the Duchess of Portland was interested in his vase, and he hoped to sell her the Correggio and a colossal Jupiter head, too. He considered the three of them 'the cream of all the Virtu I have ever possessed in my life'.

In Naples Sir William was packing up all, selling his horses, and letting his country houses for the year he intended to be away. In England, a change of ministry finally brought Charles Greville employment. He became Treasurer of the Royal Household. His younger brother, Robert Fulke Greville, a most assiduous courtier, had advocated Charles for this useful post. It was in the King's personal gift, so future changes of

ministry were immaterial. Greville took up his duties on 22 February,
and on the same date moved back into King's Mews. He cut a strange
figure at Court, his pretensions and his joyless mien being kindly
received only for the sake of his popular brother. Still, he could
comfort himself with the adoration lavished upon him by Emma,
and the eagerness with which she drank in news of the Court. Her
main amusement was walking round Paddington Green, looking at
the ducks in the three ponds there, and watching the carriages going
past her windows on their way to London.

By 14 August 1783, Sir William was in London, at Nerot's Hotel in
King Street, Mayfair. He made Emma's acquaintance very soon after
his arrival. So struck was he by her 'exquisite beauty' that he forgot his
debts and commissioned Reynolds to paint her portrait. The first sitting
was in the month he arrived, and there were a further spate of sittings
at the beginning of 1784. In April 1784, Mary Hamilton heard that Sir
William had been often at Sir Joshua Reynolds' house recently, that 'he
escorted my Cousin Chas Greville's Mistress, in a Hackney Coach', and
that Sir Joshua was painting 'this Woman's picture for him to take to
Naples'. Mary intended to 'have some entertainment in plaguing Sir
William with this information'.

Sir Joshua was an old friend of Sir William's. He had painted his
picture twice – once, on his last leave, as part of a group portrait of
members of the Society of Dilettanti, who were shown toasting Sir
William on his introduction to the Society. Sir Joshua was an integral
part of the 'set' Sir William saw on his leaves in England. The set
included Sir Joseph Banks, Mrs Garrick, Horace Walpole and Lord
Pembroke, and they shared an interest in science and the arts. Reynolds'
picture of Emma as a Bacchante is not a success. Emma looks as if she
has been squeezed into the frame, and most unlike the maenads of Sir
William's Greek vases in Naples. It was her likeness to them which
prompted him to commission the portrait of her in this guise. Still,
Sir William paid, and the picture was duly sent to Naples and much
admired by connoisseurs.

How did Sir William appear to Emma in 1783? He was fifty-three
years old. Though he felt himself in 1782 to be growing old 'apace',
he could still boast that he bore 'fatigue much better than those who
are much younger and fresher'. 'The crows feet are deep in my face,'
he told Georgiana Countess Spencer, following his wife's death. Still,
the description which his friend Sir Nathaniel Wraxall gave of him in
1779 may stand as a description of the widower Emma met in 1783.
'In his person, though tall and meagre, with a dark complexion, a very
aquiline nose, and a figure which always reminded me of Rolando in

"Gil Blas", he had nevertheless such an air of intelligence, blended with distinction, in his countenance, as powerfully attracted and conciliated all who approached him.'[3] Emma may well have felt awkward before such a personality at first.

Her shyness wore off, and her life became enhanced by Sir William's presence in London. She speaks, in the summer of 1784, of the gratitude she feels to him. He effected the reintroduction of Romney into her life. Sir William sat, in December 1783, to Romney for a portrait in which he wears the Star of Bath, emblem of his knighthood. At the same time, Emma's name reappears in Romney's Day Books, and one of the paintings for which she sat was a Bacchante. The inference is plain. Sir William was not satisfied with the Reynolds Bacchante. On one of his visits to 'The Fair Tea-maker of Edgware Row', Emma spoke wistfully of her visits to Cavendish Square. Sir William had a talent for kind, practical action. He arranged that Romney should paint an alternative portrait of Emma as a Bacchante, to join the other in Naples. Emma is depicted as running, laughing, encouraging a dog beside her. Emma's association with Romney resumed. From this December till March, 1786 when she left London, the artist painted her constantly. Greville no doubt noticed the difference in Emma's spirits, after her sittings for the Romney Bacchante. With his finances on a more even keel, he decided to afford her a pleasure which could benefit him, as has been described.

It is a mark of the admiration Sir William felt for Romney that he gave up seven different days to sit to him. Ever since his arrival in London he had been involved in a flurry of visits to all the relations and friends who clamoured to see him. Clubs and societies demanded his attendance. The King and Queen at Windsor thought of him with affection and wished personally to express their sorrow at his loss. In a great many activities Sir William was accompanied by his favourite, Greville. Emma had no bone to pick with him for dragging her beloved away. Still, Sir William made time to visit Edgware Row periodically. He told Greville that Emma's beauty 'often had its effect' on him. These visits had an effect on Greville, too – and a salutary one. He wrote to his uncle, in 1785, 'I know you thought me jealous of your attention to her.' He was spurred on by his jealousy to show Emma a good deal more attention himself. Emma did indeed have reason to 'allways think of [Sir William] with grattude', as she wrote in 1784.

In November, Sir William was introduced by Greville to the elderly Duchess of Portland at Bulstrode Park, where she spent most of her days playing cards with her equally decrepit friend, Mrs Delaney. Horace Walpole describes the Duchess as 'a simple woman, but perfectly

sober, and intoxicated only by empty vases'.[4] Sir William and she
had something in common, then. After preliminary negotiations for
the vase had been conducted, Sir William set Charles free from the
wearisome task of helping him charm the old ladies. He employed
instead Mary Hamilton, who proved a far more willing aide. In Sir
William's letters to Mary, from January to June 1784, he apologizes for
employing her as his go-between. In fact, it was Mary who did almost
all the hard work, which resulted in the Duchess buying what is now
called the Portland Vase, together with four lesser pieces for eighteen
hundred guineas.

Charles Greville may have been released from the ardours of executing
this sale because of his political problems. In December 1783, the uneasy
coalition between Fox and North, which had brought him employment
in February, ended with the defeat of the India Bill. George III had given
his famous permission to let it be known that whoever voted for the
bill was no friend of his. Pitt then formed an administration. In January
1784, when Parliament reassembled, Fox and North commanded an
Opposition majority. Charles Greville resigned, and, as Lady Craven
coyly tells us, 'in consequence of this retirement, many of his leisure
hours were bestowed on me'.[5] She notes at the same point that, while
having 'an elegant taste for the fine arts, he had indulged [it] too much
for the narrow limits of his fortune'. This scapegrace peeress had had
such a flagrant affair with the French Ambassador to London in 1773
that few continued to speak to her. She was evidently well served by
having to listen to Greville's complaints of his poverty following his
resignation. Emma, in 1791, refused to visit Lady Craven in London.
Fury over her affair with Greville, rather than the prudery which Horace
Walpole suggested, may have been the reason.

From December 1783 till March 1786, Emma sat to Romney for
portraits four or five times a month. He also painted her into the
historical pictures he painted for his own pleasure. If she was not
present, he could conjure up some appropriate expression of hers
(with the help of his sketch-book) for whatever character he was
painting. This was certainly the case with the Shakespearean scenes
he painted in late 1786 and 1787, after she had ceased to sit to him;
Cassandra and Miranda, for instance, have the features of Emma. Of
the likenesses of Emma which were definitely painted during the second
series of sittings, perhaps the finest work is *The Spinstress*. This work was
commissioned by Greville, and sittings had commenced by April 1784.
Robinson, a pupil of Romney's, tells us that the artist 'first caught the
idea [for the pose] from observing a cobbler's wife sitting in a stall'
on one of his afternoon sorties into the country with his sketch-book.

He also observed Emma practising 'the country craft' of spinning in Edgware Row. Greville and Romney sit at a sturdy table while Emma sits at her wheel, set a little apart from the gentlemen, drawing out the thread with the shuttle in one hand. She is listening intently to her beloved Greville, who has turned to address a remark to her. Sir William stands beyond Romney, gazing intently at Emma. Clearly, her 'exquisite beauty' is having its effect on him. Emma complained in 1786, 'I cant stir a hand, a legg, or foot, but what he is marking as graceful & fine.' Some have claimed that Greville is the standing figure, but to suggest that Greville ever looked at Emma in that searching, soulful manner, or that Romney is the youthful figure conversing with Emma, is folly. These lightning sketches are unmistakable portraits of Sir William and Charles Greville.

Romney broke his usual rule, of having his sitters come to him, on 21 April 1784, on which day his Diary has the appointment, 'Mrs Hart at 10 Edgware Road'. His son tells us it was his practice to make only a light sketch of Emma's attitude, when beginning a portrait, and to use a model or layman to flesh it out. There can be little doubt that he came to Edgware Row on this day, with the attitude of the cobbler's wife in mind, to make this light sketch. As Patricia Jaffé says in her catalogue to the 1972 exhibition of 'Lady Hamilton' at Kenwood, it gives the impression of 'having been made in the open air outside a simple country house such as Greville's must have been at Edgware Row'.

It was not the difficulty of transporting the spinning-wheel to Cavendish Square which prompted Romney to break his rule. He wished to capture the sense of contentment Emma felt in her home. The finished portrait, which has chickens scrabbling in the dirt round Emma's feet, in fact loses much of the touching quality of the first sketches. In place of the intent figure bent over her work, there is a fine lady, plying her wheel with the amused air of Marie-Antoinette at her dairy. Greville evidently liked the finished work, referring to Emma more than once as 'the original of the Spinstress'. This did not, of course, stop him from leaving it at Romney's house for others to covet.

There is a typical Grevillean coda to the story of this painting. In 1788, a Mr Christian Curwen offered to buy it. As it was still on reserve for Greville, Romney informed this other patron of the offer. Greville was still in debt to him for every painting of Emma he had commissioned. Nevertheless, Romney said, if Greville still wanted it, he would turn down Curwen's offer, keep it for Greville, and 'postpone the payment till it might suit Mr Greville's convenience'. Greville wrote to protest he did indeed want it, only 'I find myself daily so much poorer.' In fact, he suggested that Curwen should buy the picture, on the condition that he, Greville, should have the option of repurchasing it (an odd use of the term) when he should be in funds. Curwen was persuaded to agree to this, and, in turn, he imposed his own condition that, should this occur, Romney should paint him another picture of Emma as a replacement. Greville wrote to tell Romney of Curwen's condition, which he knew 'would be agreeable to you'. He expressed blithe satisfaction that he did not have 'repeatedly [to] benefit by [Romney's] sacrifices'. Here he referred to the occasion on which Romney had lost a buyer for the *Circe*, through keeping it on reserve for Greville. Unsurprisingly Greville never considered himself in quite so satisfactory a financial position as to 'recover what I now lose with regret'. Curwen paid one hundred and fifty guineas for the picture.

Romney mentioned to his son 'a scheme he had contrived for illuminating the theatres, by throwing the light upon the stage from above; by which the actors would be seen to greater advantage and with more effect'. He applied this scheme in his paintings. The pictures known respectively as *Lady Hamilton at Prayer*, *Lady Hamilton as St Cecilia* and *Lady Hamilton as a Vestal*, painted about this time, and the head of Miranda, painted in 1786, all show Emma gazing upwards, most expressively, with a strong light from above throwing her features into bold relief. The pose and the lighting mean that her chin, a weak feature, is obscured, and her lovely eyes emphasized, to her 'greater advantage'. In the portraits of this time we see Emma and Romney joining to produce the effects of theatrical realism with which he experimented in later years.

Other paintings Romney was producing in 1784 were illustrations to his friend Hayley's poem, *The Triumphs of Temper*. Hayley had offered it for illustration to Romney at the time of its composition in 1780. The poem tells the story of a young dressmaker, called Serena, who had a turbulent life, due entirely to the excesses of her temper, and who won happiness at last by curbing it. It makes dull reading today, but was much admired on publication and ran into many editions. Such ladies as the Duchess of Devonshire took its moral temporarily to heart. Hayley tells us that Romney, 'in despite of his many avocations', had finished four of the ten plates which appeared in the sixth edition, 1788, within two or three years after the first publication of the poem in 1780. Emma modelled for some of these, including *Serena in the Boat of Apathy*, and, more cheerfully, *Serena Reading the Gazette*. Emma admired Hayley's poem greatly; she found its allegorical dwellings on the advantages of good temper most pertinent to her own life.

No doubt she referred to this 'bible' after a stormy quarrel which she had with Greville in May 1784. The repentance she felt has been detailed in the last chapter. She was eager that he should follow his pursuits at home 'or else whare, for your absence has taught me that I ought to think my self happy if I was within a mile of you'. However diverting she found Cavendish Square, however often Greville appeared with Sir William at Edgware Row, she still felt neglected, and envious of the amusements Greville indulged in without her. Moreover, a separation from Greville, long planned, which was to last two whole months, was about to occur. Emma was no doubt in a highly nervous state when she raged and fumed.

Greville had certainly been amusing himself extensively without her in Polite Society. He and Sir William dined with the Stormonts in March, before going to the Prince of Wales's ball at Carlton House. Sir William's niece, Mary Hamilton, was a reluctant member of their party. When Mary acted as lady-in-waiting at Kew Palace in 1779, the Prince of Wales had been deeply smitten with her charms. She was the first to capture his susceptible heart. He wrote her long letters, signed Palemon, in which he described his love. She treated him as an errant younger brother, and reproved him for swearing and other faults. She elicited from him a most amusing character sketch of himself. 'Tho' rather too great a penchant to grow fat, ye features of his Countenance are strong & manley . . . un petit nez retrousse cependant assez anime . . . I forgot to add my uggly ears.' The correspondence was halted abruptly by Mary, when he veered in his affections and began to confide in her his love for the actress 'Perdita' Robinson.

She had not seen the Heir to the Throne since she resigned her post (for reasons of fatigue). She was now looking forward to marrying a Derbyshire squire called Dickenson. Unfortunately, the Prince of Wales 'particularly' requested her presence at his ball. She was in no mind to go. A ball dress would be an expense she could little afford; she had no ambition to be 'in the first circles'. Sir William exerted pressure on her to comply. Relations rallied round with offers of millinery and flowers, velvet for her bodice, shoe buckles. The 'carelessness of her dress' was reckoned to be her only fault. A friend explained that Mary knew 'assez bien, that she can charm without it, & she despises it'. She was pretty, intelligent, an excellent musician, and had 'saucy eyes' besides. Emma found Sir William's and Greville's affectionate relation of Mary's virtues insupportable. Her anger at Greville's neglect of her may well have been exacerbated by his, and his uncle's, attendance on Mary. (Nor did Mary think much of the time Sir William spent with Emma, referring to her as 'this Woman'.)

On 6 June 1784, Emma set off with her mother for Hawarden. This visit had been arranged by Greville to occupy the time he would be out of London. He was accompanying his uncle first to Pembrokeshire and thence to Scotland, to the Hamilton estates there. Greville was still severely displeased with Emma and her ungovernable temper. After an interview in which he forgave her, he would not see her off. He left that duty to Sir William. In her distress at leaving Greville with such unhappy memories of her, Emma tried to be gay on parting with Sir William. 'Ask him how I looked,' she directed Greville. Yet she was so distraught, 'my heart was ready to break'. She could not stop crying long enough to offer Sir William a kiss. She forgot, under the strain of parting with Greville, an important book which had instructions 'how to bile that Bark', or boil that bark.

Hawarden was not the end of Emma's journey. She had been suffering from rashes on her knees and elbows, and Mr W—, her doctor, had given her a prescription which had done little good. She referred contemptuously to his medicine as 'those things', presumably pills. A course of sea-bathing was then recommended, the favoured remedy for skin complaints in the late eighteenth century. Emma's particular complaint was probably eczema, which is nervous in origin. At the bathing resort to which she went, she was given the treatment held to cure scurvy, eczema and a host of associated complaints. The 'Bark', to which she refers, was Peruvian Bark, which was boiled in water. The infusion, known as 'tang', was drunk or applied to the affected areas. Salt water, however, was considered the essential part of the cure. It was drunk. Most discreetly and awkwardly, sufferers bathed in it, with the aid of a 'bathing-house', which an attendant rolled down to the sea, and from which the client then emerged into the water, clad in a cumbersome long shift. Sea-water was heated at home, in Emma's case, for her to rest her elbows in it.

At Hawarden, Emma's object was to fetch 'little Emma' away from her grandmother. She repaid Mrs Kidd five guineas that she had 'laid out' on the child – 'I would not take her away shabbily.' Greville had decided that the child should now leave the care of her great-grandmother. Though Mrs Kidd survived till at least 1791, she may well have complained of the burden she felt little Emma to be on a woman of her years.

With little Emma, Mrs Hart and her mother went to Chester. They stayed here with Mrs Burt, who recommended to them the bathing resort of Parkgate, and the lodgings of a Mrs Ladmore there. Emma was distinctly worried about going to a resort which was so near the place of her birth. She knew Greville would think it indiscreet. The resort, also port for Ireland, lay only four miles west of Denhall, below the village of Neston on the Wirral Peninsula, as has been mentioned.

But Mrs Burt warned against the expense of Abergele, the more distant resort Greville favoured. His second choice, Hoylake, had only three houses and not one fit for a Christian, Emma reported.

Possibly it was now that Emma's mother, going right into Lyon country, changed her name to Doggin, soon altered to Cadogan. Possibly she feared being recognized and conclusions drawn about the small child with her husbandless daughter. No doubt Emma had some marvellous story about a husband lost at sea for the lady with whom they lodged at Parkgate, when they arrived there on 12 June. This was a Mrs Darnwood, whose husband was a customs officer, and the house can still be seen, distinguished by the design 'NELSON' picked out in black pebbles on a yellow ground in the front garden. Faced in rough stone, it stands at the foot of a terrace looking out to sea.

Emma wrote constantly to Greville. Her letters reveal the growing love she felt for her child. From 'poor Emma' in the first letter, the child becomes a 'great romp', then 'this guidy wild girl . . . you dont know how I love her'. Greville dashed her hopes that the child might live with her at Edgware Row with a cruel reminder of 'agreaments'. Emma had earlier agreed to put the two-year-old child in the boarding school Greville proposed. Now she had discovered that 'when she comes & looks in my face & calls me "mother" . . . I then truly am a mother.'

She had no choice but to 'come in to all as you propose', she wrote to Greville. She might love her wilful, affectionate, blue-eyed daughter. Financial considerations rendered impractical all choice between giving up her child 'intirely' to Greville, and giving up Greville for her daughter. By 27 July she was back in London with her mother and with Emma, awaiting Greville. With her beloved's return would also come the dreaded moment when she would lose her child to Mr and Mrs Blackburn's establishment in Manchester. She tried to 'come in' to Greville's 'whay a thinking' and believe 'Hollidays spoils children', to think, 'O Greville if her poor mother had ever had the luck & prospect, merly in haveing a good edducation that she has, what a whoman might she have been.'

The dread and anticipation she felt as she awaited Greville found physical manifestation in a 'rash out all over me and a fevour'. She says she was eight days ill. 'I dare say I should have been very dangerously ill iff it had not come out,' she says with some self-importance. She spoke more truly than she knew. The crisis was over, and she had sloughed off her maternal feelings. Greville occupied all her heart once more.

The letters tell the story in Emma's words. She wrote on 15 June, when she had reached Parkgate:

I bathe & find the water very soult. Here is a great many laidys batheing, but I have no society with them as it is best not. So pray my dearest Greville, write soon & tell me what to do as I will do just what you think proper & tell me what I am to do with the child for she is a great romp & I can hardly master her. I dont think she is ugly, but I think her greatly improved, she is tall, good eys & brows & as to lashes she will be passible, but she has over grown all her cloaths. I am makeing and mending all as I can for her. Pray my dear Greville do lett me come home as soon as you can for I am all most broken hearted being from you, endead I have no plasure nor happiness. I wish I could not think on you, but if I was the greatest laidy in the world I should not be happy from you so dont lett me stay long.

She wrote again on 22 June:

Parkgate
June 22 1784

My ever dear Greville,

How teadous does the time pass a whay till I hear from you. I think it ages since I saw you & years since I heard from you. Endead, I should be miserable if I did not reccolect on what happy terms we parted, – parted yess, but to meet again with tenfould happiness. Oh, Greville, when I think on your goodness, your tender kindness, my heart is so full of grattitude that I want words to express it. But I have one happiness in vew which I am determined to practice & that is eveness of temper & steadyness of mind. For endead, I have thought so much of your aimable goodness when you have been tried to the utmost that I will, endead I will, manege myself & try to be like Greville – endead I can never be like him. But I will do all I can towards it & I am sure you will not desire more. I think if the time would come over again I would be different. But it does not matter, there is nothing like bying expearance, I may be happyer for it hearafter & I will think of the time coming & not the time past, except to make comparrasons to shew you what alterations there is for the best – so my Dearest Greville, dont think of my past follies, think on my good – little as it has been & I will make you amends by my kind behavior; you shall never repent your partiality – & if you had not behaived with such angel like goodness to me at parting it would not have had such effect on me. But I have done nothing but think on you since & O Greville, did you but know when I do think, what thoughts – what tender thoughts, you would say Good God & can Emma have such feiling senceibility – no. I never could think it, but now I hope to bring her to conviction & she may now prove a valluable & aimable whoman – true, Greville & you shall not be disapointed. I will be every thing you can wish. But mind you Greville, your troo great goodness has brought this at bear, for you dont know what I am. Would you think it Greville? – Emma – the wild unthinking Emma is a grave thoughtful phylosopher. Tis true Greville & I will convince you

I am when I see you. But how I am running on – I say nothing abbout this guidy wild girl of mine: what shall we do with her, Greville, she is as wild & as thoughtless as somebody when she was a little girl, so you may gess how that is. Whether you will like it or no there is no telling but one comfort is she is a little afraid of me. Would you believe on satturday whe had a little quarel, I mean Emma & me & I did slap her on her hands & when she came to kiss me & make it up I took her on my lap & cried. Now do you blame me or not, pray tell me. Oh Greville, you dont know how I love her, endead, I do. When she comes & looks in my face & calls me "mother", endead I then truly am a mother, for all the mother's feelings rise at once, & tels me I am or ought to be a mother, for she has a wright to my protection & she shall have it as long as I can & I will do all in my power to prevent her falling into the errors her poor once miserable mother fell into. But why do I say miserable. Am not I happy abbove any of my sex, at least in my situation, does not Greville love me, or at least like me, does not he protect me, does not he provide for me, is not he a father to my child. O why do I call myself miserable: No, it whas a mistake & I will be happy, chearful & kind & do all as my poor abbilitys will let me to return the Fatherly goodness & prottection he has shewn. Again, O my dear Greville, the reccolection of past scenes brings tears to my eys, but the are tears of happiness. To think of your goodness is two much. But once for all, Greville, I will be grateful. Adue.

It is near batheing time & I must lay down my pen and I wont finish tell I see when the post comes, whether there is a letter; he comes in abbout one a clock. I hope to have a letter to day.

I must not forgett to tell you my knees is well as I may say there is hardly a mark & my elbows is much better. I eat my vittuels very well & I am quite strong & feil hearty & well & I am in hopes I shall be very well; you cant think how soult the watter is & there is a many laidys bathing here. But, Greville, I am obliddged to give a shilling a day for the batheing house & whoman & twopence a day for the dress; it is a great expence & it fretts me wen I think of it. But wen I think how well I am & my elbows likely to gett well, it makes me quite happy for at any rate it is better than paying the doctor. But wright your oppinion freily & tell me what to do. Emma is crying because I wont come & bathe, so Greville, adue tell after I have dipt. May God bless you, my dearest Greville & believe me faithfully, affectionatly & truly yours only

Emma Ht.

She wrote again three times that week. Why did not Greville write to her? 'If you knew my uneaseyness you would.' She sent her love to Sir William, or 'Pliney' as she called him. (The nickname derived from Sir William's points of resemblance to the Roman naturalist and volcanic expert, Pliny.)

'Can you, my dear Greville, no you cant have forgot your poor

Emma already,' she wrote in her next letter. He had said he would
be happy to see her again. 'There as been some little pleasure as well
as pain & endead, did you but know how much I love you, you would
freily forgive me any former quarels for I now suffer for them & one
line from you would make me happy.'

At last she received a letter. She wrote back merrily, saying that her
daughter was 'much oblidged to you for remembering her & she hopes
you will give her a oppertunity of thanking you personally for your
goodness to her. I think you wont be disappointed in her, tho mothers
– Lord bless me, what a word for the gay wild Emily to say – should
not commend, but leave that for other people to do.'

This presumption – that with Emma would return her child to
London – prompted a swift reply from Greville.

Unkind Greville, yes I have got your letter but why do you scold me;
if I wrote scral & ill, it was with thinking with two much kindness on
you. You have mad me unhappy by scolding me; how can you when you
know my dispotion, when you know it breaks my heart to be scolded &
speacily by Greville, but I wont think you meant it ill-natured, tho you
have maid me unhappy & if you had killd me, your kindness to my poor
Emma would make me forget it for, endead, my dear Greville, I love you
two well to neglect you in any one point, so pray forgive me – & has to
your goodness in regard to agreaments, endead I will come in to all as you
propose: I will give her up to you intirely; do what you will with her, I
here sollemnly say that I will never break from my word. You shall take
her, put her there where you propose, lest any quarels, tho I hope there
will be none – hope she shall stay whear you propose putting her. Lett
what will happen I give her up to you to act as you think proper by her.
Take her, Greville & may God reward you for it, tho her mother cant. All
as I desire is that if you will lett me take her home when I go to stay tell
you come to see her whilst she is there. Nobody shall see her, tho neither
you nor I need be ashamed of her, but if you dont like that, I will give it
up, so you see, my dearest Greville, what confidence I put in you. Now
scold me, unkind Greville, how can you do so. Pray write to me derectly
& wright kind. Give my dear kind love to Sir Willm say everything from
me that you can for endead I love him. I should not now wright in such
a hurry only if I dont send it of by 4 o clock I cant send it of tell Tuesday,
so dont think I cant spare a hour, yes, 6 hours, all my whole life I could
spare to do any thing for Greville, so God bless you, my dear Greville. Mrs
Ladmore is gone to live at Chester or I should have gone there, that is my
reason as I am at Mrs Downwards, but it is the cheapest place I could gett
for she thinks nothing a truble, she eat soult watter 4 or 5 times a day for
me to wash my elbows in, but pray lett me come to town before you if
it is only a day or two, you know my reason. It may be some comfort to
you peraps to know that my elbows & knees is allmost well & I never

was better in my life, so Greville, if you will be happy to see me, you will find me in good health, handsome & fonder & kinder to you than ever. So my dearest cruil Greville, why did you scold me, I would not have scolded you at so great distance, but I will forgive you & I say again you shall see me every thing you can wish & I will be allways yours ever affectionatly & sincerely

E. H.   Adue.

Greville had made his point. He wrote again in kinder vein.

Parkgate
July the 3ʳᵈ 1784

I was very happy, my dearest Greville, to hear from you as your other letter vexd me, you scolded me so, but it is over & I forgive you. I am much oblidged to you for all the kind things you say to me & I am very happy to think we shall meet soon again, happy, good humerd & chearfull. I will be so & I think there is no fear of you. You dont know, my dearest Greville, what a pleasure I have to think that poor Emma will be comfortable & happy & Greville, if she does but turn out well, what a happyness it will be & I hope she will for your sake. I will teach her to pray for you as long as she lives & if she is not grateful & good it wont be my fault but what you say is very true, a bad dispotion may be made good by good example & Greville would not put her any whear to have a bad one. I come in to your whay a thinking Hollidays spoils children; it takes there attention of from there scool, it gives them a bad habbit, when the have been a month & goes back, this does not pleas them & that is not wright & the do nothing but think wen the shall go back again. Now Emma will never expect what she never had, so I hope she will be very good, mild & attentive & we may have a deal of comfort. O Greville if her poor mother had ever had the luck & prospect, merly in haveing a good edducation that she has, what a whoman might she have been, but I wont think. All my happiness now is Greville & to think that he loves me makes a recompense for all, for if he did not love me would he be so good, kind & affectionate, No, tis imposible, therefore I will have it so, I have said all as I have to say abbout Emma yet, only she gives her duty & I will now tell you a little abbout my self. I have not took but 2 of those things from Mr W – as the sea watter has done me so much good I have drunk a tumbler glas every morning fasting, walked half an hour & then bathed & breakfasted. I have had the tang approyd to my knees & elbows every night going to bed & every day washed them twice a day in sea water & the are just well, therefore, as long as I stay I had better go on in my old whay for I can take Mr W's prescription at home, but not sea water, tang etc. I am very well, looks well, has a good appetite & is better than ever I was in my life. I have no society with anybody but the mistress of the house & her mother and sister. The latter is a very genteel yong lady, good nattured & does

every thing to pleas me; but still I would rather be at home, if you was
there. I follow the old saying, home is home if ever so homely. I must
go to diner therefore I will say no more but that I long to see you & dear
Sir W. Give my kind, kind love to him, tell him next to you I love him
abbove any body & that I wish I was with him to give him a kiss. Dont
be affronted Greville, if I was with you I would give you a thousand &
you might take as many as you pleased for I long, I mean I long to see
you. I sopose you will scold next. Adue. I hope to have a letter from you
this next week. We have been a month from home today, Greville, its a
great wile. My mother gives her comp^{ts} to you & Sir W & say everything
that is kind or will render me dear to him; to more than you can say my
heart with gratitude assents & I must ever remain yours ever affectionately
& sincerely

    E. H.

P.S. Good by, my dear Greville, I hope we shall meet soon, happy &
well. Adue. I bathe Emma & she is very well & grows. Her hair will
grow very well on her forehead & I dont think her nose will be very
snub, her eyes is blue & pretty, but she dont speak through her nose,
but she speaks countryfied, but she will forget it. We squable sometimes,
still, she is fond of me & endead I love her for she is senceble, so much
for beauty. Adue I long to see you.

So Emma and her mother returned to London, with 'little Emma'
as companion till she went off to her 'scool'.

Edgware Road
Tuesday August 10 1784

I received your kind letter last night & my Dearest Greville I want words
to express to you how happy it made me, for I thought I was like a lost
sheep & everybody had forsook me. I was eight days confined to my room,
very ill, but am, thank God, very well now, & a deal better for your kind
instructing letter & I own the justness of your remarks. You shall have your
appartments to your self, you shall read wright or set still just as you pleas,
for I shall think my self happy to be under the seam roof with Greville & do
all I can to make it agreable with out disturbing him in any pursuits that he
can follow, to employ him self in at home or else whare, for your absence
has taught me that I ought to think my self happy if I was within a mile
of you, so as I could see the place as contained you, I should think myself
happy abbove my shear. So, my Dear G, come home & you shall find your
home comfortable to receave you, you shall find me good, kind, gentle &
affectionate & every thing you wish me to do I will do for I will give myself
a fair trial & follow your advice for I allways think it wright, therefore will
own myself wrong & begin again on a sure fowndation that shall ensure

happyness for ous boath. Dont think Greville, this is the wild fancy of a moments consideration, it is not. I have thoughraly considered everything in my confinement & I say nothing now but what I shall practice.

I must now inform you abbout my illness. My dear Greville, I had a rash out all over me and a fevour & I should have been worse if I had not had the rash out, but I think I am better for it now for I look fair & seems better in health than I was before. I dare say I should have been very dangerously ill iff it had not come out. Pray my dearest Greville, do come to see me as soon as ever you come in to town, for I do so long to see you, you dont know & it will make me so happy, I mean if you should come but to town before diner, do come because I now you will come at night. I have a deal to say to you when I see you. Oh Greville, to think it is nine weeks since I saw you. I think I shall die with the pleasure of seeing you. Endead, my dearest Greville, if you knew how much I think of you, you would love for it, for I am allways thinking on you, of your goodness, in short Greville, I truly love you & the thought of your coming home so soon makes me so happy I dont know what to do. Good by, my ever dearest Greville, may God preserve & bless you for ever, pray yours ever affectionately & sincerely

Emma

My kind love to Sr Wm & tell him if he will come soon, I will give him a thousand kisses, for I do love him a little. Emma is very well & is allways wondering why you dont come home; she sends her duty to you. Good by, my dearest Greville, pray, pray come as soon as you come to town. Good by. God bless you. O how I long to see you. Adue[6]

CHAPTER FOUR

Machinations

Greville returned to London on 17 August 1784, to find Emma fully recovered and once more acting as Romney's model and 'inspirer'. It would be interesting to know whether she confided her distress about her child, or the fact that she was stowed away in Edgware Row, to her 'friend, and more than father'. Probably Emma kept her own counsel, or turned for comfort only to her mother at this difficult time. Emma was not someone who naturally 'took things hard'. Nevertheless, she was nineteen, and daily playing a maternal role to her child in the full knowledge that at some time close at hand 'little Emma', the object of her attentions and affections, would be lost to her. 'Little Emma', when aged twenty-eight, was to write of her inability to desist from thinking of Emma as her mother – 'my misfortune, my memory traces back circumstances which have taught me too much, yet not quite all I could have wished to have known'. As she had seen Emma only briefly since she was a two-year-old in Edgware Row, these troubling, shadowy memories were evidently of that seaside holiday and term at Edgware Row when Emma was briefly her loving mother.

Sittings at Cavendish Square proceeded apace through the remainder of 1784, interrupted only by the absence of Romney in September. It was during this period that their partnership – Romney would 'request' Emma to imitate those powerful emotions of the mind which he wished to paint', and she would then animate him to 'the grandest efforts of art' – was at its most fruitful. There are fewer and fewer entries for other sitters in Romney's Day Books as the months go by, till in December 1784 there are appointments only for 'Mrs H.'[1] Just which of the finished portraits and sketches of Emma Romney was working on cannot be known. Between August 1784 and April 1786, he completed paintings today known as *Emma in a Straw Hat*, *Alope*, *Ariadne*, which indeed he may have begun at this time. He also painted Emma veiled and kneeling, with her hand outstretched. By the addition of a 'sensitive plant' from a nursery, on Hayley's suggestion, Romney made the painting a study in *Sensibility*.

Romney was enraptured by his model. He later wrote to Emma:

'There are a great number of Ladys of fashion setting to me . . . but all fall short of the Spinstress. Indeed it is the Sun of my Hemispheer, and they are the twinkling stars.' The language of this compliment, besides informing us of Romney's high opinion of the painting, also shows the element of courtly love present in Romney's and Emma's relationship, even before Emma's ascension to honours which were to lead Romney to speak of his 'divine lady'.

By the end of December, Greville had found a home for 'little Emma' with a Mr and Mrs Blackburn, 'near the Palace Inn, in Market Street Lane', in Manchester. There the child was dispatched, to be reared and later educated with the Blackburns' two daughters (described some years later as 'near her age'), under the aegis of Mrs Blackburn, in whom Greville had 'full confidence', as he had in her husband's discretion. Entries in Day Account Books Emma kept between 27 October 1784 and 21 February 1785 suggest that little Emma was dispatched some time between 5 December, when a Mrs Jones was paid the generous sum of £3 3s 0d, and 13 December, when Molly Lunn and Ann, or Nelly, or Nancy, Murphy arrived at Edgware Row and were paid a year's wages in advance.[2] Satisfied that thus all traces of the child's residence at Edgware Row had been removed, Greville wrote with contentment to his uncle, 'There is not in the parish so tidy a house as ours, it being Christmas Day.' His feelings about Emma's child and about the separation of Emma from her child which he had brought about are recorded some eight years later. 'The natural attachment to a deserted orphan may be supposed to increase from the length of time she had been protected. I have avoided any such sentiment by having only found the means to indulge so amiable a sentiment in Emma.' Greville took enormous trouble to justify his behaviour when he felt he had behaved badly, although no one but himself was levelling charges at him.

Greville had returned from his travels with his old thoughts of marrying an heiress reawakened. His absence of ten weeks away from Emma's lulling charms, the bracing climate of Scotland and his uncle's supportive company had combined to awaken ambitious thoughts in him. It is clear that Sir William would have preferred to see Charles realize his ambitions in politics, rather than in marriage to an heiress. Charles convinced him that he honestly felt that neither the Opposition party, to which he nominally adhered, nor the ministry of Pitt, was exactly adapted to his political line. Sir William was to write to him in desperation when Pitt's ministry looked to run and run, urging him to try for office. 'Why not serve the King & be of no party?' Greville knew he did right to eschew the political hurly-burly out of which ministers rose. 'I am too poor to accept a small office, & not likely to be enrolled among those of great abilities.'

Sir William had to agree that marriage to an heiress was the only other obvious way to acquire the thousands a year his nephew deemed would bring happiness. Greville twisted this agreement to seem like advice when he wrote to his uncle, 'To forego the reasonable plan which you and my friends have advised is not right.' In fact, whatever Greville's friends had advised – and Emma wrote in 1786 of friends of his who had 'long wished me harm' – Sir William spoke out shortly after his long bout of Greville's company against the ambition his nephew nursed. Escorting his niece, Mary, away from an evening at Mrs Garrick's house near Hampton Court, with 'no other light than that of ye Stars', they talked of Mary's impending marriage to plain Mr Dickenson, and Sir William approved her choice. Supposedly still with reference to Mary and her John, he said, 'of people's marrying merely for ye sake of a rank or an eligible establishment without paying any regard to principles, disposition, temper, &c, &c', that 'it was in his opinion neither more or less than a legal prostitution'.

If Sir William's enthusiasm for Greville's plan was not great, the hopeful suitor himself had no doubts. Nor can there be much doubt as to why he delayed so long in answering Emma's letters from Parkgate, and objected so vigorously to her suggestion that 'little Emma' should join the London establishment. That Emma, herself an encumbrance now that he meant to marry, should try to encumber him still further was insupportable. Nevertheless, he did her the justice to note that it was not through any failings of hers that he felt tempted by richer horizons in which she had no place. The letter which Emma received on 9 August, of which she said 'I want words to express how happy it made me,' laid out a plan whereby Greville felt he and Emma could 'keep on' together till he married. Poor Emma, of what use were all her resolutions to gain Greville's approval against such schemes as these? Unhappy Greville, as he chafed against the restrictions of his poverty.

It exacerbated Greville's feelings of poverty still more to find that, while his uncle had almost certainly appointed him his heir, he had, apparently, no intention of making that news public. Until it was public, Greville could not use his 'prospects' as bait for an heiress. And what family of wealth and position would look at a suitor with only £500 a year? So he was stymied. Without wishing to attribute the worst of motives on every occasion to Greville, we may infer that he proposed himself as a companion on the trip to Wales, wishing to prevent Sir William from selling the estates and purchasing an annuity – as he was more than half minded to do. In offering to 'watch' Sir William's estates, he drew on himself a powerful amount of correspondence from Mr Meyrick, the agent in Wales whom Sir William had newly appointed. Greville undoubtedly hoped some word would be spoken, indicating that it was sensible for the future heir to get to know the property, but Sir William persisted in supposing that Greville was acting altruistically.

The main worry for Greville was that Sir William's unaccountable reluctance to name an heir might have a very good reason behind it. His uncle might not have dismissed the idea of a second marriage, and, with it, a son and heir; he might then think it both needless and unfair now to name an heir. It was no accident which set King George and Queen Charlotte, at the latter's drawing-room of 19 August, to ask Sir William his intentions. Charles's brother, Colonel 'Wellbred' Robert Fulke Greville, was the King's favourite equerry and as such accompanied the King on his lengthy progresses round the seats of these noblemen unlucky enough to live within reach of Windsor. The Queen told Sir William she had been instructed by the King to 'fish out' whether he meant to marry again, and the King asked bluntly, 'Well, and who shall you make your Heir? I suppose your nephew Mr Greville?' There can be little doubt Their Majesties were encouraged in their curiosity by Robert, always his brother's champion. Mortifying both to Their Majesties and to Charles, standing by, were Sir William's replies. To the Queen he said he should be careful whom he chose, and to her rejoinder, 'I fear you have a bad opinion of our sex,' he said he had been so happy with 'the late Lady Hamilton' that he should be fearful not to meet again with the same fate, if he remarried. To the King, he said 'he should certainly keep that secret to himself, that no one had any claim on him as it was not a paternal inheritance but the gift of his wife'.

So Greville was none the wiser, though for the few weeks that remained of Sir William's stay in England he followed always at his heels, ready to bite at any hint about the disposition of his uncle's fortune. An evening at Lady Stormont's in Portland Place when the family gathering was enlivened by the presence of Sir William, Charles, Robert Fulke Greville and Charles Cathcart, is typical of many evenings on which Emma was left alone. On this occasion, Sir William said it made him appear 'an old Man, to be surrounded with such *well grown* Nephews & Nieces, & what was more mortifying, to be a *Great Uncle*'. However lightly he spoke, he found time, between drawing-rooms, visits to Windsor, meetings of the Royal Society, and breakfasts with his relations, to make his will and deposit a copy with Mr Hamilton of Lincoln's Inn. Then belongings – family china, a portrait of himself by Reynolds – came from the house in Wales which he had emptied now that Catherine was no longer alive to sigh for it. Giving these to

Mary Hamilton, he suggested she bring her Dickenson out to Naples (he had asked her to come alone shortly after Lady Hamilton's death). Despite his stirring talk of the benefit of travel – 'nothing opened the mind more, it was beyond conception how it furnished ideas to those who had natural taste & observation' – he did not win Mary to the idea. He set off without companion on 11 September, for the solitude he dreaded.

Greville was out of London when Sir William went to Edgware Row to make his farewells to Emma. As we piece together this meeting from references to it in the Hamilton-Greville correspondence, it seems Emma was distraught at Greville's absence. Sir William had 'many tears to wipe from those charming eyes'. Emma told Greville of the conversation which followed. Sir William's 'expressions of kindness to E, & the comfort you promised to her in case anything happened to me', wrote Greville to his uncle, 'made such an impression on her that she regards you as her protector & friend'. Sir William was evidently thinking of Greville's plan to marry when he promised Emma his support, should his nephew 'die, or slight her'.

Sir William was to say of Emma later: 'when I was in England . . . her exquisite beauty had frequently its effects on me'.[3] When he spoke of the effects of Emma's beauty on him, he was exact. It was the physical beauty of the figures painted on his Greek vases, as much as the vases' forms, that gave him such sharp satisfaction in their study. Intoxicated by beauty in art, he was also sexually aroused very quickly by the beauty of those around him. As a young man and, by his own admission, 'mad for' Lady Diana Spencer, he found himself alone at night with three Misses Swan in their drawing-room, their father snoring in his dressing-room next door. 'The eldest was a little coy at first but grew tamer . . . the youngest quite passive, but what could I do with all three? After I was raised to a certain pitch I was obliged to go one of my usual walks towards Temple Bar,' Sir William wrote to a friend.[4]

In Naples, Sir William delighted to watch, once with the Duca di Casanova, a traditional entertainment of the Kingdom, where handsome naked youths dived repeatedly into the Bay for coins. Casanova records that the Minister was among those Englishmen who asked for the entertainment to be repeated with naked girls.[5]

A young English girl came to him for advice, wishing to marry a Catholic, Guido. Sir William relates, 'I take her hand, the poor thing squeezes it when she thinks of Guido, and cries, and in the middle of all this distress the devil will have it that . . . and I grow confoundedly confused in all my councils.'

No doubt, Emma's beauty produced a similar state of confusion in Sir William. He may have spoken or acted a less chaste part than he protested to his nephew. What is clear is that he meant nothing by the warmth of feeling that came over him on these occasions. As he wrote to Greville, there was no reason for his nephew to feel jealous of his attentions to Emma.

Blithely unaware that Greville had decided he was 'as partial' to Emma as his nephew was himself, Sir William went off on 11 September in his travelling chaise with 'all ye convenient contrivances' to bask on the other side of the Alps in the Italian September sunshine. Greville pursued his destiny. His first step towards marriage was to put his financial affairs in order. In September he sold the house in Portman Square, which he had built as a speculation, at such a considerable loss that he owed its builder a large sum. As the purchaser of the house did not buy the collection of paintings and the two antique statues with which Greville had 'made it pretty', Greville had to dispose of these, as well as a large cellar of wine. The wine he stored in Romney's capacious basements; the pictures and statues he offered to the Duke of Rutland in December 1784, advising that nobleman not to let 'the money you have destined for virtu burn in your pocket', after the Duke was outmanoeuvred by another collector in some purchases. Greville offered his whole collection, of twelve years' making, for such sums as he owed his builder. Negotiations took time, but by March 1786 Greville's builder had his money.

The other outstanding debt Greville wished to clear was some £2,000 which he owed for some 'Hubberston engagements'. In January, he thought of a plan to clear himself of the crippling interest, if not of the debt itself. He proposed that the bankers he shared with Sir William, Messrs Ross and Ogilvie, should loan him money wherewith he might settle the Hubberston business. If Sir William would stand security for the loan, then the bankers would charge a low rate of interest. So that Sir William would not suffer, if Greville died or if the bankers called in the loan, Greville proposed depositing with his uncle his prized collection of minerals, which he valued at three times the sum of the loan. Greville was reluctant to take the simple step of selling this collection, whereby he need not involve his uncle in his affairs at all; the collection had not reached that stage of completion where it might fetch its optimum price. Incidentally, Greville wrote, it was indifferent to him whether the minerals were physically lodged with himself or his uncle, and he was happy to look after them for Sir William. Rightly Greville said he 'distinguished favour and business'. The nominal possession of minerals which seemed likely to remain in Greville's care is unlikely to have excited Sir William. Greville was well aware that this 'distinct branch of collecting' had no interest for his uncle. He may also have suspected that his uncle placed little reliance on his estimate of the minerals' value. Nevertheless, Greville proposed this plan in January 1785. He may have felt that Sir William was unlikely to refuse him, since he was, again, distinguishing 'favour and business', corresponding extensively on his uncle's behalf with Meyrick in Wales.

In the same letter of January 1785, Greville spoke for the first time of a third matter that needed settling before he could realize his dream of marriage. He spoke at length of Emma. He began by extolling her adaptability. 'She is naturally elegant, & fits herself easily to any situation, having quickness & sensibility.' He spoke of her pride and independence. 'On the least slight or expression of my being tired or burthened by her' she would give him up and 'not even accept a farthing for future assistance'. He then effectively says that he is 'burthened' by her. 'If I was independent I should think so little of any other connexion that I never would marry. I have not an idea of it at present, but if any proper opportunity offer'd I should be much harassed, not know how to manage or how to fix Emma to her satisfaction.' He ended, 'Give me your opinion honestly how you would act in my situation. If I followed my own inclination, advice would be unnecessary.'

To these recommendations of Emma's suitability as a mistress, to these hints that it would not be disagreeable to Greville if his uncle offered to take Emma off his hands soon ('I can keep on creditably this winter,' he wrote), Sir William made no reply, contenting himself with answering those parts of the letter which concerned his affairs in Wales. Unknown to his nephew, Sir William was occupied with thoughts which precluded him taking any interest in Greville's hint that he take Emma as a companion.

Sir William had met in Turin, after his arduous journey over the Alps, one Lady Clarges, the widow of a City baronet, Sir Thomas, who had died in July 1783. Staying at Rome some time on 'virtu business' with James Byres, the lady reappearing there, Sir William had furthered his acquaintance with her. By February 1785, Lady Clarges and a Miss Carter were in Naples to distract him from the 'deluge of blood' which accompanied the Royal winter slaughters, and from his other occupations, such as redecorating apartments in the Palazzo Sessa, and helping the Queen in a scheme to make an English Garden. Thoughts of engaging to take Emma on were far from his mind when, on 22 February, Sir William was moved, in one of those 'moments of admiration' which so affected him, to suggest that Lady Clarges take over the empty apartments of Lady Hamilton. 'The Devil fetch me if I meant to propose to her,' he wrote spiritedly to Greville, relating how the widow had misunderstood his offer, and gravely replied she had determined never to change her state.[6] To Mary Hamilton, however, he wrote more circumspectly in May. 'If Lady C. had been of the same mind with me I verily believe I should have been married. I was not in the least in love, but she seemed the quiet companion that would suit me, particularly as her passion for Musick equals mine . . .' Sir William could afford to consult his own wishes, six hundred miles removed from the conventions of the English Court, and, after twenty years at Naples, on such a footing there that anything was permissible to '*il cavaliere Hamilton*'. It will not go unnoticed that the qualities he valued in Lady Clarges were exactly those which had made Lady Hamilton such a comfort to him. However, he consoled himself with the thought that Lady Clarges' refusal had spared him the charge of her four children.

Greville at first loftily ignored his uncle's lighthearted account of his misunderstanding with the widow. He wrote early in March only of Pitt and politics, and of his own renewed determination not to be a 'firm supporter' of either party. Then, on 10 March, he took up his pen again and wrote an impetuous warning against being trapped into marriage. 'Of the 60 English' at Naples, 'what with widows & young married ladies', 'an amateur may be caught.' The return of Greville's brother-in-law, Sir Harry Harpur, from Naples had set Sir William's relations spinning in a renewed turmoil of fears for the Ambassador's bachelorhood. Greville decided to risk a flat refusal, rather than wait for ever for his uncle to take him up on the hints of his January letter.

He began by skirting round the question. 'I know that your heart is neither callous to friendship nor to beauty . . . it must be a very interested friend indeed who does not sincerely wish everything that can give happiness to a friend. I sincerely wish that happiness to you . . .' Then he came to the point.

On those cases in which comfort may arise you are more than myself able to realise suppositions by experiment; for the limited experiment I make I know to succeed, altho' from poverty it cannot last. If you did not chuse a wife, I wish the tea-maker of Edgware Row was yours, if I could without banishing myself from a visit to Naples. I do not know how to part with what I am not tired with, I do not know how to contrive to go on, & I give her every merit . . .

In the sale of his pictures to the Duke of Rutland, Greville had involved his uncle only minimally. In the matter of the Hubberston bond he had asked only what he considered a 'favour'. Now, he effectively asked Sir William to extricate him from the economic evils his support of Emma at Edgware Row had become, by taking on her support himself. With his next sentence, he sugared the pill, saying nobly, 'She shall never want.' He outlined a scheme whereby he could settle on her 'near £100 a year', though it was by selling a part of his virtu. If Sir William settled another hundred on her, Greville thought he could be 'as comfortable as I have been & am'. Reiterating his repugnance for his scheme, 'If I could go on, I would never make this arrangement,' Greville then brings a species of moral blackmail to his other arguments. 'To be reduced to a standstill . . . & then to be unable to provide for her at all . . . would make me miserable . . .' He completes his letter with elegance. 'Judge then, as you know my satisfaction on looking at a modern piece of virtu if I do not think you a second self, in thinking that by placing her within your reach I render a necessity, which would otherwise be heartbreaking, tolerable & even comforting.'

In this long letter, Greville speaks only of the economic burden Emma has become. He is careful not to mention his own plan to marry, once Emma is out of the way; he speaks only of Emma's future. He does not repeat his cry of January, 'I am not quite of an age to retire from bustle, & to retire to distress & poverty is worse.' Such sentiments might awaken caution in Sir William about the restrictions Emma's establishment as his mistress in Naples might place on his own future. He might also be led to wonder just why his nephew was so keen to wish Emma, this barrier to marriage, on him, dismissing other futures open to Emma such as other protectors and retirement into the country or a convent on the grounds, respectively, that 'she would not hear' of a connection with anyone 'that was not liked by her', and that she was 'too young and handsome'.

Sir William wrote a somewhat worried assent to the plan. Greville, in his letter of 5 May, then revealed that economic distress was not his major consideration in wishing to dispose of Emma.

> If things remain as they are I shall, to be sure, be much straitened in finances. I shall be so whether she remains or not, & literally her expences are trifling; yet when income is very small a trifling expence is felt. But, above all, I own that I think I lose opportunities of settling to advantage; when home is comfortable other pursuits are less interesting, & to sink into a retreat of this sort at my time of life is what in others I should condemn.

He felt relaxed enough to add, 'You may say that at yours it may also be absurd; every man to his idea. At your age a clean and comfortable woman is not superfluous, but I should rather purchase it than acquire it . . .'

Greville was to write of Emma in November, 'she goes on so well, & is so much more considerate & aimiable than she was when you saw her, & also improv'd in looks, that I own it is less agreeable to part; yet I have no other alternative but to marry or remain a pauper; I shall persist . . .' Greville had trained Emma to think that, on her eschewing of gaiety, on her constant self-improvement, on her making a 'comfortable home' for him, his love naturally followed. Sadly, as Greville's words show, there was no comfort, no improvement that Emma could achieve in herself, which would bring Greville to continue their liaison. One hopes that Greville's chafing at her power to sap his will to succeed in the world did not communicate itself to Emma, while the letters passed between Naples and London.

Sir William's letter, which Greville answered on 5 May 1785, contained a suggestion so shocking to Greville that he barely acknowledged the 'kind wishes' towards him and 'interest' Sir William took 'in his situation', which prompted Sir William to accept the charge of Emma. 'If I could have thought that no line could be taken but that of making E do the honours of your house, I confess I never should have dreamt of it: this is a line so different from what I have practised that I should be among the first to lament that you adopted so unwise a plan.' What Greville had in mind was something on the lines of Edgware Row. 'If you had given her any of your villas, only making it a decided part that she had a home distinct from your house, whether her visits were frequent or rare it was immaterial, her home would be distinct.' Sir William, however, had said he 'could not resist taking her into his house entirely'. Greville bewailed his uncle's intentions. 'You would lose the greatest advantage from her disposition; she is not led by interest but by kindness, & she appreciates favours from the intentions. You would be like the prodigal, depriving yourself of the means of showing attention.'

Greville pressed his point harder, describing how he had 'directed' her 'pride and vanity' to her happiness, so that she was 'totally clear from all the society & habits of kept women', and curbed of all desire for 'giddiness & dissipation'. 'In short, this habit, of three or four years acquiring, is not a caprice, but is easily to be continued' – if Sir William would only hide her away, as Greville had done. The nephew had not quite taken the point that his uncle wished for a companion, a new interest, quite as much as he wished for a mistress. He had written to Banks, on 20 February, à propos of the English Garden scheme, 'As

one passion begins to fail, it is necessary to form another one; for the
whole art of going through life tolerably is to keep oneself eager about
any thing. The moment one is indifferent on s'ennuye . . .'[7]

Greville spoke of the 'duties of the connexion'. 'It is madness to be
a slave to pleasure, & if she did not expect more than you chuse & had
no reason to doubt fidelity, there would be no fear on that head, & as
to running after other men, if once she has taken a line, & is sensible of
good intentions to her, she may now be trusted, & ten times more if left
entirely to herself,' he adds, again urging Emma's confinement. 'What
you say is true,' he ends his disquisition on the subject of Emma's sex
life, 'so beautiful a person cannot be long without a protector . . . but
it is not her wish to run the gauntlet.'

Evidently, Sir William had made some discreet reference to the
possibility of Emma resuming, in Naples, the promiscuous life she had
left off for Greville, and to the possibility that he, a man of fifty-five,
might satisfy her less adequately than a younger man. Greville's words,
'it is madness to be a slave to pleasure', awaken interesting thoughts
about Emma's sex life with him. However, as the purpose of his
remark, as of the whole letter, was to reassure his uncle that Emma
was 'tamed' of her former ways for good, he may have dissembled on
this point.

After much justification for his presumption in proposing that Sir
William show him 'a preference which you must at one or another
time . . . shew to somebody', on the grounds that, 'in my present
situation . . . having nothing to settle, how could I expect a prudent
family to adopt me?', and that Sir William had already spoken 'kindly
of your intentions towards me', Greville closed his letter: 'I shall only
add to this long letter that taking E. is no part of the request, tho' it is not
impossible I should put the question to a lady now totally inaccessible
whose fortune is what I mention . . . if you dislike my frankness I shall
be sorry, for it cost me a little to throw myself open . . .'

It has been suggested – in fact, it has been asserted by many – that
Greville sold his mistress, Emma, to his uncle. Let us consider.

The lady Greville had firmly in mind was the Honourable Henrietta
Willoughby. She was the younger daughter of his erstwhile neighbour in
Portman Square, Lord Middleton, and had been presented that season.
Charles was, as ever, confident when all the odds were against him.
He relates that she had beauty and a good disposition, but makes no
mention of the fact that other suitors might be attracted by these
charms, and by her fortune. Yet the few mentions of Charles made at
this time by young ladies of fashion like Fanny Burney and his cousin,
Louisa Lady Stormont, make it clear they thought him a fusty old virtu

bore, without humour. One wonders whether the eighteen-year-old Miss Willoughby, in the midst of the gaiety of her first season, would have felt very differently. It can only have been Charles's capacity for self-deception which made him think she favoured him. While many men found much to approve in Greville's odd character, Emma was almost alone among women in appreciating his doubting, affectionate nature. Yet for illusory hopes of happiness with a putative bride, she was to be given up.

Care should be taken to observe the sequence in which Greville asked for his uncle's help in the bond, then offered his uncle Emma, and then asked for a letter to show Lord Middleton, as yet unnamed, that he was his uncle's heir. Though all these requests were interwoven, as described above, Greville did not 'sell' Emma, as has often been intimated, to his uncle, in return for either money – i.e. the bond – or for a promise of an inheritance. Sir William was no eager 'buyer'; he more or less had the goods foisted upon him. There was even an element of moral blackmail in Greville saying that taking Emma was no part of his demand to be furnished with a letter announcing he was his uncle's heir, and then going on to say he meant to propose to the unnamed Miss Willoughby shortly. As Sir William makes clear in the letter which follows, his response to Greville's letter of 5 May, he was prepared to do Greville the favour of taking Emma, as he was prepared to do him the favour of giving him the letter for Lord Middleton. He would, no doubt, have done more, so earnestly and altruistically did he wish Greville's happiness. He most certainly did not see his future acquisition of Emma, troublesome as he feared it might be, as a *quid pro quo* for the Middleton letter. Indeed, he tried his best to make Greville give up his marriage plans and 'keep on' with Emma.

Sir William wrote, on 1 June 1785,

Was I to die this moment my Will, which I made in England and left with Hamilton of Lincoln's Inn and brought a Copy here, would show that you are the person I esteem most – but I never meant to tell you so as the changes in this life are so various that no one can answer for himself from one moment to another. For example, had I married Lady C., which might have happened, it must have been a cruel disappointment to you, after having declared you my heir. I only made my Will, as every one ought to do, in case of accident, but as I have struggled through many difficulties in life and am now by Lady Hamilton's goodness secured from want, nay, have enough to live comfortably shou'd I be dismissed from His Majesty's Service, I shou'd not chuse to put anything out of my power. To be sure, so far I am selfish and I have lived long enough to experience that most people are so, but was it not for the thought of your profiting on my death (which according to the course of nature must happen before your moment arrives many years) I should not hesitate in selling the Welsh Estate and purchasing an annuity for my life. Being a younger Brother myself and having made my own fortune and Being at liberty to dispose of it as I please at my death when I can no longer enjoy it, I shall have a satisfaction in its going to a younger Brother whom I love and esteem more than any man on Earth . . .

As to E., was I in England and you was to bring your present plan to bear and she wou'd consent to put herself under my protection, I wou'd take her most readily for I really love her and think better of her than of any one in her situation. But, my dear Charles, there is a great difference between her being with you or me, for she really loves you when she cou'd only esteem and suffer me. I see so many difficulties in her coming here, should you be under the necessity of parting with her, that I can never advise it. Tho' a great city, Naples has every defect of a Province and nothing you do is secret. It would be fine fun for the young English Travellers to endeavour to cuckold the old Gentleman their Ambassador, and whether they succeeded or not would surely give me uneasiness. My regard for E. is such that if she leaves you and retires in the country, which I suppose she would do was you to marry, I wou'd willingly make her an allowance of £50 a year till your circumstances enable you to provide better for her. I do assure you when I was in England tho' her exquisite beauty had frequently its effects on me, it would never have come into my head to have proposed a freedom beyond an innocent kiss whilst she belong to my friend; and I do assure you I should like better to live with you both here and see you happy than to have her all to myself, for I am sensible that I am not a match for so much youth and beauty.[8]

This letter more clearly shows Sir William's humanity, sometimes mistaken as mere worldliness, than any other document of his writing. Part of that humanity, as much part of it as his concern for Emma's feelings, is the earlier indecision he exhibits as to whether it might not be more prudent, if less entertaining, simply to contribute to Emma's keep somewhere in England. Sir William, not surprisingly, had 'cold feet'. He was not a private individual. He wanted reconfirmation from Greville of Emma's reformed character before he actually offered an invitation which, tempt him as it might, he could not 'advise'. His first impulse had been to have Emma 'do the honours' of his house – that is, entertain the English who gathered at the Palazzo Sessa in such numbers that Sir William referred to his house as 'the King's Arms'. On reflection, it had occurred to him that no English lady of distinction would attend where someone of Emma's position was hostess. For the Neapolitan nobility, less nice in their distinction, she would do very well, but there were the King and Queen, with whom Sir William spent so such time, to consider. The British Minister might lose his favoured place in Their Majesties' favours if he led the English community in scandal. Of course, if Sir William could bring it off, none would be more delighted than he, as his final words, 'have her all to myself', reveal. But Greville must advise him.

Sir William's enclosure, the letter declaring Greville his heir, elated his nephew. Having his letter for Lord Middleton, he hardly noticed his uncle's doubts about the wisdom of taking Emma, simply repeating his former advice to stow her away in:

> one of your villas, or rather take a small retired house on the Hill at Naples, very small; she will not want to go about, & going to dine or at any other hours, to your villa or house . . . will make a party of what . . . would be daily habit . . . As to Englishmen there is nothing to fear; left to herself she would conform to your ideas . . . let her learn music or drawing, or anything to keep her in order, she will be as happy as if you gave her every chance of disipation.

He dismissed the notion that the best plan would be for him to come with Emma to Naples. 'To what would it lead?' Thinking that settled, Greville then passed on to the interesting subject of Emma's psychology, and how best to manage it to Sir William's advantage. She 'takes easily any hint that is given with good humour. I have often heard people say you may do anything by good humour, but never saw any one so completely led by good nature . . . I believe she would die before she yielded to ill-treatment,' he wrote. Thus he disposed of Emma's impetuous temper. He turned to the business of making the plan substance. 'If you could form a plan by which you could have a trial, & could invite her & tell her that I ought not to leave England, & that I cannot afford to go on, & state it as a kindness to me if she would accept your invitation, she would go with pleasure.' He urged promptitude: 'I could not manage it so well later; after a month's absence from me [summer holidays were to part Emma and Greville shortly] she would consider the whole more calmly.' He spoke briefly of his feeling for Emma: 'if there was in the world a person she loved so well as yourself after me, I could not arrange with so much sang froid.' He closed the subject by reiterating that Emma would cause no scandal. 'I am sure I would not let her go to you, if any risque of the usual coquetry of the sex being likely either to give uneasiness or appearance.'

Greville's whole mind was on the marriage he felt to be fast approaching. He had tossed his hat into the ring and sent off Sir William's letter to Lord Middleton, he informed his uncle excitedly, now revealing the identity of Miss Willoughby, to 'prove that it was not a pretence which

I assumed'. As he wrote, he was in daily expectation of a reply. He told his uncle a little of what he had said in his covering letter.

> I have said that I communicated it to him as to a friend, being desired not to publish it; that you had given me leave to make what use I pleased of it, & if it had been of a nature to be certain of being of use that I should have communicated it to him first, in hopes that it might be useful to me, as I have ever been of opinion that there was not a more amiable family, or a more interesting daughter, that I could not be buoyed up by a smile of fortune & become presumptuous. If Fortune had always been bountiful that I should have been a more frequent visitor at their house . . .

He had not actually made a proposal of marriage, he told his uncle. 'If their partiality for me should get over the real objections [that he was a suitor with only £500 'and some incumbrances'] which they might start, they may lead my letter into that consequence; if not, it will drop without a refusal being necessary.'

Despite these words of caution, though he wrote 'distant & imperfect as the prospect is', Greville felt optimistic. Later in his letter he spoke of the Welsh estates, saying he was glad he had exerted himself in their interest before he knew he was to be heir to them, 'least you should think my zeal increased with personal interest'. Here, as so often, Greville sought to justify himself against charges which only he dreamt of. Outlining plans for the estates which would benefit less the present than the future owner, he wrote, 'If it was not building on your intentions further than you propose, & should my letter lead to my present settling, I should incline to settle about Pembroke . . . unless I could find some part in Devonshire or Cornwall [in Sir William's lands there], where I could bring to profit some manufacture of china. If I went to Wales I would bring it there and promote my plan for increasing the industry of the natives . . .'

In this, as in his announcement that the elder Miss Willoughby's dowry had only been £20,000 after all, Greville ran counter to two claims he had made in his letter of 5 May – that he would not 'tax' his uncle for anything in his lifetime, and that he would not trouble him for anything less than a £30,000 prize. He was, perhaps, too elated by the prospect of his nuptials to notice his inconsistency.

Emma, unaware that her future with Greville might soon end, went with her mother to 'some bathing place for six weeks'. Charles went with his brother on a long-planned tour of North and South Wales, and Cornwall. No letters survive of those which passed between Greville and Sir William during these summer months of 1785. What is clear is that Sir William did not send any invitation to Emma, and Greville's letter did not receive the warm welcome from Lord Middleton which he desired. He had told his uncle he proposed, in that case, to go to Edinburgh; 'my pretence shall be chemistry with Dr Black,' and live there 'cheap & retired'. There is a reference in his next extant letter, that of 11 November, to their 'last correspondence', in which Greville would seem to have informed his uncle of his decision to hold by that plan, and Sir William would seem to have consented to take Emma.

While Greville was still away, a most disturbing event occurred at Edgware Row. Mrs Cadogan had a stroke. Greville returned from Cornwall to find 'the menage just as I expected . . . it was not so severe an attack as I understood . . . but anything which the faculty stile paralysis is alarming'. Mrs Cadogan was 'by no means recover'd' when Greville, after a bare ten days at home, had to go to Warwick to take office as mayor and give his mayor's banquet.

Greville felt the blow his departure was to Emma, 'alarm'd and distress'd by her mother's illness'. He wrote to his uncle from Derbyshire, having moved on from Warwick, on 11 November, 'it was not kindly meant, but it will turn out well . . .' He spoke more warmly of Emma in this letter than in any other. It was with real regret that he wrote, 'it is less agreeable to part'. Nevertheless, he only wrote to tell Sir William that Mrs Cadogan's illness must delay Emma's departure till the spring. 'I have no other alternative but to marry or remain a pauper.' It would seem he had meant to inform Emma of his wish that they part on his return from his tour. Her mother's illness gave her a small extension of blissful ignorance. 'You may suppose that I did not increase Emma's uneasiness by any hint of our last correspondence.'

In this time of uncertainty and worry, we hear of one event which afforded Emma some pleasure. Greville brought his friend, Gavin Hamilton, to dinner one evening. Hamilton, long based in Rome, whence he had supplied Greville with his two antique statues and such of his collection of paintings as had not been supplied by Sir William, was in England to settle estates in Scotland lately acquired on the death of his brother. It seems Greville brought Hamilton to Edgware Row specifically to admire Emma's beauty. Hamilton, a leading painter in the fashionable genre of classical history, the fortunate excavator of Hadrian's Villa at Tivoli, a painter much influenced and excited by Greek forms, duly gave praise.

He says he has not seen anything like her in G.B., & that she reminds him of a person in Rome whom he admired much, but that she was deficient in the beauties of the mouth, & that Emma's is both beautiful and uncommon. He has been meditating for a subject; he says he shall not rest until he has prevail'd on her to sit; you may suppose she was flattered, & told him she put him at once on her list of favourites, because you had spoke of him as a person you regarded & also because he bore your name.

Greville proceeded, after his stay at Warwick, where he improved relations with his brother, Lord Warwick, on to Caulke Abbey in Derbyshire, the home of his sister and brother-in-law, Lady Frances and Sir Harry Harpur. Greville told Sir William that he intended taking his young nephew, Harry, who was on bad terms with his father, to London, and lodging him with the Middleton family. Perhaps, when he wrote this, Greville still had hopes of winning the Honourable Henrietta.

Sir William, from Naples, wrote a letter to Greville, on 8 November, in which he made no mention of Emma, beyond a courteous remembrance. He did speak of the Romney Bacchante, which, after much delay, Greville had finally dispatched to him, with four other pictures. It would appear, from correspondence between Greville and Romney in 1788, that these four other pictures were also by Romney, and also of Emma. Greville had asked his uncle yet another favour, namely to take off his hands the payment of all the portraits of Emma which Romney had done to that date (excepting one, *Emma in a Straw Hat*) on Greville's commission. Along with Greville's other 'reductions', which poverty had forced upon him, he had given up his 'scheme' of a series of portraits of Emma. What better plan could there be than to let Emma's likenesses further kindle Sir William's desire for her? Emma did not stop sitting to Romney, of course. Though Romney's Diary for 1785 is lost, Robinson, pupil to the painter, gives evidence that Emma attended the studio in that year. There are regular entries for her in the 1786 Diary. Presumably, she was sitting either at the painter's own request, or for portraits commissioned by other patrons. By 1786, she was sufficiently well known as a model of Romney's for the *Gentleman's Magazine* to mention her.

The other news Sir William imparted in his letter was that he was feeling impoverished. The apartments he had had decorated in the spring offended his eye, they were so badly done. At what was to be a cost of £4,000, he had decided to have the apartments redone. This cry of poverty may have alarmed Greville into thinking his uncle meant to avoid taking Emma. Equally, he may have heard the news that Miss Willoughby was planning to award her £20,000 to Richard Savile, second son of the Earl of Scarborough. (They were married in 1787.) Whatever his reasons, on 3 December Greville waited no longer for Sir William to invite Emma. He thought no more of how disagreeable it would be to part from her. He told her himself of his plan to go to Scotland for some months and wrote to his uncle of what then ensued.

> She naturally said that such a separation would be very like a total separation, for that she should be very miserable during my absence, & that she should neither profit by my conversation nor improve in any degree, that my absence would be more tolerable if she had you to comfort her, & that she wished you was not so far off, as she would ask you to take her as a guest during my absence, as there was not a person in the world with whom she could be happy with, if I was dead, but yourself, & that she certainly would profit of your kind offer if I should die or slight her, & that was the consideration which often comforted her when she look'd forward to the chances which might separate her. [Greville's account of Emma's part in this conversation, his report that she, *sua sponte*, thought of appealing to Sir William, is to be regarded with suspicion.] I told her that I shou'd have no objection to her going to Naples for 6 to 8 months, and that if she really wished it I would forward any letter she chose.

On Greville's return in the evening, Emma had 'settled every thing in her own mind that she will go with her mother only . . . that she would not be troublesome . . . very happy in learning music & Italian & etc . . . provided she was under your roof and protection'. Greville told her that she would be so happy that he would be cut out. To this Emma replied, confusedly, that if Greville did not come for her,

> she would certainly be grateful to you; but that neither interest or affection should ever induce her to change, unless my interest or wish required it, & that you could comfort her, altho' she made all the distinction of age, but that she had seen enough to value a real friend wherever she could find one, and that you had shown more real friendship to her than any person in the world beside myself, & therefore you was, after me, the nearest to her heart.

It is useless to speculate about the feelings which Emma expressed to Greville as opposed to how he expressed them to his uncle. In the letter she gave Greville on the evening of 3 December, however, though part of it is evidently composed by Greville, other parts show her suspicious of, and openly battling against, just such plans for her future as Greville and Sir William had laid.

It runs as follows:

Edgware Road, London
3 December 1785

My dear Sir William, emboldened by your kindness to me when you was in England, I have a proposal to make that I flatter myself will not be disagreeable to you. Greville (whom you know I love tenderly) is obliged to go for four or five months in the summer to places that I cannot with propriety attend him to, & I have too great a regard for him to hinder him from pursuing those plans which I think it is right for him to follow; & I know it is necessary for him to keep up his connexions in the world; – and as you was so good as to give me encouragement, I will speak my mind. In the first place, I should be glad if I was a little more improved than what I am, and as Greville is obligded to be absent in the summer he has out of kindness to me offer'd, if you are agreeable, for me to go to Naples for 6 or 8 months, and he will at the end of that time fetch me home, and stay a while there when he comes, which I know you will be glad to see him.

He therefore proposes for me to sett of the first of March next, as he will sett of then for his entended tour in Scotland, and I could not bear the thought of staying at home by my self when I know if I come to see you (which will be the greatest pleasure on hearth, Greville excepted) I shall be improving my self and making the time pass agreable; at the same time he thinks for me to go by the Geneva coach, and if you will lett your man that was in England with you meet me there to conduct me to Naples, I shall be glad; and if you will allot me an appartment in your house that I might be under your protection while I am there, and lett Greville occupye those apartments when he comes, you know that *must* be; but as your house is very large, and you must, from the nature of your office, have business to transact and visiters to see, I shall always keep my own room when you are better engaged or go out, and at other times I hope to have the pleasure of your company and conversation, which will be more agreable to me than anything in Italy. As I have given you an example of sincerity, I hope you will be equaly candid and sencere in a speedy answer as we are confined for time, and no further correspondence will be necessary, as you may depend on me, if you approve of it, setting off from London at the time I mentioned in the former part of this letter, and I shall be perfectly happy in any arrangements you will make, as I have full confidence in your kindness and attention to me, and shall long for the time when I can assure you in person how much I am, my dear Sir William, your obligded humble servant, or affectionate Emma, which you like best.

Who could have resisted such a charming appeal? Noticeable among the other improvements, which meant so much to Greville and Emma herself, is her increased level of literacy since her letter 'what shall I dow?' of 1782, which initiated her life with Greville, and even since those Parkgate letters of 1784. Sir William replied promptly to Greville's hint, 'She has not a doubt of the pleasure you will have to receive her,' and wrote to assure Emma it was so. He accepted gracefully the charge his nephew, under 'the absolute necessity of reducing every expence to enable me to have enough to exist on, & to pay the interest of my debt without parting with my collection of minerals, which is not yet in a state of arrangement which would set it off to its greatest advantage', had thrust upon him.

Greville, in the letter in which he enclosed Emma's appeal, was so confident his uncle would not reject the plan laid for him that he spoke at length of travel arrangements. 'I . . . have got the refusal of 2 places in the coach which will set out the end of Feby. or the beginning of March,' he wrote, mentioning that Sir William might ask his eminent friend, Horace Bénédict de Saussure, the Professor of Natural History at Geneva, 'to be of use to her'. He spoke of Emma's delight in sacrificing 'anything you dislike . . . if asked kindly, & you may leave her every opportunity of doing it unknown to you'. He spoke of her lack of avarice. 'I am sure there is not a more disinterested woman in the world, if she has a new gown or hat, etc, it is easy to make a little novelty go far, & all that pleases her is to have that little as sensible and genteel people wear, & of the best quality.' As for 'the little excesses which I have experienced', a propensity to make herself 'bare of pocket money', by sending funds to 'poor relations in the country, for whose care she professes herself grateful', that was to be praised.

Mentioning the possibility that, despite all Emma's virtues, her residence in Italy might not be a success, Greville wrote that Sir William could, nevertheless, 'have an experiment without any risque'. 'She will have profited by seeing a little of foreign parts; she will have improved herself . . . she may come home.' (As Emma's letter shows, she had been told a most deceitful tale, 'he will at the end of that time fetch me home'.) Greville then ended his assurances as to the temporary nature of Emma's visit by saying, 'if either by marriage or by office I shall become more at my ease, my first concern shall be to provide for her, whether she is with you or not'.

Perhaps some hint from Sir William that a man of fifty-five was not past his prime prompted Greville to change his former tune, that Emma would not mind sexual neglect. He wrote his encomium: 'a cleanlier, sweeter bedfellow does not exist . . .' He added: 'You need not fear domestic duty, women . . . very often take omission of duty as proof of inconstancy, or of neglect, or diminution of affection, & therefore resent it.' On the tricky question of mistress passing from nephew to uncle, Greville had this to say:

I have never told our story, therefore my conduct has never been judged
from my own statement. People who do not live with us are as indifferent to
us as we to them . . . Those who know us take us with more discretion . . .
we only open on a subject guardedly . . . they will have discretion not to
renew enquiry; those who are not in intimacy, cannot take the liberty . . .
in the case of Emma . . . a young person under your protection is all that
is necessary . . . altho' all the world should know both her & me, they
will . . . investigate the nature of the connexion, & without any agrement
you will find Emma discrete . . . is pleased if she thinks all the world not
in her secret . . .

Greville ended his letter by instructing his uncle, 'You must enable
me to pay their journey . . . let Cottier be at Geneva . . . by the 10th
or 15th of March.' There was little else, of a practical nature, to discuss,
once Sir William had written to encourage Emma to come to him.
Greville supplied Emma with the linen her modest wardrobe lacked.
Sir William sent £50 as bidden. Emma continued to sit to Romney.
The first of March was the date set for her departure to Naples, as
for Greville's to Edinburgh. A trunk containing both Emma's and her
mother's clothes was sent by sea.

A brief extension to Emma's term with Greville was provided by a
change of plan. Kindly Gavin Hamilton, returning to Rome, engaged to
escort the inexperienced ladies as far as that city. On 13 March, Emma,
her mother and the painter departed, and Greville wrote that, by selling
pictures and one of his statues, he had 'cleared Emma and myself of
everything connected with our establishment'. His parting with Emma
had left him so blithe and gay, he offered his congratulations to Sir
William, without a thought as to his own bad taste, on the desirable
future that was to be his. 'You will live in comfort with the prettiest
woman confessedly in London.' And Greville left for Edinburgh to
study chemistry.

CHAPTER FIVE

Emma in Italy

On 13 March 1786, a Tuesday, Emma, Mrs Cadogan and Gavin Hamilton committed themselves to the perils and discomforts of the journey to Italy. Two at least of the party – who can guess at the thoughts of that most reserved of women, Mrs Cadogan? – had little taste for the adventure. Gavin Hamilton had felt more than half inclined to abandon his painting career, his excavations and Prince Borghese's patronage at Rome for his estate in Lanarkshire. Greville, reluctant to lose his Roman 'dealer', 'decided' Gavin to return. Emma's feelings can be imagined, as the Dover packet forged its way across the Channel, and the prospect of England – and of Greville and Edgware Row – receded. In October, the enchanted season when Greville had promised to fetch her from Naples, she saw her salvation.

While this odd trio journeyed down through France in the coach of the Swiss carrier, M. Dejean, Sir William was busy in Naples. In late December 1785, one of his Royal 'foster-brothers', Henry Duke of Cumberland, had arrived to spend the winter in Naples, together with his Duchess and her gaming-mad sister, Lady Elizabeth Luttrell. If the Royal party delighted the Neapolitans with the constancy of their attendance and the formality of their dress at the public balls, the Accademic di Ballo, the Duke plagued his brother's Minister with daily demands for entertainment. The King and Queen were living quietly at Caserta, the vast, chilly palace at the foot of Monte Tifatini, some sixteen miles from Naples. Maria Carolina was lying-in for the seventeenth time throughout January and February. After the birth of Princess Clothilde, she developed an infection of the breast. She was ill throughout March and April after she had 'one of her breasts laid open . . . the incision is very deep'. The Cumberlands' demands for reception at Court were necessarily irksome to all. Sir William, in attendance on Their Sicilian Majesties at Caserta – he saw each of Maria Carolina's children born – had to devise other entertainments for the Cumberlands, when they drove out from Naples. He led them on tours of the extensive gardens – a whole river was dammed for a cascade – and of the 'court within court, and quadrangle within quadrangle' which composed the squat brick palace of Carlo Vanvitelli's creation.

There were other 'Foreign Travellers of distinction' at Naples to tire Sir William, prior to Emma's arrival, each with their letter of recommendation which, he felt, 'entitles them to expect some acts of hospitality'. Among them was the celebrated Hester Thrale, newly married to her second husband, the music-master, Gabriel Piozzi, who carried a miniature pianoforte about Naples in a carriage to advertise his profession. He and his wife were resident at Naples from November 1785 to February 1786. Another member of Samuel Johnson's circle, Philippina Lady Knight, had come in May 1785 to Naples to cure a convulsive stomach. She and her daughter, Cornelia, found the city so economical that they did not resume their European wanderings till May 1786.

Though these, like all travellers of all nationalities, battened on the celebrated English Minister for entertainments and information about the locale, they did not stay at the Palazzo Sessa. Various hotels in the Chiaia, a quarter of Naples made smart by the seventeenth-century Spanish viceroys, accommodated them, according to nationality. The English flocked to the Crocelle and to the Albergo Reale, for instance. As Sir William's house was also in the Chiaia area, only two steps from these hotels, this separate residence did not breed any noticeable independence in the travellers. They were often with the Minister by breakfast. Still, there was a small saving on bed-linen.

In the second week of March 1786, a lady, the Honourable Mrs Damer, came to Naples and did stay at the Palazzo Sessa. Anne Damer, daughter of General Conway, had stayed at the Palazzo Sessa in 1782 during Catherine's last year of life. She naturally did so again, though Sir William had no doubt of the talk it would engender. He told Greville, in a letter written on 7 March, that the widow – Damer had shot himself in 1776 – would be with him shortly and would stay no more than a fortnight. Anne Damer was, at thirty-seven, despite a regrettable enthusiasm for rouge and for private theatricals (she had an inaudible voice), still modish enough to attract – perhaps a little too modish. She was one of the Whig ladies who, led by the Duchess of Devonshire, shocked Society by canvassing in the streets for Fox in the 1780 election. She wrote Latin and Greek, she was a fine musician, and was fast becoming an accomplished sculptress. According to Horace Walpole, her work in marble resembled that of Bernini. This paragon was still occupying the late Lady Hamilton's apartments and going about in Sir William's carriage when Emma arrived late in April. Emma's imminent arrival had not for a moment deterred Sir William from again thinking of marriage. On 30 May, he informed his niece Mary that, if Mrs Damer had been content to live 'chiefly' in Naples, and take him as he was, he might have been married. However, the lady's reluctance to live out of England, and her theatrical nature which required a husband to play the part of 'dying lover', decided him in the end against going to a proposal.

Sir William saw no reason why Emma's presence in his house should discourage him from thoughts of matrimony, as and when opportunities arose. Far from seeing Emma as a charming and permanent alternative to a wife, in a letter to Greville written on 25 April he made it clear that he was not at all eager for Emma's arrival. He stressed that her residence would be a temporary charge on him, and emphasized that with Greville lay the final responsibility for his mistress, discarded though she might be.

> The prospect of possessing so delightfull an object under my roof soon certainly causes in me some pleasant sensations, but they are accompanied with some anxious thoughts as to the prudent management of this business; however, I will do as well as I can, and hobble in and out of this pleasant scrape as decently as I can. You may be assured that I will comfort her for the loss of you as well as I am able . . .

Sir William was, for once, not amused by his nephew's covetous designs on him. He had signed a bond, in which he was named joint security for the loan from Ross and Ogilvie, whereby his nephew might clear himself of his Hubberston debts. Foolish, scheming Greville had declared that signature worthless without a witness's approval, and had sent another bond. Though Sir William signed this and sent it to his nephew with his letter of 25 April, he was incensed at Greville. In this bond he was named principal in the loan, and his nephew only joint security. 'I trust to your well known probity to secure me against all accidents as far as you can,' he wrote with a degree of sharpness unusual in his correspondence with his nephew. Emma's arrival seemed part and parcel of Greville's selfish schemes. Now that he had been landed with Emma, Sir William ended his letter severely, 'you will, I daresay, turn your mind seriously to the improving of your fortune, either by marriage or getting into employment.'

Greville, free of Emma, secure of his loan, could afford to shrug his shoulders at such a mild display of wrath. As for Sir William's declaration that Emma was to be an interlude only, time would tell. Sir William himself might consider her presence in his house no barrier to marriage, but her presence would be effective in another way. No lady of distinction would visit where a woman of Emma's type lived. Mrs Damer, who departed shortly after Emma's arrival, was to be the last of the artistic widows who led Sir William to dream of recapturing the quiet felicity of his days with Catherine.

On 27 March Emma and her companions reached Geneva and were met by Vincenzo Sabatino, Sir William's head footman, and possibly also by Abraham Cottier, Sir William's valet. Emma was flattered by this attention to her comfort. Perhaps it was as the party rested by the shores of sparkling Lac de Genève that Gavin Hamilton made some sketches, which Sir William possessed by 1798, of Emma reposing on a couch. His large paintings of Emma as a Sibyl and as Hebe may have been later worked up from these sketches. There is no record that she sat to 'kind and liberal' Gavin – so Fuseli described him – at any later date.

The increased party made the journey over Mont Cenis and the 'sublime' Alps under the experienced care of Swiss *voiturins*. For a fixed sum, these guides provided chairs in which travellers were carried, mules to which the baggage was strapped, and paid for all the travellers' meals (excluding breakfast) and lodgings during the journey into Italy. From Turin, travelling *cambiatura*, Emma and her companions proceeded down through the plain of Piedmont, into the Grand Duchy of Tuscany, to Bologna, and then into the Papal States. At Rome, in mid-April, Gavin left the party, and the ladies exchanged public conveyance for Sir William's own travelling chaise. Traversing the miasmic Pontine Marshes on Pope Pius' splendid new road, by the last week in April Emma's and her mother's long journey into foreign climes neared completion with their arrival at Terracina, frontier town to the Kingdom of the Two Sicilies.

However little Emma may have observed during the last six weeks, however much her thoughts were only of Greville (her letters to him 'on the road' do not survive), the beauty of the coastal road along which the carriage now proceeded past the 'ever furious' sea between Terracina and Fondi, and the purple mountains whose bulk blocked the eastern horizon as the road turned inland, must have impressed her. Then there was the excitement of crossing the River Garigliano in a ferry-boat; there were tantalizing views of coastal bays and of distant islands to occupy her before they reached Capua. The vermin infesting the shacks which served as posting-inns along their way no doubt also made their impression on Emma. Seasoned travellers slept in all their clothes and did not get between the sheets. After Capua, the Campagna Felice, or Blessed Land, with its rich earth and poplars, festooned in Virgilian fashion with vines, rolled before the travellers' eyes. Lemon trees, mulberry trees and verdant market gardens, together with a notable increase in habitations, marked the approach of Naples. Now, there came into view, eminent beyond olive groves and fields of green wheat, the twin-peaked mass of Vesuvius, Sir William's passion, emitting its patterns of smoke.

Through the fine Porta Capuana, its round towers built up about with tenements, its piazza congested with wagons and stalls and further confused by a multitude of shouting, idling, singing Neapolitans, Emma entered the most delightful city on the shores of the Mediterranean on her twenty-first birthday. The carriage wound its way along the Via dei Tribunali, the ancient decumanus of the city, south down the celebrated Via Toledo, to the Largo di Castello, the hub of the city, being 'a vast place . . . surrounded on all sides by houses'. Nearby was the Royal Palace, the 'great citadel by the sea' or the Castel Nuovo, and the Bay itself. The carriage turned to the west, along the other great thoroughfare of Naples, the hilly Strada di Chiaia. Shortly after the bend in the road above which the roseate Palazzo Cellamare reared, the carriage turned back east into the side of the Pizzofalcone hill, and into the narrow Vico di Cappella Vecchia di S. Maria. As Henry Swinburne observed, 'In the heart of the city the streets are narrow, and, on account of the great elevation of the houses, gloomy and close; they are paved with square stones of dark coloured lava.' The Vico was little more than a yard, with the church of S. Maria on its south side and a 'spinning grotto', where rope-makers worked in what George Lord Herbert called a 'majestic' cavern of rubble through a door to the north. A Roman *porta*, with inscription, gave on to a second yard. Here, Emma and her mother descended, and, beneath a vaulted passage at the yard's eastern extremity, they passed through the portals of the Palazzo Sessa and into its open courtyard.

Emma told Greville she was very glad she had arrived on her birthday. All that day, she had been exceptionally low-spirited, thinking how far she was from Greville on a day when he had 'used to smile on me and stay at home & be kind to me'. Sir William did all he could to cheer her. One hopes he gave her a glass of champagne, a drink she had probably not tasted since the days with Sir Harry, but was to adore later. While only porter and other beers were drunk at Edgware Row, Sir William imported fine wines from France, as well as hogsheads of cider and porter from England. 'Cribb'd, cabin'd, and confined' as Emma had been for the last five years, a life of spacious apartments, carriages, 'a pack of servants' and constant company – going far beyond what she might have enjoyed at Uppark – now opened before her in the 'native city of the Zephyrs', where 'the excessive heat of the sun' was 'tempered with sea breezes, and with gales, wafting the perfumes of the Campagna Felice'.[1]

The Palazzo Sessa – four white walls rising three storeys high above a courtyard – had housed monastic orders from the eleventh century

till shortly after Sir William's arrival in Naples. Among the distinguished abbots of this community had been Pope Marcello II, Cardinal Francesco Buoncompagni, Archbishop of Naples, and Monsignor
Perelli, famous for his stupidity.[2]

In 1767 the monks ceased to walk in the cloisters which ran, behind
an arched façade, beneath the upper storeys of the building. The abbey
was suppressed in the clerical purges instigated by the then Prime
Minister, Tanucci. Part of the building was converted to the uses of
a secular school – the major part was acquired by the Marchese di
Sessa, and transformed into the Palazzo Sessa. For 804 ducats a year
(about £150), Sir William had leased since then from the marchese
the entire southern length of the building, that to the right of the
courtyard entrance, and the adjoining half of the western length above
the entrance.

His apartments were approached by a stone staircase concealed in
the arched cloister directly opposite the courtyard entrance. On the
first floor, visitors went up three shallow steps to their left to enter
Sir William's lower apartments. From a small hall a narrow corridor,
with a vaulted, painted ceiling and with windows looking out on the
courtyard below, ran along the entire side of the *palazzo*. At the back
of the corridor wall, and also reached from the hall, a series of three
large rooms, all with views of the Bay beneath and Vesuvius beyond,
gave on to one another. These were the apartments where Sir William
conducted his official business.

The first room, designated 'First Ante-chamber' in an inventory of
1798, was the room where persons on business attended the Minister's leisure. They waited in a room whose decoration, with pilasters
wreathed with ivy and ceilings picked out with bright paint according
to Adam designs, rather than the tables and screens Sir William imported
from England, prompted Goethe in 1787 to describe the rooms in the
palazzo as 'furnished in the English taste'. It was a motley crew who
waited here. Apart from representatives of governments and banks,
there were booksellers ('Whatever rare books there are in Naples,
the antiquarians must bring to me first,' Sir William told the artist,
Tischbein), artists of all kinds in need of patronage, and a stream of
often ragged vendors of the curious. Tischbein tells us that 'People
knew he loved odd objects.' It was not only vases the Neapolitans
brought. Tischbein records, among other 'strange products of nature'
which Sir William bought, a polyps or Medusa's head. Once set in a
glass container, the monster's slow writhings fascinated the Minister for
a considerable time. Rarely a day went by, Tischbein tells us, without
some new freak being offered to Sir William.

The polyps, and other purchases, were accommodated in the 'Next Room', so designated in the inventory, to the 'First Ante-chamber'. Visitors on His Majesty's official business were marched through to the library, where it would appear Sir William's secretaries, Smith and Oliver, spent their days. Visitors on more congenial business remained in the 'Next Room', which, we understand from Tischbein, was Sir William's personal study. The room was, at the date when Emma arrived in Naples, less full of black glaze and terracotta than it had been or was to be in later years. Sir William did not begin seriously to build up his second, and infinitely superior, collection of Greek vases till after excavations at Nola in 1791. Still, there was plenty to attract the eye, and to provide hours of entertainment for Sir William and his guests. Tischbein, recording the many hours he spent there from 1787 to 1798, declared, 'I have never seen a more pleasant room . . .' there were specimens of lava in one cabinet, facsimiles of medals from the Vatican collection in another, telescopes at the window trained on Vesuvius, and antique terracottas and cameos dotted about such surfaces where maps of the Kingdom of Naples or curious books did not lie.

In this room Sir William breakfasted, spent hours of the day, and more often than not returned, after dinner on the upper floor, for an hour or two more with his objects. Tischbein tells us, as further evidence of the very idiosyncratic nature of this room, that on the walls were inscribed various precepts for life, one being, '*La mia patria è dove mi trovo bene*', or 'My homeland is where I feel at home'. (This sentiment outraged various English visitors.) One imagines these mottoes were written up in gold lettering along the cornices of the walls. The walls themselves were buried under a variety of paintings, hung apparently in a 'confused, chaotic manner'. In fact, each work in the room was carefully selected, and favoured for a particular association which it had for Sir William. Paintings honoured for their intrinsic merit or value were kept for other rooms. Here, besides the *Laughing Boy*, then ascribed to da Vinci, there was a rough sketch dashed off by Lady Di Beauclerk (née Spencer) of her children, rolling about on the ground. This held a high place in Sir William's affections for the success with which the artist had broken all the rules. Eruptions of Vesuvius, painted by Pietro Fabris, the artist of the engravings in 'Campi Phlegraei', also featured here. But so did a picture of a ferry-boat on the Volturno river, a reminder of shooting parties in that region. As Tischbein said, 'the whole seemed chaos, but, if you looked closer, you could recognise the sensitivity and sensuality of the inhabitant who had brought together these expressions of his taste . . . The walls showed his inner life . . .'

The library, adorned with paintings and books, gave on to the corridor, at the head of which stood a water closet. Across the corridor, extending along the western side of the *palazzo* above the entrance, the rooms were apportioned to Emma and her mother on their arrival – 'a very good establishment of 4 rooms, very pleasant, looking to the sea . . .' First came a large sitting-room, in white with gold stars and wreaths on the ceiling. Two similar rooms followed. From the last of these, however, there opened a charming little room, with a fireplace. From one of its windows, the view was of the Chiaia. From the other, one looked down on the blue bay, divided at the foot of the hill into twin gulfs by the Castel dell'Ovo on its miniature peninsula. This jewel-like chamber, its ceiling painted blue and decorated with golden stars and harps, still today brings to mind the enchanted room of Curdie's Princess, and other chambers of fairy-tale.

Sir William had decorated the staircase, as it proceeded up to his upper apartments, with heads of the philosophers, Democritus and Heraclitus – the one laughing at the world, the other weeping for it. Between them was a picture by Luca Giordano of a Neapolitan playing the guitar with a parrot and monkey perched on either shoulder, and a ram and an ass at his side. In 1801, when Sir William sold this painting, he notes that 'Luca was out of humour with his Countrymen'. This 'hasty picture' was 'a Satire on them'; they were all 'Imitators, Talkative Asses, and contented Cuckolds,' or *'Simii, papagalli, cucci, e cornuti buoni'*.[3]

On the upper floor, Sir William entertained guests who had come for pleasure rather than business. The rooms were laid out on a similar pattern to that of the floor below. Where Emma's apartments lay on the lower floor, Sir William had his bedroom. Mrs Damer no doubt occupied the late Lady Hamilton's bedroom and sitting-room or boudoir, which also lay in that quarter. Reception and entertainment of guests took place in three rooms above Sir William's business quarters. In 1770, Lady Anne Miller wrote of her attendance at a 'Musical Assembly' in these rooms that she could have fancied herself at an assembly in London. Though she was, in the main, referring to the considerable numbers of English people present, the rooms, too, were English in ambience. However, the room on to which the last of these three rooms opened, the 'new apartment' which Sir William was so occupied by in 1785, was anything but northern and English.

Sir William had completed the room by the time Emma arrived, for Cornelia Knight saw and described it before she left Naples in May 1786, calling the room a 'boudoir'. Tischbein, who knew the room well from 1789 on, describes it more accurately as a 'balcony room'. Sir William had built, on to the corner of the southern and western sides of the *palazzo*, what would today be called an 'observation tower'. Half of the circular room was formed by a balconied window which 'went right around the corner'. One could, simply by turning one's head, take in an enormous sweep of land and sea, Tischbein tells us excitedly. Cornelia Knight confirms that, from this novel picture-window, her host had a 'magnificent view of the bay'. Goethe said the view 'may well be unique. The sea below, Capri opposite, Mount Posillipo to the right, near by the promenade of the Villa Reale, to the left an old building of the Jesuits, in the distance the coast line from Sorrento to Cape Minerva – probably nothing comparable could be found in the whole of Europe and certainly not in the middle of a great city.'

The other half of the circular tower was, as Tischbein says, 'decorated in a very surprising way'. Sir William had had the walls and the doors 'covered with great mirrors' in which you could see reflected all the surrounding area. Cornelia Knight again confirms: 'The bay, by moonlight, appeared to great advantage, and sometimes the full moon seemed to emerge from the crater of Mount Vesuvius. On other nights it was curious to see the lighted boats employed in the tunny fishery . . .', and the strange marine life of the bay, reflected in the mirrored walls. As Tischbein says, sitting on the brocaded cushioned seat which ringed the mirrored boudoir, 'one felt as if one were sitting outside on the top of a rock, on the crest of a cliff above sea and earth.' Here, Sir William loved to sit and read, and Tischbein gives us a vivid picture of his interrupting the Minister here. Sir William, in a moment of solitary contentment, was stretched out along the cushions, a book in his hand. He was laughing aloud at something which seemed more than usually foolish in the book he was reading.

In this and the other upper rooms, Sir William gave his concerts and entertained the *corps diplomatique*, the Neapolitan nobility and other visitors – whether they came to dine, to make music, occasionally to dance, or just to pass an idle hour. Here, Sir William, entranced by Emma's beauty – which he thought much improved in the two years since he had seen her – gave up all appointments in the first days of her residence to breakfast, dine and sup with her. His rancorous letter to Greville was a thing of the past. 'I cannot move a hand or a foot or a legg but he is marking it as graceful,' Emma wrote fearfully to Greville on 30 April.

The 'pack of servants' who attended this uneasy couple no doubt watched events with interest. Most of them had served Sir William many years. There was Gasparo, or Gasperino, Russo, the major-domo, who had a tendency to get above himself. (Lady Hamilton apologized in 1782 to her husband for not papering a room; she had thought Gasparo had had 'one of his ideas', but in fact the order emanated from Sir

William himself, away at Caserta.) There were two footmen at least
– Vincenzo, Emma's escort, and Salvatore Baldi – besides a character
called Gaetano, who may have done the cooking. This simple operation
– mainly boiling *maccheroni* and fish – took place on the upper floor.
(In 1776, Sir William suspected Gaetano of poisoning Jack, a pet
monkey whom the Minister had trained to look at virtu through a
magnifying-glass, 'to poke fun at antiquarians'. All the servants hated
poor Jack.) In Naples, it was the custom for men to do all the domestic
work – 'even to the making of the beds', the traveller Samuel Sharp
wrote in 1772. Besides these domestics, Sir William had on his pay-roll,
apart from the faithful Cottier, another 'man', Ambrogio Curnier, two
English secretaries, Smith and Oliver, and Emma soon acquired a doting
maid. Then there were coachmen, grooms and *volanti* – indispensable
servants who ran in front of the household's carriages in the streets
to clear a path. Perhaps some among these last doubled as the 'band'
referred to by many visitors to the house. Sir William, early on in his
residence in Naples, took three or four 'musicians' into his house. Thus,
a quartet, for him to join or just listen to, might always be available.
Where wages were low and living cheap, such luxuries were practised
by all. The musicians in question were probably drawn from the streets
of Naples, where little groups of songsters and fiddlers were to be found
at every street corner.

Few of these gentlemen would have slept in the house. Neapolitans
preferred the independence of board wages, generally. Those that did
'live in' may well have slept on the staircase. Such was the custom in
the *palazzi* of the indigenous noblemen – Fuga and the other architects
having omitted to provide servants' quarters. Curnier, we know from
letters of 1787, rented his own apartment – with balcony – from the
Marchese di Sessa. No doubt Smith and Oliver did for themselves
similarly. Possibly, some of the servants slept by Sir William's basement
treasure-house or 'lumber-room'. Here were to be found rejected vases,
surplus pictures and a chaotic hotch-potch of curiosities; sarcophagi,
candelabra and antique busts were among the exhibits. Here, Sir William
kept, besides inferior works, such works of art – ancient and modern
– as the King of Naples would have been unhappy to learn were in
foreign hands. The lumber-room was by no means shown to all; the
Emperor Joseph of Austria and the poet Goethe were among the few
who rated the treat.

In the first few days of Emma's residence in these strange surroundings, Sir William did all he could to cheer her. He took her to the play
at the Teatro dei Fiorentini, a veritable flea-pit, and to the San Carlo,
the famous opera house whose name honoured Ferdinand's father, its

founder and now King of Spain. Every Friday, at dusk, the nobility of Naples proceeded in their carriages – horses and carriages were their consuming passion – along the esplanade below the Chiaia called the Villa Reale. Emma having arrived on the Thursday, the very next day Sir William prevailed on a rich nabob, Sir Thomas Rumbold, to take him, Emma and Mrs Cadogan out to join the throng. Though Emma wrote to Greville, 'I find it is not either a fine horse, or a fine coach . . . can make [me] happy', she nevertheless enjoyed the treat, and was much flattered by the admiration she aroused, with her English dresses and blue hat. She was delighted with a white satin dress, 'with India painting', which Sir William gave her – 'cost 25 guineas'. Despite her real unhappiness and worries about her future with Greville, Sir William's admiration did not really trouble her. 'He will never be my lover,' she wrote on 30 April and felt that settled that.

> I have a great regard for him as the uncle & friend of you, & he loves me, Greville. But he can never be anything nearer . . . He never can be my lover . . . he loves me now, as much as ever he could Lady Bolingbroke. Endead, I am sorry, for I cannot make him happy. I can be civil, oblidging, & I do try to make myself as agreable as I can to him. But I belong to you . . .

Emma was interested by the life around her. Her susceptible heart was touched by the unhappiness of the nabob, Sir Thomas Rumbold. He was nursing a son 'who is dying of decline . . . poor young man, he cannot walk from the bed to the chair'. The boy's stepmother, 'like a tender-hearted wretch', had left her husband 'with his heart broken', and gone off to Rome, taking the coach and all the English servants, to have a gay time there. Emma made fast friends with Sir Thomas. He was the first of many to respond warmly to Emma's practical kindness. Every day he 'brought is carridge or phaeton, which he as bought hear . . . & shows ous a deal of civilities . . .' He was to write to her on his return to England.

Emma looked forward, as she wrote to Greville on 30 April, to visiting Sir William's *capannina* or little cabin at Caserta shortly. There was also the prospect of bathing and going out in Sir William's sailing boat from his villa at Posillipo. She had visited this house, the day before she wrote, and pronounced it 'a very pretty place'.

The term 'summer-house' is most suitable to describe this little house, comprising only three rooms and a kitchen. It lay vacant through the winter. Then, from May to September, Sir William, and now Emma too, spent the hot hours of the day here. They drove out from Naples in time to dine at two, and spent the afternoon sailing, 'rolling in the waves', or investigating what the *piscina*, or rock-pool, which Sir William had excavated for purposes of marine observation, had to offer. Rich as the waters were then, nautilus, sea-lemons and sea-oranges, and an assortment of weird crustacea were usually captive. For shade there was a huge Venetian blind, which could extend like a sail over the semi-circular terrace with its ornamental parapet which topped the rock. Two large doorways in the side of the house nearer Naples gave on to the flat roof of a secondary structure. On this terrace, Sir William had constructed a *giardino pensile*, or hanging garden. Here he, and now Emma, entertained guests, under a canopy of vines, with wine and fish and fruit. Behind them, the craggy hill of Posillipo rose steeply, while in front the Bay teemed with boats and fishermen leaving the harbour of Mergellina. The shore road from Naples below was only navigable by carriage up to the casino. The rock on which the house was built blocking further passage, a tunnel had been cut through the rock for those who wished to proceed further on foot. The daily traffic, the women colourful in their Marian red veils and blue dresses, passing in one side of the rock, and emerging the other side, still voluble, amused the terrace party above. Knowing Sir William's liberality, boys would gather beneath the house and beg him to throw money into the sea, so they might show their agility in diving for it. Tischbein mentions that they also wrestled, sometimes huge, writhing groups of them, on a very high wall – again to entertain the Hamilton party. Perhaps the wall in question was part of the beautiful Palazzo Donn'Anna, crumbling, overgrown ruins in Sir William's day, which stood directly to the north of the casino, almost in the Bay. The Neapolitan youths were nothing if not intrepid.

Perhaps it was here, at Posillipo, before they drove back to Naples in the evening, that Sir William attempted to break the illusion under which Emma was labouring. It was certainly on the day he showed her Posillipo, 29 April, that he spoke to her of Greville. Perhaps trying to obtain her favours from gratitude, he told her he had made his will and left everything to his nephew. 'That made me very happy for your sake,' Emma wrote simply to Greville. If he was in need of money immediately, she went on, he need only write and she would procure him some. 'I am afraid I distressed you but I am sure Sr. W will send you some,' she wrote brightly, unaware of what Sir William had already done for his nephew. When she told Sir William that she must, with her allowance, help Greville and send him money for his journey to Naples in the autumn, it was not lust but pity which made the old knight kiss her, and tears come into his eyes. He told her she should command him in anything, and did not attempt further to rupture her illusions that day. Emma wrote her not unhappy letter to Greville the following day.

On 1 May, however, Emma had such a disturbing conversation with Sir William that she took up her pen to add to her letter before the post went.

> I have onely to say I enclose this I wrote yesterday & I will not venture myself now to wright any more for my mind & heart is so torn by different passions that I shall go mad, onely Greville, remember your promise, October. Sr. Wm. says you never mentioned to him about coming to Naples at all, but you know the consequence of your not coming for me. Endead, my dear Greville, I live but on the hope of seeing you & if you do not come hear, lett what will be the consequence, I will come to England. I have had a conversation this morning with Sr. Wm. that has made me mad. He speaks half I do not know what to make of it, but Greville, my dear Greville, wright some comfort to me, pray do, if you love me . . .

If Emma's physical form was admired for its resemblance to the antique, Catullus himself would have admired Emma's facility for expressing the different lover's passions in such swift succession.

Sir William had been put in a difficult position by Greville's false tale to Emma. He had been prepared for a woman who, 'on the least neglect [from Greville] will accept your offers . . . She must have in her mind a stronger impression of the chances [of Greville and herself not meeting again] than she expresses but she says she would not put herself in the reach of chances with any person but yourself.' Later in that letter of 20 January, Greville related how Emma had turned down Henrietta Willoughby's brother, though he 'persecuted her to accept his proposals', on the grounds that he was 'young & giddy'. If Emma did talk of accepting Sir William should Greville neglect her, we may be sure she meant it only as idle lovers' teasing, and Greville misrepresented her levity. Sir William, when he made Greville's intentions of neglect plain to Emma, found himself with a lady whose virtuous devotion to Greville was impenetrable. Judging by Emma's words, 'half I do not know what to make of it', Sir William found it difficult to make her proposals.

Emma's world, meanwhile, was turned upside down by the bald statement that Greville, her knight in shining armour, had no intentions of appearing in October. She had written as follows on the thirtieth:

> I dreaded setting down to write for I try to appear as chearful before Sr

Wm. as I can & I am sure to cry the moment I think of you, for I feil more & more unhappy at being separatted from you, & if my total ruin depends on seeing you, I will and must in the end of the sumer, for to live without you is impossible. I love you to that degree that at this time their is not a hardship opon hearth, either of poverty, hunger . . . or even to walk barefooted to Scotland to see you, but what I would undergo. Therefore, my dear, dear Greville, if you do love me, for God sake and for my sake, try all you can to come hear as soon as possible . . .

Though she sent off these sheets with her horrified, scrawled addition of the next day, Emma must have felt how inappropriate were such sentiments when Sir William had just revealed Greville's perfidy. The balance of her happy, flirtatious relationship with Sir William was disturbed. She was nervous and embarrassed with him now. Her last line, 'wright some comfort to me do . . . if you love me, but onely remember you will never be loved by anybody like your affectionate Emma', reads as if Emma was now convinced, despite herself, that 'the chances . . . of not meeting again' with Greville were high. The degree to which she felt his deception cannot be exaggerated. Nevertheless, she persisted in holding off Sir William. He wrote to Mary Dickenson a month after Emma's arrival,

I have a *female visiter* from England, that occupies a part of my House, that is *a deed* without a *Name*; I shall say no more but that it is probable the visit will not be of long duration . . . Tho' appearances are not always true – with regard to my present situation, if you knew the circumstances, Even you would not blame me, & no one knows better than you what is realy right or wrong . . .'[4]

Poor Sir William had indeed been 'sold a pup' by his beloved Greville.

The hot weather descended on Naples. The nobles had cast off the fur cloaks and muffs they had worn against the piercing winds of winter before Emma's arrival. Now they prepared, literally, to sit out the summer. Samuel Sharp described this operation. 'They sit in chairs, with only a thin callico gown, for hours together, some days, wholly occupied in wiping off the sweat that runs in channels down their bodies.' The nobles of Naples were naturally prone to inactivity. If they stirred themselves, it was only to 'sit still' by the side of their beloved sea, and 'snuff it up as a man takes rappee', Sharp declared. They lived what today might be called a 'minimalist' life, horses and carriages being the dukes' and counts' and princes' passion, lovers that of their ladies. 'When they are provided,' says Sharp of the horses, 'they do as they can for the rest.' The King and Queen kept only a small Court, and the salaries were bad. Their estates did not interest the nobles, though the soil in certain valleys in the Kingdom was so rich that farmers used the iron part of a spade, like a hoe on a long pole, to turn it.

Uninterested themselves in agriculture, the nobles let out all their land, but always in small packets – so grudging their tenants 'a better livelihood than roots and brown bread'. (As a result of this obduracy, the nobles were forced to take payment in corn, oil, and wine and had the bother of selling these themselves.) Without parliamentary elections, racehorses, expensive country-houses or gardens, or demands on their purse for education – or any of the expenses and occupations of nobilities in other countries at this time – they had sufficient money and all the leisure in the world to live their urban, idle life. Naples, which they were deeply attached to anyway, had perforce to be the beginning and end of their world. The horses, on which they lavished such sums, could only bear them into other countries for six months at a time, and by special permission of the King. If they remained away longer, their estates were seized.

Intrigues of the most banal kind naturally filled their *vita otiosa*. The ladies, after the first year of marriage and the birth of the heir, were entirely occupied with their *cicisbei*, or lovers. Lady Knight said, 'some of these connections were undoubtedly innocent, but all are indelicate.' Samuel Sharp went further. 'Many people in England imagine the majority of Cicisbeos to be an innocent kind of dangling fribble; but they are utterly mistaken in the character.' In fact, after a lady had made her choice of *cicisbeo*, he thereafter played much more the role of a second husband than of an exciting lover, and she spent all her time deceiving him. Emma no doubt adored the stories Sir William, who loved an anecdote, had to tell of the farcical scenes which ensued.

The *lazzaroni*, the sixty thousand unemployed 'loafers' of Naples, were, perhaps, the most striking sight in Naples – if only because they were forever in the way. Like the nobles, they adored their city. (Returning to Naples, the poet Goethe was once startled by a young guide who emitted a banshee howl of joy as they crested a hill and saw the city beneath them.) They considered, like the nobles, all other towns and parts of the Kingdom of Naples inferior to their own. They adored, almost as much, 'snow or iced water, and lemonade'. As today on the streets of Istanbul, the cry of 'Iced water, fresh cold water!' echoed all day in the streets of Naples. The Kingdom's revenues, derived mainly from a tax on the thousands of foreign visitors who came to Naples, were substantially augmented by the state monopoly of ice. Provided with this necessity, living otherwise on a little fruit and bread, the *lazzaroni*,

despite their ragged and often naked state – they adorned their person
with religious tattoos – appeared happy. In the summer, they slept on
the streets. In winter, they retired to the Christian catacombs below the
Palace of Capo di Monte, where they huddled together for warmth.
If they wished for money, there were a hundred jobs in the porterage
way awaiting them. They often irked foreigners by their refusal to stir,
for any money, when they thought it was too hot. Lazing by the side
of the Toledo or prancing in and out of the water at Mergellina, they
had a most developed sense of their own dignity. After all, if the chief
pleasure of the King of this land of plenty was to imitate their habits
and occupations, to such a degree that he was dubbed *Il Re Lazzarone*,
what reason was there for them to bow to any man?

In such a country, where, insensibly, the moral code was relaxed
for all, where Goethe was to declare, 'everyone lives in a state of
intoxicated self-forgetfulness, myself included,' Emma stood firm against
Sir William's advances through May, through June . . . Gifts of a black
Rubens hat, with feather trim, and sliding fans did not alter her mind.
In July, she was still blindly, obdurately, playing her virginal role. James
Byres in Rome had perhaps got wind of how matters stood in the
Palazzo Sessa, when he wrote to the Bishop of Killala on 14 June.
'Our friend Sir William is well. He has lately got a piece of modernity
from England which I am afraid will fatigue and exhaust him more
than all the Volcanos and antiquities in the Kingdom of Naples.'[5] In
July Emma wrote to Romney, at Sir William's request, to ask if he and
Hayley could come out on a visit. Doubtless, both she and Sir William
felt that the painter and poet might leaven the oppressive atmosphere.

Sir William, philosophical as ever, bore Emma's rejection of his
advances with tolerable equanimity. On 4 July, he wrote to his friend,
Sir Joseph Banks, 'A beautiful plant called Emma has been transplanted
here from England & at least has not lost any of its beauty.'[6] Banks, a
close associate of Greville, would have understood the allusion, whether
or not he had met Emma to appreciate her beauty. Sir William, who, on
Emma's arrival, was so fascinated by her beauty – 'he does nothing all
day but look at me and sigh', and point out 'my beauties' to his friends
– now turned to taking what advantage he could of her person. He sent
for another Romney of Emma 'in the Black gown . . . & I have made
the bargain with him that the picture shall be yours if he will pay for
it & he will,' Emma wrote to Greville, showing she had learnt a little
about 'art-dealing' from him. Sir William wanted the picture to join
the Romney Bacchante, and the Reynolds of Emma, which he had
hung in his new mirrored 'Gallery', as he called the room in his 1798
inventory. Besides this, Sir William was encouraging all the artists in

Naples to work on Emma in the first months of her stay. Emma wrote to Greville on 22 July, 'Their is two painters now in the house painting me; one picture is finished. It is the size of the Bacante setting in a turbin, a turkish dress, the other is in a black rubin hat with fethers [the hat Sir William had bought her in May], blue silk gown, etc. but as soon as these is finished ther is two more to paint me.' Angelica Kauffmann, if she came to Naples from Rome, where she was resident, was to paint her, and the cameo artist, Marchant, was 'to cut a head of me for a ring'.

While Emma was under his care, Sir William did what he could to further the ambition she had expressed from London, to be 'improved a little more'. He had, by 22 July, provided her with 'a language master, a singing master, music etc, etc . . .' Unfortunately, her progress in these subjects was not now of particular interest to her. As she wrote to Greville,

> but what is it for, if it was to amuse you I should be happy, but Greville, what will it avail me. I am poor, helpeless & forlorn. I have lived with you 5 years & you have sent me to a strange place & no one prospect, me thinking you was coming to me; instead of which I was told I was to live, you know how, with Sir W. No. I respect him, but, no, never, shall he peraps live with me for a little wile like you & send me to England, then what am I do to, what is to become of me.

Earlier in this letter she repeats her cry, 'I find life is unsuportable with out you. Oh my heart is intirely broke. Then for God sake, my ever dear Greville, do write mee some comfort. I don't know what to do, I am now in that state I am incapable of any thing.' She was, in fact, resigned by now to the idea that Greville had done with her, though she could not help writing to him as if some happier outcome might transpire. At the beginning of her letter she had faced reality: 'As soon as I know your determination I shall take my own measures. If I dont hear from you & that you are coming according to promise, I shall be in England by Christmas at farthest, dont be unhappy at that, I will see you once more for the last time.' At that point, however, her resolve to be calm broke down, at the thought of that 'last time', and she wrote as detailed above. Her words on the folly of beginning a connection with Sir William are revealing. Her betrayal by Greville had made her cautious and suspicious of all men, but she was now considering, if only to dismiss, the idea of accepting Sir William's offer. After fourteen letters from her to Greville had gone unanswered – Greville was faithful to his promise to Sir William that he would 'neglect' Emma – she was now accepting that Greville had cast her off, and thinking of a future without him.

Interestingly, she could not alter her tone, despite her altered feelings for Greville. She writes in the same friendly, high-spirited way about her life in Naples, as she would have done if she were assured of Greville's love. She writes excitedly of the admiration an old friend of Greville's from Vienna – Prince Dietrichstein – has for her. 'He is my cavaliere servente or chechespeo which you like.' The Prince wants a picture of her by Kauffmann, he walks at her side in the Villa Reale, 'he dines with ous often.' She records the admiration of another gentleman, Lord Hervey, and calls him 'a lover of mine'. Lord Hervey, heir to the outrageous Earl-Bishop, Frederick Augustus, fourth Earl of Bristol and Bishop of Derry, was a worthy son of his father in so far as he caused sexual scandal wherever he went. Emma was entranced by the galaxy of distinguished gentlemen who gathered around her. 'I walk in the Villa Reale every night, I have generally two princes, two or 3 nobles, the English minister & the King, with a crowd beyond us,' she solemnly informed Greville. No longer did she merely view the nobility of Naples from Sir Thomas's carriage. The evening of 22 July, for instance, 'I have a conversazyeone tonight & a concert.' She had the King of the Two Sicilies 'in my train' at the opera, which she and Sir William attended most nights. Greville, who had declared Emma cured of all wish for 'casual admiration', must have shaken his sage head over her exuberant expressions of gratification ('what will surprise you I am remarkably fair that everybody says I put on red & wite'), and over her description of her free and entertaining life ('I am going to Paysilipo to diner . . . I bathe every day . . . we had a small deplomatic party & we was sailing in our boat . . .'). All his prophecies to Sir William of the disasters that would ensue if Emma were not kept locked up in a villa had fallen on deaf ears. Here was Emma writing importantly, 'We have had dreadful thunder & lightenen; it fell at the Maltese minister just by our house & burnt is beds & wines etc. etc. I have now perswaded Sr. Wm. to put up a conducter to his house; the lava runs a little but the mountain is fery ful & we expect an irruption every day.' Alas, Emma did not have time to tell Greville 'my ideas of the people of Naples'. One gathers these might at least have been her own opinions, judging by her next words, 'But Greville, flees, & lice their is millions.'

If Emma was gratified by the court which the nobles of Naples paid her, it was the King's admiration which really excited her. Ferdinand was in her train every night, and, on Sundays, when it was the custom for all Naples to go to Posillipo, 'he allways comes . . . before the casina in his boat to look at me.' Emma and Sir William, and some members of the *corps diplomatique*, were out sailing in the Bay. 'The K. directly came up, put his boat of musick [a barge full of musicians] next us & made all the French horns & the wole band play, he took off his hat & sett with his hat on his knees all the wile & when we were going to land, he made his bow & said it was a sin he could not speak English . . .' Elsewhere in this letter, she writes, 'the King as eyes, he as a heart, & I have made an impression on his heart, but he told the Prince, Hamilton is my friend & she belongs to his Nephey . . .' Greville's own heart must have sunk at these words. Emma went on defiantly, 'all our friends know it, and the Prince desires his best compliments to you'.

Sir William needed all his notable urbanity to stand by while Emma aired her devotion to Greville. On the other hand, Emma's naive excitement over Ferdinand's admiration of her must have amused him. Sir William had seen this ungainly Bourbon, with his protuberant eyes and the disfiguring bulbous nose which earned him the nickname *Il Re Nasone*, court a hundred ladies in his time, among them the celebrated Sarah Goudar. Ferdinand's declaration that loyalty to Sir William prevented him from more than mere admiration of Emma must have relieved Sir William. Sarah Goudar, an Englishwoman who had run a 'gaming hall' in Naples, was among several ladies who had been banished from the Kingdom – on the Queen's orders. Maria Carolina felt no sexual jealousy of Ferdinand's ladies. She only feared them for the ascendancy they might acquire over her husband – an ascendancy which she wished to reserve all for herself. (So strange was the relationship between King and Queen that Ferdinand would accede to any request by Maria Carolina if she showed off her fine, white hands to him as she asked.) In November of this year, Sir William wrote his private opinion of the Royal couple to the Foreign Secretary. 'Ferdinand', he wrote, was 'diffident of acting for himself . . . but at the same time is jealous to a degree of others acting for him. His Majesty's habit of dissipation has taken such firm root' that there was little probability, 'nay, scarcely a possibility of His ever . . . applying seriously to business. The chase in winter and parties of sailing or fishing in summer call out his Majesty every day, at Sun Rising, and keep him out till it sets.' By the time he attended Council with his ministers, 'at which the Queen always assists', he was 'more or less fatigued with the dissipation of the day'.

Maria Carolina was known in Naples as *polpett mbocca* (or Rissole-in-the-mouth), supposedly on account of the Habsburg physiognomy which made her, when she spoke, gobble like a turkeycock. On the other hand, she had 'a very good understanding, is sensible that, unless she applied to the business which the King avoids, the whole State

would be in confusion . . .' She 'gives up the greatest part of her time
daily in looking minutely into every paper & in preparing matters for
the dispatch of business when she meets the King in council at night . . .'.
With the aid of the English-born General John Acton, who, though
only Secretary of War and Minister of the Marine, had become the
'universal Channel' for all business, and 'may truly be esteemed Prime
Minister of this country', the Queen 'generally carries every part' of her
wishes. Having lost the taste for intrigue when she discovered the heady
excitement of politics, she took only the occasional lover, and spent the
rest of her time with her children. Sir William's conclusions about this
Kingdom of Misrule were that, though since Acton's arrival in 1779
'this Country has greatly improved, from the large experience I have
had of the Neapolitan character . . . no great change can be effected
during this corrupt bigotted generation, unless good faith and a better
education were universally introduced.' The Kingdom was, internally,
in 'a state of total stagnation'.[7]

Emma could think herself fortunate that the Queen did not take
exception to her 'pasteboard king' husband's admiration of her. Prince
Dietrichstein had enthused to the Queen of Emma's charms, but she
felt only interest in the new arrival. 'The Queen likes me very much
& desired Prince Draydrixton to walk with me near her [in the Villa
Reale], that she might get a sight of me,' Emma wrote to Greville.
Perhaps it was to forestall any risk that the King's passion might become
dangerously hot, and the Queen grow to 'like' Emma less, that Sir
William intended taking Emma on a tour of Capri, Ischia and the other
islands. 'We shall be a whay a little while,' Emma wrote to Greville. 'I
should feil pleasure in all this if you was heare, but that blessing I have
not & so I must make the best of my lot.'

In fact, bad weather would seem to have delayed the expedition.
On 1 August, Emma wrote again from Naples. 'We have a deal of
rain hear & violent winds, the older people hear never remember
such a summer.' The King was 'sighing for' her, and besieging her 'in
a round about manner', she wrote, but she now appeared conscious of
the danger of incurring the Queen's wrath: 'we keep the good will of the
other part mentioned abbove [Emma had written that the Queen was
'very poorly with a cold', and added with innocent self-aggrandizement
that she herself had one 'pretty much like it'] & never gives him any
encouragement'. The interest Royalty took in her, increased though it
was, now no longer preoccupied Emma's thoughts. She was writing to
Greville in answer to a letter in which he had advised her to 'oblidge
Sr Wm.'.

'I will not answer you,' wrote Emma, strong in her indignation,

for Oh if you knew what pain I feil in reading those lines when you advise
me to Whore nothing can express my rage, I am all madness, Greville, to
advise me, you that used to envy my smiles, now with cooll indifferance
to advise me to go to bed to him, Sr Wm. Oh, that's worst of all, but I
will not, no I will not rage for if I was with you, I would murder you &
myself boath . . .

Earlier in the letter, she had written, sadly, 'I allways knew, I have ever
had a forebodeing, since I first begun to love you, that I was not destined
to be happy . . .' Now, her cold and a headache inflaming her misery,
she wrote,

nothing shall ever do for me but going home to you. If that is not to be,
I will except of nothing, I will go to London, their go in to every excess
of vice tell I dye a miserable, broken hearted wretch & leave my fate as
a warning to young whomen never to be two good, for, now you have
made me love you, made me good, you have abbandoned me & some
violent end shall finish our connexion . . .

Disbelief that Greville could have altered while she was constant,
overcame Emma. 'If it is to finish, but, Oh Greville, you cannot, you
must not give me up, you have not the heart to do it, you love me I
am sure & I am willing to do everything in my power that you shall
require of me . . .' Commenting on the death of Charles's nephew,
Lord Brooke, she fell into self-pitying mood, 'poor little boy, how
I envy him his happiness,' but optimism reasserted itself towards the
end of her letter. She still wrote as if Greville were going to come for
her. 'We shall all go home to England in 2 years & go through Spain
& you will like that.' Imperiously, she went on, 'pray write to me &
dont write in the stile of a friend but a lover, for I wont hear a word
of a friend, it shall be all love & no friendship. Sir Wm. is our friend,
but we are lovers.' These strong words were belied, however, in the
postscript. 'Pray write for nothing will make me so angry & it is not
to your interest to disoblidge me, for you dont know the power I have
hear, onely I never will be his mistress. If you affront me, I will make
him marry me. God bless you for ever.' If these last words showed an
awareness of the potential of her charms, and consequently a certain
loss of the sweetness which was such an attractive feature of Emma's
early personality, she was a worried woman. These words also show
that Emma was now seriously considering Sir William as a protector.
He had charms such as a popular personality, a carefree approach to
life, and money, which Greville could not offer – and where Greville
condemned Emma's ebullience and vanities, Sir William only laughed.

Nevertheless, it was to Greville that Emma's heart was given, and Emma had told him of Sir William's offer to settle £100 a year on her. Surely he would have her back on such terms? She awaited an answer. None came.

Just when Emma unlearnt the lessons of purity which Greville had instilled in her, and went to bed with Sir William, cannot be known. Certainly by October, Sir William and she had formed a tentative connection. Perhaps during that postponed August trip to the islands which ringed Naples, Emma, 'fell'. Sir William remarked to Joseph Banks in a letter of September, 'My visitor, for you must know I have one, is as handsome as ever & in tolerable spirits considering all – it is a bad job to come from the Nephew to the Uncle but one must make the best of it & I long to see poor Charles out of his difficulties.' The phrasing of the sentence suggests that the liaison had begun.

By 24 October, Greville was writing to his uncle that 'now you owe your present situation to your attentions, & not to any unfair advantage, & on her part there can be no plea but free choice . . .' Then Greville goes on, puzzlingly: 'no part do I lament the ostensible use you made of my name.' It would seem that what decided Emma to favour Sir William was the information he gave her that Greville had begun to plan to cast her off in early 1785. All three, Emma, Sir William and Greville, felt – despite her surrender which had been so eagerly awaited – dissatisfied with the situation in October. There was no thought then that Emma's liaison with Sir William would be a lasting affair. Greville's letter shows that the plan on hand was to settle Emma with her mother somewhere in England, with Romney as trustee of the money Sir William would make over to her. So stood matters in October.

There is an interesting postscript to these events. A foreseeable consequence of Emma beginning an affair with Sir William while still hoping Greville would come back to her was that she had pretended to Greville that she was still playing Artemis, the chaste, while she was fully launched on an Aphrodisian career. Sir William had undeceived Greville, who wrote back in this October letter: 'I have often told her that I never expected from a woman a power to withstand favourable opportunity & a long siege, but that any secrecy on the subject to me would be considered as arising from a wish of acting a part.' (Earlier in the letter he wrote that 'keeping the same dramatis personae in a play . . . places a woman particularly awkward, as she generally considers herself call'd on to act thro' the part, and rest her justifications on the exaggerated complaints of duplicity & cruelty.') This was not necessary 'where the above expectation is delivered, & if attempted to be concealed, can only be for the purpose of assuming a false appearance, & in her case her frankness will be a merit, & will put her intercourse on the proper footing.' As far as Greville was concerned, that disposed of that.

In November, he counselled Sir William to make sure Emma did not miss any chance of a young man returning from Naples to England who might make her a 'favourable' offer. 'At any rate,' Greville wrote concernedly, 'she will have the good sense not to expose herself with any boy of family; she must look to from 25 to 35, & one who is his own master.'

CHAPTER SIX

My dear Sir William

In the passages of his November letter quoted in the last chapter, Greville wrote with apparent confidence that both Emma and Sir William were resolved she should depart for England in the spring of 1787. (The awesome journey over the 'sublime' scenery of the Alps was not readily undertaken in winter.) However, other passages in this same letter indicate that Sir William regretted he could not save the situation. If, as Greville had acknowledged in October, 'when her pride is hurt by neglect or anxiety for the future, the frequent repetition of her passion balances the beauty of her smiles,' without Emma Sir William would be left ageing and lonely again, albeit in peace. He may have expressed his regret to Greville, or simply agreed that, as Greville had written in October, Emma would have been 'a charming creature . . . if she had been bless'd with the advantages of an early education'. A shame that, with all the resources at his disposal and with his interest in disseminating such knowledge as he had, Sir William should not have the chance to rectify the sad state of Emma's education. For want of a little decorum in her behaviour, she was destined to waste away in a country cottage with her mother, the cynosure only of ignorant villagers, where so much more might have been made of her.

So, one imagines, Sir William might have mused to Greville. Or perhaps Greville was so keen to keep Emma at bay in Naples, he indulged in some wishful thinking. At any rate, in this November letter, interspersed with the instructions for the proper management of Emma's return to England, there was careful advice for Sir William on that hoary old subject which Greville so loved – the proper management of Emma herself.

Sir William should play her like a trout, he instructed. Working on the pride which was so strong in Emma, he might keep her from 'meanness' – the type of behaviour now stigmatized, in divorces, for example, as 'uncivilized' – and also from 'bombast'. By this, Greville meant Emma's tendency to 'fly at the mention of truth' when it was unpalatable, and make grand gestures when a reasoned response was required. 'No absolute dependence can be given by man,' Greville reflected soberly, to any woman's declarations or intents; 'the springs of action are so much in the extreme of sublime to low . . . there is to them no interval between plain ground and the precipice.' Appeals to Emma's pride, or sense of dignity, were nevertheless the best carrot with which to entice her away from unpleasing behaviour. (Shrieks of unhappiness and a determination to return to England where an appeal to Greville in person might do more than all the letters in the world could do to win him back, naturally, came under this heading.) Especially with young women, Greville assured his uncle, 'interest [self-interest] has much more rarely weight than pride.'

Greville, the keen student of Emma's psyche, had dwelt on the advantages to Sir William of Emma's selflessness in October: 'she has not a grain of avarice or self-interest. On the contrary, she has a pleasure in sharing her last shilling.' Greville was also enthusiastic about another facet of Emma's vivid personality. 'I have always said that such a woman, if she controul her passions, might rule the roost and chuse her station,' he had written in October. Then, his admiration was only incidental – latent, even. His point was that Sir William, by giving Emma her freedom, would find that she needed much 'more management'. With her character, she had naturally 'followed up' the line he had allowed her. In October Greville's attitude to Emma's snatching at liberty was: 'Give her an inch and she'll take a yard.' In his November letter, he took a different line. Perhaps he had received a hint from Sir William that he particularly relished Emma's belief in herself, and her competitive urge to outshine others in all fields.

This November letter was the last of the many documents we have reviewed in which Greville set down his prescient, and obtuse, thoughts about Emma Hart. It seems fitting that the last words about her personality which he wrote should be a eulogy. He wrote that what would cause Sir William trouble, of all Emma's quirks, was her 'passion for admiration'. 'It is not troublesome as she is satisfied with a limited sphere,' he added swiftly, and repeated his advice of October that, 'by [Sir William's] constantly renewing very little attentions', Emma would be happy and good-tempered. Then Greville played with fire and titillated Sir William's imagination, and his own, with thoughts of what Emma could achieve, given the opportunity.

> She . . . is capable of aspiring to any line which would be celebrated, and it would be indifferent when on that key whether she was Lucretia or Sappho or Scaevola or Regulus; anything grand, masculine or feminine, she could take up, and if she took up the part of Scaevola, she would be as much offended if she was told she was a woman, as she would be, if she assumed Lucretia, she was told she was masculine.

So Greville wrote. One wonders whether he or Sir William noticed

that, with the determination which he ascribed to Emma to become
what she willed for the sake of admiration, he necessarily ascribed an
absolute want of moral sense. But then, Greville was never much
occupied by questions of morality, nor was his uncle, however they
might wrangle over the niceties of business transactions. Sir William had
the kinder and more sympathetic nature, but the principle of self-interest
flavoured all his doings quite as inexorably as it did Greville's. He is
unlikely to have thought the grandeur of Emma's conceptions, at which
Greville hinted, cause for fear, merely for amused applause.

We return to Naples, or more properly to Sir William's little cabin
near the Royal Palace of Caserta, at the foot of the Apennines to the
north of Naples. Here the Hamilton household arrived some time
before 11 November, following the Court, which would remain at
Caserta as usual till March and the end of the wild-boar season. On
arrival, Sir William and Emma were grimly preparing to sit the winter
out in forced companionship till news should come that the gentian
flowered again on the alp. When Greville's November letter reached
the house in early December, his advice and encouragement for the
ordering of the relationship may still have been premature. Shortly
before Christmas, however, an abrupt change came over Emma's feeling
for Sir William, and a joyous rapprochement took place between them.
So much we infer from a series of letters Emma wrote to Sir William
between 26 December and 18 January 1787, when he was away hunting.
Emma had determined to love Sir William and remain in Naples. That
it was her decision, that Sir William was merely delightedly acquiescent,
emerges strongly from the letters – as much from her requests that he
forgive her past behaviour as from her remark, 'you told me to stop
tell Jany, and then I should feel [the cold], and today has fully proved
it'. So she wrote on 8 January 1787.

This resolve to remain in Naples was the first decision of importance
that Emma took in her life. Until now, her 'friends' – Sir Harry, Greville
and, to some degree, Sir William – had taken charge of her fate. Perhaps
she, too, was awed by her departure from the harum-scarum style in
which she had previously got by. She referred, in her letter of 26
December, to having got her 'wisdom teeth . . . now', adding, 'I will
try to be ansome and reasonable.'

What had occurred that Emma should write, on 26 December,
'certain it is I love you & sincerely & endead I am appreensive
two much for my own quiet, but lett it be. Love as its pleasures
& its pains. . . .'? Only a month before, all thoughts had been for
her departure from the Kingdom of the Two Sicilies. Now, that
departure was in the shadowy future, Greville a shadow in the past,

and Sir William's appreciative, courteous figure was centre of Emma's stage.

There is no record or evidence for what at last brought Emma's troubled relationship with Sir William to this happy new beginning. That Sir William was equally contented with Emma is clear from her letter of 18 January: 'I have just received your dear sweet letter. It has charmed me. I don't know what to say to you to thank you in words kind enough. Oh how kind! Do you call me your dear freind? Oh, what a happy creature is your Emma! – me that had no freind, no protector, no body that I could trust, and now to be the freind, the Emma, of Sir William Hamilton. . . .' Yet there are two clues, both of which suggest that the inception of this fine new romance was marked by a stormy quarrel, with Emma expressing her intention to vacate the Kingdom immediately.

The significance of Emma's remark that Sir William had suggested she stay till January should not escape us. What indication is there in Greville's letters that there was any plan for Emma to return earlier than the spring of 1787? It would suggest that Emma had suddenly – and wildly, in view of the weather conditions – decided to go. The move to Caserta very likely played its part in that.

Naples would have seemed an agreeable enough place to Emma to await her departure for England. On 4 November, with the King of Spain's name day, the *opera seria* began, and the Teatro San Carlo was doubly illuminated. In Naples, there were the Accademie di Ballo which the Cumberlands had graced. There was the constant entertainment the streets provided, be it a show of Pulcinella or a funeral cortege with a widow tearing her hair and grinding her teeth, as was mandatory. Above all, in Naples there was Sir William, Emma's *preux chevalier*, to sigh over her beauty, bring friends to admire it, and generally to escort her where and when was her pleasure. If he had to attend at Court, the Royal Palace was only a few minutes' walk from the Palazzo Sessa, along the Mole and past the Castel dell'Ovo out on a promontory. If Sir William went there to walk on the Royal terraces overlooking the Bay, and point out the signals from the cone of Vesuvius smouldering across the water to the Queen and her daughters beside him; if he paid visits to General Acton, Minister of the Marine and of War; if he occasionally visited the old Prime Minister, Caracciolo, whose return from Sicily had so greatly enlivened the gaiety of Neapolitan society, if not the quality of politics; well, these were but a few hours in the day. We may take Emma's word for it that he danced attendance on her the rest of the time.

Life at Caserta was quite a different affair. One imagines that a very

few days' existence at the 'little cabin' made Emma extremely eager
to leave the Kingdom as swiftly as she could. The house stood in a
remote position, close to the Great Cascade which tumbled down the
steep foothills of the Apennines. Nearby was the English Garden, which
lay outside the Royal Park, by Sir William's choice, to the right of the
great basin of marble into which the Cascade finally plunged con brio.
The Royal Palace, to which a succession of marble channels and smaller
pools led the waters from the great basin, was fully three miles distant,
as were most of the other courtiers' villas.

Charming as the bosky surrounds might be, and interesting as was the
view of the distant palace blocking the plain with its bulk, the house was
run-down, ill-kempt and, as Sir William assured his sister and his niece,
extremely uncomfortable after Catherine's death. Sir William had used
it only as a place to sleep and rest between the arduous bouts of slaughter
with the King which constituted their mutual daily winter delight. Sir
William, in fact, adored his winter season at Caserta. He expressed his
view of the matter in 1780 when the Royal Family moved there: 'I
prefer infinitely passing a day in a free air, with the sort of anxiety that is
excited by the expectation of a huge boar or wolf, than to be at the most
pompous ceremony that can be imagined in the most luxurious city.'

If Emma had heard him express such opinions during her first weeks
at Caserta, one feels she might have struck him. If the secluded position
of the house, the lack of entertainment after all that Naples offered, and
the rustic squalor of living conditions conspired to make her long for
England, Sir William's constant absence on his shooting parties was no
doubt the straw on which Emma's temper foundered. From dawn to
dusk she was left alone, just as Lady Hamilton had been before her,
whom Sir William had described in perplexed tones as 'living like
a hermit' at Caserta. Emma, however, was not one to draw down
the reproach, as had Lady Hamilton from her frank Scots friend, Dr
Drummond, of 'vegetating at home',[1] if she could avoid it. Sir William
was in duty bound to escort the King where the King would go. Emma
was, by virtue of her unofficial position, not her sex – the Queen was
sometimes forced to watch the sport from a palisade – ineligible to join
the Royal parties. The prospect of staying at home in the rambling house
– far from really being a cabin, it could house fifty people – throughout
November, December, January and February, while Sir William went
cheerfully off in his thick coat and boots every morning, not surprisingly
did not appeal. Emma announced her revolt and her intention to make
for England immediately.

Greville had written in his November letter that 'Mutual sacrifices
constituted proofs of regard.' Sir William was perhaps startled out of

the complacency with which he had regarded his *capannina* and the entertainments for ladies there – walks and music – by some frank comments from Emma on the subject. There was little sacrifice that he could make in the way of staying at home to entertain Emma. However, it would seem from Emma's letters that, in the compromise that followed swiftly on Sir William's realization that Emma was indeed feeling real neglect, various forms of entertainment were arranged for her. Among these were visits from Sir William's friends, like Hackert, the favoured German landscape painter who lived closely with the Court at Caserta. Then there were music lessons from the teacher, Gallucci, who had been a performer earlier rated by that fine musician, Lady Hamilton. There was Graefer from the English Garden to bring his woes about the jealousies of the Italian Royal gardeners, and to discuss plans to design a Grand Conservatory. Above all, there was the feeling that Sir William understood, and regretted his absence from her side. When he accompanied the King on an expediition to the distant game reserve of Persano in January 1787, which was to be of two weeks' duration, he arranged for Emma to return to Naples. And, all the time he was absent, sometimes for a few nights, sometimes just for the day, Sir William left Emma to deal with the variety of business (of a non-diplomatic kind) which arose. This occupation was evidently a great pleasure to her, no less for the sense it gave her of importance than for the human interest it provided. In Emma's letters beginning on 26 December, the compromise is seen to be working very well.

It is difficult to say whether the love which Emma declares for Sir William gradually evolved from the success of the compromise, more gratitude than love. The evils of the alternatives that had been open to her when she chose to remain in Naples must have come finally home to her, when she was happy and settled enough to consider them quietly. She had every reason to feel gratitude to Sir William, and Emma had an almost morbid regard to favours shown her. Nevertheless, one must bear in mind that Emma had always felt immense admiration for Sir William and for his position. Even in the last few months, whatever the difficulties, that admiration had not lessened. They say that imitation is the sincerest form of flattery because the purest form of admiration is emulation. Emma's letter to Greville of August 1786 imitates Sir William's turns of phrase when she speaks of being 'closely besieged' by the King. She adopts his concerns when she speaks of being '7 weeks in doubt' whether little Lord Brooke, the neglected son and heir of Greville's brother by his first wife, was dead. (One imagines Emma had more pressing doubts than the fate of poor George.) Emma would certainly have aspired to emulate Sir William on the hunting field, too,

had she been permitted. (The only lady shot of whom we hear is Lady
Craven, but, as our informant is that unreliable lady herself, we need not
place much faith in the story.) As it was, the letters of the winter of 1786
and 1787 show Emma taking Sir William for her model in all things.

The most marked way in which she imitates him is in her adoption
of his philosophical attitude to life. For someone of her mercurial,
nervous disposition, Sir William's system of sitting back and relaxing
at every possible opportunity proved difficult. (She wrote that she
found long walks and music 'soothed' her.) Yet she shows herself in
these letters determined to persevere, and 'controul her passions'. It
was the unspoken condition on which her position at Sir William's side
was assured. 'If sometimes I am out of humer,' she wrote to him on 26
December 1786, 'tell me, put me in a whey to be grateful to you for
your kindness to me, and believe me I never will abuse your kindness
to me, and in a little time all faults will be corrected, I am a pretty
whoman, and one can't be everything at once . . .' Emma, in effect,
had grown up. Valiant attempts at forbearance and a sober resolution
to please Sir William are new grace notes in her adult personality. In
the last letter of the series, written at the end of January 1787, Emma
set down, in her new reasonable manner, the reasons why she should
love her new protector: 'my dear Sir William, my friend, my All, my
earthly Good, every kind name in one, you are to me eating, drinking
and cloathing, my comforter in distress. Then why shall I not love you?
Endead, I must and ought, whilst life is left in me, or reason to think
on you.'

With the blossoming of this new relationship, a most satisfactory
sexual relationship developed, to judge by the tenor of Emma's remarks
in her letters. Interestingly, Emma speaks more frankly of sex to Sir
William than she ever did to Greville. Love with Greville had been a
spiritual affair, on Emma's side, perhaps. Greville had not encouraged
discussion of sex, witness Emma's Parkgate letter: 'I long, I mean I long
to see you. I sopose you will scold next.' Even when recommending
Emma to Sir William as a delightful sexual partner, all he could bring
himself to say was that she did not offend any of the senses. Sir William
was less naturally fastidious than his nephew. Besides, he belonged to a
generation which expressed itself coarsely at times. Greville could never
have written, as Sir William did of his old friend, Lord Pembroke, in
1780: 'with him . . . Sh-cum-sh is the beginning of love and kiss my
A—e is the end of it.' Emma speedily adapted to these new mores.

On 9 January 1787, she wrote from Naples of some men who had
suffered some sexual misadventure: 'Sure they wont die. Oh Lord!
endead I never will bite your lips nore fingers no more. Good God!

What a passion they must have been in. . . .' There are constant references to Emma's wish to warm Sir William in her arms. After four years of solitary nights – and one wonders whether with Lady Hamilton's 'low spirits', and her tendency to 'brood so much over bodily distresses', went a passionate nature – Sir William must have felt revitalized by Emma's yearnings for his elderly body. The subject of mortality fascinated him, as it did his contemporary, Horace Walpole. Sir William, this very year, 1786, accurately meted out for himself seventeen more years. Some years later, Greville's sister, Lady Frances Harpur, declared that her uncle looked as thin as a stick, and the unkind Earl-Bishop called him a piece of walking *verdantique*.[2] Sir William, we can take it, was not robust in appearance in 1786, aged fifty-six. Nevertheless, if he was lean, he was not withered. His estimate in 1782 that he could stand fatigue better than many younger men held true now again, if it had faltered in the years after Catherine's death.

It was unfortunate that, just when Sir William and Emma had embarked on their happy relationship, the shooting season was in full swing. Still, it had brought them together. Emma now affirmed it was 'right I should be separated from you sometimes, to make me know myself, for I don't know till you are absent how dear you are to me . . .' On 19 December, Sir William was with her at Caserta, for he went to Court to tell the King and Queen of the Two Sicilies of the sad death of the Princess Amelia of England. Maria Carolina no doubt made gratifying remarks of regret. She openly wept throughout a Court reception which took place on the anniversary of the death of one of her children in 1777. Ferdinand is unlikely to have been much moved. It is difficult to forget the blithe mode in which he had grieved the death of Maria Carolina's elder sister, once his intended bride. Etiquette forbade him to go shooting. To while away the wasted day, he dressed up one of his more comely gentlemen of the bedchamber as the corpse of the Habsburg Archduchess, and stuck chocolate drops on the courtier's face to simulate the smallpox from which the Princess had died. With Ferdinand as chief mourner, the funeral procession, with 'Maria Josepha' laid out on an open bier, wound solemnly through the public apartments of the Palace at Portici. 'Entering at the time,' Sir William had informed the Foreign Secretary, 'I became an eyewitness of this extraordinary scene.' The death of an unknown English princess would hardly have moved Ferdinand more.

On 25 December, all Naples was in a religious fever. The *presepii*, those extravagant representations of the scene in the Bethlehem shed which could cost families who prided themselves on their cribs – mother of pearl and jewelled inlay were considered commonplace

– half their yearly income, excited the greatest attention; fireworks and illuminations came a close second. The King, who went regularly twice a day to pray in the marble chapel at Caserta, was perhaps one of the few lay Christians in the Kingdom to celebrate Christmas with true piety. The same day, however, he took Sir William – whom the *lazzaroni* grieved to think, as a heretic, could not go to heaven[3] – from Emma to accompany him on a three-day shooting expedition in the Apennines. One wonders if Emma's thoughts wandered, when she was alone, to past Christmases at Edgware Row, or whether she had succeeded already in barring all thought of Greville from her mind.

Sir William, an assiduous but never obsequious courtier, went with the King only a few miles distant from Emma, to a charming Belvedere, or hunting lodge, in the middle of a village called S. Leucio. Nearby was an enclosure in the crater of an extinct volcano where wild boar awaited His Majesty's and his gentlemen's pleasure. S. Leucio shared with Naples a very dear place in the King's heart. Here he was wont to flee the formality of Court life at Caserta.

While Maria Carolina surrounded herself in the public apartments of the monumental Palace with forty German maids, according to Lady Craven, and, according to more reliable witnesses, with her children and a few favoured intimates, Ferdinand lived in his entrancing little Palace, calling from its yellow stuccoed balustrades to the countrymen of the village below to come and chat to him.

In later years, Ferdinand was to establish a famous silk factory here, and to make S. Leucio one of the finest 'model villages' in Europe. At present, the finest thing about the Belvedere was its superb view, matched only by an even more beautiful Belvedere further up the Volturno valley. The River Volturno meanders slowly and deliberately along the green pasture, in front of the parterres of both Belvederes. Behind, an extraordinary landscape of low, smooth hills recedes into the remote distance with, it seems, never a mortal soul or flower to disturb the brown and purple scree. Here, under arctic conditions this winter, with the pasture deep in snow, the Volturno all but choked with ice, and the hunters themselves on the hill knee-deep in snow, with a savage wind whistling over the Apennines direct from Russia, Sir William and Ferdinand pursued their sport.

Emma whiled her time away with visits from 'Don A. and Hackert & Garly' in the evening of Christmas Day, though she assured Sir William 'all my heart and soul was torn from me' when he went away earlier in the day. She wrote, on the next day, that she felt better, 'perche? the day after to moro . . . I shall have you with me to make up for past pain.' Possibly her visitors had had something to do with lifting her spirits, too. She was expecting 'Garly' again as she wrote.

Emma's visitors were carefully selected by Sir William to satisfy her 'passion for admiration'. 'But chastely, always chastely with your best friend's wife', as Giraudoux's Ajax admonishes, was the condition on which they came. Dashing young princes do not feature. Graefer, with his new wife from Chester and his worries about the irregular payment of the salary which the Queen merely spoke of paying him, was a relaxing companion in that he spoke English only – poor Graefer's inability to master Italian compounded his problems. Most of Sir William's circle had a tendency to begin a sentence in English, use a French word or two in the middle for the telling phrase, and finish off in Italian. Tiny, witty Abbé Galiani, who belonged more to the set of the Baron de Talleyrand-Périgord, Ambassador to Naples from Galiani's beloved Paris, was the finest practitioner of this style. He was said, with Caracciolo, to be witty to his fingertips, as he further enlivened his conversation with emphatic Neapolitan gesticulations. Emma's Italian was not at this date sufficiently fluent to allow her to understand the swifter conversations without effort. With her imitative ear, however, she had made surprising progress in eight months, and now she applied herself to her lessons, whereas on 22 July she had written: 'I have a language-master . . . but what is it for?' The anonymous *Memoirs of Lady Hamilton* tell us that 'a confidential monk' came to the house 'to attend her . . . who passed as her tutor in the languages', Italian and French, which we may believe, if we doubt the assertion that the monk was also Emma's confessor.[4] Stories that Emma had her education at a convent can be dismissed. Copious references throughout this series of letters and in letters of following years prove she had all her tuition – be it dancing, singing or languages – at home. It was the accepted mode, at Naples, for foreigners to have their tutors to their homes or lodgings. By August 1787, when tuition in Italian had given way, thanks to Emma's fluency, to her devoting one hour a day to reading the language, she wrote, 'there is a person comes a purpose'. In this person, we may see the *Memoirs*' 'confidential monk'.

The admiration of Sir William's friends for her growing 'accomplishments' – French and Italian were hallmarks of the noblewoman's education – drove Emma on, as much as the practical need to communicate. The Cavaliere Angelo Gatti, who was a constant visitor to the Palazzo Sessa, thought Emma spoke Italian so well in January 1787 'that he sitts 2 hours together and taulks to me'. If that experience was rather wearing – the next day Emma provided a third, Don Andrea, to take a share of conversation when Gatti dined with her – Gatti's admiration was very satisfying. (He said, also, that Emma was 'so accomplished, so kind', as she repeated delightedly to Sir William.) Gatti, a Florentine and once Professor of Medicine at Pisa University, had lived in Naples since 1778 on the urgent wish of the Queen of the Kingdom herself. As the French chargé d'affaires at Naples, Baron Dominique Vivant de Non, wrote in 1782, Gatti was best known for intrigue and for inoculation – he introduced the latter into Naples and it introduced him.[5] The Queen called him from her brother the Grand Duke's domain, originally to treat the Royal Family, after smallpox had ended the circumscribed life of the imbecile Don Filippo, Ferdinand's eldest brother and the natural heir to the Kingdom of Spain. (He had passed his time escaping his chamberlains' wardship and pursuing ladies of the Court, like Pan the Nymphs, through the public apartments of Caserta. Interestingly, he shared Ferdinand's fetish about hands, deriving even greater pleasure than from his amorous sallies in having fifteen or sixteen gloves placed, in order of size, on his hand.)

Gatti's inoculations proved so successful that all the religious doubts which had occupied the Kingdom while they awaited the outcome vanished. The Kingdom implored him, now regarded as a divine healer, to remain and work his magic on every one of them. The Queen's offer of a large pension and diamonds decided him, and Gatti graciously consented to remain, on the condition he hold no official position. It is not known whether he ever practised medicine again; the 'trivial intrigues' of the Court, which Sir William loathed, and natural history, a love Sir William shared, kept him much too busy. Emma, at least, was thrilled by his stories of the Queen's dislike of Maria, Royal Duchess of Gloucester, in Naples this winter. Gatti 'had it from a whoman abbout Court'.

That most reserved of men, Philip Hackert, came constantly to admire Emma while she was at Caserta. When she retired to Naples in January, we find him again there, dropping in from his apartments in the Palazzo Cellamare further up the Strada di Chiaia. One feels it may have been more than simply a wish to oblige his first patron in Naples, Sir William, which prompted this attention. Emma was greatly flattered by his visits. Vicariously, she enjoyed his intimacy with the King and Queen, and with lesser mortals too. 'Hackert was full dress'd going to Skavronskys [Skavronsky was the Russian Ambassador] last night,' she breathed on 5 January, 'the Duke of Gloucester was to be there . . . but not the Dutches nor the children.' The only disappointment was that Hackert showed no gift for gossip about his Royal masters, though he taught the Princesses drawing, and was so relied on by Ferdinand that he had little time away from his Royal duties. Besides making what amounted to a pictorial record of the Kingdom's splendours – these, in Ferdinand's eyes, included the arsenal, a new frigate, and all his game reserves – Hackert was given the care of some new-fangled oil-lamps at Caserta and the job of transporting that precious inheritance, the Farnese marbles, to Naples. Perhaps Hackert felt little temptation to gossip about a master who happened, by a lucky chance, to prefer his style of landscape painting to all others. Photographic realism is an anachronism which describes this style better than the title generally given to the school which Hackert founded, *vedutismo topografico napoletano*. As is generally known, Ferdinand paid Hackert in a novel manner, by the palm or yard of canvas he painted. This accounts for the vast stretches of clear sky which brood above each scene he painted. What is usually ignored is that Hackert would accompany the King for an entire week's sport when about to paint one of the game reserves, such was his dedication to the precise record. It is a pity his admiration for Emma's beauty did not lead him to abandon landscape temporarily and leave us an accurate record of her to complement Romney's soft portraits. Sadly, no portrait is known.

On 28 December 1786, Sir William returned to Caserta where Emma waited to 'settle & comfort' him, and receive him 'with smiles, affection and good humer'. So she wrote on the twenty-sixth. She had learnt her lesson, that 'Sir William minds temper more than beauty,' as she later expressed it to Romney. However, after only five days, when Sir William was expected at Court to attend the 'Grand Gala of Baciamani' (or Kissing of Hands) which inaugurated the New Year, Sir William was off again, this time for a fortnight. The Queen, being pregnant, remained at Caserta with her children.

Sir William and the Royal party travelled down to Persano, one of Ferdinand's most remote game reserves, on the specially extended road from Salerno, there to iron out who were the great men of the day, and to discuss their achievements. Such was the staple conversation on these trips, Sir William told Nathaniel Wraxall. By great men, great shots were meant. Emma went to Naples till he should return. She was not idle. On the fifth, she had already caught up on the major topics of the New Year, chief among which was the flight of Jane Lady Lanesborough with Mr King (not yet her second husband), leaving unpaid debts to half Naples, including General Acton's cook and Sir William's tailor. 'In short, there innumerable villanys is more than I am able to recount,' wrote Emma, burning with indignation. Clark, the cicerone and portrait painter, a constant visitor to the Palazzo Sessa, had suffered, too. In fact, the only person who would seem not to have reached into his pocket for the erring pair was Sir William himself. 'You are the onely person to have acted towards them with good sense,' wrote Emma approvingly, 'but you always do right in everything.' Lady Lanesborough was, in fact, notorious. One is glad to note that in August Lady Sophia Butler, one of the daughters who trailed round Italy after their mother, Lady Lanesborough, stepped off at Milan and married a Marchese Luigi Marescotti. Or perhaps Lady Lanesborough sold her to get out of difficulties there.

Emma took up the cudgels next on behalf of Ambrogio Curnier, 'your man'. He had come to see Emma in great distress about a threat from his landlord, the Marchese di Sessa, to increase the rent he paid for his room. 'That fellow [the Marchese, owner of the eponymous Palazzo] must be the nastys creature living after all the benefit he has had from you,' Emma wrote, 'to go to impose on that poor man for the sake of a few ducats more.' The Marchese, who also wanted more if Curnier was to continue to enjoy the view from his balcony, would, Emma urged Sir William, soon be routed by a few words from Gasparo to his opposite number in the Marchese's household. A few words from him in writing to Gasparo would settle it, else Curnier would be turned out. Emma had to write again on 8 January after another visit from Curnier before she could write gratefully on the tenth, 'Cuny's duty to you, and thanks about the Marquis Sesos – (you may look big upon it.)'. No wonder that when Emma took such trouble over the household's affairs, they petted her. Gasparo insisted that in the cold weather she should have dinner upstairs, so that the food would not freeze on its way down to the next floor, and that it should be eaten by the warmth of a fire. The major-domo excused this unwarranted extravagance in an otherwise unused room – Emma and her mother stuck to their own apartments when Sir William was away – on the grounds that 'a fire in that room must be to air it well'. Vincenzo, one of the lackeys, brought her chocolate and her letters to her bedside in the morning. Emma wrote on 12 January: 'the wind made me so sleepy that I slept till eight a clock, and was fast asleep when Vinchenzo brought your letter, and I read it in bed, and gave it a good hug.' (She went on: 'But I wished you had been there. But I gave it a kiss or 2.') No doubt Vincenzo was envied his morning duty by his fellow servants. 'If you was to know how kind everybody behaves to me, you would love them,' Emma sighed with pleasure.

Life was taking on an enchanting hue for Emma. She was secure of Sir William's infatuation with her charms, and perhaps, more importantly, of his fondness for her. He sent her short notes from Persano to reassure her, as well as to give her a detailed account of his sport. Emma, more dutiful than Greville or Sir Joseph Banks, who both found these accounts very 'boaring', wrote enthusiastically: 'I wish I had been at your post, I should like to see you shoot.' As January began to turn 'excessive cold' however, and reports came from Persano of bad days' sport, Emma may have felt glad she was relatively snug in Naples. The *European Magazine* carried this report from Naples on 13 January 1787: 'For some days past we have had the wind blow from the North with great violence. Yesterday the country and the mountains in the neighbourhood were covered with snow, and it has since frozen, which is very rare in this climate.' Emma confirms that on 8 January the ice was lying about the blocks of lava which paved the streets of Naples. She must have been astonished by the sight of Vesuvius' snow-clad form, puffs of vapour still testifying to the inner heat within. 'Today,' she wrote, 'it is impossible to keep oneself warm.' Poor Emma.

She ventured out, nevertheless, to sit for her portrait on the eighth to 'Coletalino'. Deciphering Emma's wild guesses at the spelling of Italian friends' names can be difficult. The name of the owner of the Naples house she spells 'Sestes — I can't spell this names write' one day, 'Seso' the next. One notes, however, that even after Sir William has given her the orthodox spelling, she still spells it wrongly. Emma simply did not think spelling mattered. 'Garly', who visited her at Caserta, may well have been Garbi, who had painted her by 1798. In the instance of 'Coletalino', however, we are on sure ground when we recognize in that misnomer the artist Costanza Coltellini. Costanza was one of a delightful quartet of sisters, who all lived together in the 'Casa Coltellini', watched over by an elderly aunt. They undoubtedly needed a chaperone. Their house was 'a port of storm for artists, literati, and travellers of rank, who vied to enjoy the charming society of these interesting ladies'. Interesting they certainly were. If Costanza painted, Rosina drew; they would show their recent work to visitors, or perhaps a composer would play a new piece on the harpsichord or accompany Annetta in a new song. Some man of letters might recite from a new work, or a traveller recount a droll anecdote about some foreign part. So the impresario, Don Ferrari, tells us in his *Anecdotes*, and it was infinitely preferable to the normal run of *conversazioni*, which rivalled the English rout-party for ennui.

Undoubtedly the star attraction of the Casa Coltellini was the eldest sister, Celeste. Ferrari says that if he had been a Mussulman, he would have married all four sisters, but Celeste alone he calls the 'pearl of Naples'. Not only was Celeste beautiful; she was a superb actress and singer. Before she and her sisters settled in Naples, in 1781, she had been called to every opera house in Europe to perform. (In the course of these travels, on which her sisters often accompanied her, the ugly Florentine rasp was lost, Ferrari records with relief, and thereafter their voices were agreeably dovelike.) In Naples, where Celeste came for the opera season of 1781, she showed that 'she was certainly the most natural, talented and perfect actress that could be desired.' Sir William, we know, was an admirer, for among the pictures he catalogued in 1798 was her portrait. No one, till in 1792 Celeste married the Swiss banker Meuricoffre, who lived in Naples, was more than an admirer, however. In relying on her talents alone to keep her position as 'first woman' at the Teatro dei Fiorentini, Celeste showed her superiority to the Neapolitan opera singers. They had not noticeably improved in the direction of sexual sobriety since the days of Charles III, when they were only allowed to come within the city limits on the days they were actually singing in the theatre. One feels that Emma, with her developed notions of prudery, would have balked at going to the house of an opera singer, had Celeste's virtue not been well known.

In fact, there was evidently a certain amount of décolletage in the portrait Costanza Coltellini was painting for Sir William. It was a miniature, to be set in the lid of a snuffbox, so 'it will be seen a great deal, and those beautys that only you can see shall not be exposed to the common eyes of all,' Emma wrote firmly, informing him that it would not be so interesting if it was too naked. She consoled Sir William by saying it would be a very good likeness. 'Others may guess at them [her bosom], for the are sacred to all but you,' she went on confusingly. 'I wish they was better for your sake,' she wrote further, in time-honoured womanly fashion. 'But I should not know how to mend them if I cou'd tho' you don't like sugar loaves.' A priest on Ischia was later to beg this snuffbox from Sir William.

If Sir William had fault to find with Emma's figure – and that she may have been a touch luscious for perfection in his eyes at this date is suggested by a letter of 1790 – he was alone in his view. Goethe, in March 1786, called her figure 'perfect'. When Emma went to the theatre, or went out in her carriage or on horseback, people in the streets nudged each other and exclaimed, 'Look at her, there. What divine beauty. She's a Madonna.' The musician Ferrari actually used the term *vergine*. He explained that this compliment was paid on the strength of beauty and goodness; ladies with several children were just as much contenders as anyone more likely to be *vergine*. Before he saw Emma, Ferrari relates, he doubted the reputation that went before her. Celeste Coltellini invited him to dinner, probably some time in January, to hear and meet an English girl 'whose voice touched everyone's heart and whose beauty outshone that of the Venus of Medici'. Ferrrari says he smiled disbelievingly. Celeste assured him he would see she had not said enough. Ferrari arrived on the appointed evening and found Emma, 'the most beautiful creature' he had ever seen. He writes in ecstasies of her for pages. As Ferrari left Naples before the Carnival in 1787, and Celeste only returned from an engagement in Vienna in the autumn of 1786, it seems reasonable to assume that this dinner took place in January 1787. (Emma was, of course, otherwise at Caserta, and, moreover, Sir William would very likely have accompanied her, if he were on hand.) Sir William almost certainly authorized and encouraged the display which Emma gave at the Casa Coltellini of her newly trained voice. As we know, she had had a singing master since July at least. If her lessons lapsed after she realized there were other plans for her stay in Naples besides improvement, by December 1786 she was taking lessons regularly from Gallucci, 'from nine to ten' in the morning on 8 January, and singing to Sir William's friends who came to visit her. As with her Italian, their encouragement and expressions of amazement at her progress in singing spurred her on. A 'voice' was another part of the lady's education she craved. The admiration Ferrari expressed also excited Emma, because he was a discerning judge, deemed capable by the Court composer Paisiello of conducting the opera for a performance or two.

Ferrari tells us Emma sang some Scottish airs 'with such gusto and wish to amuse; she articulated the words so well and so clearly that she pleased not only the English present, but all the foreigners, even though they did not understand a word.' This airing of Emma's voice at the Casa Coltellini was, in effect, Emma's baptism by fire in the font of the musical centre of Naples. Ferrari's opinion of her voice is likely to have been echoed by the other judges: 'Although her voice was not yet fully trained, yet it was by nature sonorous, mellow and true.'

When Sir William's friends admired her voice, Emma was delighted. On 14 January 1787, she was guest of honour at a veritable banquet – 'such a profusion of diner that it is impossible to describe' – which the English banker, Mr Hart, held at his house. One wonders if Signora Hart, an Italian lady who threw aside her nun's vows to marry and then could not obtain forgiveness from the Pope, was present. Emma does not mention her but only an abbé, a 'very genteel man', a friend of Andrea's and 'an Englishman I did not know'. (As Sir William was to write in February, there was a plethora of English tourists in Naples that winter – one reason why he stayed so much at Caserta.) They were all very polite to Emma, she records, especially the voluble banker himself. Though by this date Hart's sight had gone, he nevertheless 'produced me as a specimen of English beauty', Emma says. It was rather exhausting, sitting next to him at dinner, as he would try and help Emma to everything on the table (which she would not have

minded at all, only 'poor man could not see'.) After dinner, which one
hopes did not end in too much of a mess, the infatuated man went and
got a song which 'fourty years past' had been written for Lady Sophy
Ferner. He had translated it into English and 'would sing it'. When he
came to 'dymond eyes and pearl teeth', he looked at Emma and bid his
friends do the same. He 'is quite gone', Emma wrote, and intended to
dedicate his translation to her, 'just as if I was the most perfect beauty
in the world'. 'And so the all admired me', she wrote happily.

Hart came panting round to the Embassy later in the evening to hear
Emma sing. She made him 'allmost cry' with three songs – favourites
of Sir William's – by Handel. With songs by Piccinni, father of *opera
buffa*, and Paisiello, however, she had even more of an effect. 'He could
not contain himself, for he says he never saw the tragick and comick
muse blended so happily together.' (*Opera buffa*, designed originally as
an intermezzo to *opera seria*, was tragi-comic.) *Opera buffa* was, indeed,
far better suited to Emma's gift for sketching a variety of different, and
opposing, moods than grand opera, which required the performer to
'hold' a mood for protracted periods. Sir William, however, at this date
and for some time to come, hoped that Emma would learn to sing
the Handel arias and Mozart and Vivaldi he preferred as well as Lady
Hamilton had once done. Conscientiously, Emma worked at what he
wanted, but, with comic songs, she relaxed. Where once the house had
echoed to the sad strains of a 'Funeral March for Hector' which Lady
Hamilton had composed herself, now it rang with the more licentious
and light-hearted arias of the contemporary comic favourites. The
servants no doubt preferred Emma's style. Not that her talents for the
less serious kind of opera meant she was slapdash or light-hearted in her
application to her lessons. We have a quaint picture of Emma practising
her solfeggio or scales before Hart. He was struck by her ability to hold
her notes, and go from high to low note 'so very neat'.

When Emma rejoined Sir William at Caserta on 17 January, she could
look back on a glorious fortnight in which she had dazzled, and held her
own among a crowd of critical strangers, and in her own right, without
a protector's canopy. Proof of her achievement was perhaps given her
when she paid a visit to a convent in Naples on 10 January. This
was a regular form of entertainment for ladies in Naples, Neapolitans
and foreigners alike. The convents were under the jurisdiction of the
Queen, who herself paid the twenty odd establishments visits in turn
throughout the course of the summer. As the nuns in the convents were
generally noble ladies who had not found a husband, and made up for it
by doing themselves very comfortably, these visits were not the penance
one might imagine. When gentlemen visited monks at monasteries like

the Certosa of S. Martino, they found the arduous ascent up the hill above Naples, which it shared with the Castle of S. Elmo, well worth it. (Once, after a magnificent dinner, Henry Swinburne was dismayed to be led to another room, in which even more sumptuous arrays of game and viands awaited the guests. Fortunately, it was a jest on the Abbot's part, and all the fish and beef and venison haunches were made of water-ice.) When Emma sallied out, her 'clear white dimity and blue sash' hidden under fur wraps, to the Convent of Donna Romita, she found they had 'all the good things to eat, and I promise you they don't starve themselves.' The Donna Romita was where the most aristocratic of Neapolitan nobility housed their spinster daughters, the ecclesiastical historian Galante tells us. The nun with whom Emma spent most of her time at the fine walled convent, close to the church of S. Angelo of the Nile, with its 'beautiful garden', was a member of the ancient and noble Neapolitan family of Acquaviva.

Beatrice Acquaviva appeared to great advantage in the convent habit, Emma thought, and added to its 'becoming' effect with a muff, several diamond rings, and 'a good deal' of unspecified 'finery' besides. She told Emma she had heard of her attentions to the poor. At Edgware Row Emma had 'a pleasure in sharing her last shilling'. Now Emma was enabled to indulge her taste for philanthropy more liberally. Sir William was soon to settle to give her £150 a year, and £50 for washing. 'Your good heart would melt at any trouble that befel me,' said Beatrice, 'and partake in one's greef or be equally happy at one's good fortune.' Emma found her quite charming, not surprisingly, and 'something in her eyes vastly alluring'. They were not the eyes of a nun at all, Emma thought innocently. The mere fact of being a nun did not deter Neapolitan ladies from the intrigues which their counterparts in the world enjoyed. Indeed later in her letter Emma says that there was 'not one word of religion' spoken all the time she was at the convent, by Beatrice or her two sisters or the other fifty-eight nuns. So we are at liberty to doubt the fair Beatrice's chastity, but not her admiration of Emma. She kissed Emma's lips, her cheeks and forehead, said 'charming creature' constantly, and said she read Emma's heart in her angelic countenance.

Despite all the compliments paid her, Emma was growing to miss Sir William more and more. She could only get so much enjoyment out of reciting to him her triumphs and other news that might appeal to him – on 5 January, she had told him the Baron de Talleyrand-Périgord's house had caught fire. Sadly, in view of the rivalry between the French and English sets, only one room had been 'very much on fire', and the Ambassador himself was anyway villeggiaturing with Paisiello on Ischia.

On 14 January, she told Sir William she was angry with him for not having written. 'When I have no other comfort then your letters, you should not cruely disapoint me . . . I don't feil right without hearing from you . . .' Previously, her complaint had been that he wrote her only one or two lines. Luckily, a letter came on the fifteenth, the letter which she kissed in bed and which 'charmed' her, calling her Sir William's friend. She had said 'Pattienza' on the ninth when she heard Ferdinand was not thinking of bringing his party back from Persano as yet. Now she longed to see Sir William. The independent life she was leading in Naples had tired her.

She was delighted to return to Caserta on the sixteenth, and to be reunited with Sir William. On Thursday morning, the eighteenth, he had to go off again, probably to S. Leucio, for a further three days of extirpation, but Emma was content. She had discovered that she really loved him. His absence had confirmed it. 'One hour's absence is a year, and I shall count the hours and moments till Saturday, when I shall find myself once more in your kind dear arms, my dear Sir William.' Emma took a long walk, as she was now accustomed to do in the gardens surrounding the house, during which she reflected and found life was good. On her return, she added to her letter words of gratitude to her friend for 'having given me the means to amuse myself a little, if in your absence I can be amused', with her music lessons. 'I owe everything to you, and shall forever with grattitude remember it.' With injunctions to look after himself – fatal accidents from others' guns and from wild-boar tusks were on her mind, one imagines – Emma closed this most touching series of love letters with the words, 'I send you a thousand kisses and remember last night how happy you made me, and I tell you Satturday night I shall be happier in your presence unmixed with thoughts of parting.'

Emma Hamilton, artist's model extraordinary. Seen here as Circe in a
painting by George Romney

Charles Greville, by George Romney. Sir William Hamilton's nephew and Emma's first love

Emma, modelling for Romney, when she was living as Greville's mistress in Paddington

Emma in triplicate by Hugh Douglas Hamilton. One of many portraits resulting from Emma's journey to visit Sir William Hamilton in Italy

George Romney, self-portrait. Emma described the artist as her 'friend and more than father'

⑤

Sir William Hamilton, British Minister in Naples for forty years, by Reynolds. 'I will make him marry me,' said Emma – and she did

(7)

(above) Emma, Lady Hamilton, when she was secretly pregnant by her lover, Admiral Nelson. By J. H. Schmidt

(below) Mrs Cadogan, Emma's mother and constant companion. By Norsti

(7×)

The Hero. By William Beechey

CHAPTER SEVEN

Surprising Transformations

In the early months of 1787, as they moved between Naples and Caserta, Emma and Sir William consolidated the friendship that had grown up between them. Their friends and servants must surely have thought them an odd couple. Sir William, advancing in years if still of sinewy height and of fine beaked profile, looked grey beside healthy, blooming Emma.

At the Palace, the Queen doted on her children. The King went hunting. At a Royal performance, a singer, Savario Savilla, expired in mid-song at Their Majesties' feet. In February the almond-blossom and gilly flowers peppered the hill of Posillipo. It was Lenten Carnival time in Naples. The Carnival, in February, had grown odious to Sir William after twenty years' exposure to its excesses. Emma, if she were not putting on a show of sophistication, no doubt enjoyed the hurly-burly. No one was safe from the confetti onslaughts of the crowds. When the Queen, heavily pregnant, went out in her carriage during the 1786 Carnival, she had a placard begging clemency. The atmosphere was as charged as that of any Kali festival today in India.

That Royal couple, William Henry, Duke of Gloucester and Maria, his Duchess, were still in Naples. Poor William – with his pale, short-sighted eyes, and delicate complexion and health – found that the southern climes alleviated his asthma. (Maria, his Duchess, had been rewarded for her temerity. She early alienated other members of the Royal Family by driving her carriage into the inner courtyard at Hampton Court Palace, a Royal privilege, before she married William.) For all his formality of manners and slow speech, William had a certain native wit. When he was a boy, his impatient mother said to him '"Thinking". And pray what were you thinking?' He replied 'I was thinking what I should feel if I had a son as unhappy as you make me.'[1]

On 16 March 1787, Duke William sent a message to Sir William at Caserta, saying he would come to Caserta that Sunday. He had heard of the changes in Sir William's domestic affairs. Sir William had commented on them on 17 February to Charles Greville. 'Our dear Em. goes on now quite as I cou'd wish, improves daily, & is universally beloved. She is wonderfull, considering her youth & beauty, & I flatter myself that E. and her mother are happy to be with me, so that I see my every wish fulfilled.'

The Duke of Gloucester very much hoped to have the honour of meeting Sir William's 'little friend', though we may doubt whether he intended his Duchess to accompany him. For Emma's sake we must hope that the meeting took place – she would have been thrilled to meet a Royal prince, even if he did not spring straight from the pages of a fairy-tale. No doubt Sir William was happy to provide the introduction the Duke wished, if only to give himself a breathing space. He wrote to Greville irritably, 'Tho' I cannot say I have here the least real business, no man on earth can be more constantly occupied than I am at this instant, what with my attendance on His S. My . . . & . . . attentions to the Gloucester family, & a most numerous concourse of English & foreign travellers recommended to me.'

In March, an interesting event occurred. The poet Goethe, already celebrated for his *Sorrows of Young Werther*, came to Naples. He had fled Weimar in disorder and at dead of night, leaving only a note for his patron, the Duke. From Rome he set off with Wilhelm Tischbein for Naples, Tischbein to try and get commissions, Goethe to enlarge his Italian experience.

The poet wandered the streets of Naples in amazement, intoxicated by the very atmosphere. 'Either you were mad before, or you are mad now,' he said to himself. 'I seem to be a completely different person whom I hardly recognize.' He admired the trees loaded with oranges, which hung over the walls on either side of the road to Naples. He watched fish of strange appearance being hauled up, young water-melon sellers hawking their wares, and 'horses decorated with artificial flowers, crimson tassels and tinsel. Some horses [which pull the bright red and gilt one-horse carriages] wear plumes on their heads, other little pennons which revolve as they trot.' He saw a child's coffin go by, covered with rose-coloured ribbons. 'At each of its four corners stood an angel, about two feet high, holding a large sheaf of flowers over the sleeping child, who lay dressed in white.'

Philip Hackert, generous man, welcomed Goethe at his apartments in the old palace of Caserta. After an evening where assembled ladies and lords seized the charcoal from Tischbein's hand and daubed each other with beards, Hackert took Goethe to meet Sir William Hamilton and Emma. This was more to the poet's taste, and he went several times to the Caserta house. It was on 16 March, the day on which the Duke of Gloucester wrote to Sir William, that Goethe recorded the first-known performance of what were destined to be called Emma's Attitudes. Just what these were, we shall learn shortly. First, it must be emphasized that the Attitudes were a show for favoured eyes only.

How highly Sir William regarded Goethe, we cannot know. If he understood him to be only a German friend of Hackert's, he was lucky in his audience. Goethe, disciple of Winckelmann, was at this date thrilled by the human form, as a contemporary writes. Here was the ideal spectator for the classical drama Emma and Sir William had wrought in the long winter evenings. Let us take our seats beside Goethe and settle to watch the show as he describes it.

> Sir William Hamilton . . . has now, after many years of devotion to the arts and the study of nature, found the acme of these delights in the person of an English girl of twenty with a beautiful face and a perfect figure. He has had a Greek costume made for her which becomes her extremely. Dressed in this, she lets down her hair and, with a few shawls, gives so much variety to her poses, gestures, expressions, etc., that the spectator can hardly believe his eyes. He sees what thousands of artists would have liked to express realized before him in movements and surprising transformations – standing, kneeling, sitting, reclining, serious, sad, playful, ecstatic, contrite, alluring, threatening, anxious, one pose follows another without a break. She knows how to arrange the folds of her veil to match each mood, and has a hundred ways of turning it into a head-dress. The old knight idolizes her and is quite enthusiastic about everything she does. In her he has found all the antiquities, all the profiles of Sicilian coins, even the Apollo Belvedere. This much is certain: as a performance it's like nothing you ever saw before in your life. We have already enjoyed it on two evenings.

Later writers describe Emma's Attitudes more closely, but none so vividly as Goethe. Many accounts confirm his remarks that Emma let down her hair, and pulled a few shawls about her to surprising effect. It seems she used her sweep of chestnut hair to curtain the arrangements of shawls she made beneath, and hid her figure with a shawl while she adjusted a leg or an arm – from kneeling to suppliant or praying position, for instance. Witty Horace Walpole apostrophized Emma as Sir William's (or 'old William's') 'Gallery of Statues'. That expression is the key to Emma's poses, and the key to the reason why she so delighted eighteenth-century 'virtu men', as she glided from one pose to another.

William Hamilton, when he first came to Italy, had been described by Walpole as 'picture-mad'. Once esconced at Naples, as we know, he turned his attention to what were then called Etruscan vases. He bought Neapolitan genre paintings but no longer invested in Old Masters. Like

many a virtu man in Italy before him, his attention was distracted by
the wealth of Greek and Roman sculpture which Italy housed.

If Emma were to appear today, drape her shawls and her hair about
her and take up the pose of Agrippina scattering the ashes of Germanicus,
what would be the reaction? Few would recognize the allusion, and
those who did would hardly find it interesting. The cultured world of
the eighteenth century, however, had only recently seen for the first
time the collection of wall-paintings from Pompeii and Herculaneum
and statues of such scenes as are now familiar to us from museums
and reproductions. Emma moved through pose to pose in a climate
foreign to our own – a climate in which all spectators were indelibly
imbued with the classical taste and sense and smell. Goethe does not
specifically tell us that Emma's Attitudes were derived from antique
models. However, his references to the Apollo Belvedere – a household
name – and his claim that Sir William has found in her all the antiquities
agree with what later writers say the Attitudes represented. Among a
host of other characters, Hebe, Juno and Bacchantes are invariably
mentioned. Interestingly, male statues also provided inspiration. In
1794 an artist called Rehberg drew Emma from life performing her
Attitudes. He gives a good idea of her cashmere or Amaranth shawls
and of the two varieties of Greek dress she wore – a loose shift,
and a tunic. Wearing the tunic, she represented male characters of
antiquity – Pylades, Orestes sacrificing to his sister, Oedipus blinded.
Remember Greville's prophetic words: 'She . . . is capable of aspiring
to any line which would be celebrated . . . anything grand, masculine
or feminine . . . if she took up the part of Scaevola, she would be as
much offended if she was told she was a woman, as she would be, if
she assumed Lucretia, she was told she was masculine.'

As we have seen, Emma had a large cast of marble characters on
which to draw for her Attitudes. But how did this performance first
arise? What led Sir William to coach Emma, as he evidently did, in
this part?

It has been mentioned that Sir William looked on Emma much as
the ancients looked on their hetaerae or mistresses. A large part of their
duties was to entertain their male protectors – Aspasia, Pericles; Thais,
Alcibiades. So Emma sang and attitudinized for Sir William, calling to
mind not only the nymphs of classical legend but the ladies of classical
history who similarly sang or danced.

Isaac Gerning, a German writer who visited Naples in 1796, tells
us mysteriously that the Attitudes arose out of an instance of a poor
restoration of the arm of a Pallas (Athene).[2] What he means, presumably,
is this. It was the fashion in the 1770s and 1780s to make torch-lit

expeditions to the Royal Galleries of Rome and Naples. Cavaceppi and Gavin Hamilton were only two of many artists who restored ancient torsos and limbs to what they fondly believed were their former glory. William Hamilton was among the few who questioned this renovation, and preferred to see the marbles and bronzes in their unrestored state. It is easy to imagine Sir William tut-tutting over some Pallas from Herculaneum, and gesturing towards the offending arm. Emma says 'Like this, you mean?' and strikes the appropriate attitude and correct position. Sir William is bemused by her likeness to the Pallas, and asks her next to play the part of Andromeda. He did not need to know Ovid's Pygmalion to see that Emma's impersonation was inspired. Let us assume that he then coached her to a point where she could flow from one attitude to another. We know already that Hart, the banker, thought Emma like 'Juno', majestic and noble in her bearing. Winckelmann might have been writing of Emma when he said of Juno: 'She may be known . . . by her large eyes and an imperious mouth,' – and again, 'The beauty in the expression of her large, roundly arched eyes is like that of a queen who wills to rule.' *Deae . . . incessu patuit*, as Virgil says of Dido. (She had the bearing of a goddess.) Emma was tall and slender. Imagine her with that long, glossy mane of chestnut hair, dressed simply, as Sir William preferred, in a white gown with perhaps a cashmere shawl to ward off noxious draughts, fluttering about the Royal Gallery in the deceptive torch-light. She could easily play the startled faun, or the Bacchante surprised bathing. Is this a wholly unprecedented species of drama, as all accounts of it lead us to believe? Not entirely. In 1778, some cousins of Sir William's, the Cathcart sisters, had seen a show called 'Pygmalion', in which a 'statue' came to life and sang and danced.

Goethe tells us that there was an earlier stage to the performance he saw. On a visit to the Palazzo Sessa, he was shown that treasure trove, Sir William's lumber-room. Goethe was much intrigued by 'a chest which was standing upright. Its front had been taken off, the interior painted black and the whole set inside a splendid gilt frame. It was large enough to hold a standing human figure.' Goethe was told that that was what it was meant for. 'Standing against this black background in dresses of various colours, [Emma] had sometimes imitated the antique paintings of Pompeii or even more recent masterpieces.' Paintings by Caravaggio and Reni, with their dark backgrounds, spring to mind. 'This phase . . . is now over, because it was difficult to transport the apparatus and light it properly,' Goethe records. Imagine Emma standing in the chest, with book in hand, posing as the famous *Portrait of a Woman Reading* from Pompeii. The modern-day spectacle which springs to mind as emanating from the Attitudes is, of course, Isadora Duncan's Greek dance. As we do not know Emma's feelings about the performance she gave, it is worth considering Isadora's emotive outpourings. 'Into the body, harmoniously developed and carried to its highest degree of energy, enters the spirit of the dance,' Isadora wrote. A friend commented in 1901: 'In her "Narcissus", wearing a tucked-in white tunic showing an admirable knee . . . the spectator seems to see her reflection in the clear water. And . . . one actually feels the refreshing contrast of the hand, with the liquid element.'[3]

In ancient theatre, the drama that comes nearest to Goethe's description of Emma's performances is the pantomime, or Saltatio. (Greek choruses bear some resemblance, in that they danced and sang a host of different reactions to the stage action in one choral ode. They were many, however, and their chant, not their dance, was their raison d'être.) Pantomime was a late invention of the Roman stage, *circa* 22 BC; W. A. Beare describes it thus: 'the central figure was the masked dancer, who performed scenes . . . from mythology . . . in dumbshow, while appropriate words were sung by a chorus.' He adds: 'our evidence is that the essential attraction of pantomime was the supple, artistic, expressive, passionate, sometimes exquisitely lascivious movements of the dancer.' Juvenal wrote on pantomime, and Sir William had probably read him; Noverre, a celebrated ballet master, read in the library of Sir William's friend Garrick a mass of literature on pantomime in 1760. All of these, no doubt, contributed to Sir William's conception of the Attitudes. Let us not forget, however, that, as Kirsten Holmstrom has written, the foundations of this mimoplastic art were laid in Romney's studio at Cavendish Square, when Emma posed as Greek heroines at the painter's direction.

In May, Goethe returned to Naples from his quest in Sicily, for the Ur-pflanz or Primal Plant, and saw Sir William's treasure vault. On this occasion, on 27 May, he praised Emma as before: 'Sir William Hamilton and his Fair One continue to be very friendly. I dined at their house, and in the evening, Miss Hart gave a demonstration of her musical and melic talents.' He describes the vault and the chest. Then, mysteriously, he launches into a diatribe against Emma, making comments which, he says himself, 'a guest who has been so well treated ought really not to make'. 'Our fair entertainer', he writes, 'seems to me, frankly, a dull creature. Perhaps her figure makes up for it, but her voice is inexpressive and her speech without charm. Even her singing is neither full-throated nor agreeable.' Professor Weitz, a great Goethe expert, argues that Goethe inserted this entry of 27 May to meet editorial requirements when in 1816 he was preparing *Italienische Reise* ('Italian

Journey') for publication. Weitz's thesis is that Goethe had since met Marianne von Willemar, also of modest origins. To placate her, he tempered his praise of Emma.

What Emma thought of Goethe we do not know. From Tischbein's portrait of Goethe in the Campagna, it seems unlikely that Emma would have found him attractive, with his broad brow and oxlike neck. It may, by the way, have rankled with Goethe that Tischbein laid aside his portrait of the poet to paint Emma as Iphigeneia in a scene from Goethe's play of that name. Emma looks out from under a veil or shawl draped, cowl fashion, over her head. This is the first picture of Emma inspired by her Greek Attitudes.

Tischbein, Goethe's companion, was soon to become an intimate member of the Hamilton set in Naples. In June Philip Hackert came to Rome with the Cavaliere Venuti, owner of a priceless, though mutilated, Ulysses. Their mission was to remove the fabulous Farnese marbles from the Palazzo Farnese, now the French Embassy in Rome, and convey them to Naples. In early July, the baggage wagons got under way and Tischbein went with them. He rested, after the exhaustion of the journey, at Sir William's villa at Posillipo. 'There is really no more glorious place in the whole world. After lunch a dozen boys went swimming in the sea. It was beautiful to watch the groups they made and the postures they took during their games. Sir William pays them to give him this pleasure every afternoon.' Later, he went for a row with Sir William. 'I like him very much. We talked on many topics; I learned a great deal from him, and look forward to learning more in future.'

The burning summer wore on. The Queen was pregnant; the King shot African quails on Capri. Tischbein had another meeting with Sir William and Emma. A ship protecting coral fishers captured a Turkish vessel which had attacked, and brought it prisoner to Naples. Six Turks were killed and one wounded. The Madonna protected the Christians from injury, Tischbein told Goethe. Among the prisoners taken was a young Moorish girl. The Neapolitan captain took valuable jewellery from her; thousands of people rowed out 'in boat after boat' to see her and the others. Several 'fanciers' offered to buy her, but the captain meant to keep her. 'I also rowed out every day,' Tischbein wrote, 'and once I met Sir William and Miss Hart there. The latter was very moved and cried, at which the girl also started crying.' Emma too tried to buy her, but the captain was obdurate. The people of Naples loved Emma for her soft heart.

Sir William and Emma were living in a dream. As Goethe wrote in March, 'Naples is a paradise; everyone lives in a state of intoxicated self-forgetfulness.' Emma had forgotten her past. Sir William threw caution to the winds, and, in August and September, led his nymph on a *villeggiatura* or a tour of country villas as his acknowledged consort. With glee, Emma relates the adventures they had together in an excessively long letter to Greville. She begins it in August, and ends in December 1787.

The first place to which Sir William takes her, at the end of July, is the country villa of the Duca di San Demetrio, the King's favourite gentleman of the bedchamber. This villa at Punta di Sorrento commanded a magnificent view of the Palace of Tiberius on neighbouring Capri, and views of the plain stretching from beneath Vesuvius to the sea. Emma declared she 'never pass'd a happier ten days except Edg..re R..d'. Emma describes their daily routine:

s/ ?
> In the morning we bathed, and returned to a fine sumer house, where we breakfasted. But first this sumer house (in) on a rock over the sea, that looks over Caprea, Ischea, Procheda, Vesuva, Porticea, Paysilipo, Naples, &c., &c., &c., the sea all before ous, that you have no idea of the beauties of it. From this little paridise after breakfast we vewd the lava running down 3 miles of Vesuvua and every now and then black clouds of smoak, rising in to the air, had the most magnificent appearance in the world.

Emma adds that she has made some drawings from it. 'I am so used to draw now,' she says airily, 'it is as easy as A B C.' Some would say she had not mastered that. When they are at Naples, she goes on, they dine every day at Villa Emma at Posillipo, and she makes two or three drawings. After only a year of her company, Sir William has named his *petit palais* after her. He laughs at her, she says, and says she shall rival him with the mountains now.

After breakfast at the Sorrento summer-house, at which we may be sure Emma made a hearty repast, she turned to more serious affairs. She had her singing lesson – 'for Sir Wm. as took a musition in to the house. But he is one of the best masters in Italia.' This was Giuseppe Aprile, from Apulia, who had been first man at the Teatro San Carlo – Burney, in 1770, reported him to be 'the crack of Naples', although, he added, he was said to have a thin voice and to embroider overmuch. Later, when Burney heard Aprile for himself, he approved his shake and his 'taste and expression'. Author of some excellent exercises, he turned to teaching only after a long career in which he sang in all the German and Italian theatres. Sir William did Emma a great service in taking this castrato, Aprile, now just short of fifty, into his house to be tutor to her alone. There is perhaps a touch of the eunuch invading the harem about the proceedings.

After Emma's lesson, she and Sir William rode on asses all about the countryside – a chance for Emma to display her vaunted equestrianism founded at Uppark. They paid visits. It must have been a quaint sight for their hosts – Sir William grizzled and lanky atop a donkey; on her jogging mule beside him, Emma in radiant health with wisps of her long hair escaping her hat and veil. At three they dined. All the varieties of shell-fish netted in the Bay were at their disposal. Figs, grapes, apples, hams, *polpette* and pâtés, *maccheroni*, quails and small songbirds; the diet was little different from that of the Pompeians who feasted near Sorrento in AD 79 when destruction overtook them.

After dinner, our heroic pair sailed about the coast, then returned and dressed for the *conversazione*. This very Italian entertainment was, one young man thought, only just preferable to an English rout-party. In Naples, there would be seven or eight a week, and two or three on the same night. By the light of flambeaux, the nobility climbed to the *piano nobile* of the host's *palazzo*. They then walked up and down a series of rooms exchanging greetings, drank a glass of lemonade, and then made their farewells. On they went to the next *palazzo*, where they soon saw all the people who had been at the last *conversazione*. Not least among the chronic dissatisfactions with this form of evening party was the fact that the hundreds of carriages which waited to take departing guests on to the next venue clogged the narrow streets of Naples. As each arriving guest had to be dropped exactly at the *palazzo* entrance, frequently long queues of carriages tailed back round several street corners.

Emma was not as yet used to *conversazioni*. This visit to San Demetrio's villa was one of her first experiences of this type of party. Fortunately, there was only the one in the neighbourhood each night, so the guests came prepared to be entertained for the evening, and music was the order of the day. Emma tells Greville that they had Sir William's 'band of musick' with them. These were the two or three among his servants who could make up a quartet when required. As darkness fell on Sorrento, the concert began in one room. In another, Emma sat and received all the nobility. 'I sung generally 2 searous songs & 2 buffos [*buffo*, or comic]. The last night I sang fifteen songs. One was a recatitive [recitatif] from an opera at St Carlo's. The beginning was Luci Belle sio vadoro, the finest thing you ever heard, that for ten minutes after I sung it, there was such a claping that I was oblidged to sing it over again.' Emma was not averse to blowing her own trumpet, when she thought she merited it.

She goes on: 'I sung after that one with a Tambourin in the character of a young girl with a raire-shew [raree-show, or a box of tricks], the

pretist thing you ever heard. In short, I left the people at Sorrento with
their heads turned. I left some dying, some crying & some in despair.
Mind you theis was all nobility as proud as the devil. But we humbled
them.' It is interesting to note here that Emma speaks of performing 'in
the character of' a young girl. She belonged to the Garrick school of
acting, the founder of which believed in using every facial and bodily
muscle to emphasize the passions behind the spoken words. Garrick had
exceptional control over his features. More classical actors impassively
recited the words, bestowing solemnity and weight upon them by their
grave demeanour. One can imagine Emma entering with every carefree
gesture further into the part of the young girl.

Emma's Italian had improved by leaps and bounds. She showed off
about it no end. Talking of the nobility, she says, 'I paid them, I spared
non of them, tho I was civil and oblidged every body. One asked me
if I left a love at Naples that I left them so soon.' Emma pulled her lip
at him and asked, pray, did he take her for an Italian woman who had
four or five different men to attend her. 'Look, Sir, I am English,' she
affirmed proudly, 'I have one cavalere-servante & I have brought him
with me,' pointing to Sir William. 'But he never spoke another word
after this: for before he had been offering himself as Cavalere Servante.'
Her admirer said she was a rare woman.

After their victorious *villeggiatura*, on 4 August Sir William proposed
to take Emma up to inspect Vesuvius, the volcano which was smoking
ominously and emitting what Emma called 'cascades of liquid fire . . .
red-hot', which ran into a deep cavern. 'I fancy we shall have some very
large eruption soon, as large as that of 67,' Emma said knowledgeably.
'I wish we may,' she added. She had not seen the devastation such
events wrought on the villages which the Neapolitans would build
on the lower slopes of the volcano. Emma and Sir William were to
dine at two and set off at four. At Portici they were to mount asses
and arrive at the top as dark fell, returning to Naples about two in the
morning.

In Naples there was now much to occupy Emma. 'Sir Wm. is very
fond of me & very kind to me; the house is ful of painters painting
me.' Who these were, we cannot know, but Emma tells us later that
'all the artists is come from Rome to study from me.' Perhaps it was
Gavin Hamilton who spread the news of Emma's beauty with his
sketches of her seated figure. Perhaps it was Goethe. At any rate, Sir
William now had nine pictures of Emma '& 2 a painting'. Nor was
he content with the pictorial image alone. The celebrated jeweller,
Nathaniel Marchant, was cutting Emma's head in stone, 'that is, in
cameo for a ring'. One artist was modelling her in wax, another in

clay. Under such pressure, Sir William was forced to fit up a room that was called 'the painting-room'.

Were the tensions of their first months together resolved? 'Sir Wm. is never for a moment from me,' Emma declares. 'He goes no where without me. He as no diners, but what I can be of the party. No body comes with out the are civil to me; we have allways good company.' From this proud summary, we can deduce that there were some ladies and gentlemen who preferred not to come but to be uncivil about Emma elsewhere. There had been further changes in the domestic arrangements. Now Emma lived 'up stairs in the same apartment where he lives, and my old apartments is made the musick-rooms where I have my lessons in the morning.'

Emma ran on to tell Greville of more territorial expansion. 'Our house at Caserta is fitting up eleganter this year, a room making for my musick, and a room fitting up for my master [Aprile], as he goes with ous. Sir Wm. says he loves nothing but me, likes no person to sing but me, and takes delight in all I do and all I say so we are happy,' she ended contentedly.

She rambles on, enthusing over her visit to the summit of Vesuvius. The lava was coursing five miles from the top. 'The mountain is not burst is ignorant people say it is.' There was a wooden hermitage half-way up, where an extraordinary Frenchman dwelt. In him Mrs Piozzi, the year before, had recognized her old hairdresser from London. He was accustomed to welcome such visitors as reached his eyrie with most delicious omelettes. On this occasion Emma and Sir William found him in dire distress. The 'finest fountain of liquid fire falling down a great precipice' set fire to trees and brushwood in its path. 'We saw the lava surround the poor Hermits house & take possession of the chapel,' in spite of all the pictures of saints and religious prophylactics which adorned it. Such was the fury of Nature.

'For me I was inraptured,' Emma breathes. 'I could have staid all night there & I have never been in charity with the moon since for it looked so pale and sickly ... the light of the moon was nothing to the lava.' They met the Prince Royal, Charles, whose tutors would only take him a little way up and whisked him down swiftly. Emma and Sir William asked him how he liked it. '*Bella ma poca roba*' was his response. 'Pretty, but nothing great.' If they had only taken him five hundred yards higher, he would have seen 'the noblest sublimest sight in the world'. Emma had imbibed wholesale Sir William's vocabulary of praise.

She followed her scorn at the cowardice of the Prince's tutors with another jibe at the folly of her host nation. 'O I shall kill myselfe with laughing.' A sixty-year-old prince, from one of the best families of Naples, came to visit. He had never left his city. 'When I told him I had been to Caprea,' Emma wrote, 'he asked me if I went their by land; onely think what ignorance. I staired at him and asked who was his tutor.'

About the third week of August, the Hamilton ménage returned to the Palazzo Sessa. That young reprobate, Lord Hervey, was again in Naples, due shortly to commence his duties as Envoy to the Court of the Grand Duke of Tuscany. Meanwhile, he whiled away his time making passionate love to the young Princess Roccafiorita, whose husband was absent on his estates. The pressing nature of his suit came soon to the ears of General Acton, who wrote a stiff note to Sir William, desiring him to stop this whipper-snapper in his tracks.

'I must tell you', Emma wrote afresh to Greville, 'I have had great offers to be first whoman in the Italian opera at Madrid where I was to have six thousand pound for 3 years.' This was news to make Greville sit up. Six thousand pounds was a colossal amount of money, considering Emma and her mother were at present living on a sum of a hundred and fifty pounds a year for clothing and sundries, and fifty pounds for washing. Emma turned down the offer. Not from reasons of affection for Sir William or from pride that she was not of the opera-singer class did she spurn Madrid, however. 'I should not like to go into Spain with out I knew people their & I could not speak their language,' she wrote sensibly. Another reason was that Gallini, commissioning dancing master of the London Opera House, had been in Naples, engaging artistes. 'Tho I have not bee persuaded to make a written engagement, I ceartainly shall sing at the Pantheon & Hanover Square [two celebrated concert rooms], except something particular happens.' Gallini had sworn to get up a subscription concert for her if she would not engage for the opera. (Even Mrs Sheridan, née Elizabeth Linley, was permitted by her husband occasionally to sing at subscription concerts.) Emma wished to think it over before she decided. Sir William's view of the matter was that he would 'give me leave' to sing at Hanover Square 'on the condition Gallini as proposed' – namely, two thousand pounds. Would Sir William pocket this substantial sum? Emma does not go into further detail. There is something extraordinary about Emma's detailing of these offers. Only a year earlier, nobody knew or cared if she had a pretty voice. Now the impresarios of Europe courted her, their offers confirm her assertions that audiences wept and applauded wildly when she sang. Her master, Aprile, has to take a large share of the credit, but clearly she responded to tuition. Sir William now paid Aprile 'a great price on purpose that he shall not teach any other person'.

It was now September. The Queen had been delivered of a boy, Leopold, in August. He was to become her favourite child, though she had a mammary disorder after his birth.

An English ship, skippered by a Captain Finch, had been awaited eagerly. The seamen listened to a concert where Emma sang. 'They says Miss Hamilton is a fool in singing in comparison to me,' she jeered. Miss Hamilton was daughter to Sir William's clerical brother, Frederick. 'So says Sir William, but I don't know,' she wrote, with a reversion to modesty. 'It is a most extraordinary thing that my voice is totaly alterd, it is the finest soprano you ever heard, that Sir William shuts his eyes & think one of the Castratos is singing . . . my shake or tril, what do you call it, is so very good in every note, my master says that if he did not feil & see & no that I am a substance, he would think I was an angel.' Triumphantly, she announces: 'I have now gone through all difficculties. I solfega [or sing a solfeggio, scale] at first sight & in reccatative famous.'

'Sir William is in raptures with me' was the sum of the whole. 'He spares neither expence nor pains in anything.' She catalogues the various expenses to which her admirer is put. Besides Aprile who teaches her three times a day, at eight a.m., before dinner (about three p.m.) and in the evening, there was a French master, the Queen's dancing master (Le Picq) three times a week; and then Emma read Italian for an hour a day with a person who came 'a purpose'.

Fortunately, Sir William believed in leisure and pleasure as firmly as he believed in disciplining the mind. Straight after Emma's first singing lesson and dancing lesson, he had the phaeton at the door, and drove her out for two hours. No doubt the villagers round about Naples and Caserta grew accustomed to the solemn procession of the carriage in its search for fresh routes.

Besides all her lessons, remember, Emma had artists beseeching her at every hour to lend them her shining countenance for a moment. There were now five painters and two modellers 'at work on me', at Sir William's request, and a picture of her 'going to the Empress of Russia', no less. It is extraordinary how far and how fast Emma's reputation as a beauty travelled. Presumably, the Russian Ambassador Skavronsky had made mention of the British Minister's 'friend' in his dispatches home, and Catherine, that curious monarch, had then asked for a likeness to be sent to her.

Besides acting as model to the world and improving her talents, Emma was kept busy entertaining. When she wrote that they had a 'good society' at the Palazzo Sessa, that did not include any of the powerful aristocratic ladies of the Court. Among them were the

Princess Belmonte, an aged lady who, despite her years, had a host of young favourites dangling at her feet, such was the magnetism of her personality. La Belmonte would never have deigned to grace an embassy where one of Emma's class presided. Small matter if Naples was not aware of Emma's exact origin – so far as they were concerned she had arrived, a Greek nymph from Mount Ida, without known antecedents. The ladies of the Court could still make a pretty good guess at her previous circumstances. The Marchesa di Solari, who first came to Naples in 1791, was told that the Queen 'more than once expressed herself in a tone of great discontent, that a man, honoured with an important mission, an English minister, should live publicly with a prostitute taken from the very streets of London'. Where the Queen did not go, her ladies did not go either, so the company at the Palazzo Sessa, if good, was mostly male. One cannot imagine that Emma minded too much. With her mother a quiet chaperone in the corner of the room, she responded to the licentious mood which prevailed at Sir William's convivial table.

In November, Emma and Sir William hosted a diplomatic dinner. Among the many envoys, ministers and ambassadors seconded to the Court of Naples, Sir William was on particularly good terms with M. de Sa, the Portuguese Minister. M. le Baron de Talleyrand-Périgord, the French Ambassador, was a music-lover like Sir William, and kept a rival box at the Teatro San Carlo – a double box so that there was room for supper to be served at the interval. All the French gathered there, as the English viewed the opera from Sir William's box. Skavronsky was another music lover. It seems doubtful that these ambassadors' wives accompanied their spouses to the Palazzo Sessa. They missed a thrilling show.

They were sixty to dinner. Such large numbers were quite common in Naples, where, generally, only foreigners gave dinners at all. The Neapolitans ate frugally at home and reserved their wealth for a great show of carriages and horses on the Toledo; naturally, they welcomed the treat of dinner out, and there were few refusals. After dinner, Emma sent the coach and her compliments to 'the Banti who is first whoman at St Carlos'.

Brigida Giorgi Banti, aged thirty-one and a Bolognese by birth, was particularly noted for her bravura style. Daughter of a street singer who played the mandolin, in 1779 she married Zaccaria Banti, a dancer in London. She went as a pupil to Mr Piozzi, but he became so exasperated by her want of application that he declined to teach her further. This did not halt her career. The Banti agreed to come and sing at Emma's concert. Emma describes how she felt 'in a little fright' at the thought of performing with this famous singer. 'She placed herself close to me, but when I begun all fear whent a whay & I sung so well that she cried out, just God, what a voice, I would give a great deal for your voice.' The company applauded vigorously. It was of consequence that Emma should appear well, for Sir William wished to show her off to a Dutch ship's company, and its captain Commodore Melvile. There being no Dutch Embassy at the Court of Naples, Sir William generally did the honours for those patriots who came from Holland. The Banti sang a song after Emma and did not get half so much applause. 'Poor Sir Wm. was inraptured with me, for he was afraid I should have been in a great fright.' Emma was finding fast that there was little which frightened her bold spirit. She takes a childish delight in recounting her triumphs to Greville.

An enjoyable consequence of her glittering performance was that Commodore Melvile was so 'inchanted' with Emma that he put off his voyage onwards for a day, and invited Emma aboard for a dinner 'that nealy surpasses all description'. Emma proceeds to describe the pomp with which she was welcomed aboard.

Sir William, Emma and Mrs Cadogan processed down to the Mole where stood the Dutch ships – one a sixty-gunner, the other a frigate. The Commodore and Captain and four more of the senior officers waited to conduct them in a longboat out to the ship. 'The 2 ships was dresd out so fine in all the collours, the men all put in order, a band of musick & all the marine did their duty.' As they passed the frigate, she fired all her guns in salute, and twenty cannon roared as they went on board.

The company sat down thirty to dine, with Emma at the head of the table, mistress of the feast. She was 'drest all in virgin wite & my hair all in ringlets reaching all most to my heals'. Her hair was now so long, Sir William assured her she really looked and moved like an angel.

The dinner went on till half past five, to Emma's dismay. There was a great opera at the San Carlo that night, in honour of the King of Spain's name day. The San Carlo was to be illuminated and everyone 'in great galla', as Emma phrased it. On this day, 5 November, the winter season opened. For the occasion, Emma had the finest dress made up 'on purpose, as I had a box near the K & Queen'. The gown was of purple satin; the petticoat which peeped out was white satin, trimmed with crêpe and spangles. She had a lovely cap from Paris, 'all wite fethers', to top this dazzling creation, and her hair was to have been delightfully dressed. Emma was on her mettle. She meant to outshine every other lady in the theatre.

The best laid schemes o' mice an' men gang aft a-gley. At half past five, the Commodore and Sir William, who had evidently put away quite an amount already, would have another bottle to drink to the 'Belle ocche [beautiful eyes] of the loveliest whoman in the world as the cald me'. Emma was torn between gratification and anxiety. All opera-goers had to be at their posts when the Royal party entered their box, resplendent with mirrored glass and candles. Finally Sir William was persuaded to leave the table. The boat was put out. After the frigate and sixty-gunner boomed a valedictory salute, the riotous party arrived on shore, to the curious gaze of *lazzaroni* loafing on the quayside. The Hamilton trio and the Commodore and the five other officers crowded into one large coach anyhow, and tumbled out at the opera house in a great flurry of hats and legs.

They reached the Minister's box just in time, and throughout the evening the Commodore and other officers 'attended my box all the time and behaved to me as tho I was a Queen'. Sir William had written fondly to Banks a month earlier, 'She will rival Madame Mara [a famous opera singer in London] with her singing soon.'[4] Where there was an example of ambition achieved, Emma was swift to follow.

In November, the Hamilton household moved to Caserta, where all remained till 28 December. Every day, Emma and Sir William walked in the Queen's Garden. The botanic garden and a species of Ferme Ornée were coming on apace. The *cavaliere* Gatti came to stay for a week, and brought with him a prophecy from Padre Antonio Minasi, who lived on the slopes of Vesuvius and drew its smoke patterns for Sir William. He said in a week or a fortnight the mountain would open on the Portici side, 'and carry all that place a whay'. Even at Caserta there were signs that a great eruption was due. Emma was talking to Graefer in the English Garden when 'all of a sudin their rose such black collums of smoke out of Vesuvus attended with such roaring that I was frightened.' There was a dreadful noise 'just like cannons in ones ears'.

Emma took one of her maids up on the leads of the house at night, and showed her the strange sight of Naples seen very plain in the light of a great fire on the mountain. The throes were succeeded by red-hot cinders which fell all over the mountain. Teresa – 'who is a great biggot' – fell down on her knees when she saw the fire. 'O Janaro [Gennaro], Antoino mio,' she cried (according to Emma's report), invoking the two patron saints of Naples. Emma fell to her knees too, in mockery, and called, 'O Saint Loola mio, Loola mio,' which was nonsense. Teresa got up in a great hurry and said, 'Ebene signora la vostro excellenza non credo in St Janaro evero' (Well, your excellency, I see you don't believe in St Januarius). Emma replied, 'No Teresa evero per me Io credo se voi prega all Loola mio se stesso Cosa' ('No Teresa, quite true. I think if you pray to Loola, it's all the same'). Teresa looked at her and said to be sure her mistress read a great many books and must know more than she, but did not God favour Emma more than her? Emma denied it. 'O God says she, your excellency is very ungrateful, he as been so good as to make your face the same as he made the Blessed virgins and you dont esteem it as a favour. . . . You are like every picture of her.' 'Greville, its true,' Emma exclaims, 'the have all got it in their heads I am like the virgin & the do come to beg favours of me'.

It is interesting to consider what style of Madonna was familiar to the Neapolitans, so that we may imagine how Emma came to be mistaken for such an august personage. Raphael's early series of Madonnas and lady saints was doubtless familiar from many copies in the churches. The type Emma referred to was evidently one of the veiled variety, as the following anecdote makes plain. Two priests came to the Hamilton house at Caserta. Sir William had Emma put 'the shawl over my head and look up'. One priest burst into tears straight away, kissed her feet, and said God had sent her into the world for a purpose. If Raphael's picture of Saint Catherine looking up from under her shawl is considered as the type of female religious men deemed divine, then one can imagine the effect Emma had on the priest. Remember, also, that Romney saw the likeness between Emma and Raphael's saints, and adapted many of Raphael's designs to accommodate Emma's figure. If Emma dressed as Sir William wished, in clear celestial colours; if she indulged in the little charitable tasks among the poor which won their affection; small wonder this innocent populace thought the girl who had come among them so suddenly was a person of semi-divine origin.

Emma ended her long letter – and the year, 1787 – with some very down-to-earth requests of Greville. Would he ask Mr Macpherson for a shawl for Emma? Her own were quite worn out 'now as I have such a use of shawls . . . Sir Wm. is quite miserable for I stand in atitudes with them on me.' She asks for four or five prints of 'that little Gipsey picture with the hat on'. (Sichel attributes this picture of Emma in a hat with oranges to Opie. But it is not known when he might have painted it, except that it was prior to Emma's departure from England in 1786.) Sir William wanted one and she had also promised prints to two other people. She thanks Greville for two hats, but added that she had given the black one to Madam Vanvitelli (wife of Luigi, son and successor to his architect father, Carlo). It was too small. What man can know the disappointment of the ill-fitting hat?

Emma ends her letter, 'Mind you, your Uncle Fred's daughter cant sing so well as me,' and adds some unwelcome news. 'We shall be in London this Spring twelve months; we are going to Rome

this spring. Adio & believe me more your friend than what you
are mine.'

She then adds a postscript. She means to write to Greville's brother,
Robert Fulke, next post about White, a soldier servant he had sent out
to Naples to get employment. 'I have assisted them [White and his
wife] a good deal & will more.' She sends love to '[Heneage] Legg[e],
[Sir Joseph] Banks and Tolemach [Tollemache] etc. etc. & tell them
to take care of their hearts when I come back; as to you'. Emma jokes,
'you will be uterly undone but Sr Wm. allready is distractedly in love
& endead I love him tenderly. He deserves it.'

With what mixed emotions Greville must have received this lengthy
epistle. He was no doubt pleased that Emma was so well established
away from him, but her triumphant descriptions of her success surely
irritated him and confirmed his suspicions that, if Emma were given
her head, she would go far beyond what he saw to be her sphere.

Sir William praised Emma to Greville in terms almost as generous
as those she used herself. On 18 December, he wrote from Caserta:

> We are here as usual, my dear Charles, and I am out almost every day
> on shooting parties, but I find my house comfortable in the evening with
> Emma's society. You can have no idea of the improvement she makes daily
> in every respect – manners, language, & musick particularly. She has now
> applied closely to singing 5 months, & I have her master (an excellent one)
> in the house, so that she takes 3 lessons a day; her voice is remarkably fine,
> & she begins now to have a command over it. She has much expression, &
> as she applies chiefly to the solfeggia, she will be grounded in musick, &
> there is no saying what she may be in a year or two; I believe myself of
> the first rate, & so do the best judges here, who can scarcely believe she
> has only learnt 5 months.

On another tack, he wrote: 'I can assure you her behaviour is such
as has acquired her many sensible admirers, and we have a good man
society, and all the female nobility, with the Queen at their head, show
her every distant civility.'

If this is contrary to what the Marchesa di Solari would have us
believe, Maria Carolina was no doubt too regal to show her disdain
publicly.

In January 1788, Emma wrote to Greville again, with some money
enclosed for her uncle. This might be William Kidd, Mrs Cadogan's
brother, but seems more likely to be Mr Moore of Liverpool, whom
one of Mrs Cadogan's sisters, Amy, had married. Emma was not one to
let her relations go hungry while she enjoyed good fortune. There was
never any mention in her letters, however, of little Emma, immured in

her Manchester school with no holidays. It cannot be expected; Emma had closed her heart up against that tie when her infant daughter was sent off from Edgware Row. She does say, however, that Sir William has given his niece Mary Dickenson, née Hamilton, 'a choaking' for some remarks about Emma. 'He told her I was necessary to his happiness . . . no person should come to disturb me.' On 7 February, Mary wrote from Taxal, Derbyshire, to quell her many relations' anxieties. Her first remarks show how ignorant London was of the reality of Naples, and how wild its surmises.

> I know there was a report which gained credit of my Uncle Wm's being married, but I gave it none, as I was certain he would have communicated his *intentions*, as he places ye most unlimited confidence in me. I recd a long letter from him, a few days ago, dated Jany 8th, from Caserta . . . I have *reason now* to apprehend he will never marry. He tells me that his health is better than it has been for some years past . . . he is . . . much taken up with the Queen of Naples' English garden at Caserta.

'His domestic hours have many charms to interest him,' she concludes ominously.[5]

Emma was now the companion of Sir William's hours, a needed prop at his side when the fatigue of the Bourbon Court overburdened his composure, a delight on which his tired eyes could feast at the end of a bustling day.

That Emma had undergone something of a transformation is apparent from further items in her newsletter of 8 January. Greville's friend, George Saunders, architect, visited Naples. He had not seen Emma since Edgware Row days, 'He was surprised at the stile he saw me in, and the attention that is shewn me, and the magnificence of my dress.' He was 'astonished' by her voice and by her fluency in Italian. 'But I love to surprise people.' Emma's singing lessons had borne great fruit. Paisiello, that agreeable, convivial composer, had given her a duet to work on and perform at the Carnival. This was honour indeed. 'We give a great concert, and I sing it with the first man of the opera.' This was probably the great tenor, Casacelli. The song was *'Per pietà da questo istante non parlarmi, O Dio d' Amor'* (For pity's sake speak to me no more, O God of Love). She informs Greville it 'makes every person cry'.

In the spring, Rome beckoned as it does all those today who know the mauve charm of the wisteria falling in rich clusters over its walls. What the purpose of this trip was, we do not know. Perhaps Sir William merely wished to show Emma the sweets of the papal city, perhaps he took her to be painted by the artists of the day. Perhaps he led her round

the scenes where those dramas of classical history took place – the hill
where the Roman geese shrieked their warning that the invader stood
below, the palace where Caesar's Julia flaunted her body before her
lovers, the steps up to the Capitol where Caesar himself was slain. By
early summer, with minds enriched and, perhaps, Attitudes increased,
the pair were back in Naples.

Sir William wrote to Banks on 19 August 1788. 'Otiosa has ever been
the epithet attached to Naples . . . really the climate does incline one
to be perfectly idle . . .' At some point, perhaps on Emma's birthday,
Sir William made her a most sumptuous present. 'She so long'd for
diamonds that, having an opportunity of a good bargain of single stones
of a good water & tolerable size, I gave her at once £500 worth.' Sir
William was not a rich man, and this present cost over twice the yearly
allowance he made Emma and her mother for 'cloths & washing'. It
proves that Emma by now was well lodged in his affections. It also
indicates that Emma and Sir William now entertained together on a
grand scale. In January she had written: 'The English is coming very
fast, and you can't think how well I do the honours.' Emma had come
far beyond Greville's suggestion that she be kept confined in a villa on
the hill.

The Queen gave birth to another child, the King continued to hunt
and General John Acton tried to keep the fluctuating fortunes of the
Kingdom of Naples within some measure of order. Among other
reforms as Minister of the Marine and of War, he made the King
dissolve his favourite company of Lipariote soldiers. In their green
and gold costumes, they were a decorative addition to the shooting
preserves, but of little military use.

The English Garden came on apace. A Mr Malcolm of Cricklewood
sent plans for a glass house; there was no properly seasoned wood to
be had in Naples and he would send it. This excellent plan fell by
the wayside due to the hopeless state of the Garden's finances. The
King had recently taken over the superintendence of the plot from his
spouse. Having had no interest in the affair, and threatening to plough
the whole up and sow it with Indian corn, he changed his tune. Having
held that God gave land of quite sufficient beauty as it was, he began to
be violently interested in the project. He was now to be seen walking
'arm in arm' with Graefer. However, Sir William could not induce him
to pay for Malcolm's goods. The matter became most embarrassing. Sir
William and Emma continued to sit each day in the Garden and drink
a dish of tea, while controversy raged about them.

There were worrying reports from England all through the year 1788
of George III's insanity. The King rambled in his bed with periodic

recoveries and relapses. Sir William was not merely upset that the monarch should be incapacitated. He had been a friend to George III, owing to the intimacy of his mother and the King's father, since childhood. Indeed, he was often referred to as the King's foster-brother. No doubt Emma betrayed some becoming sensibility as the reports worsened. She was always genuinely sorry for and kind to the sick.

A tragedy closer to Sir William's heart even than the madness of his monarch occurred in 1788, and was broken to him by Charles Greville in November. Young Charles Cathcart, hopeful sprig of Sir William's sister, Jean Lady Cathcart, died on his way to China. He was to lead an embassy to Peking and negotiate trading contracts between England and China – a matter of the first importance and a great honour for young Charles. His 'Scotch ardency' and practical intellect had taken his uncle, Sir William's, fancy; he made him his heir after Greville when he made his will in 1784. Now he was deeply upset. Charles's sister, Louisa Lady Stormont, proposed that she and her other sisters, Mary Graham and the Duchess of Atholl, and Lady Cathcart, put on 'Bombazeen' gowns with black satin ribbon 'because it *felt* deeper mourning than silk . . . I think it would be comforting.'[6]

For the Bourbon family, there was bad news, too. In December 1788, Gennaro and Carlo, sons of the King and Queen, contracted smallpox and died. In the same month, Ferdinand's father, the King of Spain, died and Ferdinand's elder brother, Prince of the Asturias, succeeded as Charles IV.

In the spring of 1789, Sir William took advantage of a lull in the affairs of the Two Sicilies to make an expedition to Puglia, or Apulia as the province is now known, the heel of the boot of Italy. This was the only part of the Kingdom which he had not as yet explored. *Travels in the Two Sicilies* by Henry Swinburne, 1776, was his guide, and a good one it proved. Swinburne's descriptions and comments on the poverty and barren wastelands were amply borne out by what Sir William saw himself. The province had never recovered from the eruption of Vesuvius in 1769 and the famine which followed.

Emma accompanied Sir William on this trip. He had not advised it but 'she is so good there is no refusing her'. As it happened, her presence on the expedition was in many ways disadvantageous to Sir William. Where a single man might have stayed every night in the monasteries which littered the way, the pair of them were condemned to carry heavy baggage and strike camp every night. Yet no doubt the gipsy life had its attractions. Perhaps Emma sang as they sat by the light of the fire, the only beacon in a blackened night.

Sir William meant to pick up a few antiquities emerging now from the excavations which were prosecuted as soon as the King removed the embargo on digging in 1786. He found a little intaglio of Greek sculpture at Canosa 'just like Emma'. By now, the archaeologist was merged with the man, as Emma was merged, in his eyes, with the goddesses of antiquity. Other finds were a large intaglio of the head of Hercules, and a fine vase at Bari. He found, to his disappointment, that almost everything excavated was sent direct to the capital. Fortunately, he was able to buy a 'very extraordinary collection' of vases recently excavated within the year – 'the drawings . . . are most excellent . . . many of the subjects from Homer'.

The tour lasted thirty-two days. In this time, Sir William and Emma ranged over the length and breadth of Puglia. Sir William informed Banks that they went a great part of the way on foot, the roads were so bad. He adds that Emma took notes – 'She is as clever as she is Beautiful.'[7] To Bari, Taranto, Brindisi and Foggia they went, touring the boot of Italy in a loose loop. The towns were little more than villages, the life to be observed more primitive than anything Emma had known even on the Wirral Peninsula. They rested more than a day in one place for only ten of the thirty-two days; during the remainder they travelled 'slowly from morning to night'.

It was a fatiguing trip for a man of fifty-nine, even if he was in good health. The rest of the summer, Sir William and Emma lived quietly. They bathed and sailed and dined at Villa Emma, at Posillipo. Their intimates, Gatti, Hackert and Tischbein, visited them. They made music and read quietly in the evenings. As we heard from the maid Teresa, and the 1815 *Memoirs* bear her out, Emma was a great reader. Having come to it late, she only read the more. Sadly, however, we have no record of what she read at this date.

When they had no business on hand, Sir William and Emma strolled in the English Garden, which they hoped would one day be 'among the first in Europe'. The King had ordered a good house to be built for Graefer within the Garden wall. Noting the King's other plans, Sir William writes to Banks. 'You will laugh when I tell you that one of the first things the King wishes Graefer to do in the garden is to make a labyrinth.' This was considered a very old-fashioned idea. Horace Walpole in *The Gardenist* writes that the latest thing was a serpentine wood. Sir William was at a loss where to find a plan for the labyrinth. The only one he knew was on an antique medal.

The Pulcinella King, as Ferdinand was sometimes known – after the puppet of Italian *commedia dell'arte* – made a joke at George III's expense. He called him a poor king of straw who could not do what he liked. Sir William was so relieved by his foster-brother's return to health, he minded no jibe. On the King of England's birthday, he wrote on 2 June 1789, there would be such a sirloin of beef on his table as he was sure had never appeared before at Naples. He had invited all the English Factory (an enterprise of a Mr MacKinnon). There would be his best wines to drink His Majesty's health, which were not by any means despicable. Sir William forewent the pleasure of syrupy Lacryma Christi and other local wines and imported superior vintages from France.

There can be no doubt that Emma enjoyed herself on that occasion. It marks a departure from Sir William's habit of inviting a mixture of nationals, and a cheerful disdain for the opinion of others as to his liaison. The English bidden to the dinner would swiftly tittle-tattle about the Embassy in their letters home. Sir William had forged such a companionable bond with Emma during their exertions in Puglia, he now threw caution to the winds.

CHAPTER EIGHT

We give no Scandal

Sir William's reaction on his return to Naples after the Puglia trip was to send Greville what amounts to a statement of his intentions towards Emma. They were not as promising as she might have hoped. On 26 May 1789, he wrote:

> [Emma's] conduct is such as to gain universal esteem, & she profits daily in musick and language. I endeavour to lose no time in forming her, & certainly she would be welcome to share with me, *on our present footing*, all I have during my life, but I fear her views are beyond what I can bring myself to execute; & that when her hopes on that point are over, that she will make herself & me unhappy; but all this entre nous; if ever a separation should be necessary for our mutual happiness, I would settle £150 on her, & £50 on her mother, who is a very worthy woman; but all this is only thinking aloud to you, & foreseeing that the difference of 57 and 22 [Sir William was in fact fifty-nine, Emma was twenty-four] may produce events; but indeed, hitherto her behaviour is irreproachable, but her temper, as you must know, unequal.

Sir William concludes by saying that he will visit England next spring. 'How we shall manage about Emma is another question.'

Meanwhile, events outside the Kingdom of the Two Sicilies were moving fast, while Naples slumbered idly. On 14 July 1789 in France, the people stormed the Bastille. Reports and rumours of bloodshed and carnage reached Naples. Maria Carolina feared for the safety of her elder sister, Marie-Antoinette. Ferdinand feared for the might of a fellow Bourbon family. In Naples, there were few signs of any republican or revolutionary movements at this date. When they came, it was to be from the ranks of young nobles, charged with altruistic fervour. The day had not yet come, either, for émigrés to leave France and flock to asylum in Naples.

The event of most significance in the Neapolitan calendar was the death of the Prime Minister, Caracciolo, in December 1789. This left the way clear for General Acton to assume the highest office, in addition to his ministerial posts. He moved into the Segretario, opposite the Royal Palace in Naples, a fine military building. From now on, he was without dispute the most important channel in the Kingdom

– through whom all petitioners, all politicians and all administrators must pass before they reached the ear of the King. England was of great importance to his appointment. Acton, though born in 1736, in Besançon in France, and educated abroad, traced his roots and a baronetcy which he was to inherit in 1791 to estates in Shropshire. He always had in mind retirement to that western part of England, and his policies betrayed the affinity he felt with England. While Caracciolo, like most Neapolitans, had seen his allegiance as being to the Head of the Bourbon House, the King of Spain, Acton wished to form an alliance by treaty with England.

The King did not notice the shift in Acton's policy-making. He had never personally had good relations with his father. Now that his brother, Charles, was King of Spain, matters were somewhat ameliorated. There was talk of His Catholic Majesty sending an ambassador to Naples – the last such had been withdrawn ten years before. No doubt Ferdinand felt vague pleasure, even wrote to urge such a step, but a resumption of relations with Spain would not much affect his Kingdom. As long as he had a gun in his hand and dogs to scent out game, he rarely questioned the government of the day.

Maria Carolina was less happy. Her allegiance was to her brother, Joseph, Emperor of Austria. With the rupture of relations between Naples and Spain, she had ensured that Naples was in fief to Austria. Her plan was for one of her elder daughters to marry their cousin, the Hereditary Prince of Austria. Acton had originally been her protégé, but recent events had shown her that he was not as malleable as she had thought. He had ceased to be attracted by her charms. They may not have had an affair, but she had certainly written him some very compromising letters. He had those as a defence against her, while she had no string by which to pull him about. He continued to work for the good of the Kingdom, and, as he saw it, this would be improved by alliance with England.

Sir William, naturally, was delighted by Acton's tentative moves in the direction of England. What did Emma make of it all, or did she not trouble her head with politics? One thing we can be sure of – she learnt from Sir William, that loyal subject, that the interests of the Hanover monarchy were paramount. Then she was preternaturally patriotic, as many exiles tend to become. They judge the faults of the country they inhabit against the virtues of the country of their origin. As she was not received at Court, nor was there any reason for her to visit the Segretario, where the business of government was conducted, she probably had only confused notions of what was happening.

We hear from Banks of the matters with which it was thought

Emma should occupy herself: botany in the English Garden, and the pursuit of intellectual information. 'Her mind, when once stored with instruction . . . will certainly last as long as she stays on this side heaven.'[1]

Emma was probably more agitated by a rumour which Banks repeated to Sir William, in October 1789: Charles Greville was thought to be going to pay a visit to Naples. Sir William was seriously discommoded by this information, false though it proved to be. 'It will be to me rather awkward, not that I have one grain of jealousy in my composition and Emma has good sense enough to see to whom she has the greater obligation.'[2] Emma was probably disappointed that the rumour came to nought. Few women can resist the spectacle of past and present lovers treating each other with suspicious courtesy.

When Greville's visit did not materialize, Emma continued happily to entertain visitors to the Embassy: whether with her Attitudes or singing or dancing with a tambourine was unimportant. The point was that with her performances she took a large burden of the duty of welcoming strangers off Sir William's bowed shoulders. By now, aged fifty-nine, he was feeling his years.

We have a most amusing account of the visit to Naples of the Lutheran minister and poet, Herder. He describes an odd occasion at the Palazzo Sessa, to which he was introduced by Tischbein. As a Protestant clergyman, he had been asked to marry an English couple at the British Embassy. Having officiated, he expected some fee to be paid in token of his services. The thrifty English saw no reason for it. Perhaps this experience at the Embassy coloured Herder's view of Emma's Attitudes. He watched with the Dowager Duchess of Weimar for some time as Emma went through her poses, and confessed himself a little bored. Perhaps this communicated itself to Emma; at any rate, all at once she began to concentrate all her wiles on Herder. No doubt the rest of the audience was highly entertained as she gestured lasciviously as a Bacchante in front of the embarrassed pastor. Medea threw the poisoned robe around Herder, her Creusa. The pastor wrote indignantly home to his wife, Caroline. She was nearly as straitlaced as he, and commiserated with the husband who was an idol to her but now the laughing-stock of Naples.[3] This is the first taste we have of Emma's anger and swift revenge when piqued. It was a trait in her which Sir William thought amusing, no more. It was to lead her into trouble later on.

In late 1789, an illustrious party arrived in Naples, more kith than kin to Sir William. Elizabeth Duchess of Argyll was the leader, and her health the reason for the trip. She was accompanied by her son, the Duke of Argyll, by her daughter and son-in-law, Lady Augusta and

Henry Clavering, and their baby daughter, and by another daughter, Lady Charlotte Campbell. The Duchess had, by a previous marriage to the Duke of Hamilton, links with Sir William, who was grandson of the third Duke.

In this old lady were the remains of the beauty which had wedded Miss Gunning, Irish granddaughter of an Irish peer, to two of Scotland's premier dukes. When she and her sister Maria (later Lady Coventry) came to London, the capital went wild. A militia was detailed off to escort the young ladies and keep them from harm when they went out to walk in the Mall. Crowds stood about the railings to watch them go by.

The beautiful Duchess was as good as she looked. Augusta, her daughter, was no beauty but had 'pretty colouring and a spirituelle expression'. She ran off with Clavering after a masquerade. Sensibly, the Duchess accepted the match. Another daughter, Elizabeth, was unhappily married to Lord Derby. Her mother was strong in support.

The Duchess had been ailing for some years. She was now fifty-six and seriously weak. Lady Augusta was pregnant with a second child. The party were thus fairly inactive. No doubt they spent more time taking airings in the Villa Reale or sitting in their *salone* with the windows open, 'snuffing up the air', than viewing the antiquities.

Sir William, as all others, admired the Duchess. He found, to his delighted surprise, that she looked very favourably on Emma. The Duchess may well have known something of Emma's liaison with Sir Harry from her son, the Duke of Hamilton, Sir Harry's great friend. Perhaps the Duchess saw something of herself when young in Emma, fêted as she was on every street corner. It seems that Emma confided to her friend some of her history. The Duchess is likely to have taken her part against Greville. In a famous legal action called the Douglas Case, a certain Archibald Hamilton claimed the Duchy of Hamilton, which the Duchess's eldest son held. Charles Greville took it into his head to support Archibald. She was not pleased.

With the Argylls in Naples this winter were Francis Lord Elcho and his wife. Again, there was a link between them and Sir William. Susan, Lady Elcho was granddaughter of the fourth Duke of Hamilton. No doubt Francis Lord Elcho, a noted agriculturalist, found much to interest him in the Neapolitan agronomy. More interestingly, Lady Elcho told a friend the next winter that 'altho' Sir W. H's public situation would not permit him to declare it, there was no doubt of his being married to Mrs H., that he had presented her to them on that ground, & that the behaviour of both parties confirm'd her belief of its being so.'

Was Sir William merely using the licence afforded to him by the

remote situation of Naples to *impose* his mistress on his friends? Or did
he, by now, have different intentions to those which he had outlined
to Greville in May 1789? Was he seriously thinking of marrying Emma?
Had he, in fact, married her, as Lady Elcho insists? Emma was to affirm
much later that she had been secretly married for two years before
the official date in 1791. No such marriage exists in the Register of
the English Church at Naples for this year. That Emma was now
considered presentable to everyone, we know from Lady Charlotte
Campbell's reminiscences of Emma at this date. However much the
Duchess, her mother, may have taken to Emma, she would not have
presented her to her young daughter if she had not judged it seemly.
So, leaving the vexed question of marriage alone, from the date of the
Duchess's visit and her sanction of Emma, Sir William took courage and
allowed the presumption that Emma was his wife to go unchallenged –
in Naples, that was. A French visitor in January 1790 wrote of Emma
that she was believed to be secretly married to Sir William.

In England, Sir William made sure that there were no illusions about
his relationship with Emma. We may take his word for it that he was
still *de iure* a widower, if *de facto* Naples believed him a married man
again. In April 1790, he told Banks:

> was I in a private station I should have no objection that Emma should
> share with me *le petit bout de vie qui me reste*, under the solemn covenant
> you allude to, as her behaviour in my house has been such for four years
> as to gain her universal esteem and approbation – but as I have no thoughts
> of relinquishing my Employment and whilst I am in a public character, I
> do not look upon myself at liberty to act as I please, and such a step I think
> wou'd be imprudent and might be attended with disagreeable circumstances
> – besides, as amidst other branches of natural History I have not neglected
> the study of the animal called Woman, I have found them subject to great
> changes according to circumstances and I do not like to try experiments
> at my time of life. In the way we live we give no Scandal, she with her
> Mother and I in my apartment, and we have a good Society. What is to be
> gained on my side? It is very natural for her to wish it, and to try to make
> people believe the business done, which I suppose has caused the report
> in England. I assure you that I approve of her so much that if I had been
> the person that had made her first go astray, I wou'd glory in giving her
> a public reparation, and I would do it openly, for indeed she has infinite
> merit and no Princess cou'd do the honors of her Palace with more care
> and dignity than she does those of my house; in short she is worthy of
> anything, and I have and will take care of her in proportion as I feel myself
> obliged to her. But as to the Solemn League, *Amplius Considerandum Est.*
> Now, my Dear Sir, I have more fairly delivered you my Confession than
> is usually done in this country, of which you may make any discreet use

you please. Those who ask out of mere curiosity I shou'd wish to remain in the dark.[4]

In May 1790, while the Argylls were still in Naples, Sir William wrote to his niece, Mary Dickenson. A proposed visit to England had to be postponed owing to 'the very unsettled state of Europe, which makes it improper for any of his Majesty's Ministers to think of stirring from his post at this moment'.

Sir William goes on:

I have deferred my journey until next Year. I do assure you I was truly sensible of your kindness & affection to me which you shew'd in your last letter, & which ought to have been answered long ago. Emma read it & wept over it. I do assure you that her goodness of heart is such, & her conduct has been such for four years she has resided with me, that I shoud not hesitate, was I in a private character, to put the law on the side of our Connection. But as I have experienced that of all Women in the World, the English are the most difficult to deal with abroad, I fear eternal tracasseries, was she to be placed above them here, & which must be the case, as a Minister's Wife, in every Country, takes place of every rank of Nobility.

As it is, many seek Emma's acquaintance, & we have the best company in Naples at our house. The Duchess of Argyle & that family doat upon Emma, & really she gains the heart of all who approach her. You would be surprised at her having learnt so much in 4 years. She is perfect Italian, begins to speak French tolerably, & sings certainly better than any English woman I ever heard. I have enlarg'd upon this subject because I thought you wished I shou'd . . . I can figure to myself your happiness in the family way . . .[5]

A rather amusing story about Mrs Cadogan – and there are few enough stories, amusing or not, about her – may be attached to the Argylls' visit to Naples. That old trickster, Angelo, was told it by a duke ('to whom I made my obeisance on lately meeting him in Bond Street'). In this duke we may see the Duchess's son.

When I was at Naples, Sir William Hamilton had a casino at Portici, some little distance from Mount Vesuvius, as he was in the habit of approaching the crater as near as he could venture. He often took up his residence there expressly for that purpose, and was engaged on one occasion that had particularly attracted his attention. I was left alone to dine with Lady Hamilton and her mother, who had followed her from England. In the course of conversation, after dinner, when speaking of the excellence of the lacryma christi, a famous Italian wine, the mother ejaculated, 'Oh! as how I had but some English gin here!' The duke, who luckily had taken some with him, directly forwarded his servant to his hotel at Naples for it. At his return,

the madre, delighted with the vero gusto, by her frequent tasting did not a
little convince his Grace of the improvement the juniper berry had upon the
vulgar tongue (in which she particularly excelled), and the glass increasing,
she said, 'she had not never enjoyed the good creature [gin] since she left
England; it was far betterer than all your outlandish wines.'[6]

In early 1790, there was another interesting visitor to Naples. This
was the Comte d'Espinchal, who fled France when the disturbances
first arose. He came to Naples to stay with a friend, the Baron de Salis.
Since 1782, this last had been organizing the shambling orders of the
Neapolitan military.

The Comte adored Naples. It was said of him, by Mme Vigée-Le
Brun when he lived in Paris, that there was no one who could reap so
much enjoyment from the daily doings of the city, nor be so perpetually
busy all day long doing nothing. At Naples he scampered in and out of
the French Ambassador's box at the opera, visited a clutch of friends
in a morning, and made time to see Emma perform her Attitudes and
dance a tarantella all in one day.

He gives us an interesting glimpse of the milieu in which the Attitudes
were performed. M. le Baron de Salis gave a dinner on 28 January:

The company was . . . almost entirely composed of foreigners . . . The
Duchesse de Guiche and the Duchess of Nivenheim sang Italian airs to
our great pleasure. Mme Hart, English, superbly tall and with a heavenly
figure, has been living for several years with the chevalier Hamilton, the
English Minister, to whom she is believed to be secretly married. She also
sang at this concert with infinite taste. After an excellent repast . . . there
was dancing till the theatre began. I much enjoyed watching a very free
and voluptuous dance, having something of the Spanish fandango about
it, called the Tarentella. The misses Amici, Neapolitan bourgeoises, and
extremely pretty, danced it marvellously, but Mme Hart added a volupté,
a grace which would set on fire the coldest and most insensible man. This
Mme Hart, who is one of the most beautiful creatures I have seen, is of
obscure origin. Nobody knows from what state the chevalier Hamilton has
plucked her. Apparently, it is to please her benefactor, a great Lover of the
arts and of antiquity, that Mme Hart has learnt to execute various attitudes.
She dresses in Greek or Roman style, adorns herself with flowers or covers
herself with a veil, and thus attired gives a living spectacle of masterpieces
of the most celebrated artists of antiquity. She is very obliging and gave
a performance to a little group of us. You have to have seen her to
conceive to what degree this lovely figure enabled us to enjoy the charms
of illusion. If I were the chevalier Hamilton, I would review all Olympus;
I would see often Hebe and Venus and the Graces, sometimes Juno, very
rarely Minerva. To vary my pleasures, a rich boudoir would offer me an

impassioned and tender Cleopatra welcoming Mark Antony and sometimes a woodland cabin would show Alcibiades frolicking with Glycera.[7]

What must be noted here is the fact that the figures Emma chose to represent were not, in their statuesque form, dressed in a *chiton* or *peplos*. Venus or Aphrodite was draped about only on her hips. Statues or paintings of Hebe and the Graces show more flesh than drapery. The erotic quality of these Attitudes, many of which were concerned with sexual anecdotes of antiquity, is thus shrouded in Emma's shawls and draperies. Let there be no mistake: the gentlemen who saw her perform were busily imagining her naked. But only to Sir William did she show her 'beautys'.

D'Espinchal's account of the tarantella as danced by Emma is interesting. This is a dance of Sicilian origin, which is accompanied by beating of the tambourine. Catherine Hamilton had her maid sing Sicilian songs to Dr Burney in 1770.[8] While the Attitudes exhibited Emma's classical, noble aspects, the tarantella was a peasants' dance, a heady, intoxicating experience for performers and audience.

With the winter of 1790, the celebrated artist Mme Vigée-Le Brun came to Naples to add to the catalogue of paintings of Emma. She came from Rome to search out commissions, and her first client was the musical Skavronsky, who wished her to paint his wife. It is said of Mme Skavronsky that she never moved from a day bed where she lay, nor ever was seen in anything but an undress, or chemise. When asked by her poor husband if she would not put on some of the jewels with which both he and her lover uncle, Prince Potemkin, loaded her, she only sighed and said, 'What is the use? I see no point.' To lull her to sleep at the end of her tiring day, a servant girl crouched at the foot of her bed and told her the same story time without number.

On the second day of painting Mme Skavronsky, Mme Vigée-Le Brun was interrupted by the tall, urbane figure of Sir William Hamilton. He had heard that she was in Naples. Could he persuade her instantly to paint Emma for him? Vigée-Le Brun did not yield to this determined onslaught. Only after completing the Skavronsky commission did she paint Emma – in all, four times. For Sir William she painted a bust of Emma as a turbaned Sibyl. The full-length version she painted for the Duc de Brissac. Following his murder in 1792, she took this painting about with her through Europe to advertise her talents. 'She calls [it] her Masterpiece,' Sir William noted in 1801.[9]

Vigée-Le Brun also painted a very kittenish picture of Emma as a Bacchante *couchée*. Emma lies on a tiger-skin, like Elinor Glyn. The painter notes in her memoirs that Emma had 'a great quantity of beautiful chestnut hair which could cover her entirely and as a bacchante, with her hair spread out, she was admirable.' In the other picture of Emma as a Bacchante, she dances with a tambourine before Vesuvius. The *Herculaneum Dancers* are the model for this picture, that charming frieze only a few inches long but one of the finest objects from Herculaneum. In Vigée-Le Brun's painting, the treatment of Emma's hair and her russet colouring, the Pompeian tints of her dress and of the background, combine to make this a most evocative portrait of Emma at this date.

Vigée-Le Brun tells us, falsely, in her *Souvenirs*, that it was she who was responsible for persuading Emma to wear Grecian clothes – she says the Attitudes were at first marred by Emma's modern dress. As we know, Goethe had seen Emma in a Greek tunic in 1787. However, another story – concerning Emma's vulgarity in dress – may have some basis. Vigée-Le Brun was painting Emma at Caserta, and two ladies visiting the Hamiltons, the Princesse de Monaco and the Duchesse de Fleury, sat solemnly watching her all morning. All were in transports over Emma's beauty. She wore only the thin tunic which she has on in the Bacchante *couchée* portrait. The luncheon hour came and the ladies, who were all expected for the meal, waited while Emma changed. When she re-entered the salon she was so hideously dressed – in her own fashionable clothes – that none of the ladies at first realized who she was.

The Bacchante *couchée* pose is not unlike that of Romney's *Calypso*, which he sold to the Prince of Wales. For all Vigée-Le Brun's vaunted originality, she was no great innovator where Emma was concerned. Vigée-Le Brun, however, was well satisfied, especially with the *Sibyl*.

Seventeen-ninety-one dawned, and matters were soon on a very different footing from when Sir William had written to Greville that he would not marry Emma. Plans were being made for the Hamilton ménage to visit London while the Royal Family of Naples visited Austria.

On 10 February 1790, Maria Carolina's brother, the Emperor Joseph, had died, leaving a tattered Empire. Another brother, the Grand Duke of Tuscany, succeeded Joseph as Leopold II. Eight days later, the Princess of Württemburg, Leopold's daughter-in-law and new Crown Princess of Austria, died. With these changes, there came more, beneficial for the Neapolitan Bourbons. It was decided that Francis, the Crown Prince, should now marry Maria Theresa, the eldest Princess of Naples. His younger brother, Ferdinand, the new Grand Duke of Tuscany, was to marry her younger sister, Luisa. Maria Carolina was delighted with these engagements, which promised well for the future of Naples. The two weddings were to take place in Vienna. At the same time, Francis, the Hereditary Prince of the Two Sicilies and Duke of Calabria, was to exchange vows with but not formally marry the Emperor Leopold's eldest daughter, the Archduchess Maria Clementina. As they were only fourteen, the marriage was to take place later.

Prince Ruspoli, the Austrian Ambassador to Naples, delivered the formal demands for the hands of the two Neapolitan Princesses on 12 August 1790, accompanied by bejewelled portraits of the Archdukes. Maria Theresa was fortunately unaware that her fiancé, Francis, spat blood. She was prepared to 'love him passionately', and hoped only to emulate Philemon and Baucis in the length of her married life. Luisa was 'completely transformed' by her 'happiness'. Her mother judged she would be 'more absent-minded, less deeply attached but more cheerful' than her sister. Neither of them had pretensions to beauty. On the other hand, they had been taught drawing by Angelica Kauffmann, Hackert and Tischbein, and had other accomplishments.

Paisiello conducted the choir in the Royal Chapel for the betrothal ceremony. Pardons were liberally distributed among the people, and grants made to unmarried girls and families in need. The Kingdom was appropriately cheerful.

On 21 August 1790, the Royal Family sailed for Trieste and Vienna, amid reproaches from the *lazzaroni*, who begged them to return soon. After the pomp and ceremony of the weddings, the Neapolitan Royal party went on to Frankfurt for Leopold's coronation as Emperor, and to Pressburg for his coronation as King of Hungary. With a visit to the Pope at Rome, the Royal party did not return to Naples till March 1791.

Sir William waited only for the King and Queen to return to their capital before he embarked on his journey to England. In January 1791 Emma had written to Greville, and the knell of doom had sounded for any hopes he might have had that marriage between her and his uncle was not to be. She writes first, as if to tantalize him, of her sense of sadness at the Duchess of Argyll's death. 'I never had such a friend as her, & that you will know when I see you & recount to you all the acts of kindness she shew'd to me; for they where two good & numerous to describe in a letter . . .' The Duchess had died on 29 December 1790, on her return to Argyll House in London. Her coffin was taken to Argyll in Scotland in a hearse pulled by six horses and attended by a quantity of mourning coaches. Her husband and daughters were too afflicted by their loss to attend the sad procession northwards.

Emma then goes on to reproach Greville for suggesting that, for the sake of the conventions, she and Sir William should lodge separately when in London.

You need not be affraid for me in England. We come for a short time, &
that time but be occupied in business, & to take our last leave. I don't wish
to atract notice. I wish to be an example of good conduct. & to show the
world that a pretty woman is not allways a fool. All my ambition is to make
Sir William happy, & you will see he is so. As to our separating houses, we
can't do it, or why should we? You can't think 2 people that has lived five
years with all the domestic happiness that's possible, can seperate, & those 2
persons, that knows no other comfort but in each other's company, which
is the case I assure you with ous, tho' you bachelors don't understand it.
But you can't imaggine 2 houses must seperate ous. No, it can't be, and
that you will be a judge of, when you see us. We will lett you into our
plans & secretts.

Next, Emma details a ball of great dimensions given at the Palazzo
Sessa. 'Sir William will lett you know on what a footing we are here
[i.e. that they were as good as married]. I had near four hundred persons,
all the foreign ministers & their wives, all the first ladies of fashion,
foreyners & neapolitans, our house was full in every room.'

Sir William gave great thought to Emma's appearance. Following
his judgement that simplicity was most effective, he dressed her in
white satin, with no colour about her but her hair and rosy cheeks.
She was without powder, as it was the first 'great assembly' they had
given. 'All the ladies strove to outdo one another in dress and jewels,
but Sir William said I was the finest jewel amongst them.' To mark
the occasion, which seems to have been Emma's official introduction
into the Neapolitan social whirl, Sir William had 'the Banti', the tenor
Casacelli and two others to sing. Since that date, the Palazzo Sessa had
become the epicentre of social life. 'Every night our house is open to
small partys of fifty or sixty men & women. We have musick, tea etc.
etc. & we have a great adition lately to our party, we have a new Spanish
ambassador & his wife & we as made a great frendship & we are allways
together. She is charming.'

Emma ends her letter with a moving coda, and with a certain distant
dignity towards her former lover.

Think then after what Sir Wm. as done for me if I should not be the horrid
wretch in the world not to be exemplary towards him. Endead I will do all I
can to render him happy . . . I shall allways esteem you for your relationship
to Sir Wm. & haveing been the means of me knowing him. As to Sir W. I
confess to you I doat on him nor I never can have any other person but
him. This confession will please you I know . . . Emma.[10]

Hardly had Greville received this blithe missive than his friend

Heneage Legge dispatched a letter to confirm his worst forebodings. First Legge describes the Elchos' assumption of a marriage between Emma and Sir William; then he notes the appalling effrontery with which Sir William proposed Emma as nurse and companion to Mrs Legge. Mrs Legge 'is not over-scrupulous in her manners and sentiments beyond the usual forms establish'd by the rules of society in her own country', Legge informed Greville stiffly. However, 'as she was not particularly inform'd of any change in Mrs H's situation, she had no reason to think her present different from her former line of life, & therefore could not quite reconcile it to her feelings to accept these offers of friendship & service, tho' there was no doubt of their being kindly intended'.

As a result of her stiffness, Mrs Legge saw little of Sir William. Heneage was not so nice in his notions, and went to the Palazzo Sessa a good deal. His report of the ménage there is as full as it is interesting. This is the last glimpse we catch of the five-year liaison which had proved so happy that marriage was now to follow.

Let us quote it in full:

The language of both parties, who always spoke in the plural number – we, us & ours – stagger'd me at first, but soon made me determine to speak openly to him on the subject, when he assur'd me, what I confess I was most happy to hear, that he was not married; but flung out some hints of doing justice to her good behaviour, if his public situation did not forbid him to consider himself an independent man. Her influence over him exceeds all belief; his attachment exceeds admiration, it is perfect dotage. She gives everybody to understand that he is now going to England to sollicit the K's consent to marry her, & that on her return she shall appear as Ly H. She says it is impossible to continue in her present dubious state, which exposes her to frequent slight & mortification; & his whole thought, happiness & comfort seems so center'd in her presence, that if she should refuse to return on other terms, I am confident she will gain her point, against which it is the duty of every friend to strengthen his mind as much as possible; & she will be satisfied with no argument but the King's absolute refusal of his approbation. Her talents & powers of amusing are very wonderfull; her voice is very fine, but she does not sing with great taste, & Aprili says she has not a good ear; her attitudes are beyond description beautiful and striking, & I think you will find her figure much improved since you last saw her. *They* say they shall be in London by the latter end of May, that their stay in England will be as short as possible, & that, having settled his affairs, he is determin'd never to return. She is much visited here by ladies of the highest rank, & many of the *Corps diplomatique*; does the honours of his house with great attention & desire to please, but wants a little refinement of manners, in which, in the course of six years, I wonder she has not made greater progress. I have all along told her she could never change her situation for the better, & that she was a happier woman as Mrs H. than she would be as Ly H., when, more reserved behaviour being necessary, she would be depriv'd of half her amusements, & must no longer sing those comic parts which tend so much to the entertainment of herself & her friends. She does not accede to that doctrine, & unless great care is taken to prevent it I am clear she will in some unguarded hour work upon his empassion'd mind, & effect her design of becoming your aunt. He tells me he has made ample provision for her, in which he is certainly right, and with that she ought to be content. It must be unnecessary for me to caution you against ever telling them that I wrote to you on this subject, nor should I have done it, if I had not been sure that you are not apprised of the state they are in, & the unbounded influence she has gain'd over him & all that belongs to him.

Well, was it a case of Chorus Girl Weds Elderly Aristocrat? Had Emma's beauty and youthful zest prevailed over Sir William's notion of what was due to his rank and family? We can be fairly certain that Emma had been, as Sir William reported in 1789, eager for the marriage for some time. There was, however, no one else in Naples or London connected intimately enough with the couple that they could exercise much sway one way or the other. Mrs Cadogan, who was on excellent terms with Sir William – they were probably not far removed in age from each other – no doubt wished for the match. Greville, as probably, disliked the idea. There was always the threat of an heir to displace him, although Sir William's first marriage had proved fruitless. From Emma's letter of January 1791, we may judge Greville had written to point out some imaginary objections she should have to the match. Sir William's relations in England perhaps did not relish the idea of welcoming Emma into their ranks, but few of them had influence over him. The King and Queen of Naples had no direct jurisdiction over the British Minister. In fact, the sole master of Sir William's fate was His Britannic Majesty, and to him Sir William was returning to beg his permission to the marriage. So, in effect, Sir William made up his mind to marry Emma, uninfluenced by any considerations but those of his own comfort and happiness.

There were factors that played a part in his decision, if they were not crucial. The appointment of Sir William Eden to succeed Sir James Graham as Ambassador to Spain had been a blow. Sir William had specially written to the Foreign Secretary, to plead his own case for promotion to Spain; Sir James, after all, had gone to the more important Court from Naples. The fact that he was passed over in favour of Eden did not, perhaps, surprise Sir William. It was an end to his hopes of promotion, however, and set the Minister at last to think seriously of spending the rest of his life in Naples. What could be more agreeable than to have Emma at his side for that span?

Lastly Sir William was an honourable man. He saw the justice of Emma's wish to gain security of tenure by marriage. Later this year he gave to Lady Spencer a frank account of his decision to marry Emma.

> A man of 60 intending to marry a beautifull young Woman of 24 [Emma was 26] and whose character at her first outset of life will not bear a severe scrutiny, seems to be a very imprudent step, and so it certainly would be 99 times in 100, but I flatter myself I am not deceived in Emma's present character – We have lived together five years and a half, and not a day passes without her having testified her true repentance for the past.

In her position as Sir William's mistress, she has 'naturally been subject to frequent mortifications . . . her sensibility is so great that her health has been often affected by it. In short', Sir William finished, 'I have at length consented to take off these difficulties, and as the world calls it make an honest Woman of her.'

As if he felt dissatisfied with this long explanation, Sir William added, 'I do assure your Ladyship that Emma is out of the common line.'[11]

CHAPTER NINE

English Leave

The Hamilton clan in London were up in arms about Sir William's rumoured intentions towards Emma. By 8 February 1791 Greville's brother Warwick had heard that Sir William was to be in London in April or May. His mother, the Dowager Countess, hoped from this that 'the Reports' of her brother's marriage were not true. Emma was perhaps unlucky in her opposition. Apart from the strange rupture of relations between the Dowager Countess and her Lord, there was little of scandal in the Cathcart, Stormont and Greville annals. Sorrow, with childbirth deaths and early fatalities, there was in plenty. Only the previous December, Sir William's niece, the Duchess of Atholl, had died while pregnant. Though news of a wedding is generally held to offset the pain of a funeral, the Hamilton clan were not minded to think so on this occasion.

While they prognosticated and ruminated in London, 22 April 1791 found Sir William and Emma, with Mrs Cadogan as chaperone, in Venice. Sir William had no doubt thought fit to turn aside from the customary route via Turin and over the Alps, that Emma might see this legendary city. One wonders if she adopted the stately dress worn by Venetians and foreigners alike. The Marchesa di Solari describes it. The ladies wore a gown of rich black velvet, with a long train to the skirt and coloured body and sleeves. A black silk veil covered the head and shoulders; crossed about the neck and waist, and trimmed with lace, it fell tastefully behind on the black skirt. It was 'very becoming when properly put on',[1] the Marchesa notes, and Emma, with her fresh complexion and bright hair, would have looked enchanting.

Sir William had not waited for the King and Queen to arrive in Naples, but had met them and formally taken leave of them at Florence. He had also had the satisfaction of renewing his acquaintance with the Emperor, Maria Carolina's brother Leopold and formerly Grand Duke of Tuscany. All had treated him with gratifying regard.

In Venice, he moved in no less interesting circles, and here Emma was of the party. Charles Philippe Comte D'Artois, afterwards Charles X, was in the lagoon Republic with a large party of French émigrés. Many of them were known to Sir William from visits to Naples, among them the Marquis de Vaudreuil and the Polignacs. The Duchesse de

Polignac had been a great favourite of Marie-Antoinette's, though this 'did not prevent their being amongst the first to forsake the royal family and emigrate' (Morrison).

Leaving the mists and the émigré population of Venice to drift where they would, the Hamilton party pressed on to Brussels. Greville had been asked to leave word here of where he had found them joint lodgings in London. With good reason Greville may have ground his teeth and stabbed his pen point into the paper as he wrote of the success of his mission. It was not a task tactfully entrusted to him. At Brussels, too, Sir William found a blunt letter from his niece, Mary Dickenson, asking his intentions.

On 16 May, Nerot's Hotel in King Street saw the arrival of our party. It had been Sir William's invariable custom, on his leaves in England, to proceed direct to one or other of his nieces' salons and there take up the silken cords of London holiday. On this occasion, his relations had some time to wait before they saw him.

There was an amusing letter from an old schoolfriend, the Earl-Bishop. This eccentric milord was an indefatigable traveller. An Anglican bishop, he once represented himself as a Catholic divine at the gates of some solitary convent in Italy; there he was feasted, and revered, and escaped without the truth coming out. The many Hotels Bristol in Italy and Switzerland commemorate other laical experiences. In Siena, he once threw, from his hotel room, a tureen of steaming pasta over an advancing procession of the Host. On occasion, he dressed in a mixture of purple and gold of his own devising, sometimes in a coloured silk coat and a white hat. There was never an episcopal sign about him, nor 'in his Conversation the least degree of gravity'. Sir William was to remark in 1795, 'Wherever he goes he carries mischief with him.'

In 1791, for a miracle, he was in Ireland, and extremely keen that Sir William and Emma should visit him there. He wrote from Ballyscullin on 25 May that he would send a warrant for his friend if he thought it would bring him.

> You shall have musick every day or no day, you shall see the Giant's Causeway by sea & by land, you shall see extinguished volcanoes & almost burning ones, you shall have grouse-shooting or not as you please, you shall fish on salt water or fresh just as you like best, I will meet you where you please, & bring you to the most romantick & perhaps the most sublime scenery you ever saw; only come, & do not disappoint yr old friend & school-fellow.

Sir William did not avail himself of this delightful invitation. He was playing a strange game in London. His sister, Elizabeth, saw him and remarked that he looked thin and stooped, 'but just in his usual Spirits, & wherever He Is, the Life of the Company'.

'His *Lady* is *not* his Wife', Lady Frances Harpur informed Mary Dickenson with relief. Sir William told the Dowager Countess Warwick that 'being a Publick Character at Naples, He did not think it Right to marry Mrs Hart; from respect to his King'. Lady Warwick said that was very proper, but added that she hoped he thought there was 'something owing to Yourself!'

'Oh! as to that,' Sir William answered, 'the first object is to be Happy.' Then 'in raptures' he expatiated on 'the Charms, Talents & Accomplishments of Mrs H & said she was the Happiness of his Life'. However, he was *not* married.

The Dowager Countess was told that Emma had 'never appeared in his Liveries, had her own Carriage & separate Establishment; but at Naples is well received'. Lady Frances told Mary that Emma was 'always at Sr W. Hamilton's Parties, & visited by English ladies, of Character, at Naples; who Here cannot take notice of Her; but she was always introduced as Mrs Hart'.

Sir William and Emma were by now ensconced in lodgings in Somerset Street. 'She is in a Manner seen by all who visit Sr Wm. The Mother sits in a Corner of the Room, & does not take any part in the Conversation.'

What are we to make of Sir William's denial? We know from Legge's letter to Greville of January that 'she gives everybody to understand that he is now going to England to sollicit the K's consent to marry her . . . she will be satisfied with no argument but the King's absolute refusal of his approbation.' Sir William certainly had much business to do with his Welsh estate to attend to in London. 'He has not a Moment to Himself . . . Several Persons from Wales . . . being in Town.' Transaction of this business was the purpose for which he had requested this leave. Had no agreement between himself and Emma about marriage been reached? Or was he merely fending off his inquisitive relations till he had had audience with the King? (Emma must have been on tenterhooks, waiting for that interview.) Certainly, in May there were strong doubts, if not on Sir William's part, whether a marriage would take place.

While Sir William dealt with Welsh business, Emma had gone at once to her dear Romney at Cavendish Square. Hayley describes the elevating effect her visits had on the artist's 'sinking spirits'. 'The fair Emma . . . surprised him by an early visit one morning in a Turkish habit, and attended by Sir William Hamilton. Romney had ever treated her with the tenderness of a father, which she acknowledged on this occasion with tears of lively gratitude, in announcing to him her splendid prospect of being soon married to Sir William, and of attending him to the Court of Naples. The joy of a father, in the brilliant marriage of a favourite daughter, could hardly exceed that of my friend on this occasion.'

Sir William had come with Emma for a purpose. On 2 June at '½ past 9' Emma returned to the artist's studio for the first of a series of sittings, thirty-six in all, which were to occupy her and Romney till September. Several paintings resulted. By 19 June the Prince of Wales had met Emma and commissioned two paintings of her, one as Calypso, stretched in a chrysanthemum tunic before a cave. The Calypso is now at Waddesdon and cast into the shade by Reynolds' portrait of Elizabeth Linley or Sheridan as St Cecilia which hangs next to it. Emma does not look markedly older or different from her earlier portraits by Romney. A charming Bacchante where Emma, hair and eyes wild, gleefully holds a Greek vase aloft, also dates from this summer. 'I dedicate my time to this charming Lady,' Romney wrote on 7 July. 'They are very much hurried at present, as everything is going on for their speedy marriage, and all the world following her, and talking of her.'

Romney painted her, during June and July, as Joan of Arc. This was to hang in Alderman Boydell's Shakespeare Gallery, as was a Constance which he never began. This volume of projects shows how eager Romney was for Emma's company, how quick was his nervous disposition to find pretexts on which to keep her soothing presence by him. As Emma was undoubtedly the most talked of woman in London this hot summer, there was also kudos and a hope of high prices being paid for likenesses of her. 'At present, and the greatest part of the summer,' he wrote to Hayley contentedly, 'I shall be engaged in painting pictures from the divine lady. I cannot give her any other epithet, for I think her superior to all womankind.'

Romney relaxed his rule of walks and frugal suppers to dine at Somerset Street with Emma and Sir William three times during July and August. On hearing Emma sing from Paisiello's Nina, he was so moved, he wanted to rush down to Eartham and bring Hayley back to hear it. He found her acting 'simple, grand, terrible, and pathetic'. 'The whole company were in an agony of sorrow.'

There were visits outside London to be made during the sultry month of August. In June Sir William had not been eager to pay a visit to Warwick Castle, perhaps from loyalty to Charles Greville, who was now on permanent bad terms with his brother. He spoke of visiting Mary Dickenson and her John in Derbyshire in August, and in July wrote to confirm this plan. 'Sir W. H. & E. H. appearing to be separate must be so in your house, & I mean to bring with me a man & a maid-servant.' Emma, he mentioned, was by herself a good deal, as he was so often and so urgently required at various soirées. He still expressed doubts about marriage. 'Sir W. H. is one thing, & the King's Minister at Naples, another.' This was no polite parleying. Sir William was generally frank with his niece, and was by now convinced that she was no enemy to Emma. He was evidently still in two minds about the wisdom of remarriage. Emma, no doubt unaware of this, wrote to thank Mrs Dickenson for her invitation. She had been busy match-making on behalf of Eliza, Mr Dickenson's sister, while her own future was still in doubt. A gentleman named the Chevalier Palombi was in the offing, and Emma had seen him. He would be with the Dickensons the following week, and she and Sir William would follow. 'I hope to shew you that you have not pleaded in a Wrong Cause,' Emma wrote. 'In short, Madam, I am the happiest Woman in the World!'

The visit to Taxal in Derbyshire passed off well. Emma no doubt made herself agreeable to Louisa, the Dickensons' four-year-old daughter. Lady Frances Harpur wrote to Mary on 9 August, saying she was glad Mary had seen Sir William '& had time for Conversation, – tho' probably the *Lady* was in the way', she added cattily. Mr Dickenson at least, did not think so, as will transpire. 'I believe it likely she may be our Aunt,' Lady Frances continued. 'My Mother in her last seemed to fear it; do you think it likely; I *own I think not*; for making a *Shew* of Her *Graces & Person to all his acquaintance* in *Town*, does not appear a *preliminary for Marriage*.' Lady Warwick had perhaps heard rumours from Naples, where it was commonly believed that Sir William and Emma were married, but secretly.

Sir William and Emma continued to keep his concerned relations guessing, by the very openness of their association. From Derbyshire, they proceeded to Herefordshire to visit the connoisseur Payne Knight, to Wiltshire, to Henley and back to London via Twickenham. Their host in Wiltshire was Sir William's eccentric kinsman, William Beckford, their lodging his mansion, Fonthill. He was recently returned from ten years' exile, in Portugal and France, where he had lived like a king, sublimely uninterested in the real King's fortunes.

The great jet d'eau just in front of my salle à manger window, which window is almost as large as that of a Cathedral . . . I waved my wand and behold – a garden as green as in the month of May – full of wallflowers and Larustine, primroses and violets started up on the Terrace . . . What care I for Aristocrates or Democrites? I am an – Autocrate – determined to make the most of every situation . . .

He had not as yet begun to build his celebrated tower or abbey at Fonthill. However, he had sixteen or eighteen people to keep the beautiful walks in the garden in order, 'three Men cooks and a confectioner', ten men, including his pet dwarf named Perro, behind the chairs to wait on guests. There was a 'large, choice, and costly library' for Sir William's pleasure, 'one apartment filled up wholly in the Turkish style with large mirrors, ottomans and divans . . . Sideboards and cabinets, the work of the best artists, and combinations of the more precious metals with jewellery, and the most expensive and dazzling objects, met the view on all sides.' If the situation of Fonthill Splendens was not perfect, 'erected', as it was, 'on the margin of a standing piece of water at the bottom of a hill clothed in wood', this was soon forgotten by all but its owner. Beckford, however, ruminated on the ill effects of the site of the house till discontent prevailed and he caused the whole to be sacrificed in 1801.

From Fonthill Sir William and Emma went to Bath. Sir William wished to see his old friend Georgina Dowager Countess Spencer. She had decided it would be better if she did not meet Emma, and had gone off to Longleat. From here she wrote to ask him his intentions, which prompted his letter already quoted.[2]

Bath was the fashionable place to be in August. They had reached the city 'filled with Workmen, dust & lime' by 10 August, as an entry in Lady Elizabeth Foster's diary makes clear. Lady Elizabeth was the delightfully pretty daughter of Sir William's old friend, the Earl-Bishop. Separated from her Irish husband, she was closest friend of Georgiana Duchess of Devonshire, and lived much at Devonshire House. Together, these beauties set the town by its ears, despite sorrowful protests from Lady Spencer, Georgiana's mother. They were at present in Bath to nurse Georgiana's sister, Harriet Lady Duncannon. The Duchess of Devonshire was also resting after having given birth, to the grim pleasure of her spouse, to the Marquess of Hartington. This noble infant had a 'separate establishment' outside Bath, where his mother visited each day. Her other children, young Georgiana and Harriet, were with her in Bath, under the excellent supervision of Miss Sarah or 'Selina' Trimmer. The Duke stayed away. (When he was betrothed to the dazzling Lady Georgiana Spencer, Mary Hamilton found her 'very *chatty*', but 'not one word spoke the Duke to his betrothed, nor did one smile grace his dull visage.')

If Lady Spencer did not wish to meet Emma, the Duchess of

Devonshire and Lady Betty had no qualms. The latter confided her impressions to her journal.

> Having just seen the celebrated Mrs Hart, who by an extraordinary talent has, as Lord Charlemont says, found out a new source of pleasure to mankind, I cannot forbear mentioning the impression which she made upon me. She was introduced last night to the Duchess of Devonshire by Sir W. Hamilton. She appeared to be a very handsome Woman, but coarse and vulgar. She sung, and her countenance lightened up – her *Buffo* songs were inimitable from the expression and vivacity with which they were sung. Her serious singing appeared to me not good – her voice is strong, she is well taught, yet has a forced expression and has neither softness nor tenderness. Her voice wants flexibility.
>
> This morning she was to show her attitudes. She came, and her appearance was more striking than I can describe, or could have imagined. She was draped exactly like a Grecian statue, her chemise of white muslin was exactly in that form, her sash in the antique manner, her fine black hair flowing over her shoulders. It was a Helena, Cassandra or Andromache, no Grecian or Trojan Princess could have had a more perfect or more commanding form. Her attitudes, which she performed with the help alone of two shawls, were varied – every one was perfect – everything she did was just and beautiful. She then sung and acted the mad scene in *Nina* – this was good, but I think chiefly owing to her beautiful action and attitudes – her singing except in the *Buffo* is always in my mind a secondary talent and performance –
>
> In the evening she came again but we ought to have closed with the morning. She looked very handsome certainly, and she was better draped than the first evening, but her conversation, though perfectly good-natured and unaffected, was uninteresting, and her pronunciation very vulgar. In short, Lord Bristol's remark seems to me so just a one that I must end with it: 'Take her as anything but Mrs Hart and she is a superior being – as herself she is always vulgar.'
>
> I must however add, as an excuse for that vulgarity and as a further proof of the superiority of her talents that have burst forth in spite of these disadvantages, that Mrs Hart was born and lived in the lowest situation till the age of 19, and since that in no higher one than the mistress of Sir W. Hamilton.

Whatever Lady Elizabeth and her father thought of Emma, one of the Devonshire clan was pleased with her. Some years later, when the Duchess of Devonshire was in Naples, she wrote to her daughter, Georgiana, to say she was seeing a good deal of her 'old friend, Lady Hamilton'. Perhaps Emma and young Lady Georgiana found a common interest in charity. When some poor children were seen outside the Devonshires' lodgings in Bath, Fanny Burney writes, Lady

Georgiana had to be forcibly restrained from asking them all up and giving them a nourishing tea. Her grandmother persuaded her to be content with showering coins down on the startled idlers.

Some time in August, Sir William took Emma on a tour of Strawberry Hill, the gothic mansion belonging to Horace Walpole. Their names are recorded in the Visitors' Book. A housekeeper stood by while visitors gaped. On this occasion, the visitors were at ease with the collection, for Sir William had collected and sent to his old friend quite a few of the exhibits on show.

On 17 August, Walpole wrote some lines on Emma into his diary 'on Mrs Harte, Sir William's pantomime mistress, or wife, who acts all the antique statues in an Indian shawl . . .' People went mad about her wonderful expression, 'Which I do not conceive; so few antique statues having any expression at all, nor being designed to have it'. Walpole did Emma's rapturous critics the courtesy of admitting he had not as yet seen Emma perform her Attitudes. This crusty old gentleman succumbed like all others to Emma's charms when he met her at the Duke of Queensberry's villa at Richmond. No Attitudes were performed, but he admired enormously the acting which accompanied her *Nina*. When the Hamiltons had returned to Naples, Sir William wrote to Walpole: 'You can not imagine how delighted Ly H. was in having gained your approbation in England.'[3]

One more journey which Emma and Sir William made together before they returned to London was to Park Place, near Henley. Here Sir William grew up; here old friends, the Conways, now lived. Anne Damer was daughter of the house, though not present on this occasion. Emma 'delighted' old General Conway and his wife, Lady Ailesbury, at their home, one of the finest seats in England, with her Attitudes – 'Such consummate art in the management of her draperies' did she display. Lady Ailesbury thought her taste in ordinary dress 'atrocious', however. One can picture the faintly odd scene at this, the last of the bridal visits. Lady Ailesbury sits, doing the worsted work for which she was famed. General Conway dozes in a chair while Emma prances about the room, and Sir William looks on benignly. Sir William and Emma returned to London on 16 August.

At some point during the visit to London, Mrs Cadogan made an expedition to Manchester. She went to see little Emma, Emma Carew as she was now known, presumably to see that she was well settled and lacked for nothing. Miss Carew, nine years old now, must have been surprised by the appearance of this elderly visitor, never dreaming it was her grandmother. Mrs Cadogan 'saw her situated to her satisfaction', Greville tells us. Miss Carew remained where she was, and the only

record of Mrs Cadogan's visit lies in the child's accounts. 'Filligree box
for Mrs Hart by order of Mrs Cadogan ... £2. 12s 6d'. Inevitably
the visit made the child 'evidently more anxious'. It was an unhappy
situation. Did her daughter's circumstances worry Emma? Or was she
too much taken up by the still undecided question of marriage?

On 22 August Romney was made happy by a visit from Emma. He
had been hoping since the sixteenth for this treat, but had hardly dared
expect it. Before she and Sir William left London, he had perceived 'an
alteration in her conduct to me. A coldness and neglect seemed to have
taken place of her repeated declarations of regard.'

On the twenty-second, Emma smiled on Romney. It is possible that
her coldness, if the sensitive painter did not imagine it, had been due
to worry about the question of marriage. The round of visits on which
Sir William took her assuaged her fears. On the twenty-third, and then
again and again till she left London, she sat to Romney. The painter
was made reckless by the renewal of their friendship. He gave a party.
'She performed in my house last week,' he writes to Hayley, 'singing
and acting before some of the nobility with most astonishing power;
she is the talk of the whole town, and really surpasses every thing
both in singing and acting, that ever appeared. Gallini offered her
two thousand pounds a year, and two benefits, if she would engage
with him, on which Sir William said pleasantly, that he had engaged
her for life.'

Mr Dickenson came to London at the end of August to arrange his
sister's departure with the Chevalier Palombi, her new husband, to Italy.
He wrote a diary-letter to his wife, which gives our only account of
the last few days before the marriage between Sir William and Emma
was solemnized on 6 September. 'My Dearest Love,' he writes on 29
August:

> You know what London is, & how difficult it is to command time ... I
> went to Emma & staid an hour with her & her Mother. She told me that
> she had laid down such a plan for her conduct, on her return to Naples,
> as she was satisfied wd ensure to her universal respect & the approbation
> of Sir Wm. She knew that it wd be in her power to make him happy,
> that gratitude, inclination, & every consideration wd compel her to do
> everything in her power to please him, & She was certain shed do it.
> I told her that the eyes of many people were upon her, that I rejoiced
> to hear of these determinations as I ardently wished that She & Sir Wm
> should be perfectly happy; that I could see it would be very easy for her
> to keep up in him that warmth of attachment which he entertained for
> her, & that I hoped that he would find Emma & Lady H. *the same* ...
> I was speaking of Sir Wm to Emma & said how much I admired him

& added that I loved him. She assured me that there was no love lost for that he liked me as well. She read me a very affecte letter of his to her from Windsor. The King joked him about Em. at a distance & gave a hint that he thought he was not quite so religious as when he married the late Lady H.

Thus tacit consent for marriage was given, to the relief of all. Queen Charlotte, however, refused to receive Emma at Court, which surprised no one.

'Emma told me yt her marriage is to take place on Tuesday, therefore I shall not leave town till this day Sent,' Dickenson continued. 'A demur was made by the A. Bp of Canty about a special license owg to an expression in Sir Wm's application, therefore it must be solemnised in a Church. Lord Abercorn is very anxious about it, & his Wife is dying, therefore they are afraid lest he shd be prevented from attending.' Lord Abercorn, head of one branch of the Hamilton family, had taken to Emma and agreed to stand witness.

Emma sat to Romney further, on 4 and 5 September. He was painting her head for that connoisseur, Mrs Cadogan. Romney was very pleased with it, and we may see this head in the charming and gay oil, sometimes named *Euphrosyne* or *Mirth*. He meant to send it to Mrs Cadogan when it was finished, but it was still among his canvases in 1800.

She also found time to sit to young Thomas Lawrence. Lawrence had heard much of 'this wonderful woman . . . Mrs Hart . . . I hear it is the most gratifying thing to a painter's eye that can be.' He was scornful of Romney's pictures of her ('feeble, – more shew the artist's feebleness than her grandeur'); he determined to make his mark himself.[4] For the Marquess of Abercorn, soon to be witness to the Hamilton marriage, he painted a full-length portrait of Emma as *La Penserosa*, which was exhibited at the Royal Academy in 1792. Besides this, there exists a very fine drawing in the British Museum – black and red chalk and stump. Of another work, we will hear later.

At last, 6 September dawned; a disparate party was assembled and proceeded to St Marylebone Church in the Marylebone Road. Weddings were customarily small at this date – Lord Herbert, for one, was staunch in his refusal to have more than the witnesses required for the occasion at his nuptials. The Hamilton wedding was marked by informality. Emma took time in the midst of her preparations to send a very correctly expressed note to Mr Dickenson. It was the last communication she was to make in her spinster state.

Dear Sir, Forgive me but I have not had a moment's time to answer your kind note. Lord A. & Lady C. have gone to dress and return in a quarter of an hour, they have ordered their coach at nine o'clock and we shall then be glad to see you, and I assure you I feel unhappy at not having had more of your company, but you have seen the Bustle we have been in since you have been in town, you shall have the things this afternoon. I write on this scrap of paper as I can't find a sheet in the house, and Sir Wm is out, but you will forgive it as I would not make you wait, and I write in such a hurry that you will not be able to read it. Adio.

Assembled at Marylebone were Mrs Cadogan, the Marquess of Abercorn, Louis Dutens, secretary to the English Minister at Turin and a dilettante, possibly Charles Greville and John Dickenson.

In their presence 'The Right Hnble Sir Willm Hamilton of this parish, Widower and Amy Lyons of the same Parish, Spinster' were duly married. Without delay, they repaired to Romney's studio, where the painter took Emma's likeness for one of the most elegant portraits he achieved. It is known as *The Ambassadress*, and Emma sits at her ease in what is surely her wedding dress. With a large blue hat tied with a scarf and boasting a plume, and a voluminous white dress tied with a sash, she gazes sweetly out from a landscape in which Vesuvius is eminent. This was the last portrait Romney painted of Emma from life. She took a 'tender leave' of him, and was off.[5]

The deed was done and the *Gentleman's Magazine* and the *European Magazine* noted it, the first giving, in addition, fulsome descriptions of Emma as 'a lady much celebrated for her elegant accomplishments and great musical abilities'.

CHAPTER TEN

The Fatigue of a Dinner of Fifty

According to the 1815 *Memoirs*, on the day that Sir William Hamilton was married, he had a private interview with His Majesty, by appointment. The King, in course of conversation, mentioned the report that was circulated respecting the intended nuptials of the Ambassador, adding with a good-natured smile, 'But I hope it is not true.' To this his Excellency immediately rejoined, 'May it please your Majesty, the ceremony took place this morning.' The remark, if made, was jocular. Sir William had secured his sovereign's tacit consent to the match at Windsor in August.

Two days later the newly-weds set out for Naples. The Continent was in a state of flux. In Paris, a new era had dawned. The National Assembly had agreed on a constitutional code, and the King and Queen were released from their prison in the Tuileries. They held Court three times a week. Crowds gathered to see them pass through the gardens on their way to Mass, as they had always done. 'Mme Elizabeth, the King's sister,' however, 'looked as if she was going to spit in the people's face. The King himself came rolling along and looked as if he did not care a farthing about it if they would but let him alone . . .'

So Lord Palmerston, a witness to the endless deliberations in the Assembly over the constitution, viewed the matter. He lodged in the Hotel de l'Université and, about 10 September, was joined there by Sir William and the new Lady Hamilton. Sir Charles Blagden, Secretary of the Royal Society, had written to Palmerston that the happy couple 'talk of passing through Paris'. Sir William no doubt wished to see for himself what was reported so wildly in the foreign press. And what woman has ever been able to resist the lure of a Paris hat?

In Lord Palmerston, Sir William and Emma had a fine guide. He had been watching events in the French capital since July, and may even have carried letters, like Thomas Pelham, from Charles James Fox to the Leaders of the Assembly, counselling moderation. Palmerston was intrigued by Emma. He wrote to his second wife, Mary, mother of the statesman, on 14 September:

Sir William and Lady Hamilton are arrived at this hotel and are to stay a few days. I have been introduced to her and had a good luck to be the

means, by speaking to Monsr. Noailles, of getting them placed yesterday
in the Assembly. She is very handsome but not elegant, her face is very
much like what I have seen in a fine old portrait and she wears her hair
something in that style. She seems very good humoured, very happy and
very attentive to him. I am promised an exhibition of her performances
that have been so much talked of . . .

Four days later he wrote of the great public rejoicing which the
Assembly had decreed to celebrate the acceptance of the constitution.

About six o'clock a very fine balloon went up with a man in it, which
succeeded very well and went directly over Paris. At night the illuminations
of the buildings and gardens of the Tuileries and Louvre and of the Champs
Elysées, which is a vast piece of ground planted with trees adjoining to them,
were by much the finest of the kind I ever saw and the whole scene with
the immense quantities of people and music and dancing in every corner
exceeded every expectation I had formed. No carriages were permitted
to be used in any part of the town the whole day so that the fatigue was
very considerable to those who wished to see it all. I was all day with the
Hamiltons and Monsr. de Noailles and we succeeded very well. About ten
o'clock Lady Hamilton and the rest of the party went home after returning
from the Champs Elysées . . .

Lord Palmerston was warm in his commendations of Emma after
spending some days in her company.

She is certainly very handsome and there is a plain good sense and simplicity
of character about her which is uncommon and very agreeable. I have
seen her perform the various characters and attitudes which she assumes
in imitation of statues and pictures, and was pleased even beyond my
expectation though I had heard so much. She really presents the very
thing which the artists aimed at representing. I have not yet heard her
sing which I am told is very remarkably good in its way. I am to do that
twice tomorrow. In the morning at the house of an Italian where she is
to practice, and in the evening at Lady Sutherland's where there is to be
a little music for her . . .

There is an odd story attached to a charming picture of Emma as
a Bacchante, framed by a garland of flowers, which hangs at Lord
Palmerston's home, Broadlands, today. In 1790, Sir Joshua Reynolds
had painted out a *Roman Charity* which first occupied the frame of
flowers. He substituted a hand and an eye, and presented it to his
friend Palmerston. This last was deeply embarrassed when he learnt
that this device was meant as 'an emblem of liberality, guided by

intelligence'. Reynolds agreed to alter the device; then his health suddenly deteriorated. Palmerston gave the canvas to young Thomas Lawrence on his return from Paris, and by 12 October 1791 the artist had made a start. Artist and patron no doubt agreed together that Emma, so recent a vision to them both, would do well to fill the garland. By late November it was finished, and by 1792 had come to rest in the dining-room alcove which it occupies today.

It seems that at a certain point during the Paris week, Emma was presented to the Queen, Marie-Antoinette. Supposedly, the Queen gave her a letter to take to her dearly beloved sister, Maria Carolina of Naples, and this letter is said to have been the last letter Marie-Antoinette ever wrote to her sister. Be that as it may, the Hamiltons had secured their Royal audience. They soon left Paris.

They were wise to leave when they did. William Beckford wrote to Sir William from Paris on 15 December: 'A thick cloud hangs over Paris at this moment, fraught with some confounded crackers. I expect an eruption any moment. The assembly knows not which way to turn themselves . . .' He ends, 'Je me prosterne au pied de la Madonne.'

On 27 September, Emma was once again in Geneva, some five years after she had last visited it under the aegis of Gavin Hamilton. Now she was in very different spirits, as a letter to Mary Dickenson makes clear.

Dear Madam, a thousand thanks to you for your kind letter, indeed I feel as if I had not deserved it, but Mr Dickenson will inform you of the hurry we were in, the last days we were in England, and believe me, the honour you have done me by corresponding with me, and the pleasure is such that I shall seize every opportunity of shewing my gratitude to you for the happiness your dear and instructive letters give me, and at the same time I hope to profit myself, for having lived five years in Italy and not having had the happiness to have had a dear Mrs Dickenson to write to me and correct me, I am afraid at first I shall be a dull correspondent, but I hope I shall mend as I go on, and now I am so happy and feel so content, that I shall have a pleasure in writing to you, and believe me before the 6th September I was always unhappy and discontented with myself; ah Madam, how much do I owe to your dear Uncle. I feel every moment my obligations to him and am always afraid I can never do enough for him since that moment. I say to myself Am I his Wife, and I can never separate more. Am I Emma Hamilton? It seems impossible I can be so happy. Surely no person was ever so happy as I am. Yes Mrs Dickenson is, but there are no more Mr Dickensons and Sir William Hamiltons in the world, to advise me, and I know you will forgive me. From Naples my letter will be more reasonable. Poor Mr D. how does he do?

Dickenson's sister had left for Italy with her Italian husband shortly
before the Hamiltons.

> She was angry the horses were not ready and sent to the pastry cook's for
> some tarts and eat all the time still she got into the coach, and, believe me,
> smiled, when Mr Dickenson, his face all bathed, could only kiss his hand . . .
> people say that insensibility is a happiness; let those that have it enjoy it,
> I don't envy them, and Mrs Palombi seems to have a good share of it.
>
> God Almighty has given you such a husband I believe there is not his
> fellow, but I would not have had you to have seen him at that time except
> it would have been to have given Mrs Palombi a good scolding. Give our
> dear loves to Mr D. and Louisa and tell them we hope to see them at
> Naples with you one of these days . . . From Naples I will write everything
> that I do and think, and make it into a packet and send it to Lord Greville's
> [Grenville's] office, and desire it to be put into the post and then I shall
> not be afraid to write long nonsense. God bless you dear Madam. May you
> enjoy all the happiness you deserve and believe me your ever obliged your
> truly grateful and sincere, E. Hamilton.

Imagine Emma's joy in her new signature, and note her strenuous
attempts to refine her prose style.

In celebration of their recent marriage, Sir William had Angelica
Kauffmann paint Emma in Rome on their way to Naples. (*Emma Lady
Hamilton as the Comic Muse* is a charming portrait: Emma holds aloft an
antique mask, as she emerges from behind a curtain.)[1]

There were difficulties to overcome in Naples, however, before
Emma could take her place at Court. We hear of these first from
Sir Charles Blagden in London, who wrote to Lord Palmerston on 8
December:

> Be so good as to convey my thanks to Lady P. for her very obliging letter,
> and inform her that Lady Hamilton is probably before this time presented
> at the Court of Naples – at least so says the letter I saw yesterday from
> that country. It states that when Sir William first went to Court, nothing
> was said about Lady Hamilton, which gave umbrage to both and made Sir
> William resolve not to attend the Court at Caserta (this perhaps occasioned
> the report prevalent in town a few days ago, that he was recalled). However,
> some days after, a messenger was sent importing that the Queen would be
> glad to see Lady Hamilton, in consequence of which, a time was settled
> for her presentation and they are both to spend the holiday at Caserta with
> the Royal Family.

Maria Carolina, having decided to receive Lady Hamilton, showed
her 'all sorts of kind and affectionate attentions', so Emma wrote to

Romney on 20 December. 'I have been received with open arms by all the Neapolitans of booth sexes, by all the foreigners of every distinction . . . in short, I am the happiest woman in the world.' She wrote further:

Sir William is fonder of me every day, & I hope I [?] will have no corse to repent of what he as done, for I feel so grateful to him that I think I shall never be able to make him amends for his goodness to me. But why do I tell you this? you know me enough; you was the first dear friend I open'd my heart to, you ought to know me, for you have seen and discoursed with me in my poorer days, you have known me in my poverty and prosperity, and I had no occasion to have lived for years in poverty and distress if I had not felt something of virtue in my mind. Oh, my dear friend, for a time I own through distress my virtue was vanquished, but my sense of virtue was not overcome. How gratefull now, then, do I feel to my dear, dear husband that has restored peace to my mind, that has given me honors, rank, and, what is more, innocence and happiness. Rejoice with me, my dear sir, my friend, my more than father, believe me I am still that same Emma you knew me. If I could forget for a moment what I was, I ought to suffer. Command me in anything I can do for you here; believe me, I shall have a real pleasure. Come to Naples, and I will be your model, anything to induce you to come, that I may have an opportunity to show my gratitude to you. Take care of your health for all our sakes. How does the pictures go on? Has the Prince been to you? write to me, I am interested in all that concerns you. God bless you, my dear friend! I spoke to Lady Sutherland about you; she loves you dearly. Give my love to Mr Hayly, tell him I shall be glad to see him at Naples. As you was so good to say you would give me the little picture with the black hat, I wish you would unfrill it, and give it to Mr Duten. I have a great regard for him; he took a deal of pains and trouble for me, and I could not do him a greater favour than give him my picture. Do, my dear friend, do me that pleasure, and if there is anything from Naples command me.

We have a many English at Naples, Ladys Malmsbery, Malden, Plymouth, Carnegie, Wright, etc. They are very kind and attentive to me; they all make it a point to be remarkably civil to me. You will be happy at this, as you know what prudes our Ladys are. Tell Hayly I am allways reading his *Triumphs of Temper*; it was that that made me Lady H., for, God knows, I had for 5 years enough to try my temper, and I am affraid if it had not been for the good example Serena taught me, my girdle would have burst, and if it had I had been undone, for Sir W. minds more temper than beauty. He, therefore, wishes Mr Hayly would come, that he might thank him for his sweet-tempered wife. I swear to you I have never been once out of humour since the 6th of last September. God bless you.

Sir William wrote a more sober account of what had transpired to his niece Mary on 15 January 1792. He first expresses his thanks for Mary's staunch support in England. 'Emma's heart is tender & gratefull & tho' mine has grown tough by age, yet it feels a gratefull emotion towards you, as it will, I dare say, to my last hour.' Then he describes their reception at Naples as:

> very flattering, and Emma has kept rigidly to our plan. She is the wife of Sir W. H. supposing him at Naples in a private Character. You know our Court & the difficulty that woud have attended my attempting to present her there. As I was aware of that, I married as you know 2 days before I left England.
>
> The Queen of Naples, informed of all my proceedings, told me she wou'd see my Wife tho' she could not acknowledge her as the Wife of the English Minister, & she received her most kindly. Emma very naturally told her whole story & that all her desire was by her future conduct to shew her gratitude to me, and to prove to the world that a young, beautiful Woman, tho' of obscure birth, coud have noble sentiments and act properly in the great World. In short the Queen of N. is quite fond of her & has taken her under her protection. All the Neapolitan Nobility have been to see her & shew her every atention & the English Ladies who are numerous here this year, are quite fond of her.
>
> I find in England some that are hungry after my place had trumped up a story that I had imposed on the Court of Naples by presenting Ly H., & that the King of England was very Angry & meant to turn me out. After 27 years' service & spending all the King's money & all my own, it wou'd be rather hard as I have not been any ways guilty & my marriage is my own private business. I fear nothing for at least we are just in England.[2]

One of the 'numerous' English ladies wrote from Naples to Lady Herries, a friend of Mary Dickenson's, to confirm this account. 'I have had Lady Hamilton with me all ye Eveng, that is of Jan. 14th, we were alone & I am more & more pleased with her.' Harriot Lady Malmesbury, travelling with her husband and a friend, reported on the situation to her sister Lady Elliot. On 10 December 1791, they had reached Naples, a foggy day made worse by rain that would not clear. On the sixteenth she wrote about a mysterious Mrs L——. 'She won't go to Caserta to see Lady Hamilton, though every soul besides herself does.'

Lady Malmesbury noted the presence, in the numerous hotels and lodgings about the Largo di Castello and the Chiaia, of the less than brilliant 'colony' of English. 'Lord and Lady Malden; Lord and Lady Plymouth; Lord Dalkeith, a natural, good-humoured boy; Lord Bruce, who is quite like Lord Ailesbury just out of the shell – which, by-the-by, is no bad comparison, for they are like unfledged turkeys . . .' At Portici, there was HRH Prince Augustus of Sussex, fifth of the English Royal Princes. This poor youth was asthmatic and his Royal father had ordered him to live in the country for his health. He had by now conceived a grand passion for Lady Anne Hatton. Perhaps it was for her sake that the plump prince lived 'entirely on potatoes and water . . . yet is quite a colossus', the Countess added sadly.

On Boxing Day, Lord and Lady Malmesbury dined at Caserta with Sir William and Emma. Lady Malmesbury had more to say of the weather than of the dinner. 'What rain!' she exclaimed to her sister. 'Perfect buckets of water accompanied with violent thunder and lightning, and now and then stopped for a few hours by a cold north wind.' In the morning at Caserta it froze hard. Then from eleven it rained for twelve hours with an interlude in the evening of 'such lightning as you never saw'.

Confined indoors, Lady Malmesbury had good opportunity for judging Emma and she was favourably impressed. 'She really behaves as well as possible, and quite wonderfully considering her origin and education . . . I believe all the English mean to be very civil to her, which is quite right.'

Others in England were strong in support of Sir William's new marriage. Lord Abercorn wrote early in 1792 to assure his cousin that 'as to any foolish reports in our newspapers, you need not rest a thought upon them . . . you have a friend that would not let you be a sufferer for want of his interposition.' The Earl-Bishop had written reassuringly from Woodstock, on 21 December 1791:

> I congratulate you, my old friend, from the bottom of my heart, upon the fortitude you have shown, & the manly part you have taken in braving the world & securing your own happiness & elegant enjoyments in defiance of them. I . . . should have been too happy in contributing to unite you had Lord Abercorn been in Ireland . . . nobody mentions your decision but with approbation; no wonder provided that they have ever seen & heard Lady Hamilton; & now I flatter myself you have secured your happyness for life, & will enjoy your otium cum dignitate, & take your dignitatem cum amoenitate for the remainder of your days, & I shall claim my old Cabin at Caserta, that I may be a witness of that permanent comfort I so often wish'd you before.

There was one shadow cast upon the Hamiltons' conjugal felicity. Charles Greville was swift to relinquish his responsibility for 'Little Emma' in Manchester. He sent to her keeper, Mr Blackburn, an order for £32 11s on Sir William's account at Ross and Ogilvie. Greville writes that he has 'taken a liberty . . . I communicate it to you instead of Ly H., because I know it would give her some embarrassment, & she might imagine it unkind in me so soon to trouble you about her protégé.' Greville explained he was short of money. There was as usual no need for him to justify his behaviour. Why should he pay for an ex-mistress's illegitimate child when it was not his and she now had a husband to support her? Greville noted, 'The natural attachment to a deserted orphan may be supposed to increase from the length of time she has been protected. I have avoided any such sentiments by having only found the means to indulge so amiable a sentiment in Ly H . . .'

On 3 January 1792, there was an enforced separation between Sir William and Emma. The King took his English friend off hunting at Persano. Sir William was 'sorry, my dear Em. to leave you in affliction: you must harden yourself to such little misfortunes as a temporary parting; but, I cannot blame you for having a good and tender heart . . . you are in thorough possession of all mine, though I will allow it to be rather tough.'

On the sixth he allowed Emma had been quite right in buying new lamps. He was glad the Prince (probably Prince Augustus) had asked to dine with her. He was furious however at unnamed 'devils in England'. They wanted to 'stir up something against me; but our conduct shall be such as to be unattackable.' He ends, 'I would not be married to any woman, but yourself, on earth, for all the world.'

The next day he was glad all went on so well with the English ladies. He sent her a boar with instructions to 'keep some to eat at home, and dispose of the rest to your favourite English . . .' He had an admonitory word about her writing. 'The cold . . . makes my hand something like your's – which, by the bye, you neglect rather too much: but, as what you write is good sense, every body will forgive the scrawl.'

Emma insisted her husband write to her every day. On the tenth, Sir William approved an expedition Emma had made to the Academy – a public ball. 'You are, certainly, the most domestic young woman I know: but you are young, and most beautiful.' Naturally, she liked to show herself a little in public.

Sir William thanked her for her 'effusion of tenderness . . . I . . . will do all I can to keep it alive. We are now one flesh, and it must be our study to keep that flesh as warm and comfortable as we can.'

On the twelfth, Sir William responded to agitated letters from Emma. If the servants did not answer her call, they would be dismissed. 'You are my better half, and may command.' Should her mother go with her to 'the English parties'? 'Very well,' responded Sir William, but not to the Neapolitan parties. 'Believe me, it will be best for her, and more to her happiness, to stay at home.'

On the fifteenth, Emma was praised for refusing to invite Prince Augustus' flame, Lady Anne Hatton, to dine, and for telling her the reason. (She was too much the libertine for the straitlaced Emma.) Sir William wrote of his meditated arrival the next Saturday: 'What say you to a feet washing that night? *O che Gusto*! when your *prima ora* is over, and all gone.'

The sixteenth brought a reply to some gossip of Emma's about the English in Naples. 'Let them all roll on the carpet, &c. provided you are not of the party.'

On the seventeenth Sir William cavilled at Emma's spelling. She must observe the distinction between 'except' and 'accept'.

On the eighteenth, it was Emma's dress sense which occupied her tireless husband.

> It was not your white and silver, alone, that made you look like an angel, at the Academy . . . A beautiful woman, feeling herself well dressed, will have a sort of confidence, which will add greatly to the lustre of her eye: but . . . for some years to come, the more simply you dress, the more conspicuous will be your beauty; which . . . is the most perfect I have yet met with . . .
>
> Adieu! my sweet Em. I rejoice that the time of our reunion is so near – *Saturday night*!

So closed these charming letters of a watchful husband away from his young wife.

As usual, with the New Year came new visitors for the Hamilton Embassy to entertain. Many too were waiting for Holy Week to begin before they left for Rome. Lady Malmesbury wrote from Naples to her sister on 11 January 1792. True to form, the weather was her constant preoccupation. It had rained, and the wind had blown continually; 'pleasant, comical' Lord Dalkeith said: 'it is like being in Noah's ark when the flood was going off, for the tops of the mountains are alone to be seen.' Lady Plymouth's windows had been blown in, shutters and all. All the English had been ill, Lord Dalkeith (heir to the Duke of Buccleuch) never well since he 'chose to lie down and sleep on the hot lava upon Vesuvius'. Lord Bruce, Lady Ailesbury's son, fell desperately in love – 'like a rabbit with a bunch of parsley' – with the Duchesse de Fleury. Otherwise, Naples was quiet.

Lady Malmesbury struck up a tentative friendship with Emma during her visit. Emma took the opportunity to spin her a tale about eighteen murderers living in the courtyard of the Palazzo Sessa in the spring of 1791. At length, Sir William had given permission for the King to 'take them up'. Lady Malmesbury gave further details. 'The battle between them and the sbirri [police] on the yard lasted three hours, in Lady Hamilton's hearing, and they killed two before they could take the rest.' Emma was deceiving her friend. This siege had taken place some twenty-five years before, shortly after Sir William's arrival. The story, presumably, seemed to Emma to gain from a later setting.

Lady Malmesbury admired Emma's Attitudes, thinking them beyond 'the most graceful statues or pictures'. She also saw Emma dance the tempestuous tarantella – 'beautiful to a degree'. She added an etymological note: 'It is not what the spider (tarantula) makes people dance without a master, but the dance of Tarentum (Taranto), and the most lively thing possible.'

By the end of January, the weather was on the turn. 'The last three weeks have been delicious – perpetual sunshine – all the banks covered with violets, the wild sweet pea, the wild Heliotrope, and all in full blossom,' wrote Lady Malmesbury. While her party made boat trips to Baiae, a new party of visitors arrived. These were the Marquis and Marquise d'Osmond and their young daughter, Adèle, later Comtesse de Boigne. They arrived towards the outset of 1792, the Comtesse recorded in her memoirs. She became a favourite playmate of the younger Royal Princesses, Maria Amalia and Marie Antoinette, who often sent for her to Portici, while the Queen formed a lasting friendship with the Marquise.

According to the Comtesse, it was during her family's ten-month stay at Naples that Lady Hamilton began to come into favour with the Queen, and Mme la Marquise was supplanted. Adèle records that she used sometimes to assist Lady Hamilton in her Attitudes. On one occasion Emma placed her on her knees, praying before an urn, and knelt beside her 'in an attitude of grief'. Then, 'suddenly rising', Emma grasped Adèle by her hair. The child turned in fright, 'which brought me precisely into the spirit of my part, for she was brandishing a dagger'. The audience broke into applause and exclaimed, 'Brava la Médéa.' Emma then drew Adèle to her and clasped her, 'as though she were fighting to preserve me from the anger of Heaven'. 'Viva la Niobé,' came loud cries from the onlookers.[3] Here is evidence that each Attitude was intended to recall a particular episode from mythology. The Comtesse mentions that the audience was composed of 'artists'. Among these may have been Frederick Rehberg, 'Historical Painter to the King of Prussia'. Sir William commissioned him to draw and publish some of Lady Hamilton's Attitudes. *Drawings faithfully copied from Nature at Naples* duly appeared in 1794. Among the drawings there is one in which Emma appears as Medea dragging one of her children. It seems probable that the Comtesse's description and Rehberg's drawing are of one and the same performance.

Sir William was excited by the progress of another work he had commissioned. He had asked Tischbein to execute designs from his new collection of vases, 'all of which were under ground 3 years ago'. The iconography of many of the vase paintings had defeated Sir William, till the Russian Minister, Italinski, offered his help. Now the first volume, he reported proudly on 17 April 1792 to Horace Walpole, newly Earl of Orford, was to be published two months hence. As tribute to Emma's resilience on the tour of Puglia in 1789, Christopher Kniep's frontispiece shows Lady Hamilton inspecting the finds of a tomb.

Sir William wrote to Orford in April in a moment of respite.

Since my return here I have been in one perpetual hurry, and the Holy Week having carried off most of the foreign travellers to Rome, it is now only that I begin to breathe . . . of upwards of 100 British travellers that have been here this winter I can scarcely name those who can have reaped the least profit, for they have lived together and led exactly the same life they wou'd have done in London. I respect Magna Charta, but wish there had been in it some little restraint upon emigrants.

He had this to say of Emma, to whose charms a doubtful Walpole had been converted in the summer:

Lady H, who has had also a difficult part to act & has succeeded wonderfully, having gained, by having no pretensions, the thorough approbation of all the English ladies. The Queen of Naples, as you may have heard, was very kind to her on our return, and treats her like any other travelling lady of distinction; in short, we are very comfortably situated here . . . You can not imagine how delighted Ly H. was in having gained your approbation in England. She desires to be kindly remember'd to you. She goes on improving daily, particularly in musick & in the French & Italian languages. She is realy an extraordinary being, & most gratefull to me for having saved her from the precipice into which she had good sense enough to see she must without me have inevitably fallen, and she sees that nothing but a constant good conduct can maintain the respect that is now shown her by every body. It has often been remarked that a reformed rake makes a good husband. *Why not vice versa?*

Among other cares that had been besetting Sir William was the health of HRH Prince Augustus, Duke of Sussex. Lady Wright's son had had

'two fits of his asthma attended with a high fever and fears for his life'
in the winter of '91. Perhaps Naples was not the perfect climate for
asthmatics, after all. The formidable Philippina Lady Knight thought,
if the sulphurous air of Naples did not do good, it did harm – 'as it is
by no means natural'. By 8 May 1792, Prince Augustus had returned
to Rome where Lady Knight considered he had 'grown too fat'.

In the summer months of 1792, Sir William and Emma had the
delightful treat of enjoying the English Garden without interruption
by visitors. Just below the Great Cascade, a gate led the interested
visitor into an enchanted world, a mile away from the formal planting
of the Royal Gardens. 'The English Garden' was a concept which
owed much to the imaginary classical landscapes of Claude Lorrain.
Sir William, knowledgeable both in the artist's works and in the
ancient wall-paintings of cool, green gardens which were Lorrain's
inspiration, had created an orderly wilderness of great beauty. The
individual specimens were doing well. A camphor tree had shot up
in three years. The melon plants were fruiting well. Almost every day
through the long summer, Emma and Sir William came to the Garden
to drink tea under the palm trees by Graefer's house.

If Sir William had complained of the number of travelling English
in April, he was confounded by the streams of couples, young men
and families who invaded Naples in the winter of 1792. There was the
Duchess of Ancaster, Lady Plymouth, the Cholmondeleys, Lady Forbes
and many more. It may have been due to the fatigue of looking after
them all that Sir William suddenly became seriously ill. Emma wrote
distractedly to Greville on 4 December:

> Sir William is out of danger & very well considering the illness he as had
> to battle with. He as been 15 days in bed with a billious fever & I have been
> almost as ill as him with anxiety, aprehension, & fatigue, the last, endeed, the
> least of what I have felt & I am now doubly repaid by the dayly progress he
> makes for the better. Luckily we are at Caserta were his convalescence will
> have fair play & I am in hopes he will be better than ever he was in his life,
> for his disorder as been long gathering & was a liver complaint. I need not
> say to you my dear Mr Greville what I have suffered, endeed I was almost
> distracted, from such extreme happiness at once to such misery, that I felt,
> your good heart may imagine. I was eight days without undressing, eating
> or sleeping. I have great obligations to the English ladies & Neapolitans,
> altho we are 16 miles from Naples, Lady Plymouth, Lady Dunmore, Lady
> Webster & several others sent twice a day & offered to come & stay with
> me, & the King & Queen sent constantly, morning & evening, the most
> flattering messages, but all was nothing to me – what cou'd console me for
> the loss of such a husband, friend & protector, for surely no happiness is

like ours. We live but for one another, but I was to happy, I had imagined I was never more to be unhappy, all is right, I now know myself again & I shall not easily fall in to the same error again, for every moment I feel what I felt when I thought I was loseing him for ever.

There were thoughts of the Wirral in Emma's mind this Christmas. She wrote to her mother's friend Mrs Burt of Chester on Boxing Day. She described the welcome the King, as godfather, gave to Graefer and his Chester wife Caroline's first child. Mrs Graefer received a gold watch set in pearls, twelve silver candlesticks, 'and sylver tea board and sylver coffey pot, sugar basen, etc etc . . .'. Emma was worried that Mrs Kidd, her grandmother, should be short of funds. In her letter to Greville, she had asked him to send her £20. Emma herself had left her £30, besides supplies of tea, sugar and other commodities when in England. With the news of Emma's marriage, family cares were now laid at her door. In her next letter, she proposed to 'say more about Mr Connor', another relation.

Visitors continued to flood Naples. An old friend was Lord Palmerston. With him came his wife and Miss Carter. They arrived just before Christmas 1792, when Sir William was recovered. On 16 January Lady Palmerston had her first encounter with Emma at a ball Lady Cholmondeley gave for her son Lord Malpas' first birthday.

> I find her not so beautiful as I expected, but certainly extremely handsome and her figure uncommonly fine. She was well dressed and there is something in her manner very good humoured and a great desire of pleasing. Sir William looks extremely ill and it puts one a good deal in mind of January and June, for I think she is beyond May. Her voice is vulgar and she and Sir W. are rather too fond, but upon the whole I think her a very extraordinary woman . . . It's an odd thing, but there are hardly any of the Neapolitans who open their houses, but the English seem to do the honour of Naples to the Neapolitans . . .

The next day the Palmerston party were among fifty-three who sat down to dinner at the Palazzo Sessa – and Sir William had had twenty excuses! 'Lady Hamilton looked extremely handsome and really does the honours uncommonly well. She is extremely obliging, without the least appearance of feeling any elevation from the change in her situation. Sir William perfectly idolises her and I do not wonder he is proud of so magnificent a marble, belonging so entirely to himself. We stayed till about 8 . . .'

Ten days later the Palmerstons went to Caserta and dined with the Hamiltons at two o'clock. 'Prince Clary and Esterhazy, the Imperial

Minister, dined there. In the evening Lady Hamilton sang, accompanied by four musicians, who live in the house, and Paisiello came from the Queen, who luckily did not wish for music that night ... Lady Hamilton looked particularly beautiful and her desire to please and her extreme civility is very uncommon. Mrs Cadogan, her mother, looks like a lady you have more often found useful than I could have ever done ...', Lady Palmerston wrote to her reprobate brother, Benjamin Mee.

On 24 February, the Palmerstons were invited to the King's Hunt at Carditello. At a very handsome breakfast, the Princess Doria and Lady Hamilton were the only other ladies. Twelve youths attended, in green and gold uniform with a red cape. They wore round hats with a feather, and a silver boar with two dogs pursuing were chased on their belts. The horses which drew the ladies' open carriages to the Hunt were 'little wild Neapolitans'. Hackert painted a similar scene, with the Queen and attendant ladies viewing the *chasse* from the safety of a palisade. Tischbein painted the figures and the lady marked 'Lady Hamilton' is placed next to the Queen. Prince Augustus is among the huntsmen.

On the twenty-seventh, Lady Palmerston heard Emma sing. She was critical.

> I like Lady H. too well not to wish that she had never learned to sing, for certainly her talents do not lie that way. Her voice is powerful but perfectly without harmony and I am sure she has no ear. She is, however, a very extraordinary character, and by her conduct proves how much she merits her great reverse of fortune. Sir William went to the King, as is his constant custom, to play at billiards.

Lady Palmerston reflected at length upon Emma a month later.

> Lady H. is to me very surprising, for considering the situation she was in she behaves wonderfully well. Now and then to be sure a little vulgarness pops out, but I think it's more Sir William's fault, who loves a good joke and leads her to enter into his stories, which are not of the best kind. She is vastly desirous to please and is very civil and good humoured to all her friends and her attention to Sir William is infinitely amiable ...

Elizabeth Lady Webster was more sparing in her praise. She had arrived in Naples in the second week of October 1792, with her husband Sir Godfrey. He was forty-five to her twenty-one, and had recently lost his seat in Parliament. According to the Earl of Ilchester, his 'gloomy and at times sullen disposition, his violence of temper, his fit of depression ... and dissipation' repelled her while 'a foolish levity of conduct consequent upon youth' made them uneasy travelling companions. Lady Webster lost no time in attaching an admirer, the Chevalier Italinski, the Russian Minister, to her side. With him and with the Palmerstons she sallied out on sightseeing expeditions. She celebrated her twenty-second birthday – 'so old and yet so silly' – dining in the Temple of Isis at Pompeii.

In January 1793 Lady Webster had an interesting event to confide to her journal. Shortly before the birth of the French Republic in September 1792, France had sent a new minister, Armand de Mackau. (The Baron de Talleyrand-Périgord had retired on hearing the news of the French King's arrest, and remained as an ordinary citizen in Naples.) Mackau had with him Hugou de Bassville, who divided his time between annoying the Neapolitans by sporting revolutionary uniforms and cockades, and delighting them by painting out the Bourbon fleur-de-lis on the Embassy's coat-of-arms in favour of a 'beauteous Minerva with her lance and the sacred cap of liberty'. The Neapolitans mistook the symbol of revolution for the Madonna. 'I am terribly bored here,' Hugou confessed.

The King and Queen of Naples refused to recognize Mackau and Hugou till November 1792, when the Convention recalled them. Then they had the shortest of audiences with the Royal couple. The King asked Mackau how the air of Naples agreed with him. When the Queen had spoken a few words to Mackau's wife, 'she smashed her fan as soon as the visitor's back was turned'.

Suddenly it was apparent that the new French Government would not tolerate even such watery defiance from the Kingdom of the Two Sicilies. By 20 November, the King and Queen knew of the Council of War that had taken place on the eighth at Genoa. M. de Sémonville, French Minister there, was 'one of the most dangerous firebrands' of the Revolution, 'translating seditious literature and scattering it throughout Italy'. 'It was decided unanimously that the French squadron should sail to Naples and Civitavecchia to attack and pillage those places.' In fact, war was threatened, if not declared.

What was the reaction in Naples? The Queen refused to retire to Castellamare and fomented alarm. The King went daily to the hunt, though Acton, now Sir John Acton, wished him to encourage by his presence 'the workmen at the docks, the troops and the militia' who were working on defence preparations. The Royal Family decided to retire to 'the massive Castel Sant'Elmo upon the appearance of the enemy. Lesser mortals were so terrified that each thinks of saving his property and moving away.'

The Queen wrote to the Marchese di Gallo, Neapolitan Minister to

Vienna, that she and the King had made violent economies. They had sold all their silver, down to the last chandelier and coffee-pot. The King had given up 392 horses and 300 dogs, and 'reduced his hunting grounds . . . Yesterday he had the wild beasts of the menagerie killed.' The Queen wrote by the light of a tin lamp.

By early December 1792, the danger was at hand. The squadron – of fifty-four sail – had left for Naples. Acton had tried to contain the danger by stipulating that only twenty-two ships could be received – the quota for friendly powers. Six ships might be admitted at Naples, Acton agreed after much bargaining; the rest must anchor off Baise.

On 12 December, a squadron appeared, smaller than that spoken of, and commanded by Admiral Latouche-Tréville. Though Mackau informed Latouche that the Republic had been recognized and only six ships could be admitted, Latouche 'refused to divide them and drew them up in line of battle, nine ships of the line and four frigates'. 'They were moored in front of my house on the Chiaia,' Lady Webster noted indignantly.

Eventually the squadron sailed for Sardinia but a storm sent them limping back to Naples for repair. All the French officers, each a firebrand of revolutionary talk, were free to land. They visited the theatres, the museums and private houses. The Jacobins threw caution to the wind and received them warmly. Guests wore Phrygian caps at dinners in their honour and drank to liberty. It was a heady time. Events reached a climax with a dinner on board Latouche's ship, the *Languedoc*, on the King's birthday. Toasts were drunk to the French Republic. A Calabrian freemason, the Abbé Jerocades, declaimed an ode to the assassin of Gustavus III of Sweden, recently murdered.

At the news of the execution of Louis XVI on 21 January 1793, all Naples went into mourning, and the whole Court attended the Requiem Mass for the King. 'Atrocious example! . . . execrable nation! . . . I should like this infamous nation to be cut to pieces, annihilated, dishonoured, reduced to nothing for at least fifty years,' wrote Maria Carolina. She was reduced to wishing death for her Royal sister.

In the early months of 1793, there were seventy-three 'straye English' in Naples. Not surprisingly, Sir William and Emma spent much time at Caserta, out of the way of their visitors' eternal demands. Here Sir William began to feel 'better & more alive than for some years passed . . . I pass my days agreably.' So he wrote to Greville on 12 March.

> Emma goes on perfectly to my mind, but she has made our house so agreable that it is more frequented than ever, &, of course, I am at a greater expence. However, I may safely say that no minister was more

respected than I am here, & the English travellers, as Lord Cholmondley will tell you, feel the benefit of our being so well at this Court, for Emma is now as well with the K. & Q. as I am, & of many parties with them.

This is borne out by the journal of Lady Webster, and also by the letters of that most fascinating beauty, who greatly enlivened Naples with her arrival on 16 April 1793, Georgiana Duchess of Devonshire. Travelling with her were her mother, Lady Spencer, her sister Harriet (newly Lady Bessborough), and her beloved rival for the Duke's affections, Lady Elizabeth Foster. Completing the party were 'the Carolines'. These were Caroline Ponsonby, aged six, Lady Bessborough's daughter, and Caroline St Jules, aged eight.

This 'French' child, Caroline Rosalie Adelaide, was, in fact, the illegitimate daughter of Lady Elizabeth and her best friend's husband, 'Canis', or the Duke of Devonshire. Though only her brother, Lord Hervey, knew it, Lady Elizabeth had spent much of her pregnancy on the island of Ischia. She had then given birth to Caroline in miserable conditions at Vietri in the Gulf of Salerno. An Archi-Prêtre des Amoureux in 'a squalid den' up a little staircase, 'dark and dirty', assisted her. Lord Hervey had been present in Naples to provide Lady Elizabeth with an excuse for her seclusion. They gave out that they were enjoying fraternal excursions to the outlying antiquities. One cannot doubt but that Lady Elizabeth saw the twin peaks of Vesuvius again with certain dread memories. Caroline, innocent babe, was, however, more than reward enough for her travail. Even Lady Spencer, who was no friend to Lady Elizabeth, adored her.

Their escort Thomas Pelham, later Earl of Chichester, attributed a long illness entirely to the strain caused by 'the whimseys of two capricious ladies', but the Devonshire House ladies were delighted with Naples. The Duchess had become a keen mineralogist in Switzerland, and found plenty of specimens to interest her in the Campi Phlegraei. 'As I don't mind scrambling I pick up a great deal myself. You wd. laugh to see me climing up hills with a hammer in my hand,' she wrote to her daughter, Georgiana.

The children were less certain if they liked Naples. Caroline St Jules was upset by the expiry of a dog put inside the Grotta del Cane to demonstrate the thick layer of carbon monoxide trapped therein. She cheered up, however, when the dog was released and recovered, and she happily cooked eggs in the hot springs at Piscarelli. At Pompeii she loved the charred loaves of bread in the baker's shop.

The Duchess of Devonshire visited Emma on her arrival, and told her daughter that Lady Hamilton, 'yr. old friend', was 'ador'd here not only for her beauty & her talents but for her Charity – they say she assists the poor to ye greatest degree . . .'

Lady Palmerston, who had been on a seafaring expedition to Capri and Ischia, called on Emma on her return to Naples. She found Emma in transports. She 'had just received the present Sir William has made her of all his diamonds on her leaving off playing at rouge et noir. Her pleasure proved she was worthy of the present and I never saw a gift better disposed. She went with us to some shops. Nothing can exceed Lady H.'s good humour and I must always think her a very extraordinary character . . .'

On 28 April, the Neapolitans forgot their fears of the French and gathered to celebrate the birth of a son, Ferdinand, to the Empress Maria Theresa, their Princess, and to the Emperor Francis II of Austria. The Royal grandfather, Ferdinand, appeared on the balcony of the Palazzo Reale to tumultuous cries from the *lazzaroni* below. He granted them the life of an assassin, like Pilate, and there were illuminations all that night and the following night. The birth of little Ferdinand was a new and tangible tie between the Royal Houses of Austria and the Two Sicilies. In these troubled times, there was need of such proof of alliance.

We have in the journals of Lady Betty Foster and Lady Webster, and from the Duchess of Devonshire's letters to her daughter, rich accounts of the *modus vivendi* of the English in the month of May 1793. The three writers have very similar reactions to the treats they were afforded. In large part, their entertainments were arranged and managed by Sir William and Emma, as we shall hear.

On 1 May, there was 'a brilliant appartment' at the Queen's in honour of her grandson's birth. Lady Webster wept 'with joy', and then on the fourth celebrated the miracle of the liquefaction of the blood of St Januarius. This miracle consisted in a lump of dried blood preserved in a glass vessel melting in the hand of a priest. The liquefaction denoted St Januarius' continued protection of Naples against the might and wrath of Mount Vesuvius, and the ceremony was taken very seriously by the people of Naples. On this occasion, the ceremony took place at the Duca di Sangro's palace, and was followed by a ball. On Sunday, 5 May, Count Francis Esterhazy, Austrian Ambassador to Naples, gave a fête in honour of the Austrian Archduke's birth. Then there were expeditions of pleasure to the outlying convent of the Camaldoli, to the ancient seaside resort of Baiae. On the eighth, it was Lady Spencer's birthday and the Carolines gave her nosegays. Her daughter Georgiana gave her a most covetable cup 'of the Naples China with Herculaneum figures'. On the ninth there was a grand expedition to one of the King's hunting seats, which was 'render'd very gay by a number of Country people & by some horse races'. Lady Webster went with the Duchess, and said wryly that 'unfortunately, the late hours of Devonshire House are transferred to the Chiaia.' They were late. Still, the King showed them 'the whole manufactory' – that is, his silk factory. 'From the Belvedere, we went to the English Garden, which is very beautiful from being in many respects unlike one.'

The King had pressed the English party to dine at Carditello, one of his country seats, where the two Carolines were wonderfully excited by the dinner-table arrangements. The table was of 'Merlin's construction', wrote Lady Webster. The places disappeared and reappeared through trapdoors at the touch of a bell. 'The middle circle of the table contain'd the dinner,' the Duchess further explained. After the dinner, the King showed the ladies 'all his cows, hogs, and pigs, and his breed of stallions'. The Duchess found time to tell her daughter how glad she was of her 'acct. of the Shawl manufactory . . . I read it to Ly. Hamilton who makes, you know, so good a use of shawls . . .' The evening was rendered gay by some regimental music. 'I like an old fool', confessed the beautiful Duchess, 'join'd in the English country dances & danced with both the Caros . . .'

On Saturday, 11 May, the English were in force at the Hamiltons' house at Caserta. Their house was not large enough to hold all, so Lady Webster, for one, lodged at Hackert's. 'Mullady sang Nina, Paisiello's music; her vile discordant screaming took off the whole effect of his simple melody.' This vicious remark was probably occasioned by the lady's enforced lodging at Hackert's. Nobody likes to be in the inferior house-party.

The Devonshires went off to Rome. Lady Webster did not linger long. She left Italinski 'much dijected' and threatening to imitate Mark Antony, who retired to Alexandria on his defeat. She left Lady Plymouth with regret. 'Tho' I am not very prudent, I think she is less so . . . Ld. Berwick remains the whole summer. [Her husband Plymouth had returned to England.] Lord Palmerston, comically enough, calls them "Cymon and Iphigeneia", for till their attachment began Ld. B was never heard to speak: love roused him.' Lady Plymouth was not long Cymon's. William Pitt, Lord Amherst, soon appeared a brighter star on her horizon.

On 2 June 1793 Emma wrote, exhausted, to Greville,

I should have answered your kind letter sooner; but I have not had time to write to any of my friends these five months, which I am sorry for, as they may accuse me of neglect and ingratitude, which, if they do it, will be a wrong accusition; for I litterally have been so busy with the English, the Court and my home duties, as to prevent me doing things I had much at heart to do.

For political reasons we have lived eight months at Caserta, that is – making this our constant residence, and going twice a week to town to give dinners, balls, &c, &c, &c, returning here at 2 or 3 a clock in the morning after the fatige of a dinner of fifty, and a ball and supper of 3 hundred. Then to dress early in the morning, to go to court, to dinner at twelve a clock, as the Royal family dine early, and they [have] done Sir William and me the honner to invite us very, very often. Our house at Caserta as been like an inn this winter, as we have had partys, that have come either to see the environs, or have been invited to court. We had the Duchess of Ancaster several days. It is but 3 days since the Devonshire family has left; and we had fifty in [our] family for four days at Caserta. 'Tis true, we dined every day at court, or at some casino of the King; for you cannot immagine how good our King and Queen as been to the principal English who have been here – particularly to Lord and Lady Palmerston, Cholmondeley, Devonshire, Lady Spencer, Lady Bessborough, Lady Plymouth, Sir George and Lady Webster. And I have carried the Ladies to the Queen very often, as she as permitted me to go to her very often in private, which I do. And the reason why we stay now here is, I have promised the Queen to remain as long as she does, which will be tell the tenth of July. In the evenings I go to her, and we are *tête-à-tête* 2 or 3 hours. Sometimes we sing. Yesterday the King and me sang duetts 3 hours. It was but bad, *as he sings like a King.*

Greville replied to Sir William about banking matters. He ended his letter, 'Tell Lady H. that I hope she does not follow the fashion of others; at the [Queen's] birthday the prevailing fashion was very unlike court dress, & very unlike a Grecian dress, & very unlike Ly H. dress, but evidently an imitation of her . . .' Emma's simple raiment during the summer months of 1791 had had a distinct effect on contemporary taste. Greville followed up his pleasant news with a typically Grevillean word of warning not to be extravagant. 'Tell her that her own country cloathing is far more adorning than all the trappings of French milliners on awkward, inanimate damsels.'

Emma and Sir William had suddenly more important things to think of than fashion and English visitors. On 20 April 1792, in the wake of the pacific Emperor Leopold's death, France had declared war on Austria. But hostilities did not at once break out, as neither nation was mobilized. The Battle of Valmy occurred on 20 September, and saw Austria and Prussia defeated. Then followed the proclamation of the French Republic and the trouble over Mackau. War was declared by France on England and Holland on 1 February 1793, a declaration which was 'highly agreeable' to George III.

In Naples, the appearance of Mackau at the Court reception of 1 May, to which our English diarists were bidden, proved the catalyst for an Anglo-Neapolitan alliance. When the King and Queen saw Mackau – they were still in mourning for the death of Louis XVI – they turned their backs. The French Foreign Minister scolded Mackau for his lack of tact; though all the foreign representatives had been invited, it had not been expected that he would attend. Miserably, Mackau awaited his successor, Maret, who was kidnapped with de Sémonville by the Austrians in July and imprisoned in the Tyrol.

On 12 July the Anglo-Neapolitan treaty of alliance was signed. The Kingdom of Naples was to provide 6,000 soldiers, four ships of the line, four frigates and four small ships of war, for operations in the Mediterranean. Neapolitan trade with France was forbidden; English ships were to protect Neapolitan merchantmen; the King could only make a separate peace with British consent. If they continued to fight, he was obliged to remain neutral. England, in return, was pledged to keep a fleet in the Mediterranean throughout the period of emergency. On the conclusion of peace, they must grant the interests of the Two Sicilies special consideration.

With the signing of this treaty, Maria Carolina began to make flattering advances to Emma. Emma's position was no longer that of 'any travelling lady of distinction'. Maria Carolina had written in February to thank Emma for the interest she took in the 'execrable Catastrophe' of Louis XVI's execution.[4] Emma was now an established favourite of the Queen's, and presented the English ladies at Court, as had never been intended. She was in a long line of women whom the Queen made her 'favourite' for a time, her intimate friend of the moment. Emma was exceptional on two counts – the length of her tenure, and the fact that she was by birth of the people and not of the Court. We must assume that the Queen was genuinely intrigued by Emma. She rarely offered friendship to no purpose, however. Her passion for information – of the greatest and of the most trivial importance – could be perhaps assuaged by tit-bits from the English Minister's wife. Naples was still such a political backwater that Sir William rarely received important information. This was changing, however, and there were to be, increasingly, opportunities for Emma Lady Hamilton to serve her 'dear dear Queen'.

In August the war declared on Britain by France in February began to affect Naples. A division of the bespoke English fleet in the Mediterranean waited, under Lord Hood, off Toulon. Toulon was still Royalist, as were many of the southern French towns – less opposed to the British than to the new French Government. In August, the army

of the Convention marched into southern France. The city fathers of
Toulon lost no time in surrendering to Lord Hood and asked him to
defend them from the army which now besieged Royalist Marseilles.

Hood decided this was the moment to ask the Kingdoms of Naples
and Sardinia to honour their alliance promises. Dispatches were made
ready for the two Kingdoms, asking for troops in return for British
subsidies. The messenger whom Hood chose to carry the dispatches to
Naples was a certain Horatio Nelson, diminutive Post-captain of the
Agamemnon. He arrived in the Bay of Naples on 11 September 1793,
and dispelled the rumour spread by a Spanish ship that the Spaniards
had captured Toulon. As Ferdinand gleefully put it, 'The Spaniard had
Trompé, Trompé!'

CHAPTER ELEVEN

Maria Carolina and Miladi

'We are in the Bay all night, becalmed, and nothing could be finer than the view of Mount Vesuvius,' wrote Captain Horatio Nelson on 11 September 1793. All Naples was delighted, the next morning, to see a ship flying the British standard, after being so long menaced by Latouche's frigates. The King was so eager to hear of the British success at Toulon that he 'came afloat and sent to me'. 'We are called by him the Saviours of Italy.'

An account is given of Sir William's first meeting with Hood's emissary in Harrison's *Life . . . of Lord Viscount Nelson* (1806).[1]

On Sir William Hamilton's returning home, after having first beheld Captain Nelson, he told his lady that he was about to introduce a little man to her acquaintance, who could not boast of being very handsome, 'but,' added Sir William, 'this man, who is an English naval officer, Captain Nelson, will become the greatest man that ever England produced . . . he will one day astonish the world. I have never entertained any officer in my house, but I am determined to bring him here. Let him be put in the room prepared for Prince Augustus.'

Nelson was equally complimentary:

'Sir William,' said he, in consequence of the dispatch made use of in obtaining the Neapolitan troops, 'you are a man after my own heart: you do business in my own way! I am, now, only a captain; but I will, if I live, be at the top of the tree.'

Nelson was much given to such trumpetings. What is surprising, in view of the endless naval visits to Naples, is Sir William's supposed assertion that he had never entertained any 'officer' at his house: Captain Finch and Commodore Melvile are two previously recorded in this book whom he did so entertain. Sir William, son of a naval man, had a healthy respect for the marine forces. It is said that Harrison's *Life* was written 'under the immediate dictation of Lady Hamilton'. Strange that she forgot her previous triumphs before naval admirers.

Whether Nelson did lodge at the Palazzo Sessa during his stay is not certain. He had his stepson, Midshipman Josiah Nisbet, with him. (He made a practice of taking his midshipmen around with him, to give them a little polish.) His purpose was achieved 'with a zeal which no one could exceed'. Not only did he obtain the 6,000 Neapolitan troops from Acton, he also procured a letter from the King – 'the handsomest letter, in his own handwriting' – for Lord Hood.

In four days Nelson was with the King three times, and dined with him once. He was sat at the King's right hand, 'before our Ambassador and all the nobles present'. After five years 'on the beach' in Norfolk, Nelson had come into his own. Of course, just because of those five years out of action, the little captain was the more impressed by what others regarded as a poltroon's court.

Nelson intended to celebrate the end of a successful mission with a visit from the King on board the *Agamemnon*. First, to breakfast came Sir William and Emma and other members of the English colony. Among them were the Bishop of Winchester, his lady and family, Lord and Lady Plymouth, Earl (actually Viscount) Grandison and Lady Gertrude Villiers, 'besides other Baronets, &c'. Nelson had to borrow much of his cutlery from the Palazzo Sessa, his ship not being designed for entertainment on so lavish a scale.

At one o'clock, the King was due to come on board and the English party embark for shore. There was to be a cannonade and the Royal Standard of Naples was ready to hoist. However, there was an abrupt change of plans. Sir John Acton sent an express to say that a French man-of-war 'and Three Sail under her Convoy' had anchored off Sardinia. 'Unfit as my Ship was, I had nothing left for the honour of our Country but to sail, which I did in two hours afterwards. It was necessary to show them what an English Man-of-War could do,' wrote Nelson gravely to his brother in Norfolk. In the flurry of departure, Nelson omitted to return a butter-pan he had borrowed from the Palazzo Sessa. He sent it some days later from Leghorn.

What effect Emma had on Nelson on this brief visit may be gleaned from an account he sent of his visit to his wife, Fanny. 'Lady Hamilton has been wonderfully kind and good to Josiah. She is a young woman of amiable manners and who does honour to the station to which she is raised.' With Nelson's departure, the Hamiltons did not entirely forget him. Sir William corresponded quite actively, and Nelson sent Emma a note the next year. However, the correspondence merely consisted in the passing of intelligence about the French fleet's movements, and assurances of mutual regard.

As Nelson's account of the English who breakfasted with him makes clear, Naples was still regularly invaded by those intrepid islanders. The Palmerstons returned on 23 December 1793, for instance. A sign of the times, however, was Lady Palmerston's discovery that quite half her Neapolitan friends were shut up. Some were imprisoned for Jacobin activities; in Naples' 'voluptuous climate', most were in convents for illicit affairs of the heart. The English were subject to no such restraint. Lady Palmerston commented on Lady Bessborough's social rota. She 'sees company on Mondays and Thursdays and Lord Grandison on Tuesdays and Saturdays'.[2]

It was at an evening party at Lord Grandison's that disturbing news closed a troubled year. A note was brought to Sir William with the news that the English had evacuated Toulon. Information that the French army was nearby at Nice decided Hood to attempt to hold the city no longer. A full report was only made available with a letter from Sir Sidney Smith to Sir William of 10 January 1794. Long before that, Maria Carolina was writing an anxious note to Emma. She had heard there were English ships at Leghorn. Had they sent any news of Toulon '*au chevalier Hamilton*'?

The involvement of the Neapolitan troops at Toulon was the first experience of war for the Kingdom of the Two Sicilies for over sixty years. The city was plunged in gloom when news came of the losses. It had been expected that the addition of the Neapolitan troops would miraculously swing the balance in the allies' favour. Sir Gilbert Elliot, however, described the regiments as 'perfectly raw', though well turned out on the German model. 'They have . . . one small fault as soldiers which is an insurmountable dislike to danger, and a determination not to incur it.'[3] When the plans were laid for a well-concerted retreat from Toulon, due to begin on 18 December 1793, the Neapolitans, led by their general, Prince Pignatelli, calmly upped and left on the evening of the seventeenth. In the confusion this caused, their losses were only rendered the heavier. Meanwhile, Admiral Forteguerri was 'in as great haste as the military'. He 'pushed off' for Naples without making any arrangements about troops or refugees. Such was the ignorance in Naples, however, that Lady Palmerston reported in January 1794: 'It seems agreed on all hands that the Neapolitans have behaved singularly well.'

The news of the Neapolitan losses did not affect the junkets on which the English were regularly employed. On 4 January 1794 Emma hosted a *Prima Sera*, to which the Palmerstons came. Sir William was away hunting with the King at Monte Dragone. The evening ended with a visit of condolence to the Princess Belmonte. The Prince had died on New Year's Day. As was the custom, the Princess sat up in a room 'with the hangings taken down, with hardly any light in the room and all in the deepest black, to see all her acquaintances'. As she had not lived with her husband for many years, this was perhaps an excess of mourning.

The next day, Lady Palmerston was of a large party which dined with Lady Hamilton. 'Nothing could do the honours better than Lady H., and few so well. The more I see of her, the more I admire her, and think her a very superior woman . . .' On the thirteenth, Sir William was back in time to escort Emma to a dinner at General Acton's. The Palmerstons were the only other English favoured by an invitation. To a grand fête given by the Hamiltons for Prince Augustus, however, all the English were bidden.

In February, with the spring flowers, Lady Webster returned to Naples to lodge at Severino's Hotel. Her only reference to the Hamilton household was that they 'were as tiresome as ever; he as amorous, she as vulgar'.

In March 1794 many of the other English went to Rome and Sir William and Emma were relieved of their agreeable house-guest, Prince Augustus. He returned to Rome to wed Lady Augusta Murray. This accomplished secretly, he proceeded to London and was granted an increase in his allowance by his fond father. He escaped with this back to his bride in Rome, where rumours were spreading of his marriage. Irate, George III discovered his son's secret only after Augustus had fled.

Meanwhile, Sir William was feeling proud of himself. He had just prevailed on Acton to send some mortars for the siege of Bastia on Corsica. The centre of the English fleet's operations in the Mediterranean had moved to this island after the disaster of Toulon, and by the end of May Bastia had surrendered. The King of England's birthday was consequently celebrated in Naples in grand style. On 21 June General Paoli, in the name of the Corsican people, tendered the crown of Corsica to His Majesty George III, represented by Sir Gilbert Elliot as his Minister Plenipotentiary. So another colony was added to the British dominions.

Meanwhile, at Caserta, Sir William and Emma were enjoying leisurely afternoons in the English Garden. Lady Spencer and her amorous, ailing daughter, Lady Bessborough, lived with them. Lady Spencer was considered something of a *bas bleu* or blue-stocking, and was a hard taskmaster to her frivolous daughters. Emma, however, she now pleased to approve, and later recalled 'the Quiet Evenings & the Handels Musick & Songs at Caserta . . .'.[4] She would never forget Emma's and Mrs Cadogan's 'kind care of my poor little girl'.

Sir William was busy in April, writing long dispatches to the Foreign Secretary about the 'terrible & well laid' plans to murder the Royal Family at Caserta, and set on fire the Royal Palace and arsenal at Naples.

French money was used for bribes, and LOMO and ROMO (from *Libertà o Morte* and *Repubblica o Morte*), political clubs with divergent aims, had collaborated. The situation was still critical when he wrote. Forty conspirators were in jail, few older than twenty-four, and some destined for public execution. The plot was well advanced when discovered, it wanted only the explosion, Maria Carolina told Gallo, Neapolitan Ambassador to Austria.

In the summer, there were two events to interest the English at Naples. On 1 June, later known as the Glorious First, Lord Howe won a major victory off Ushant. More locally, on 15 June, there was a 'formidable' eruption of Vesuvius and, a month later, 'subterraneous hisses accompanied by a sound of boiling water is heard often at the foot of Vesuvius,' Sir William informed Greville. 'It sounds for all the world like a giant kettle.'

To this eruption Emma attributed 'a violent diarea' which reduced Sir William to such a low ebb that she was much alarmed – 'notwithstanding I thought I should have gone with him.' The Queen thoughtfully invited them to her palace, the Quisisana, at Castellamare to recuperate in September.

Quisisana is an elegant pink villa commanding a heady view of the Gulf of Castellamare. Pleasant groves of camellias and olives surround it, while bulky grey hills rise above. Even in its ruined state, the ballrooms and major salons are imposing. There is a charming story attached to its name. A mythical prince, worried by his daughter's health, immured her here for some years. Whether the breezy situation or the loneliness was responsible, she recovered her health and was released. *Qui si sana* in English translates as 'Here one heals.'

Here they spent their third wedding anniversary and Sir William told Emma 'he loved me better than ever, and had never for one moment repented.' She wore a locket with his miniature and some of his hair 'next the heart'. Emma's constant solicitude was rewarded. 'Think of my feelings in that moment, when I could with truth say the same to him,' she wrote to Greville. She gave a 'little fête' to mark the occasion, inviting the Plymouths among others from Naples. 'I never saw Sir William so happy, nor never was so happy myself.'

The occasion of Emma's letter was the appointment of Greville as Vice-Chamberlain to the King. 'You have well merited it . . . May you long enjoy it with every happiness that you deserve!' Emma wrote. The appointment was the work of Greville's brother, Colonel 'Wellbred' Robert Fulke, always a favourite at the Court, and was to be the peak of Greville's career. He was still dealing in antiquities, still trying to interest Sir William in developing his estates in Wales. But, as Sir

William objected, from the improvements so far, including an Inn and Landing-place at Milford Haven, he had not received a penny in two years. 'What has futurity ever done for me?' he complained quaintly.

Emma concluded her letter with some complaints about Mrs Hackwood, her long-serving dressmaker. 'All the things were spoilt, and I had no right to pay for them.' Nevertheless, she instructed Greville to settle the bill, and asked him to send her 'an English riding hat, very fashionable'. With Lord Pembroke's death, which gave Sir William 'a little twist', she had lost her supplier of mounts for her rides about the countryside. The Queen came to her rescue, and supplied her with 'horses, an equerry, and her own servant in her livery every day'. This was only one of the marks of Royal favour. 'P.S.', she finished, 'Mother's love to you. She is the comfort of our lives, and is our housekeeper. Sir William doats on her.'

Sir William confirmed in October 1794 that he was still in good health. He blamed the bilious complaints which attacked him in the wake of the eruption on the 'sulphurous and mephitic vapour of Vesuvius that filled our atmosphere'. He and Emma were at Caserta as usual. He was shooting larks only at present, but in a few days' time the boar season began. The Court looked on him and Emma and treated them 'as if we belonged to the family'.

At the end of November, there was a curious addition to the English at Naples. This was the Earl-Bishop of Bristol and Derry. A compliment to Emma preceded his arrival. He gave a dinner in Rome and, in 'mixed company', swore that 'God Almighty must have been in a glorious mood when he made you, &, tho' in general he made but a bungling work of it, yet he had outdone all the rest in forming Lady Hamilton.'

The Earl-Bishop came to Naples with a proposal that Sir William resign his employ at Naples to Bristol's son, the amorous Lord Hervey. Hervey had lost his ministry at Florence and had been rewarded with a Government pension of £1,500 a year. Bristol proposed that this be turned over to Sir William in return for the resignation of his post to Hervey. Emma's informant, Joseph Denham, did not suppose that Sir William would be agreeable to the loss of £3,500 a year and 'all his consequence', nor would Emma like to leave Naples, 'where I hear you are such a favourite of the Queen's'. Denham merely wrote to apprise the Hamiltons of their eccentric friend's plan.

It was indeed unlikely that Sir William would favour such a proposal, but he received the clerical Earl hospitably. He spent one week at Naples and one at Caserta with the Hamiltons by turns and was still with them on 18 December. Emma wrote to Greville, 'He is very fond of me, and very kind. He is very entertaining, and dashes at everything. Nor does he mind King or Queen, when he is inclined to show his talents.' Put in mind of the Queen, Emma added, 'If I was her daughter, she could not be kinder to me, & I love her with my whole soul.' Emma ended her letter with more affirmations of her continuing love for Sir William. 'I am, as women generally are, ten thousand times fonder of him than I was . . . no quarrelling, nor crossness nor laziness. All nonsense is at an end, and everybody that sees us are edified by our example of conjugal and domestick felicity.' Polly Prim! Emma had no time to write further. She only asked Greville to send her, by the Neapolitan courier, some ribbons and fourteen yards of fine muslin or 'fine Leno. Ask any Lady what Leno is,' she added, '. . . and put it down to Sir William's account with his banker.' Emma's allowance of £200 per annum was no longer sufficient. With the Queen's favour came 'constant' attendances at Court, even twice daily – 'and I must be well dress'd'. As she wrote, Prince Augustus was once more hieing thither, and his arrival was to be the occasion of a great dinner at Court.

Emma goes into rhapsodies over the Queen and her charm – 'the best . . . friend in the world. I live constantly with her, and have done intimately so for 2 years.' Emma was with the Queen the evening before she wrote – 'we passed four hours in an enchantment.' Her friend lent her a book by Gorani, 'a vile French dog', in which the Queen's character was thoroughly besmirched. 'Don't believe a word . . . I have by reading the infamos calomny put myself quite out of humour . . .'

Prince Augustus' visit did not pass without a pleasantry from the mischievous Lord Bristol. The rotund Prince began to sing along with Mrs Billington, the celebrated opera singer, at a concert at the Palazzo Sessa. The Bishop endured this for a time with only 'a peevish pish or two'. 'At length, the interruptions became so annoying, that . . . turning to the royal singer, he said, "Pray cease: you have the ears of an ass."' Prince Augustus was not deterred. The Bishop, sickened by the false compliments paid the Prince, said to a lady who sat next to him, loud enough to be heard by everyone in the circle, 'This may be very fine braying, but it is intolerable singing.'

A story about Emma may belong to this winter too. She was sitting with the Earl-Bishop when a lady of dubious reputation came to call. The Earl-Bishop rose and made to leave. 'Don't go,' Emma said. To this he replied, 'It is permitted to a bishop to visit one sinner; but quite unfitting that he should be seen in a brothel.'

With January 1795 arrived information from Greville about Emma's 'young protégé' or 'élève'. 'I enquired particularly about her; she will not be tall nor handsome, but of a good disposition.' Greville had instructed Mr Blackburn not to raise her expectations and little Emma had consequently 'no one idea to act or think upon beyond the quiet & retired life' now hers with Mrs Blackburn and her daughters. Emma's daughter was now nearly thirteen and Greville very much hoped some 'good sort of man, either with a profession or fortune', could be brought to marry her. 'A moderate dot [or dowry] may have its effect.'

Richard Payne Knight, the author and collector, sent Emma news from abroad in January 1795, and thanked her for the elegant fragment of Greek sculpture she had sent him. Emma had congratulated him on some poetry, her dilettante side to the fore. He now took the opportunity to tell her he had attempted some verses on her own fair person. He had recently been building bridges and park walks at Downton, the Herefordshire estate where she and Sir William visited on their nuptial tour. He hoped she would grace the house soon, where he had fitted up a museum for his bronzes.

Sir William had spoken in 1794 of visiting England, but the political situation now was such as to preclude any but urgent visits. 'When a peace will permit us, we shall make you a short visit,' Sir William told Greville in March, but he was much too busy at present to pencil in a date. 'One would have thought there were such difficulties this year, that few wou'd have arrived at Naples, yet I had 74 at dinner the Queen's birthday,' Sir William grumbled. He was seriously thinking of giving up his post for a pension and continuing at Naples as a private resident. Meanwhile, Emma went on to his 'perfect satisfaction'. 'I do not believe there is any-one that the Queen of Naples loves in her heart so much.'

Sir William suffered another attack of bilious fever in April, and 'the quantity of bile he has discharged . . . is incredable.' The Queen was 'as a mother to me', Emma informed Greville. She wrote four or five times a day and even offered to come and help Emma in her nursing. 'This is friendship.'

Emma had an amusing anecdote about Lady Bath, who was staying for two days at Caserta. She was so shy that, when she gave a ball, she asked Emma to do the honours for her. 'I put her at her ease,' Emma said grandly. Her status was quite different now, as friend of the Queen, from what it had been when she arrived in Naples. Lady Bath asked all the Neapolitan ladies of the first distinction, then had 'a nervous fit and wou'd not come out of her room for 3 hours'. Emma maliciously told this story to Greville, 'as you was to have married her, I think I heard'.

Emma now directed Greville to send her some political news.

'Against my will, owing to my situation here, I am got into politicks,' she announced. It was for the Queen that she wished information. 'She loves England and is attached to our Ministry, and wishes the continuation of the war as the only means to ruin that abominable French council.'

But Emma was not wholly bound up in political affairs as yet. In May she wrote to Greville to ask, 'Is the Princess of Wales handsome? How can red hair be handsome?' She was just off with Sir William to Caserta to see Their Majesties. There was an idea that they should go to the Queen's palace at Castellamare again this summer. Of Sir William's health, there was good news. He and Emma had been staying in the Casino Merala, beneath the Castel S. Elmo, and the hill air had done him a great deal of good. Sir William confirmed his better health in July. Horseriding was the best cure.

'I don't wonder at yr getting well with such a nurse as Ly H.,' wrote William Beckford in September 1795, as usual proposing a visit to Naples. 'Who would not risk a fever to be so taken care of.' He added that Sir William's report that Emma gained 'universal esteem' was no surprise, considering 'her candid open countenance & unaffected superiority'.

Was Emma still as unaffected as Beckford declared? For four years now she had been Miladi Hamilton and for two of them the acknowledged intimate of a queen. Her letters so far quoted display some sense of her own importance, but she always tried to impress Greville. She felt it her not unwelcome duty to remind him of what he had thrown over. It is notable that no English travellers complain of unbecoming airs and graces in her – and they would have been on the watch. Perhaps Emma aggrandized her importance in the political arena; her only acts so far were to transcribe several letters from Neapolitan ambassadors abroad on the instructions of the Queen and for the benefit of the British Government.

Naturally, Beckford did not make it to Naples, though he sent ahead 'wines, linnen in a large trunk, liveries, a very fine piano, & I hardly know what else besides'. In November, 'tossed by a confounded storm in the Gulph of Valencia, & chased by a Barbary corsair', he took refuge in Alicante, an 'odd, Moorish-looking place'. The Hamiltons had engaged the best rooms in the Albergo Reale in vain, and Beckford was paying thirteen ducats a day for them. Sir William was too ill to care. Bilious fever was again making his life wretched, and only yielded in December to bleeding and a favourite remedy called James's powders.

The constant threats to Sir William's health must have told on Emma.

She was evidently accustomed to nurse him herself, probably with relief from her mother. Since their marriage, Sir William had been 'under the doctor' too often not to alarm.

Thoughts of mortality were never far from Sir William's mind in the years after Catherine Hamilton's death. It would not be surprising if Emma's thoughts, as she sat beside her recumbent spouse, turned to wondering about a future without Sir William. She cannot have failed to know that Greville was Sir William's principal heir. What were the provisions for her? Would she do best to stay in Naples? The Queen would no doubt lend her support. Out of the voluptuous climate she would be still more a fish out of water than Sir William. Mercifully, each illness passed its crisis successfully, but there was no guarantee that Sir William would not crumble under the next. He was sixty-six, no great age, but this late succession of illnesses was debilitating. Emma was now thirty-one and, it would seem, fit as a fiddle. Sir William, veteran of the Seven Years' War and pacific by nature, found the Jacobin threat to his beloved city distressing. She thrived on the political intrigue, though she had no more than a simple understanding of the issues.

Was Emma content with the daily round of Court receptions and visits from the English community? She had her music, now a pastime of ten years' standing. But in ten years had she achieved anything remarkable? She had married a distinguished member of the diplomatic service and of the English nobility. From unpromising beginnings, she had now achieved a certain fame, and she had a number of distinguished friends and admirers. From the shackles of Edgware Row, she was now effectively free to act as she pleased. As Sir William grew tired, as he saw her blossoming friendship with Maria Carolina, so he relaxed his constant vigilance. Effectively, Emma was now her own woman, though financially dependent on her husband, of course. What were her dreams?

There was no example in Naples, at least, for her to emulate. There the women were parochial gossips confined to their homes – little different from the first Greek women whose men colonized the Naples seaboard in the seventh century BC. There were a few women of power and intellect. The Princess Belmonte, the poet Eleonora Fonseca di Pimentel, and the Marchesa San Marco spring to mind. Emma's gravitation towards the Queen and their friendship was not surprising, in the circumstances. The Queen had long worked to see her political aims – the supremacy of the Habsburg House – realized. In this, England could be of aid. Emma took it upon herself to represent England abroad, to further its interests. The Habsburg Queen and the Cheshire woman cemented their private friendship in the field of politics.

In fact, the political situation did not afford either the Queen or Emma much opportunity for asserting themselves, or furthering the interests of England. As the New Year dawned, the position was this. The Kings of Prussia and Sardinia had made treaties of peace with France in the summer. This had prompted the Pope to deny access to the ports of the Papal States to all British shipping. Only Sir William's urgent representations had stopped the Kingdom of the Two Sicilies following suit. In Spain, a worried Charles IV formed a full offensive–defensive alliance with France in September. With Holland overrun in 1795, England and Austria were lone defenders of the Royalist interest against Revolutionary France. And Napoleon was about to begin his speedy and brilliant conquest of northern Italy.

The arrival of a lady called the Countess of Lichtenau diverted the Hamiltons' attention from the political situation in January 1796. Wilhelmina Rietz had for some years been the mistress of the King of Prussia, beginning her career by marrying his valet, Rietz. A separation had taken place some years earlier. The Earl-Bishop conducted an ebullient flirtation with her in the summer of 1795 in Munich and it was he who proposed her visit to Naples. Mrs Rietz could not be received by Maria Carolina, but the King of Prussia disposed of that by ennobling her. The Earl-Bishop hoped that she might prove an emissary of alliance between Prussia and Naples, and that Prussia might renege on its peace treaty with France.

Sir William thought this scheme unlikely to succeed. However, he had a brilliant notion. His collection of vases now consisted of over 1,000 specimens. Europe's unsettled state was bad news for sales of works of art. Northern Italy was being progressively plundered by the French. Napoleon's speeches to his army were strong in reference to booty – 'fruitful provinces will soon lie at your mercy; there you will find honour, profit and wealth.' It seemed unlikely that Naples would escape conquest, and Sir William's precious vases would fall victim to some French connoisseur-general. The sensible plan, then, was to dispose of the collection in advance. Wilhelmina could persuade the King of Prussia to purchase the vases, Sir William would be in pocket, and secure in the knowledge that his collection had found a good home. To this end, he and Emma entertained the Countess liberally, though both he and Emma's mother were ill in the early part of this year.

The spring came and in March Bonaparte assumed command of the army of Italy at Nice. He and his forces swept down through Italy, routing the Austrians again and again. The news of each successive victory alarmed Naples afresh. There was no help to be had from the Grand Duke Ferdinand III of Tuscany, though he was the Emperor's brother; Ferdinand had been the first sovereign to acknowledge the French Republic. In April, Bonaparte forced the King of Sardinia to surrender Nice and Savoy. Lombardy was taken next, with colossal ransoms the price of armistice for the Dukes of Parma and Modena.

Naples prepared for war. Young Prince Leopold was made Commander of the Royal Corps of Nobles, four hundred cavalry volunteers in white uniforms with blue velvet trimmings. There were so many volunteers to join the army that it increased by a third, to the surprise of the Jacobins.

The King of Naples was, however, playing a double game. In the wake of the Spanish treaty with France, Prince Belmonte, the Neapolitan Ambassador, was recalled. Now Ferdinand sent him to find Bonaparte and sue for peace. After a long hunt, Belmonte discovered Bonaparte in the valley of the Adige. On 1 June he had a conference with the General which lasted from nine in the morning till late afternoon. The outcome was that an armistice was signed at Brescia on 5 June. The four Neapolitan cavalry regiments with the Austrian army were to return home. All the ships with the British fleet were to do likewise. Bonaparte had succeeded in detaching another member from the Coalition, though the peace was not to be ratified till November.

In Naples, conversation was now no longer confined to Neapolitan amours and snippets of English Court gossip. At Court, with Maria Carolina, there were the latest French moves to be discussed. Sir William was in constant communication with Nelson, who looked to him for news of the French fleet. No one could have guessed, when Emma came out to Naples in 1786, that she was to be caught up in such political action. She still had the running of the Hamilton houses to occupy her. Now, when she stared across the water of the Bay from Villa Emma at Posillipo to the Donn'Anna, she may have felt some sympathy with that legendary princess and that hurly-burly of politics in which she moved.

Historians have sought to undermine Emma's importance in the Naples of the 1790s. Yet, the alliance between England and the Two Sicilies was of vital importance, given that the Mediterranean was the arena of war. What did Maria Carolina think of Emma? Was she merely a pawn? A channel through which to pass and receive important news from England? If that was so, she was still of importance.

How true is a story in the *Memoirs* that Emma, in a jealous rage, stormed into Maria Carolina's private chamber and slapped the sovereign hard on her lily-white cheek? And that the Queen slapped her back? This sounds like burlesque, or high comedy, yet so much of Neapolitan life was just that. Suffice it to say that no trace of such ructions exists in the affectionate letters Emma received often directly from the Queen.

Of another story, that Emma and the Queen had an unusually intimate friendship – in fact, a lesbian friendship – there is no proof. It was a natural tale for those inimical to the Queen to tell, hearing of Emma's intimacy with their enemy. (Bonaparte compared Maria Carolina to the monstrous Fredegonda.) As we know from the asterisks in Ferdinand's diary, he and the Queen enjoyed, or endured, frequent sex. Her seventeen pregnancies confirm it. Besides her earlier rumoured *affaire* with Acton, there had been many others. In 1797 the King dismissed the Chevalier de Saxe, a prince of Saxony, from his service, suspecting that the Queen and he were lovers. We might posit that the Queen and Emma enjoyed a lesbian relationship as relief from these ties, but there is no reference to it in the Queen's letters. There are only reiterations of the eternity of her friendship for Emma and England. If there was a sexual thrill to Emma's friendship with the Queen, it consisted in their excitable chant of hate against the French.

Maria Carolina's character and determined pessimism may be best seen in a letter she wrote to Emma on 21 September 1796. '*Il faut faire son devoir jusqu'au tombeau*' (One must do one's duty till the grave) was her considered reaction to the mountain of troubles about her.

Emma wrote on the same day to Greville a letter equally characteristic.

We have not time to write to you as we have been 3 days and nights writing to send by this courrier letters of *consequence* for our government. They ought to be gratefull to Sir William and *myself in particular*, as my situation at this Court is very *extraordinary*, and what no person as as yet arrived at; but one as no thanks, and I am allmost sick of grandeur.

We are tired to death with anxiety, and God knows were we shall soon be, and what will become of us, if things go on as they do now. Sir William is very well. I am not, but hope, when the cold weather comes on and we go to Caserta, I shall be better. Our house – breakfast, dinner and supper – is like a fair; and what with attendance on my adorable Queen I have not one moment for writing, or anything comfortable. I, however, hope soon to get quiet, and then I will write to you fully. Pray, setle Hackwood's account. We desire it. And send me by the bearer a Dunstable hat, and some ribbands, or what you think will be acceptable. Pray do you never think on me. He is *our* Courrier; so, pray, do not spare him. In haist, ever your sincere, &c.

P.S. I have now to-night an assembly of 3 hundred waiting.

CHAPTER TWELVE

The Protecting Shield of a British Admiral

'God knows where we shall soon be . . . if things go on as they do now.' Emma referred not only to Bonaparte's astonishing record of victories in northern Italy. More particularly, she was thinking of the confused political situation in Naples. Maria Carolina pinned her hopes of preservation on the English fleet's presence in the Mediterranean. Fierce Austrian patriot though she was, she saw that in the Austrian land forces her children's kingdom had a poor protector and she did her best to encourage firmer ties with England, despite the peace treaty between Naples and France now being hammered out in Paris. She continued her practice, established in 1795, of sending Emma any important documents that came her way for transcription and delivery to the British Foreign Office.

Lord Grenville, the Foreign Secretary, did not necessarily welcome these dispatches. With increasing urgency, he encouraged Sir William to advise the Kingdom to seek a peace. Grenville had no wish to see the British fleet kept indefinitely in the Mediterranean, merely to protect Neapolitan interests.

In Naples Acton vacillated. The Austrian defeats in northern Italy inclined him to play safe and form an alliance with France. But pride in his English heritage was distressed by the idea.

Meanwhile, Ferdinand, with Royal disregard for diplomatic protocol, engaged in a secret correspondence with his brother Charles IV of Spain. Undoubtedly Ferdinand derived a certain malicious pleasure from subverting the plans of both his domineering spouse and his Minister. He thought of an alliance with His Catholic Majesty against England, convinced of the Spanish fleet's superiority.

The British ministers abroad were vaguely aware that Spain was thinking of forming an alliance with France, in place of Britain and Austria. Ferdinand, however, showed duplicitous intelligence in keeping his negotiations secret. Sir William was kept unaware of his plans – or perhaps he made no strong efforts to discover them. The charge of pusillanimity has been brought against him with regard to the fast-moving events of 1796 and of the following years. He was certainly most interested at this date in disposing of his second, and greater, collection of Greek vases before the French could capture it. With many others in Naples, he now saw the French entry into Naples as probable. If Spain formed an alliance with France, the British fleet must leave the Mediterranean. There could be no watering and restocking with Spain and France, between them, in control of all the ports.

Emma's views on the matter, amid this confusion, were uncomplicated. She hated Jacobinism with a personal loathing for the trouble it caused her adored Queen. Anything she could do to help the Queen she would, with England a second favourite. This attachment to a foreign monarch may seem odd today. At this very date, the Anglo-American, Benjamin Thompson, was the faithful servant of Bavaria. Acton, after all, was not Italian. Mercenaries were a common feature of all European life. Nelson himself in this year was to propose that he serve the Kingdom of Naples.

In September, Emma's chance came to oblige both Queen and Country. The King of Naples' correspondence with his brother Charles of Spain came to a head. Charles set out the terms of the full offensive–defensive alliance he meant to conclude with France, and stated his intention of waging war on England. Maria Carolina was intuitive where her Royal spouse's moods were concerned. This letter arrived on 21 September. She took the letter and sent it secretly to Emma, who, after hurriedly copying it, returned it.

A Count Munster had opportunely died, leaving his courier in want of employment. On 23 September he set out for London, bearing, besides the letter for Greville and dispatches from the Queen and Acton to Circello, the Neapolitan Ambassador in London, the 'letters of consequence' Emma mentioned to Greville. These consisted of a letter from Sir William, finally stirring his stumps, to Lord Grenville, outlining the contents of Charles IV's letter.

On 10 October 1796 the peace between Naples and France was signed – with a secret clause that Naples pay an indemnity of eight million francs. The English Minister and his wife remained favourites at the Court, regardless of these formalities. On 16 October, the Hamiltons and Prince Augustus came to the Palace at Portici to make music and walk in the gardens. On 1 December, despite heavy rain and storms, the Hamiltons brought Prince Augustus to a shoot at Carditello and a dinner al fresco. On 11 December, the peace was published to the sound of a trumpet, and the 'Te Deum' was sung in all the churches. 'Nominally neutral but never in our feelings,' the Queen wrote to Emma, 'we shall give proof of this on every available opportunity.' To Gallo she reviled the French as 'the murderers of my sister . . . the oppressors of all monarchies . . . the villains who have . . . put poniard and poison into the heads of all classes . . . against legitimate authority, and', she wound up tragically, 'who have consequently blighted my existence'.

The peace brought little satisfaction to anyone. Bonaparte had insisted on its being signed for fear of Rome and Naples combining against France. 'At present we cannot wage war on Naples and Austria simultaneously.'

The evacuation of the British fleet from the Mediterranean, which began in October, caused still less rejoicing. Nelson, the last to leave Corsica, wrote to Sir William from Bastia on 1 December. He was 'grieved and distressed . . . till now . . . England . . . never was known to desert her friends while she had the power of supporting them.' In this letter he wishes that 'individually as an officer I could serve the King of Naples'.

Sir John Jervis, Admiral of the Fleet, had little option but to pull out. The supply and the health situations were critical, the political situation in the Italian states constantly altering. The fleet withdrew to Portugal, Britain's one reliable ally in Europe.

One consequence of the British withdrawal was that Sir Gilbert Elliot, till lately Viceroy of Corsica, came to Naples. He gives us a telling description of Emma in her thirty-second year. In many respects this tallies with earlier accounts, but for the first time disparaging comments are passed on her figure.

'She is the most extraordinary compound,' Elliot wrote to his wife, who had made a favourite of Emma when she was in Naples with her children the preceding year. 'Her person is nothing short of monstrous for its enormity, and is growing every day. She tries hard to think size advantageous to her beauty, but is not easy about it.' What was Sir William's view of this departure from the classic form he had so admired? In December 1795 he had told the traveller, Morritt, that he had married Emma because 'she only of the sex exhibited the beautiful lines he found on his Etruscan vases.'[1]

> Her face is beautiful [Elliot conceded]. She is all Nature, and yet all Art; that is to say, her manners are perfectly unpolished, of course very easy, though not with the ease of good breeding, but of a barmaid; excessively good-humoured and wishing to please and be admired by all ages and sorts of persons that come in her way; but besides considerable natural understanding, she has acquired, since her marriage, some knowledge of history and of the arts, and one wonders at the application and pains she has taken to make herself what she is. With men her conversation and language are exaggerations of anything I ever heard anywhere; and I was wonderfully struck with these inveterate remains of her origins, though the impression was very much weakened by seeing the other ladies of Naples.[2]

Sir William had always been amused by Emma's natural propensity for outrageous conversation. The writer Isaac Gerning gives us a clue to his tolerance, when he says that Sir William was 'jealous of Emma in the Italian way'. If he did not accompany Emma to a social occasion, he made sure she had the chaperonage of several ladies.[3] In his presence, he encouraged her in badinage and flirtation, secure in his undisputed ownership. Morritt tells us that he had 'scarce known her look the same for three minutes together . . . she mimics in a moment everything that strikes her'. Now, it seemed, there were fewer who envied Sir William his prize.

Still, the Attitudes by candlelight came up to Sir Gilbert's expectations fully. Like so many before, he was unprepared for 'the very refined taste that is necessary for the execution; and besides all this, says Sir Willum, "she makes my apple-pies".' Lady Holland also noted Emma's provincial accent in this anecdote. Lady Hamilton was lying down in the pose of a water nymph, her head resting on a Greek vase. 'Don't be afeard Sir Willum; I'll not break your joug,' said the nymph.[4] Sir Gilbert would have reported any rift in the marriage lute. We may take it that none existed. That the Attitudes continued to be improved upon is suggested by a gift from Maria Carolina to Emma: *Moeurs et coutumes des anciens Romains*. Morritt mentions 'the study she has made of characters'.

While Sir Gilbert went to Rome, Emma and Sir William spent their tenth Christmas together. They were still at Caserta when a jolly family party arrived in the Bay on 6 January 1797. 'This majestic Landscape rendered more awful still by the gilded colour that the beams of the sun reflected upon it caused me the greatest pleasure imaginable,' wrote Eugenia Wynne, aged seventeen. Together with her parents, her elder sister Betsey and a ragbag of tutors, valets and maids, she had jaunted all over Europe in the last few years, in increasing danger from the French advances. Only Mr Wynne's foresight got them clear of Leghorn in June 1796, since when they had been confined on a series of British ships.

Betsey and Eugenia recorded their impressions, often none too flattering, of the German and Italian courts they visited. They were unanimous in their approval of Naples. Being both youthful and comparatively well dowered, they found plenty of Latin admirers.

The Wynnes settled in 'a very fine Inn the Brittannia [Albergo Gran Bretagna]' and found that their 'elegant apartment' adjoined that of Prince Augustus. In the first use of the Royal Marriages Act, the King had now declared his son's marriage to Lady Augusta null, even as Augusta was recovering from puerperal fever, following the birth of a son. Augustus languished abroad, pursuing his Hebrew and music studies, not daring to return to England lest his father stop his pension. Eugenia saw him 'on the Balcon, and found him grown very fat'.

Betsey, Eugenia's elder sister, was interested in only one visitor to Naples. This was Captain Thomas Fremantle, who had distinguished himself and his ship, the *Inconstant*, in the *Ca Ira* engagement in 1795. On New Year's Day, Eugenia had been impatient. 'He is always undecided, he would and would not, she would, and would heartily, how will it end?' On the tenth, Eugenia gloomily noted progress in their courtship. The thought that her sister was to be 'soon torn away . . . bathes my cheeks with tears of grief'. Fremantle duly made his proposal of marriage via an intermediary to Mr Wynne, and was rewarded with a promise of £8,000 dowry.

Snow covered the summit of Vesuvius, while the *lazzaroni* pursued 'those insects who delight to nest in their head', as Emma and Sir William returned to Naples. On the twelfth Emma visited the Wynnes and 'insisted upon the ceremony being performed at her own house' the next day. 'She showed the greatest interest to us all . . . a charming woman.' Eugenia was so affected by the prospect of losing her sister, however, that she 'made a very stupid figure during the visit'.

The wedding duly took place at the Palazzo Sessa, both Betsey and Eugenia wearing 'a Nuptial garment (white crepe)'. An English parson performed the ceremony, and Prince Augustus himself gave Betsey away. Sir William and Emma, Sir Gilbert and Mr Lambton – '(one of the richest private gentlemen of England)' – and his wife were witnesses. A merry dinner followed with many toasts to the bridal pair. Lady Hamilton and Prince Augustus were foremost in paying them flattering attentions. The day did not end there. After a brief attendance at the San Carlo – the opera house was fully illuminated in honour of Ferdinand's birthday – the party went to the Wynnes' inn, where a Catholic priest married the wedded pair again.

Emma paid the Wynnes a visit on the next day and on the day after that. One wonders why she made quite so much of the family. That she should arrange the wedding was not inexplicable. The Wynnes had had a rough ride in Italian waters for some months, the French fleet at their heels. Emma had a kind, even romantic heart and the Wynnes would undoubtedly have incurred both trouble and expense in finding an English parson on their own. Nevertheless, her constant visits to the Wynnes and her energy on their behalf – on the fifteenth she presented them to the Queen – show a managing side of Emma that was later to come strongly to the fore. One cannot but think that, after the excitement of the affair of the Spanish letter, she was a trifle bored. Emma's efforts may well have been for Fremantle's sake. Nelson's visit and his subsequent letters had awoken in Emma a friendly feeling for all the British fleet. Sadly, Fremantle did not reciprocate this friendly feeling. In 1794 he had thought 'My lady an uncommon treat'; now he got on 'tolerably with my lady, whom I dislike'.

When Emma took the Wynnes to her Queen, they remained an hour and a half, and the Queen 'did not miss an opportunity of showing her regard and esteem for the English'. The day was not complete without a third wedding ceremony conducted by another Catholic priest, and a 'very pleasant ball' at the Palazzo Sessa. Sir William seems a shadowy figure in all this, Emma directing the whole.

She was on hand on the next day to bid the bridal pair fare-well. Eugenia wrote: 'I saluted this cruel day with my tears.' While Fremantle's ship *Inconstant* was still in sight, she could think of nothing else. However, on the Tuesday Eugenia roused herself to give an account of 'the well known and much admired Lady Hamilton. She makes no secret of the meanness of her birth, and is so little intoxicated by the splendour of her present situation, that her mother is always with her . . . she loudly says . . . that before she married Sir William she had not a gown to put on her back.'

Eugenia commented on the disparity in age between Sir William and Emma, the one past seventy, the other four- or five-and-twenty. In fact, he was sixty-six, she thirty-one. Emma's 'bloom of youth and beauty' and Sir William's stooped back made the gap seem wider to Eugenia, just seventeen. Eugenia commented on Emma's gratitude to Sir William. 'She is always employed in making him happy full of the delicate attention that the warmth and sincerity of a pure sentiment alone can make a wife capable of . . . When he is absent she talks of him with so much respect and affection . . .'

On the seventeenth, Sir William was at Persano with the King, in pursuit of a pack of wolves. Four were duly shot, but a confusion arose when Sir William averred he had shot one. This turned out not to be the case. He then wrote a memorial to the King, begging that, if he could not claim the beast which he thought he had securely killed, at least let him have it recorded in the game book. Then he would have the consolation of being able to show he had killed a wolf before he died. 'You wouldn't believe what a *piccirillo* [baby] he's become,' Ferdinand wrote to his wife.

On the nineteenth, Emma gave another ball, a grand affair in honour of Queen Charlotte's birthday. All the Neapolitan Princesses came, 'the Italian ladies manners and dresses so indecent . . . both', Eugenia commented disapprovingly. A supper for the English alone followed, with toasts and the usual hip-hurrah, followed by a grand shattering of wine glasses on the middle of the table to the loyal cry of God Save the King. The evening ended with Emma and the corncrake Prince Augustus singing a tune apiece.

Emma had arranged for her master to give Eugenia singing lessons. Aprile was now living with his old father in Taranto, so this was probably Viganoni. This, and drawing and harpsichord lessons, filled the débutante's days, when she was not expeditioning.

On 9 February, a family party went off to Caserta for dinner at the Hamiltons' *capannina* before a ball at the Royal Palace. As usual, the house was full – the Prince and the Lambtons among the guests. The ladies then 'gave the last stroke to their toilette' and off they all set for S. Leucio. The Queen greeted them together with the Princesses Maria Amalia, Cristina and Marie Antoinette, whose countenances were a mixture of 'goodness joined with timidity'. The Queen excused their gaucheness, it being the first time they had appeared in the world. Later in the day she came and took Mrs Wynne repeatedly by the hand, tears starting in her eyes. 'When I look at these innocents, when I think of the uncertainty of their future, my head swims,' she said, pointing at her children. The King, unmoved by this affecting scene, 'did nothing but jump, laugh, sing and run about to see that everybody should be well served'.

Emma opened the ball with the Hereditary Prince, and Prince Augustus of England with the Princess Royal. Pretty good for a carter's granddaughter to be in a set with three Royal Highnesses! Eugenia describes the dinner that ended the festivities, 'cold etiquette . . . entirely banished'. A sort of informal picnic was enjoyed, the company settling themselves with their plates on their knees here and there in the charming apartments. With such easy gaieties the Neapolitan Court amused itself in this year while Bonaparte pressed nearer to Rome.

News from abroad slowly filtered through, despite the lamentable state of the post. Beckford wrote, describing his Christmas fête at Fonthill. 'All your vases . . . would not contain half the liquid passed down human throats upon this loyal and festive occasion.' He was planting trees at a tremendous rate, and the great drive was to be thirty miles long. 'How happy I should feel in once more guiding you & Ly. H thro' this most singular labyrinth.' He demurs, however, at the price Sir William has set on his collection of vases, £7,000 – 'a lumping sum'. Regretfully he supposes Russia or Prussia must have them.

Nelson wrote, newly an admiral since 'the most glorious 14th February' when Sir John Jervis won the Battle of Cape St Vincent and was created Earl St Vincent. Ever concerned with honours, Nelson thought Sir William would like to know he had just been accorded the Order of the Bath. Lord Bristol, with a finger in every pie, wrote from Pyrmont in July. The King of Prussia, once a prospective purchaser of Sir William's collection, had arrived there – 'wasted to a skeleton, & his long body . . . bent almost double, looked like the bow of Ulysses.' Everywhere, the crowned heads of Europe were tottering as Bonaparte triumphed. Who had they to blame but themselves if their oppressed subjects responded with enthusiasm to the republican call? The Countess of Lichtenau was among many Royalist bandwagoners who met their Waterloo in advance. By the end of the year she was languishing in the prison of Spandau. Lord Bristol informed Hamilton of this with a cheerful callousness undiminished by memories of his licentious flirtation with the lady.

The news from Rome was alarming. General de Beauharnais of the French army seized a chance brawl and the slaughter of one of his officers to declare war on the Papal States in December 1796. He marched on Rome unopposed, while His Holiness the Pope scuttled for safety to Florence. Even now, the French army, pursuing its usual policy of battening on the conquered, was recovering strength. The one remaining thorn in the republican crown was Naples. No doubt plans were being laid for its capture.

Sir William reclined against the red velvet cushions which ringed his observatory on the world. The inscription '*Hic ver assiduum*', or 'Here spring reigns eternal', ran in gold letters along the frieze above his head. The news might be bad, but he was a philosopher. The view over the Bay and away to the twin capes of Sorrento and Posillipo was some consolation. A Tuscan wit once said that, if the devil had taken Jesus up the Castel S. Elmo road, and not up a bare Judaean mountain, 'I'm not sure he wouldn't have succeeded in seducing the Son of God.' According to an agreeable Neapolitan proverb, when God tires of the cares of this world and of the pleasures of Paradise, he opens a window in the sky and looks down on Naples, his most satisfactory creation. Who can blame Sir William for preferring a new item from the basket which the booksellers of Naples regularly brought him and a luxuriant loll in the sunshine to the fuss and bother of persuading Ferdinand to arm against the French? In 1794 he had made his position clear: 'The whole art is . . . not with anxious care disturb the sweetest hour that life affords – which is the present.'[5]

With apple pies and Attitudes, the year 1797 went by. In April, the Austrians abandoned the struggle to keep the French at bay and signed the Peace of Campo Formio. Now England had only Portugal to support her in her struggle. In Naples the disastrous news of French triumphs and of the lower classes' open adulation of their conquerors made Maria

Carolina fearful for the loyalty of the Kingdom's subjects. She banished Vanni, the feared Inquisitor of State, and the Jacobin nobles were one and all released. The *lazzaroni* were vociferous in their praise of this clemency.

With 1797 a most unwelcome pair of Frenchwomen came to Naples. These were the sisters of Louis XVI, Mesdames Adelaide and Victoire. They had lodged for a time with the Cardinal de Bernis at Rome. Graciously he supported them, though the Convention had stripped him of his fabulous pension. It was no easy matter. Lady Knight reflected that they really behaved with great condescension, considering they had been reared to think themselves next to God.[6] On the Cardinal's death, they came to their Royal kinsmen at Naples. Maria Carolina complained vigorously of the style in which they considered themselves bound to live. More than fifty families had to be turned out of the old Palace of Caserta to make way for them and their suite. Ferdinand could not abide them.

Throughout 1797, life in Naples went on at its customary relaxed pace. The saints' feasts were duly observed, twice-weekly fêtes were held at La Favorita, Ferdinand's pretty villa on the shore at Portici. In September all Naples drove, or rode, or went on pilgrim's foot to the church of S. Maria at Piedigrotta, on the shore close to Villa Emma. Tapestries and silks and satins hung from all the balconies along the route. In November, there was a good example of the peculiar diplomatic situation at Naples, where the English Minister would not meet the French Envoy, Canclaux. Ferdinand wished to invite this last to a shoot at S. Martino. (He was rather sick of the large numbers of English who crowded his table.) However, if Hamilton objected, friction with England might develop. Over such trifles, poor Ferdinand worried his poor noodle while Napoleon crushed the Austrians in the east.

Little did Emma and Sir William dream it, but 1797 was to be their last Christmas in Naples. All the street sights – the calves wandering at will, preserved from harm by the rough painting of St Francis about their necks; the stalls piled with oranges and little *ricotta* cakes, studded with candied peel; the kettles steaming with dressed *maccheroni*, golden apple strewn on top; the picturesque lemonade stalls, all gilt and pennons and flowers; the horses eating nose to nose from the hackney-cab floor where their master strewed their corn; the confusion of umbrellas and hackney drivers hurrying the horses away home when the dreaded rain descended – all this was to be to the Hamiltons only a memory a year hence.

The machinations that were to bring about their departure were in train. Maria Carolina and Acton had thrown off the pretence of observing the peace with France and, in concert, begged England to send a fleet to the Mediterranean once more. The fall of Rome only lent weight to their pleas. In March 1798, Grenville yielded. A fleet was hurriedly assembled, and Lord St Vincent made the momentous decision to appoint Horatio Nelson as its commander.

This met with some protests. Though an Englishman could write a letter addressed to 'Sir Horatio Nelson, Genoa', and, when questioned, reply, 'there is only one Nelson in the world,' there were more senior officers who felt the appointment an injustice. Many naval observers wondered whether the Admiral was not too young. It seemed as though their fears were justified. Nelson pursued the French fleet to the West Indies, and lost them. England panicked.

On 4 June – birthday of George III – Sir William invited all the English then at Naples to a grand dinner. With the arrival of the dessert, he rose to propose the King's health. All duly responded, but a somewhat despondent air hung about the gathering. Many had lately come from Rome – Cornelia Knight, the blue-stocking, and her mother, Philippina Lady Knight, among them. Sir William then announced 'the speedy arrival of a British squadron in the Mediterranean'. He had had a letter to this effect from Earl St Vincent. Despondency gave way to exhilaration. Cornelia describes the sensational effect of his speech. 'Week after week, month after month, had our eyes been directed towards the sea without ever discovering a friendly sail, unless it was some little privateer . . .' A Ragusan commanding a letter of marque which captured a French ship was loaded with praise. 'But now we considered ourselves perfectly safe under the protecting shield of a British admiral.' Cornelia goes on to praise not only Nelson ✓ and Troubridge, his second-in-command, but Saumarez and Captain Samuel Hood – in fact, all those 'fire-eaters' who have come to be known as Nelson's Band of Brothers.

Daily, Miss Knight and her mother looked out for the squadron. Widow and daughter of an admiral, they possessed 'an excellent telescope'. It was placed at the window every morning, and never removed till after sunset.

'At length,' Cornelia records, 'we perceived a group of lofty masts and sails between the Island of Capri and the furthest point of the coast beyond Posillipo.' These were the first British ships to be seen in the Bay for over eighteen months. Nelson remained on the horizon in the *Vanguard*. A sloop came in, bearing Troubridge, 'to obtain, if possible, intelligence of the French fleet under Admiral Brueys, conveying General Bonaparte and his army'. They had set sail from

Malta, which had fallen to them, but their direction was unknown. 'Sir William Hamilton had entirely failed to gain any reliable information as to their movements. The sloop then returned to the squadron, and before morning not a mast was in sight.' Miss Knight was correct; Sir William had received no information of the French fleet's whereabouts. However, he was able to provide Troubridge with a valuable document from the King, asking the Governor of Syracuse to permit the British fleet to water and restock at that port. This was strictly contrary to the treaty between the Kingdom of the Two Sicilies and France. Emma would seem to have been largely responsible for persuading the Queen to have the document written.[7]

The prospect of a meeting between the fleets now exercised 'conversation by day, and . . . dreams by night'. News came that the British fleet had touched at Syracuse in Sicily. Then there was silence.

Early in September, Cornelia was reading to her mother. She happened to turn her eyes towards the sea, and thought she discerned a sloop of war in the offing. She consulted the trusty telescope, and found she was not mistaken. A blue ensign was hoisted. This was, however, no proof that the vessel was of Nelson's squadron, as Lord St Vincent's flag was also blue. 'My attention was instantly distracted from my book, and my dear mother was rather displeased with my evident preoccupation.' Cornelia did not confess her hopes, for fear of disappointment.

At length Lady Knight, impatient with Cornelia's lackadaisical reading of the book, rose and went to the telescope herself. The sloop was nearing land. In high excitement, the book was laid aside, and alternately the ladies kept an eye at the glass. A boat put out from the shore and pulled out to the sloop. Two officers leant over the side of the latter, 'one with a gold epaulet on his shoulder'. This convinced the Knights that one was the commander of the sloop, the other a captain going home with dispatches. Observing the gestures of the officers addressing the people in the boat, Englishmen resident at Naples, the ladies fancied they could see them, 'with the commotion natural to sailors . . . depict by their action the blowing up of some ships and the sinking of others'. Thus was the news of Nelson's astonishing victory at the Battle of the Nile in Aboukir Bay first intimated to the world.

CHAPTER THIRTEEN

The Remains of Horatio Nelson

The news 'was imprudently told Lady Hamilton in a moment. The effect was a shot. She fell apparently dead and is not yet perfectly recovered from severe bruises,' Nelson wrote, gratified, to his wife in Ipswich.

Little William Hoste, a Norfolk boy, was one of the officers who brought dispatches and news of the victory to Naples. Lieutenant Thomas Capel was the other. Under the searching gaze of Cornelia Knight's telescope, they pulled off from the *Mutine* and proceeded direct to the Palazzo Sessa with an 'officer from the English Minister', the gentleman who had rowed out to meet the ship.

William Hoste, just eighteen, was received by Emma and Sir William on this auspicious day 'very kindly indeed' – the more so that he brought a letter of introduction from Nelson to Emma. Sir William took young Hoste and Lieutenant Capel off to the Royal Palace immediately to deliver the good news, while a courier proceeded with haste to acquaint the Emperor in Austria with his ally's victory.

At the Palace, Ferdinand and Maria Carolina were dining, early as usual, with their children. On hearing the news, the King left off his *maccheroni* and jumped up. Embracing the Queen, the Princes and Princesses, he cried, 'Oh, my children, you are now safe!'

Maria Carolina, not to be outdone, 'fainted and kissed her husband, walked about the room, cried, kissed and embraced every person near her, exclaiming, "Oh, brave Nelson . . . oh, Nelson, Nelson, what do we not owe to you oh Victor, oh Saviour of Italy!"' Acton expressed his joy, and a full account of the events of the Glorious First of August was made.[1]

Briefly, on the afternoon of that day Nelson had led fifteen ships of the line into Aboukir Bay, a curving, shallow bay concealing one of the mouths of the Nile. Nelson's flagship was the *Vanguard*, Troubridge captained the *Culloden*, Samuel Hood the *Zealous*, Gould the *Audacious*, Louis the *Minotaur* among other noble names familiar from past battles. It was 'a magnificent squadron, probably the finest fleet of 74's which was ever assembled'. It had been a long voyage of discovery, but on that afternoon, when the look-out in the *Zealous* saw Admiral Brueys' ships lying at anchor in the Bay, 'the utmost joy seemed to animate every breast on board the Squadron'.

The sight might have made lesser men quail. The French fleet, in a strong anchored position, comprised thirteen ships of the line – nine 74s, three 80-gunners and, in the centre of the line, the enormous *Orient* with 120 guns and over 1,000 men on board.

Brueys assumed that Nelson and his squadron would reconnoitre and attack the next day, French fashion. As Collingwood wrote later that year, Nelson's immediate entry into battle was 'a charming thing. It was the promptitude, as much as the vigour of the attack, which gave him the superiority so very soon . . .'

The British squadron's cannon were heard for the first time by the Financial Controller of Bonaparte's Eastern Army at Rosetta, one of the promontories protecting the Bay, at half past five in the afternoon. Throughout the evening, the cannon fire raged till, shortly after nine, M. Poussielgue, the Controller, saw 'an immense illumination, which told us some ship was burning . . .'. Mrs Hemans' poem 'Casabianca', or 'The Boy Stood on the Burning Deck', tells the story of a Commondore Casabianca on this ship. He would not leave his son, who had lost a leg, preferring to perish in the flames with him.

'The thunder of guns was heard with redoubled fury, and at ten o'clock the ship on fire blew up with the most dreadful explosion.' It was the floating castle, *L'Orient*, which blew. Sailors and civilians remembered that shattering noise all their lives. There followed the most profound silence for the space of about ten minutes. By 'the cold, placid light of the moon', the ship was seen slowly to disappear into the sea, taking with her in her hold over half a million pounds in bullion, silver statues of the Apostles and three tons of plate. This represented the major part of Bonaparte's looting of Malta.

The momentary lull in the hostilities was a tacit expression of disbelief in both ranks, French and English. The fighting then resumed, and did not cease till, at two o'clock the next afternoon, two ships and two frigates, the remnants of the French fleet, under Villeneuve, fled the scene.[2]

The losses were severe. Admiral Brueys lost both legs early in the battle but continued to direct the defence, his stumps in tourniquets, till at last a shot hit him in the body and cut him in two. Nelson was wounded above his blind eye, and considered himself lost. 'I am killed. Remember me to my wife,' he cried and, when led to the surgeon, insisted he 'take his turn with his brave fellows' who, dead, dying and wounded, choked the cockpit.

Convinced finally that the wound was not severe, and, ordered to lie quiet, with victory not yet secure, he wrote the historic dispatch: 'Almighty God has blessed His Majesty's arms in the late Battle.' A portrait of him done shortly after shows him in his shirt with his head freshly bandaged, a medal from the Battle of St Vincent slung round his neck. By the afternoon of 2 August, an inspection of Aboukir Bay, though littered with masts, spars and bodies, showed not a single English ship irreparably damaged. 'Victory is not a name strong enough for such a scene,' said Nelson.

Such was the stirring tale which Hoste and Capel recounted at the Royal Palace in Naples. Emerging, they found Emma sitting in a carriage. Bruises or no bruises, she was impatient to celebrate the victory with all the gusto of which she was capable. She had a bandeau round her lovely forehead with the motto, 'Nelson and Victory'. Bidding the officers join her in the carriage, Emma paraded her willing captives through the streets till night fell.

Sir William enjoyed the scene with them for a time. Cardinal Henry of York, younger brother of Bonnie Prince Charlie and last of the Royal Stuarts, had come to Naples in the wake of the French invasion of Rome. Sir William saw his carriage. Though delicacy had hitherto prevented him from acknowledging this scion of a traitorous House, he called to the Cardinal's coachmen to stop. Getting out of his own carriage, he said, 'I beg pardon of Your Eminence, but I am sure you will be glad to hear the good news which I have to communicate.' Cardinal Henry asked to whom he was speaking. 'To Sir William Hamilton.' 'Oh, to the British Minister,' the Cardinal rejoined. 'I am much obliged to you, sir; and what is the news?' When he heard, and had the presence of Captain Hoste and Capel for proof, he rejoiced. 'When you arrive in England,' he said to Capel, 'do me the favour to say that no man rejoices more sincerely than I do in the success and glory of the British navy.'[3] Perhaps this goodwill won him the pension which George III bestowed on him to cheer his old age.

'The populace', who saw Emma's bandeau and her captive officers, 'understood . . . and "Viva Nelson!" resounded through the streets,' Hoste informed his wondering mother at the Norfolk parsonage. 'You can have no idea of the rejoicings that were made throughout Naples at this time. Bonfires and illuminations all over the town . . .'

Next, Emma bore off Hoste and Capel to her box at the opera – 'Not a French cockade was to be seen.' Cornelia Knight gives a lively picture of M. de Sieyès, the French Consul, not daring to show himself on his balcony – 'and even Madame Sieyès and her pug were seldom visible.'

Capel left the next day for England. William Hoste remained in

Naples some days, sleeping on his ship but visiting the Hamiltons daily. He was in urgent need of a complete new set of clothes, as he wore all he had, the rest having been lost in the battle. Emma had him completely fitted out.

Nelson had written in his letter of introduction that he had 'brought up' William, son of an old friend, the Reverend Dixon Hoste. Emma was determined to do what she could for her celebrated friend's protégé. In a letter to Nelson of 8 September 1798, Emma endorses Sir William's praise of Hoste as a 'natural, warm' boy. 'Sir William is delighted with him, and I say he will be a second Nelson. If he is onely half a Nelson, he will be superior to all others.'[4] Emma tried to make sure he did better financially from naval service than the hero had done. An officer from the Royal Palace came one day to Hoste, bearing with him tribute from a *donna incognita*. A small box contained 'a very handsome diamond ring'. There were, besides, two hundred guineas for the brig's company, six pipes of wine and two calves – to provide a feast of Homeric proportions. As the gift came anonymously, Hoste could but answer in best naval fashion. On the Queen of Naples' birthday, which fell a few days later, he dressed his ship, the *Mutine*, completely in colours – 'which is reckoned a token of respect'.

Meanwhile, both Emma and Sir William took the opportunity of Hoste's imminent return to Nelson to write long letters for him to carry to the hero. Sir William's letter displays all his kindly, judicial temperament. He writes: 'History, ancient or modern, does not record an action that does more honor to the heroes that gained the victory than the late one ... You have now completely made yourself, my dear Nelson, immortal ... Audendo agendoque res publica crescit,' he ended. 'How proud I am of feeling myself an Englishman at this moment.' Emma wrote to Nelson that Sir William was 'ten years younger since the happy news'.

Lady Spencer was to write: 'Joy, joy, joy to you, brave gallant, immortalised Nelson.' Emma outdoes even that. This is one of Emma's most entertaining letters. Princely hyperbole follows on munificent extravagance follows on ungrudging exaggeration.

My dear, dear Sir [she begins],
How shall I begin, what shall I say to you. 'tis impossible I can write, for since last Monday [when she first heard the news] I am delerious with joy, and assure you I have a fevour caused by agitation and pleasure. God, what a victory! Never, never has there been anything half so glorious, so compleat. I fainted when I heard the joyfull news, and fell on my side and am hurt, but well of that. I shou'd feil it a glory to die in such a cause. No, I wou'd not like to die till I see and embrace the Victor of the Nile ...

You may judge, my dear Sir, of the rest, but my head will not permit me to tell you half the rejoicing. The Neapolitans are mad with joy, and if you wos here now, you wou'd be killed with kindness. Sonets on sonets, illuminations, rejoicings; not a French dog dare shew his face. How I glory in the honner of my Country and my Countryman! I walk and tread in the air with pride, feiling I was born in the same land with the victor Nelson and his gallant band . . .

We are preparing your appartment against you come. I hope it will not be long, for Sir William and I are so impatient to embrace you. I wish you cou'd have seen our house the 3 nights of illumination. 'Tis, 'twas covered with your glorious name. Their were 3 thousand Lamps, and their shou'd have been 3 millions if we had had time . . . For God's sake come to Naples soon. We receive so many Sonets and Letters of congratulation . . . How I felt for poor Troubridge. He must have been so angry on the sandbank, so brave an officer! [Troubridge's ship was marooned on a sandbank throughout the battle.] In short I pity those who were not in the battle. I wou'd have been rather an English powder-monkey, or a swab in that great victory, than an Emperor out of it . . .

The Queen . . . bids me to say that she longs more to see you than any woman with child can long for anything she may take a fancy to . . .

My dress from head to foot is alla Nelson. Ask Hoste. Even my shawl is in Blue with gold anchors all over. My earrings are Nelson's anchors; in short, we are be-Nelsoned all over. I send you some Sonets, but I must have taken a ship on purpose to send you all written on you.

On 19 September, there was a further excitement: Neapolitans had the chance to play a part in further English rejoicings. Two ships of the line appeared on the horizon. As the weather was particularly calm, a great number of boats went out to meet them. The King himself went out in one barge, a band of music from the Royal Chapel in another. Sir William and Emma were among the merry throng, another barge conveying their band. The air was thick with Neapolitan renderings of 'God Save the King' and 'Rule Britannia', and an atmosphere of jollity prevailed such as had not existed at Naples since before the French Revolution. Tugs and barges steered about each other, jockeying, with good humour, for a better place. Other spectators lined the shore, and 'rent the air with joyous acclamations'.

The commanders were Commodore Troubridge, of the *Culloden*, and Captain Ball, of the *Alexander*. The King saluted them from his barge, not wishing to tire the officers with a Royal reception. Sir William noticed some of the seamen eyeing the King and his long, bulbous nose. 'My lads, that is the King, whom you have saved, with his family and kingdom!' 'Very glad of it, sir – very glad of it,' was the laconic response.

The excitement of the merry little naval fête was forgotten when, on the evening of 22 September, the *Vanguard*, Nelson's ship, came in sight. 'It would be impossible to imagine a more beautiful and animated scene than the bay of Naples then presented,' wrote Cornelia Knight. An even greater number of boats and barges bobbed on the placid waters of the Bay. Overhead, the bowl of the sky was filled with the wings of birds which the *lazzaroni* released from wicker cages – a traditional celebration of victory. Not since Carlo III's entry into Naples had the city seen such adulation.

Some say that the Neapolitans are swift to celebrate any new turn in their city's fortunes. In ancient times, the Neapolitans hailed each new conqueror with enthusiasm undiminished by the knowledge that they had so lately fought hard against him. On this day, the people were infected with the enthusiasm of the scanty English population of their city. The Jacobin nobles and poor M. Sieyès were left to skulk at home.

Sir William and Emma were among the first to go out to meet Nelson in 'the poor, wretched *Vanguard*'. Cornelia Knight went with them. The encounter occurred about a league out at sea. 'Alongside came my honoured friends; the scene on the boat appeared terribly affecting,' wrote Nelson to his wife Fanny. 'Up flew her ladyship and exclaiming: "Oh God is it possible" fell into my arms more dead than alive. Tears however soon set the matter to rights.'

In the 1815 *Memoirs*, this scene is differently described. As the boat neared the *Vanguard*, Lady Hamilton 'began to rehearse some of her theatrical airs, and to put on all the appearance of a tragic queen'. There was a swell in the Bay. The captain of the boat, 'who saw through her affectation, exclaimed, with an oath', that she had better get up the side quickly for the safety of the boat. 'Instead of fainting on the arm of Nelson, she clasped him in her own, and carried him into the cabin . . .' (Sir William followed.)

Whatever the truth is, Emma won the Admiral's heart with her dramatic greeting. (It is fair to mention that Lord Spencer, First Lord of the Admiralty, fainted dead away when he heard the news of the victory.)

Nelson had altered considerably in his appearance since he had last come to Naples, five years before. In August he had written to Emma that he was bringing 'the remains of Horatio Nelson' to her.[5] Leaving aside the wound which he had sustained above his sightless eye at Aboukir Bay, and the fatigue consequent on six long months at sea, his right arm was a stump, his sleeve pinned across his chest, his stomach was in poor shape and, of course, his right eye was now blind.

Cornelia Knight described him as 'little, and not remarkable in his person either way; but he has great animation of countenance, and activity in his appearance: his manners are unaffectingly simple and modest.' He introduced himself to an acquaintance about this date with the words: 'I am Lord Nelson, and this is his fin,' gesturing to his one good arm.

Out came the Royal Yacht, commanded by the Bailli Caracciolo, Admiral of the Neapolitan fleet, 'draped with emblems and covered with spangled awnings'. The music of Paisiello and Cimarosa sounded over the turquoise sea. On board was the Hereditary Princess who, like all sensible ladies faced with the hero, swooned. She had more excuse: she was heavily pregnant. Ferdinand, resplendent in gold and black lace, beamed throughout. He went aboard, took Nelson by the hand, and called him his 'Deliverer and Preserver'.

Nelson then conducted him over the whole ship. Ferdinand was moved to see an injured sailor reading to another in the wardroom, and insisted on touching the Admiral's cocked hat for luck. A handsome breakfast was then produced. Cornelia Knight remarked on a little white bird 'hopping about on the table'. She was told it had come aboard the evening before the action, and had remained ever since. The Admiral's cabin was its 'chief residence', but it was petted and fed by all. It left the *Vanguard* shortly after arriving in Naples.

The Bailli Caracciolo came on board to add his congratulations to those of the civilians. It was a gallant gesture. His chief occupation in this unmartial land was to instruct Prince Leopold, aged nine, in nautical lore.

'All Naples calls me "Nostro Liberatore",' Nelson wrote proudly to his wife. 'My greeting from the lower classes was truly affecting.' Chief in practical expressions of regard, however, were Sir William and Lady Hamilton. When Ferdinand had left the *Vanguard*, Sir William promptly asked the Admiral to live in their house. Though Nelson demurred, thinking the necessary parade of officers through the house would be irksome, it was evident his health needed supervision. Accordingly he took up residence in the upper apartment at the Palazzo Sessa, where a large portrait of George III stared down approvingly at his loyal subject. (Prince Augustus had formerly lived here. One wonders if the glance of his forbidding father had not discomfited his erring son.)

Lady Hamilton, Nelson wrote enthusiastically to Fanny, was 'one of the very best women in this world, she is an honour to her sex.' The evening of his arrival was spent at the Palazzo Sessa, where three thousand candles illuminated the 'splendid occasion', and a dinner party at General Acton's followed.

Every conceivable honour was paid to the victorious Admiral. The Queen sent Prince Leopold with the Bailli Caracciolo to the dinner to express her sorrow that illness prevented her as yet from speaking her gratitude. In a letter to Emma received this same evening, the Queen wrote: 'Oh, if ever someone paints brave Nelson I wish to have it in my bedchamber . . . hip hip my dear Milady I am wild with joy.' Crowds of people followed Nelson in the streets, shouting, '*Viva Nelson!*' Little Prince Leopold hoped to stand beneath the portrait his mother was to commission and say each day: 'Dear Nelson, teach me to be like you.'

Not surprisingly, Nelson collapsed. The strain of the long search for the French fleet when 'the Devil's children seemed to have their father's luck'; the lengthy battle; his own and others' wounds; the long month spent organizing repairs and writing dispatches in the wake of the sensational victory: now, his craving for recognition assuaged, each rendition of 'See the Conquering Hero Come' balm to his spirit, Nelson retired, exhausted, to the soft pillows of the bed Emma had prepared for him.

Emma nursed him on a diet of asses' milk – shades of Antony and Cleopatra. She had attended a variety of men on their sick-beds – handsome Samuel Linley, lean Sir William. Now it was the turn of Nelson, pitifully reduced by fever. He was anyway slight. In the spring of 1797, George Matcham, his brother-in-law, wrote to him affectionately: 'Your Physical Corporeal Substance will not go much farther than a Sprat,'[6] referring to ladies who wanted to eat him up alive.

Emma was both taller and much larger than her patient. However, if she had grown in size, the lovely lines of her figure coarsened, her face was still a fair sight for a man who had seen no woman except, perhaps, the odd gunner's wife for six months. The 'Dorick' or country accent to which the Earl-Bishop had alluded fondly earlier in the year, when he hoped to come to his 'garret' at Caserta and eat woodcock pie, was possibly soothing to this Norfolk man. Mrs Cadogan was on hand, too, to supplement the nursing. Sir William, worn out himself, fell ill too and had to go to Castellamare to recuperate. It was an anxious time for Emma.

Slowly, Nelson recovered. News from Rome may have amused him. There were no lines of communication between Naples and Rome. The French General, Championnet, thus could announce with impunity that the French had been victorious in battle against the English, and decree a day of public celebration. The wily Romans politely hung out lanterns with emblems of St Michael, traditional defender of the oppressed against Satan.

On 29 September, Nelson's fortieth birthday was made the occasion ✓ for elaborate rejoicing at Naples. The Kingdom of Naples was still officially the ally of the French Republic – astonishing though it may seem. A Royal Gala was thus impossible. Nevertheless, Ferdinand sanctioned the putting aside of sables and other symbols of mourning for the day. The Austrian Minister, Count Francis Esterhazy, had already given a grand ball in Nelson's honour. Now it was the turn of the English Minister, still not entirely well, and his wife to do the honours.

Emma spared no effort, and none of Sir William's money. The fête cost him over two thousand ducats. Nelson told his wife: 'The preparations of Lady Hamilton . . . are enough to fill me with vanity.' Buttons and ribbons with the initials 'H.N.' were distributed to the eighteen hundred guests. (Remember Emma's raptures in 1790 when a select party of sixty graced the Palazzo Sessa.) In the saloon, underneath a magnificent canopy, Emma unveiled a rostral column bearing the words, '*Veni, vidi, vici*', and the names of the heroes of the Nile.

Unfortunately the ball and supper were marked by a disagreeable incident. Josiah Nisbet, Nelson's stepson, became inebriated, and accused Emma in 'intemperate language' of having supplanted his mother in the affections of the Admiral. Faithful Troubridge and another officer carried Nisbet from the room before the altercation between stepson and stepfather could become serious. Nelson wrote to his wife of Josiah's 'rough' manners. Lady Nelson, who had evidently heard an account of the evening from her son, noted on her husband's letter that Josiah would not dance on Lady Hamilton's orders.

This is the first intimation we have that Nelson had anything but a warm regard for Emma. He was not deceived, of course, as to what she had been. He wrote to his wife of the remarkable turn-about she had made. 'She is . . . a proof that even reputations may be regained, but I own it requires a good soul.'

Nevertheless, it was as Lady Bountiful Hamilton he had met her, and as wife of a man he admired.

Nelson might dally with a Dolly in Leghorn, as he had done in 1794. His wife knew nothing of the matter. Lady Hamilton, we may be sure, at this date was indeed a willing recipient of his admiration, as he was of hers, but there was no more than mutual admiration between them yet. As her sense of obligation to him – for warding off destruction – was strong, so was his to her – for nursing him back to life. They had a common cause, newfound in Emma – patriotic fervour. Both worshipped at the altar of glory. Josiah Nisbet, a sullen and suspicious youth, anticipated a stronger feeling between them.

What Sir William thought of the incident, we do not know. Lady

Hamilton made light of it in a letter to Lady Nelson. Josiah and she quarrelled sometimes, but still they loved each other and he did as she would have him. Nelson had already told Josiah's absent mother that 'the improvement made in Josiah by Lady Hamilton is wonderful'.

It may have been memories of the unpleasant scene which prompted Nelson's bad temper the next day. He wrote to Lord St Vincent: 'I am very unwell, and the miserable conduct of this court is not likely to cool my irritable temper. It is a country of fiddlers and poets, whores and scoundrels.' The man of action was understandably ill-suited to the languorous climate of *volupté* which others found so agreeable.

Nelson found relief in an expedition to Malta. Sir Horatio Nelson was now Baron Nelson of the Nile and Burnham Thorpe. Nevertheless, Sir William was 'in a rage with the Ministry', according to Emma, for not raising him to the degree of viscount. 'Hang them I say!' wrote Emma cheerfully to Nelson's wife.[7]

Just before Nelson left for Malta – he was away from 15 October to 5 November – an Austrian general, Mack, arrived. Maria Carolina had petitioned her son-in-law, the Emperor, for some commander experienced enough to muster and lead the ragtag and bobtail which constituted the Neapolitan army.

In the wake of the Battle of the Nile, Austria had launched an offensive against the French in the north. The recent alliance with Austria cheered Maria Carolina, who was reinvigorated after the English victory. She dared to hope Naples might now distinguish itself on the field of battle. Nelson had written in a letter intended for her eyes though addressed to Emma: 'The boldest measures are the safest,' a quotation from Chatham. He urged, and Maria Carolina was ardent for, nothing less than an attack on the French at Rome. Lord Grenville in London wrote to warn Sir William of the dangers of such a resolution, while the Court of Vienna dallied. Sir William's letter crossed with his, explaining that all were agreed. The Neapolitan Court would rather attack, than wait to be attacked.

A grand muster of the troops was held at the Campo S. Germano. In six weeks, the fighting force had been increased to fifty thousand men. Maria Carolina rode out to inspect them, dashing 'in a blue riding habit with gold fleur-de-lis at the neck and a general's hat with a white plume'. Tactfully, the manoeuvre in which Mack's own troops instead of 'the enemy' were surrounded was passed over. However, General Roger de Damas, formerly in the Russian service, was present to give a damning account: 'Three-quarters of the troops were only peasants in uniform who . . . barely satisfied the requirements for a simple review.'

In all the negotiations and sessions, Emma acted as interpreter and translator for Nelson. He once spent six months in France attempting to learn the language to no avail. Italian he never attempted. Spending such hours with Nelson – who often had to deal with disputes between English sailors and Neapolitans – Emma grew more and more interested in the English seamen's fortunes. She secured Captain Bowen's promotion. Hoste remembered her with gratitude all his life. Captain Ball wrote a few lines to her from Malta, to 'the best friend and patroness of the navy'. She also took it upon herself to write to Lord St Vincent. Nelson endorsed one letter briefly. Lady Hamilton had said it all – there was nothing for him to add. What St Vincent thought is not recorded.

The projected march on Rome met a severe setback the day after it had been agreed that Nelson should transport 4,000 infantry and a few hundred cavalry to Leghorn, while Mack marched direct on Rome. The King received news that the Emperor only agreed to help if the French attacked first. This caused him to falter, till Nelson told him in round terms that 'he had his choice, either to advance, prepared to die sword in hand, or to remain quiet and be kicked out of his Kingdom.'

On 21 November, Ferdinand salved his conscience with a proclamation that, as Defender of the Faith and champion of Italian liberty, he would lead an army into the Papal States to restore the Head of Christianity to his temporal domain and peace to his own country. The Queen was at last happy. Her husband, poltroon though he might be, would destroy France – she called Paris 'la moderne Sodome'. On the twenty-second, at dawn, Mack and his cavalry troops set out with the King from S. Germano.

The story of Ferdinand's capture of Rome begins well. Championnet, the French General, led a well-concerted retreat from the Holy City before any loss of life could occur. Ferdinand rode in, his Grand Constable Prince Colonna beside him, at the head of an exhausted army to the sound of bells and acclamation from the Roman populace. Captain Louis, bringing the *Goliath* up the Tiber, was privileged to see a sight unique in English and Italian history – the flag of St George flying from the Castel S. Angelo.

Ferdinand took up residence in the elegant Palazzo Farnese by the Tiber, his own inheritance with the marbles from his grandmother. Receptions were crowded with the Roman nobility and clerics. From there invitations to the Pope to return were sent out. Considering the constant poor relations between Papacy and Naples in this century, this must have been the cause of some satisfaction to Ferdinand. Thanks for the city's deliverance were offered up in all the churches, and Ferdinand, the bumbling 'pasteboard King', was a hero.

It was a shortlived triumph. Damas wrote of the Neapolitan army's condition: 'The Seven Years' War had not exhausted any of the armies in action as much as these six days' march had exhausted the Neapolitan Army.' Continual rain had rusted their weapons. A misconceived plan of Mack's to ford, rather than bridge, the swollen River Melfa had damaged wagons and many of the mules died en route.

Championnet had only withdrawn from the city the better to concentrate his forces. The King had entered Rome in triumph on 29 November. On 7 December he had to leave the city in haste, and on the ninth the French reoccupied it. The Neapolitan soldiers lost heart and suspected they were betrayed.

So they were: Mack's own aide-de-camp suppressed dispatches, and other dispatches were intercepted. In shambles Ferdinand and his army returned to Caserta. A story that Ferdinand changed clothes with the Duca di Ascoli, his equerry, may not be true, but the Prince of Migliano told how the King would implore him as he rode beside him: 'Keep your knee stuck close to mine! Don't leave me alone!' Ferdinand himself in later years would laugh at his terror on the campaign. As Harold Acton writes, 'his candour about [his *paura*, or terror] was one of his most disarming characteristics.'

The mood in Naples was now very different to what it had been in September. The Minister of War was arrested. Vanni, the Inquisitor, shot himself with a pistol. The blood of St Januarius would not liquefy. Crowds gathered below the terraces of the Royal Palace, shouting for arms to defend themselves and do to death the Jacobins. Nelson had warned Emma on 3 October, before the miserable march on Rome, that flight was the only plan possible if the French moved on Naples. Now the time for this fateful measure was at hand. The Royal Family agreed to pay a long-overdue visit to Sicily, the lesser part of the Kingdom of the Two Sicilies.

The difficulties in the way of such a plan were immense. There were only two English ships in the Bay, the *Vanguard* and the *Alcmene*. The Neapolitan sailors were suspect, only Admiral Caracciolo certain in support. The Hereditary Princess had only recently given birth to a daughter. Mesdames Victoire and Adelaide were extremely elderly. An enormous retinue, besides the ten-strong Royal Family itself, had to be embarked – and, with it, countless trunks of clothing and other necessaries. All embarkation had to take place according to precedence – even in these panic-stricken times, the Bourbon Court made attempts to preserve its dignity. The greatest difficulty was that the flight must be made in secrecy. The *lazzaroni*, with their jealous devotion to their

King, would go to insane lengths to prevent him leaving, if they had an inkling that such a plot was afoot.

By 14 December, the preparations had begun. Maria Carolina sought to allay the people's suspicions by having all the Court jewels and other valuables sent under cover of darkness to Emma. She apologized for the vast amount of luggage dispatched. 'Unfortunately, I have such a large family.'[8] Lest the people become suspicious of the constant attendance and confabulations of the English Minister's wife with the Queen at Court, Emma remained at the Palazzo Sessa. It was the first time in five years that Emma was not in daily attendance on her 'dearest Queen'.

At the Palazzo Sessa, Sir William completed the final touches to his packing. Since October, he had been cataloguing and putting in cases his picture collection. Then there were 2,000 vases to pack up. Nelson had promised to dispatch these on board HMS *Colossus*, bound for England.

Emma describes the scene vividly in a letter to Greville.

> For 6 nights before the embarkation I sat up at my own house receiving all the jewells, money & effects of the Royall family & from thence conveying them on board the *Vanguard* [British sailors acted as porters], living in fear of being torn to pieces by the tumultuous mob who suspected our departure, but Sir Wm & I being beloved in the Country saved ous.

Matters in the city reached an ugly head when a crowd, assembled beneath the Royal balconies, mistook one Ferreri, the King's courier, for a French spy, and clubbed him to death. No one was safe. Cornelia and Lady Knight remained in their apartments, waiting for the word from Nelson to embark. They did not dare go out, in case word came and they were not there.

Nelson had as many problems to tax his administrative genius in this project as in any battle at sea. He had elected to take the Royal Family on his own ship, the *Vanguard*. The Bailli Caracciolo understood this as a slight on his own skills – since he knew the waters of the Adriatic as well as his own horny hand. In fact, so reluctant were the Neapolitan sailors to go to Palermo that twenty-five English sailors had to be seconded to Neapolitan ships, the *Sannita* and the *Archimede*. Cornelia Knight met Caracciolo at a dinner party at General di Pietra's. 'I never saw any man look so utterly miserable. He scarcely uttered a word, ate nothing, and did not even unfold his napkin.' By 18 December, Nelson thought all was arranged and that the departure should take place. General Acton sent him a volley of hesitant notes, giving, among other excuses for delay, the feeding time of the Hereditary Princess's baby daughter.

On 21 December, the order was finally given for embarkation, and
£2,500,000 worth of plate, jewellery and currency were now loaded
aboard the ships. Though it was now generally known and lamented
in Naples that the Royal Family intended flight, the precise date was
unknown. In a last and successful effort to deceive, the Hamiltons, Mrs
Cadogan and Nelson 'went out to pay a visit, sent all our servants a way
& ordered them in 2 hours to come with the coach and order supper
at home'. The visit was a Grand Fête given by the Kelim, Minister of
the Grand Turk, who presented Nelson with a magnificent sable pelisse
and a Chelengk, a notable ornament of diamond osprey feathers which
revolved by clockwork on his cocked hat.

When the servants had gone, the Hamilton party attended the fête.
Emma then, according to a memorial to the Prince Regent, 'had to
steal from the party, leaving our carriages and equipages waiting at his
house'. She, Sir William and her mother then walked to the Mole.

Only Nelson, however, went to 'a secret passage adjoining to the
pallace, got up the dark staircase that goes in to the Queen's room &
with a dark lantern, cutlasses, pistol etc' – a gothic romance, indeed
– 'brought off every soul, ten in number to the *Vanguard* at twelve
o'clock'. The Queen concurred in these details in a letter to Gallo.
The Royal Family reached the Mole in safety, but in a freezing north
wind, she noted.

The party was increased by Acton, Count Esterhazy, a number of
courtiers and diplomats, and fourteen gentlemen- and ladies-in-waiting.
There were, besides, the King's confessor, his head gamekeeper, cooks
and the Princesses of France – with six attendants – to accommodate.

Muffled in cloaks, at dead of night, King, Queen and children joined
the rest of the company on the Mole. Emma mourned to Greville, 'We
have left everything at Naples but the vases & best pictures, 3 houses
elegantly furnished, all our horses & 6 or 7 carriages.'

Such are the fortunes of war. The twinkling lights of Naples, the
palm trees dim in the Villa Reale, the mass of Castel S. Elmo above
the city receded as the *Vanguard* and the other ships bore Emma and
Sir William to the perimeter of the Bay. The ships were to wait there
for a carrying wind. If the flight seemed an adventure, the loss of a gay
home of twelve years' standing must have depressed Emma's spirits.

CHAPTER FOURTEEN

Rough Justice

The morning sun saw the *Vanguard* with its precious cargo still at anchor in the Bay of Naples. The King refused to leave till his favourite hounds were brought from Caserta. The consternation of the *lazzaroni* and, indeed, of the upper classes was tempered by the general understanding of some days past that a Royal flight was meditated. During the delay Acton, no family man, was revolted by the sight of the Hereditary Princess's wet-nurse suckling the Royal infant.

A proclamation was posted on the Palace gates, declaring the King to have gone to Palermo to seek reinforcements and appointing General Pignatelli Viceroy in his absence. The fury and anxiety felt was not lessened by a rider in which Ferdinand announced that he left more in sorrow than in anger, and would not return till his subjects gave proof of their loyalty.

At seven in the evening of 23 December 1798 the *Vanguard* set sail. ✓ To add to the concern of its crowded passengers, on Christmas Eve a gale brewed up. 'It blew much harder than I have ever experienced since I have been at sea,' Nelson informed St Vincent.

So busy had the Queen been, packing up the Royal wardrobe and jewels, so careful not to alert the Royal servants to the projected departure, that no beds or linen had been brought aboard.

Emma stepped magnificent into the breach. She provided 'her own beds and linen &c., and became [the Royal Family's] slave'. Nelson had given her a cashmere shawl presented to him by the Grand Signor days before. With this costly item Emma wrapped the Queen's feet. Like an agitated Valkyrie she strode the decks, cheering here and calming there. Nelson wrote warmly to St Vincent of 'the obligations which the whole royal family, as well as myself, are under, on this trying occasion, to her ladyship'. Emma did not 'enter a bed' throughout the entire dreadful journey.

The blasting wind tore at the mainstays, and rent the side sails to shreds. Sailors stood by with axes, ready to hack the mast down if necessary. Count Esterhazy was determined to perish in a state of grace. He threw overboard a snuffbox embellished with a naked portrait of his mistress.

As the high seas heaved and the wretched ship crested colossal walls of water, Emma went in search of her husband. She found him in their sleeping-cabin, vigilant with a loaded pistol in either hand. To her astonished exclamation, he returned that he was resolved not to go to his death with the guggle-guggle-guggle of water about his ears.

Emma made no reference to this incident in a letter to Greville of 7 January. She lauded instead her mother's attentions to the King and his gentlemen, confined with numerous attendants 'so frightened & praying on their knees' in the wardroom. 'The King says my mother is an angel.'

Christmas Day dawned and the officers apologized for the want of festive fare. The storm did not abate. Six-year-old Prince Albert, Emma's favourite, ate a hearty breakfast. Soon after, however, he was taken ill. As the day wore on, he would eat no more. Though he made no complaint, he sickened alarmingly and endured a series of convulsions. At seven in the evening, he died in Emma's arms.

Maria Carolina had lost another child, a baby daughter, the year before. Albert's death was a far greater grief. 'Nature made me a mother; the queen is only a gala-dress, which I put on and off,' she was to say later. When the ship limped into Palermo harbour the next day, she could not be persuaded to join Ferdinand at the reception arranged on the quay. He had spent most of the journey discussing with his head gamekeeper the sporting prospects which Sicily afforded, and now greeted the waiting elders with equanimity.

The Hamiltons and Mrs Cadogan followed the Queen and her daughters under Nelson's escort through driving snow to the Colli Palace. A building in the Chinese style, it was ringed about with monasteries and the Archbishop's palace. For all its Chinese pagodas and decorative bells, the Colli was a damp and gloomy refuge. As no sovereign had seen fit to visit Sicily in fifty years, it was sparsely furnished. The Queen wailed that neither windows nor doors would close, and her apartments were bare of carpet and fireplace. She took to her bed, and there were fears for her life.

'I have lived long enough,' the Queen roused herself to write, while she was still gravely ill. Somewhat recovered, she deemed herself 'the most unhappy of Queens, mothers and women', in a letter to Gallo. 'Grief is killing me . . . Everything here repels me. I would prefer any other place . . .'[1] It is a measure of the extent to which her mind was disturbed that this stateswoman of long standing made no attempt to plan a political future for the Royal Family.

The Hamilton party, including Nelson, removed shortly before the New Year to a house recommended by the Queen, the Villa Bastioni. First, however, their attendance was required at Prince Albert's funeral, an occasion in keeping with the general mood of the refugees. Less welcome was an event occurring just after the move. A grand gala was held to celebrate the Royal arrival. Grief had to be set aside. As Emma wrote, 'Dear, dear Naples, we now dare not show our love for that place, for this country is jealous of the other.'

Cornelia Knight was one of few to appreciate the beauties of the Norman city. She was brought to Palermo with her mother and a clutch of cardinals. Though she was worried by her mother's exposure to the icy weather during the voyage, she was 'not less surprised than delighted at the picturesque beauty of the Sicilian coast', dense with prickly pears and tropical vegetation. 'Then, when the prospect of the city', a coronet above the Bay, dawned, 'with the regal elegance of its marble palaces, and the fanciful singularity of its remaining specimens of Saracenic architecture, it was like a fairy scene.'[2]

The Villa Bastioni had the Saracenic features Miss Knight so admired. It had the merits of privacy and a fine view of the Bay. 'Damp and no chimneys' were not so attractive. Sir William was ill for several days with his old complaint, bilious fever. Judicious doses of James's powders had, thankfully, restored him to health by early January. His main concern was for the safety of his pictures and his precious vase collection, sent to England in HMS *Colossus*.

Now, for the first time in her life, Emma spoke less than admiringly of Sir William in her letter of 7 January 1799 to Greville. She was modest about her own part, though admitting she was 'worn out with anxiety and fatigue . . .' Her comfort was 'my dear, adorable queen, whom I love better than any person in the world . . . we weep together'. Now she spoke out. 'Sir William and the King are philosophers; nothing affects them, thank God, & we are scolded even for shewing proper sensibility.'

Ferdinand cared for nothing but himself, his wife wrote frankly to Gallo. His first edict in this time of crisis was to restrict all the hunting ground for his own use. In fact, he behaved in character; but what had led to this seeming rift between Sir William and Emma? They were evidently both exhausted and dismayed by their new home – 'Africa', as Maria Carolina deemed it. United in praise for Nelson, '*Il Nostro Salvatore*', Sir William's worries for the safety at sea of his life's work, Emma's absorption in her 'dear Queen' drew them apart. As snowstorms and desolation swept the unfamiliar city of Palermo, this couple who had so long and so devotedly luxuriated in Naples were not pulling so well in harness.

Private concerns were put aside as the New Year brought unpalatable tidings of 'dear, dear Naples'. On 12 January Maria Carolina wrote to

Gallo, 'There is death in my heart.'[3] General Pignatelli had signed an armistice with the French. Though Ferdinand was enraged that his representative should so act without his Royal blessing, Pignatelli had little option. The French had beaten Mack and the Royalist forces at Capua and Gaeta, where they had attempted to defend the approach to the city. The garrisons in the castles of S. Elmo, Nuovo and dell'Ovo and Pignatelli's forces in the Royal Palace could not hope to resist the French.

Maria Carolina and Acton, once Minister for the Marine, were appalled by the next bulletin from Naples. Four ships of the Neapolitan navy had been left at Naples. A Portuguese officer, they learnt, had scuttled these ships on hearing that an armistice was menacing. If Acton was outraged by this wanton destruction of a good part of the navy he had built up, to those in Naples it was as if the drawbridge had been raised.

An unexpected bulwark of the Bourbon Kingdom now revealed itself. The *lazzaroni* presented themselves at the Palace doors and demanded arms with which to protect their beloved city. Gone were the idle loungers by the Mole who roused themselves at most to a little porterage to pay for bread and onions. This was a raging mob. The 'patriots', as the Neapolitan Jacobins were known, were defenceless against the fury of the *lazzaroni* onslaught. Ladies suspected of Jacobin sympathies were dragged naked through the streets. A flour merchant, Paggio, and a ruffian named Michele il Pazzo, or Mad Michael, directed attacks. Among these was the wholesale looting of the house and library of the erudite Duca Della Torre. The Duke and his brother, Don Clemente Filomarino, both liberal thinkers, were tied to chairs, shot, and their bodies then burnt.

The French army was a more formidable adversary. Contemporary drawings show a ragged huddle of *lazzaroni* mown down by a well-concerted fusillade from smart French officers. Soon, all the defence points and the castles of Naples were in French hands. The fighting, though fierce, had lasted only one day.

The situation cannot but strike one as bizarre. The French General, Championnet, had come to 'liberate' the people of Naples, a people who were evincing the liveliest disinclination for this act of goodwill. In the event, the liberation took the toll of two thousand lives, out of a total of fifty thousand *lazzaroni*.

The Neapolitan Revolution was thus bizarrely effected, in the absence of the very monarchy it sought to oust. On 29 January the Parthenopean Republic was declared, Parthenope being the name the ancient Greek colonists gave to the city where Naples now stands, but the restless dissatisfaction of the *lazzaroni* cast the future of the Republic in doubt. They were only held in check by curfews and stringent penalties for insubordination.

In Palermo, Ferdinand was cheered by the resistance to the French among his subjects, particularly in the provinces. Pausing a moment from his sporting forays, he gave ear to a faithful servant, Cardinal Fabrizio Ruffo. Ruffo had it in mind to go to his native Calabria and there incite the *contadini*, or peasants, to rebellion against the French.

Ferdinand gratefully accepted Ruffo's offer to rouse the Calabrians, and duly authorized him to act as his vicar-general or 'alter ego'. He signed the decree only two days after the French had secured Naples. Due to the need for secrecy and, in part, due to the depleted resources of the Royal exchequer, Ruffo took with him only eight men – a chaplain, two secretaries and an adjutant among them. In many ways, Ruffo's mission resembled the stirring march of Bonnie Prince Charlie through the Scottish Highlands in 1745. The Prince landed with only six attendants. As he sent the Fiery Cross to the glens to raise the clans under his standard, so Ruffo landed, his sole equipment a banner with the Royal arms on one side and a cross on the other, inscribed '*In hoc signo vinces*' ('Under this standard you will overcome').

Ruffo hung this banner from the balcony of a relation's country villa, and sent out an encyclical letter to all the clergy and notables of the district, inviting their support. He then sat down to await developments and the cooking of some excellent fish for his dinner. It is said that, while waiting, he went out for a stroll on the beach. To his surprise he saw the Bailli Caracciolo land in a small boat. The Admiral explained that the King had given him permission to return to Naples and attempt to preserve his estates from the pillaging French. Ruffo courteously asked the Admiral to stay and share his fish, but he would not. To his enquiry about Ruffo's own plans, the Cardinal returned a cautious reply, and the two parted.

A motley crew began to assemble under the Cardinal's balcony. By the end of February he had 17,000 supporters from every walk of life, and in March he began the journey to Naples. The series of adventures which befell Ruffo and other, less reputable Sanfedists, or Defenders of the Faith, has been well described by Harold Acton as a 'world of picaresque fiction'.

There was sad news for Sir William, meanwhile. On 10 December 1798, the *Colossus*, bearing his vase collection, had been wrecked on the Scilly Isles. One box alone was saved, on the understanding that it contained treasure. It proved to contain the corpse of one Admiral Shouldham, preserved in alcohol. The ship's crew had not

been informed of its presence on board, as it was deemed unlucky to
carry such cargo. So it had proved. 'Damn his body,' Sir William wrote
to Greville, 'it can be of no use but to the Wormes, but my Collection
would have given information to the most learned.' William Beckford
was to write in commiseration: 'I who have bowels for work of art know
how to feel the sad loss.' Incomparably finer than Sir William's first
collection safely lodged in the British Museum, this second collection
was the subject of a marine excavation in the 1970s, but only a few vases
could be reconstructed from the thousands of pottery fragments. Apart
from artistic considerations, the loss of the vases was a severe financial
blow to Sir William.

Nelson and the Royal household were cheered by Ruffo's success.
Nelson decided to seize the nettle with both hands. He sent Troubridge
and a squadron with orders to capture the islands of the Bay of Naples.
As with all operations Nelson directed, swiftness was the keynote. On
28 March Troubridge set out, in such haste that the King's letter of
authority had to be sent after him. On the thirty-first he was in
command of Ischia and Procida.

Heartened by these twin successes, Nelson laid plans for the capture
of Naples itself. His fears that Palermo would turn republican had faded.
It is said that he would go out of an evening attired as a midshipman,
with a rather larger companion, Emma, by his side, also in male dress.
They would stroll about the Marina, or harbour, and frequent the
harbour taverns. Here they would sit in their disguise and listen to
the rumours and the discussions around them. If this unlikely event
took place even once – and both were eminently recognizable – there
were more reliable sources to confirm the Palermitans' disaffection for
all things French. Nelson felt he could accompany the forces to Naples
with an easy heart.

His heart was less easy, perhaps, about a letter from his prize agent
in England, Alexander Davison. Lady Nelson was set on joining her
husband. 'Excuse a woman's tender feelings – they are too acute to be
expressed,' Davison wrote.

 A contemporary portrait shows the lady this letter brought to Nelson's
mind. Fanny looks spare with a long nose and heavy brows. A large bow
sits atop a stiff band on her hair. The very ideal of a provincial lady,
she holds a rose awkwardly to her bosom. The contrast with graceful,
voluptuous Emma need not be explored.

Besides the obvious difficulties that Fanny spoke no Italian and would
effectively leave Nelson's father without a nurse, Nelson was at any
moment likely to be called away on duty. He had already been to
Minorca this year. He wrote back to put a stop to Fanny's plan. 'I

could, if you had come, only have struck my flag and carried you back again,'[4] which would be very detrimental to the well-being of the Kingdom of the Two Sicilies, though one was temporarily seceded. He, with Emma and Sir William, was 'the mainspring of the machine which governs what is going on in this country'.

In this there is no trace of the 'attentions . . . of a lover' which Lady Spencer had remarked Nelson showed his wife in March 1798. He would not then 'voluntarily lose an instant of her society'. Nelson, perhaps, felt his rebuff was a little terse. 'If I do not write to you so often, nor such long letters as I have formerly done', he added, it was only because he had not a minute free. Lady Nelson would have been a remarkable woman if she had not pondered that communication long, wondering that he could not tear himself away from his host's and hostess's side occasionally to scribble a note.

In Naples, the Provisional Government, unaware of Nelson's plans, embarked on an orgy of republicanization of the city. The street names were to be changed to such numinous titles as 'Fortune, Triumph, Modesty, Silence and Frugality'. Naturally, everyone continued to refer to 'the Toledo' or 'the Chiaia' as they had always done. Anyone named Ferdinand was in duty bound to take a new name. The street puppet-shows were dubbed anti-patriotic and republican themes suggested. Republican masses were composed to assuage the Neapolitan fervour for 'superstition'.

Pryse Lockhart Gordon, an observer of these interesting scenes with Lord Montgomerie, left for Palermo in April. He found the Hamiltons and Nelson, newly ensconced in the Palazzo Palagonia, near the Flora or public gardens. Gordon was incensed not to be offered accommodation in this palace boasting fifty rooms. (At the Colli, meanwhile, Ferdinand had imposed a scheme of economy which required for instance that Prince Leopold share a room with his three sisters.) To be fair, the Palagonia accommodated, besides the Hamiltons, Mrs Cadogan and Nelson, the Graefer family, two English bankers from Naples and numerous secretaries.

Gordon gave an account of events at Naples to Sir William. Nelson sat, meanwhile, writing at a table in the corner. Sir William received the news 'with great sang froid', then left the room to return a few minutes later by a *porte battante*.

On his arm or rather his shoulder was leaning the interesting Melpomene, her raven tresses floating round her expansive form and full bosom. What a model for a Roman matron! but alas! poor Emma was indisposed, 'dying,' she said, 'of chagrin for the loss of her beloved Naples;' yet the roses on her cheek prevailed over the lilies, and gave hopes that her grief would not prove mortal. The ceremony of introduction being over, she rehearsed in a subdued tone a *mélange* of Lancashire and Italian, detailing the catalogue of her miseries, her hopes, and her fears, with lamentations about the dear queen, the loss of her own charming Palazzo and its precious contents, which had fallen into the hands of the vile republicans.

Nelson then came forward.

After a few trifling queries about the burning of the gun-boats, Lord Nelson said to me – 'Pray, Sir, have you heard of the battle of the Nile?' . . . '*That*, Sir, was the most extraordinary one that was ever fought, and it is *unique*, Sir, for three reasons; first, for its having been fought at night; secondly, for its having been fought at anchor; and thirdly, for its having been gained by an admiral with one arm.' To each of these reasons I made a profound bow; but had the speech been made *after* dinner, I should have imagined the hero had imbibed an extra dose of champagne.

Gordon and Montgomerie were invited to dine by Sir William.

In the evening a stranger was announced as having arrived, bearing a despatch from the Emperor Paul of Russia: the messenger was a Turk. Lady H. with her usual tact, recommended Lord Nelson, for whom the despatch was destined, to clothe himself in his pelisse and aigrette to receive the Turk: this was done in a moment. The party moved to a *salle de reception*. The folding doors were thrown open, and the Mussulman entered. The moment he caught a glance of his Lordship's costume, the slave was prostrate on the earth, making the grand salaam . . . and in testimony of his Majesty's regard, the Emperor of all the Russias desired his acceptance of a gold snuff-box, on which was the imperial portrait . . . It was superb, of chased gold; the portrait was set with large brilliants, a gift worthy of an Emperor. Lady H—, by means of a Greek interpreter belonging to the embassy, flirted with the Turk, a coarse savage monster, and he was invited to dinner the following day to drink the health of the Emperor . . .

The only memorable event which occurred at the minister's entertainment, was this warrior getting drunk with rum, which does not come under the prohibition of the prophet. The monster, who had the post of honour at her Ladyship's side, entertained her through the interpretation of the Greek with an account of his exploits . . . 'With this weapon,' said he, in his vile jargon, and drawing his shabola, 'I cut off the heads of twenty French prisoners in one day! Look, there is their blood remaining on it!' The speech being translated, her Ladyship's eye beamed with delight, and she said, 'Oh let me see the sword that did the glorious deed!' It was presented to her; she took it into her fair hand covered with rings, and looking at the encrusted Jacobin blood, kissed it and handed it to her hero of the Nile! . . .

Mrs C—s L—e, the beautiful and amiable wife of our consul-general, was sitting *vis-à-vis* to the Turk, and was so horrified at the scene (being near her accouchement,) that she fainted and was taken out of the room. Her ladyship said it was a piece of affectation, and made no efforts to assist her guest; the truth is, she was jealous of her beauty, and insinuated that, being a sister of the late Lord E.F., she must necessarily be a Jacobin. N.B. She wore green ribbons. The toad-eaters applauded, but many groaned and cried 'shame' loud enough to reach the ears of the admiral, who turned pale, hung his head, and seemed ashamed. Lord M. got up, and left the room, and I speedily followed. Poor Nelson was to be pitied – never was man so mystified and deluded!

Poor Cecilia Lock, too. She had had trouble enough since leaving England with her husband, two small children and Tiger the dog. She had never before left England and the cosy circle of her mother, Emilia Duchess of Leinster, and of her Fitzgerald and Ogilvie siblings. Palermo was so crowded with émigrés when the Locks arrived that Sir William was hard-put to find them lodgings. Lord St Vincent and others had written, hoping that he could show them kindnesses not usually due to a consul and his wife. In the unsanitary conditions which prevailed, young Emmy Lock became infested with head-lice. She was shorn and unguents applied beneath bandages. Cecilia's troubles had begun.

Her husband, Charles Lock, was a difficult young man, quick to take offence and all too eager to put himself forward when he would have done better to hang back. He was determined to make a financial success of his posting, and wrote home of plans for marketing Black Sea cattle. Emilia Leinster, uncomfortably aware of his naivety, despaired when she thought of his thrusting presence at the languid Bourbon Court.

Charles was aware of Emma's reputation as a charming beauty before he came. His brother William had penned a graceful sketch of Emma dancing the tarantella in 1791, and had said to a lady in Bath that all the pictures and statues he had seen were so inferior in grace to her as scarce to deserve a look. Unfortunately, Charles Lock took a violent dislike to Emma, which she seems to have reciprocated. Why Emma put about the rumour that Cecilia was a Jacobin is unclear. Possibly she found Cecilia's dusky good looks and youthful figure an irritant now that her own figure had lost its charms. She was unused to feminine competition, since the 'nut-brown' Italian ladies were easily outdone. (Henry Swinburne found the ladies of Palermo positively 'monsters' of ugliness.)

Though Charles Lock had not the wit to recognize it, Emma was nervous about the future. Sir William was a year off seventy and no longer healthy. He wavered constantly over his retirement, sometimes wishing to live on in Italy as a private citizen, sometimes thinking of England, now determined to continue as Minister. A cleverer consul could have exploited the situation. Lock contented himself with writing home long, vituperative screeds about the horrors of Lady Hamilton. He found that his suspicions of Emma were all too well founded, to his mind at least. At this date, he saw plots everywhere he turned. On 20 June, Nelson, Sir William and Emma embarked 'with great secrecy' for Naples. Their directive was to restore order to that city, now, all except the Castel S. Elmo, in Ruffo's hands. The Jacobins had surrendered the Castelli dell'Ovo and Nuovo and had been given leave to proceed to Toulon. Lock saw these events in personal terms only: 'I underwent a severe mortification.' He was not privy to the secret, nor invited to accompany the expedition.

If I am to be left Chargé d'Affaires it was indispensably necessary for me previously to acquire some knowledge of the principal characters and progress of events in the Revolution, which the present occasion would so intimately have made me acquainted with. But for this I may thank that superficial, grasping and vulgar minded woman whose wish to retain her husband in a situation his age and disinclination render him unfit for, has made her use every endeavour to keep me in the dark, and to make it difficult for Sir William to give up his employment at this moment, when it is requisite his successor should be possessed of so many details which a practical initiation into affairs could only give him. Sir William has ever showed a forwardness to give me an insight into the politicks of this Court, and of the mode of conducting business, but the unbounded power her Ladyship possesses over him, and Lord Nelson with her taking the whole drudgery of it upon himself, has easily prevented his intention. The extravagant love of the latter has made him the laughing stock of the whole fleet and the total dereliction of power and the dignity of his diplomatic character, has made the friends of the former regret that he retains the title of a situation, of which he has resigned the functions. I know I write too warmly, but my disappointment in a view I had at heart, must be my excuse.

So, for English company, Lock had Miss Knight and her mother. They had had an unexpected stroke of good fortune earlier in the year. A chimney-sweeper in England named Knight left his noble connections the useful sum of £2,500 on the strength of their shared name. If their lodgings were miserable – they were first housed opposite the gaol, where one prisoner playing a guitar behind his grated window could not drown the others' 'groans and lamentations' – Miss Knight could now dream of tempting Captain Davidge Gould with her fortune. The spinster poetess's passion for Gould – one of the captains of the Nile – was the joke of the fleet.

But Cornelia had little time to think of him. Lady Knight, valiant battleaxe, had not been well since the voyage to Palermo. Arrangements had been made, in the event of her death while the Hamiltons were at sea, that Cornelia should remove to their house and to the care of Mrs Cadogan, who was remaining in Palermo. This duly occurred in July.

All Naples was illuminated the night the *Foudroyant* sailed into the Bay of Naples. '*Viva il Re!*' rang out from the shore, and parties of boats rowed out to welcome the ship. A leader of the *lazzaroni* mob which had risen up against the Jacobins, the fearsome Egidio Pallio, was among the company. He told Emma he had 90,000 *lazzaroni* ready to act at the raising of his finger, but only twenty with arms. This was relayed to Nelson, who supplied forthwith a large supply of same. Meanwhile Ruffo's Calabrese troops were murdering and looting. 'The bombs we sent into St Elmo were returned & the city in confusion.'

The *Foudroyant* anchored with the other ships in the Bay. During the six weeks they spent here, Nelson and the Hamiltons remained on board. It was too dangerous to go ashore.

Nelson was immediately entangled in a violent dispute with Ruffo. On 19 June the Cardinal had accorded what the King in Palermo was to term 'an infamous Capitulation to the rebels' in the Castelli Nuovo and dell'Ovo. The Cardinal came on board the *Foudroyant* and Sir William translated to him Nelson's intention to annul the amnesty. The Cardinal stood firm. The *polacche*, or transport ships, stood ready to take the rebels to France, and it seemed Ruffo would have his way. The rebels were boarded on the *polacche*. Then, in response to furious dispatches from Nelson, the King sent word that there should be no treating with the rebels. He also sent the Duca di Salandra with orders to arrest Ruffo. The Jacobins in the transport ships, who included the Hamiltons' old friend Dr Cirillo, were brought across the Bay to await Nelson's justice.[5] Emma informed Greville that she had then sent for Egidio Pallio. It was Their Majesties' view that the people should be the defenders of the Throne. Emma told Pallio 'in great confidence that the King would soon be at Naples & that all we required of him was to keep the city quiet for ten days from that moment'. Pallio was given a hundred marine troops to aid him, and slowly the pillaging Calabrians whom Ruffo had led into the city were checked in their looting and destruction. In Naples today, Nelson's renunciation of the amnesty is still remembered with anger.

Another matter in which Nelson exercised rough justice is also remembered. On the afternoon of 24 June, the Hamiltons' and Nelson's first day in the Bay, a single boat rowed out to the *Foudroyant* with a captive, in chains and with head bowed. It was the Bailli Caracciolo. Following his meeting with Ruffo, he had proceeded to Naples and joined the Republican forces. At first the Royal party in Palermo, and the British too, were reluctant to believe in his defection. Then they decided he had been co-opted against his will. In May Troubridge dashed these hopes. In his view, Caracciolo was a firm republican, and indeed had proved it by attacking one of the Royal ships, the *Minerva*.

When Ruffo neared Naples in May, Caracciolo left the city for his country estates. The King quite sensibly insisted that his former Admiral be taken. Caracciolo knew the coasts and islands of the Kingdom better than any man living. But he was dragged from a well, where faithful servants had hidden him, on the day of the *Foudroyant*'s arrival in the Bay.

Sir William records his impressions of Caracciolo as he came on board. He looked older than his forty-seven years, 'pale and half-dead, with a long beard'. He kept his eyes on the deck, would respond only briefly when addressed. Having learnt his seamanship under Rodney, he could speak perfect English when he wished, though he was no anglophile. He once remarked, 'There are sixty religions in England, but only one sauce.' Now he asked to be tried by British officers. Instead, Nelson turned him over to Count Thurn, commander of His Sicilian Majesty's marine.

Court martial followed that morning on board the *Minerva*, the very ship Caracciolo had attempted to fire. By a majority, Caracciolo was condemned, and Nelson ordered his hanging at the foremast yard-arm of the *Minerva* for five o'clock. His body was then to be thrown into the sea at sunset. There had been a good deal of Jacobin treachery in the Neapolitan navy; this would be a warning to all.

Thurn remonstrated. It was usual to give twenty-four hours for the care of the soul. Nelson's orders remained unchanged. Sir William told Acton, 'I wished to acquiesce with Thurn's opinion. All is for the best,' he finished weakly. 'Lord Nelson's manner of acting must be as his conscience and honour dictate, and I believe his determination will be found best at last.' Others besides Sir William had grave doubts about the humanity of Nelson's decision.

At some point between the pronouncement of the sentence of death and the execution of that sentence, Caracciolo sent Lieutenant Parkinson, his warder, to petition Lady Hamilton. The Italian Prince felt deeply the disgrace of death by hanging, the sentence accorded to common criminals. He begged Emma to intercede with Nelson and have the sentence commuted to execution. Caracciolo's messenger could not find Lady Hamilton, and the sentence was duly carried out. The Neapolitan sailors wept to see the courage with which their old commander met his fate.

Maria Carolina wrote to Emma regarding 'the unhappy and demented Caracciolo': 'I can truly sympathize with your excellent heart in all its sufferings.'[6] A story that Emma had Nelson row her round the *Minerva* to observe Caracciolo's body, still warm and pendent from the yard-arm, does not hold water. The Honourable William Rushout, later Lord Northwick, was on board the *Foudroyant* and dining with the Hamiltons on the day of the execution. He emphatically denied this unpleasant story. Nevertheless, it persists in many accounts of Caracciolo's death.

Charles Lock finally found an opportunity for going to Naples on 3 July, when the King reluctantly agreed to set out for his old home. He was still childishly angry with the Neapolitans for his own defection. Lock ignored the King's humours; he went only to look out for a house for himself and his family.

Maria Carolina wrote to Emma as the latter was sailing towards Naples: 'I recommend Lord Nelson to treat Naples as if it were a rebellious city in Ireland.' Jacobin women, like Fonseca di Pimentel and Luisa Sanfelice, were to be treated with the same 'exact, prompt severity' as their male counterparts, and 'without pity'. Emma was Maria Carolina's lieutenant, or so the Queen saw it. She directed a flood of letters, or orders, to her dear Miladi, and Emma wrote back promptly. The Queen, though recovered from her earlier mental anguish, shows an uncharacteristic pusillanimity in her letters. Now she recommends no quarter for a duchess, once her lady-in-waiting; but with the next ship, Emma learns that the Queen is graciously pleased to pardon the miscreant.

Emma rejoiced in this contradictory correspondence. She wrote to Greville that she was the Queen's 'deputy': 'I send her every night a messenger to Palermo & she gives me the orders the same . . .' Lieutenant Parsons has described the daily life on board the *Foudroyant* during July and August 1799. Due to the King's presence, 'never did midshipmen fare so sumptuously . . . The day was passed in administering justice (Italian fashion) . . . enlivened by the bombardment of St Elmo.' Dinner was at noon, then Emma played the harp. Boatloads of musicians came alongside in the evening.

Emma told Greville that Nelson was the King's representative, that Sir William was 'of the greatest use to the King', and that she herself was the Neapolitan Queen's deputy. This went far beyond what Lord

Keith, Nelson's commanding officer, or Lord Grenville meant when they trusted that Ambassador and Admiral would further the goodwill existing between England and her allies.

Emma was besieged by petitions and testimonials from old friends and acquaintances who knew of her soft heart. Duchesses, countesses begged for the lives of their brothers, sons, cousins. Nelson shows himself characteristically insensitive to the pain these demands caused her. He wrote to Mrs Cadogan, or Signora Madre as she was known: 'Our dear Lady ... has her time so much taken up with excuses from rebels, Jacobins and fools, that she is most heartily tired. Our conversation is, as often as we are liberated from these teazers, of you ...' Nelson, hampered by his poor Italian, had not made many friends in the few months he spent at Naples in 1798. 'These teazers' had been Emma's friends or close associates for over ten years. Sir William's friendship with some of the rebels stretched back to 1764. It was as if their entire periphery of friends had been washed away. In a bundle marked 'some *very private* papers and of importance respecting Naples', preserved in the National Maritime Museum, there are lists in Emma's handwriting of the Jacobins and their whereabouts – at large, or prisoners in ships in the Bay.[7] Only the nucleus of Neapolitan Society – the King, Maria Carolina and Acton – remained.

A sad document, a petition from Domenico Cirillo to Emma, exists. Whether against his will or no, he had been appointed president of the legislative council. He could not deny that he had signed anti-monarchist documents. He appealed to his friendship with Emma. He had done what he could to save the English Garden. He had attended the wounded, irrespective of their politics. No answer came, and he was consigned to the Cocodrillo gaol. In October he and the other principal Jacobins were executed. What Emma felt we do not know. Sir William said frankly that he was surprised to find how little he felt for the rebels, considering he knew many of them well. What seemed the enormity of their betrayal had done much to cancel old ties.

At the end of six weeks Emma felt pleased with one achievement, even if the scenes that passed had been as 'repugnant' to her as to Charles Lock. She had enthused Pallio and the *lazzaroni* with a sense of the Queen's virtue. The nobility she informed of the lady's redemption. The Queen would see none of 'her former evil counsellors' on her return, not the ladies of the bedchamber who 'did her disonner by their desolute life'. 'All, all is changed,' and the Queen stood fair, in Emma's opinion, to become truly popular.

The King had received a warm welcome, and was 'in great spirits', Emma told Greville. 'He calls me his grande maîtresse' – she received all the ladies of the Court. Emma did not take him at his word. 'Il est bonne d'être chez le Roi mais mieux d'être chez soit,' she wrote quaintly. 'I am waiting to get quiet. I'm not ambitious of more honners.'

Nelson declared himself equally unmoved by Royal attentions in a letter to his wife of 4 August. He gave her an account, 'more from gratitude than vanity', of the celebrations of the anniversary of the Nile. The King drank his health to a volley of salutes from all the castles and the ships. There was a 'general illumination' in the evening. A ship decked out as a Roman galley with lamps fixed to the oars and all along the sides stole the show. A rostral column bearing Nelson's name stood in mid-deck, two plaster angels bore Nelson's portrait high at the stern, and a full orchestra sang the glories of the hero.[8]

Charles Lock alone of the Palermo party was unhappy. He had had an altercation with Nelson about victualling supplies. Lock foolishly accused the Admiral of making 'false' statements. 'I wish I had said "erroneous",' Charles wrote wretchedly to his father. As usual, he blamed Emma for Nelson's rudeness, forgetting that he had begun the insults. Perhaps it was frustrated rage which led him to tell Pryse Lockhart Gordon that, on the day of Caracciolo's execution, there was a roast pig at the foot of the table. 'When the head was cut off, Lady Hamilton fainted.' Recovered, she sobbed 'that it put her in mind of her dear Caracciolo'. According to Gordon and Lock, she then ate heartily, 'even of the brains'. Lock was not on board the *Foudroyant* on 29 June. Perhaps Rushout told the story to Lock.

More reliable accounts exist of a bizarre and unnerving incident which marred the Royal visit to Naples. The King was leaning over the shiprail and perceived a strange object travelling through the water. Closer inspection revealed it to be the corpse of Caracciolo, swollen to enormous size. Despite the weights attached to it, the corpse was bobbing, sightless eyes fixed ahead, determinedly towards Naples. A diplomatic sailor told the King that Caracciolo had come to seek his pardon and the remains of the Admiral were swiftly taken up and buried in the sand on shore. Much later, they were transferred with some reverence to the church of S. Lucia.

On 2 August, the situation in Naples was deemed secure, and the King and his English followers left for Palermo. Though Villa Emma at Posillipo and the Palazzo Sessa were in view from the ship, the Hamiltons had not visited their former homes. A bomb had gutted Sir William's new apartment, his rotunda, and all their houses had been pillaged. Nevertheless, Sir William kept on the houses, paying rent till the following summer, in the hope of returning with the King. In fact, this was to be the Hamiltons' last sight of Naples.

CHAPTER FIFTEEN

A Cruise with Consequences

Between the twin capes of Palermo Bay, forming a perfect half-moon, the *Foudroyant* glided on 9 August 1799. The Royal Family came out to meet the returning party in a barge, various pleasure crafts following. Order restored, the Queen gave rich expression to her feelings, clasping a rich gold chain with her miniature set in diamonds and inscribed '*Eterna gratitudine*' round Emma's neck. Sir William received the King's portrait embellished with jewels. The city's dignitaries, attired in senatorial togas, waited respectfully on the quayside to add their congratulations. A twenty-one-gun salute was fired as the travellers stepped on shore, and, after a thanksgiving service in the cathedral, fireworks and illuminations completed the day. 'Palermo was drunk but not disorderly,' the Queen wrote in gracious review of the holiday.

More honours and rewards were heaped on the *Foudroyant* party. Two coach-loads of gala-dresses were dispatched to Emma from the Royal Palace, for Emma had lost much of her wardrobe with the flight from Naples. She applied to Greville to send her some dresses from England and he informed her that ladies in London had a passion nowadays for Sicilian dresses; they all looked like nymphs. He did not, however, follow this interesting observation with any specimens of the costume described. Emma wrote to him, just before leaving the Bay of Naples: 'The Queen is looking after my clothes.'

Other gifts, rumoured to total £6,000 in value, followed in scattered showers. Sir William detailed the gifts to his friend, Sir Joseph Banks. Emma had from the Queen a dress of fine point lace, a bracelet with the Queen's portrait and hair set in diamonds, earrings of pearl and diamonds, and numerous baskets of gloves – 'just such a present as such a fine woman as Emma, for except for being a little fatter she is as you saw her eight years ago, could desire'. The King gave her a medallion with his picture in diamonds fit for a foreign minister. Sir William himself received 'a thumping yellow diamond set about with Diamonds in a ring'.[1]

Nelson's officers were not forgotten. They each received a gold snuffbox or a ring. The crew of the *Foudroyant* and Nelson's servants had 2,300 ounces of silver for division. Nelson himself did best of all.

When Charles III left for Spain, he bestowed on his son Ferdinand the sword with which he had restored the Bourbon monarchy to Naples. It originally belonged to Louis XIV, who gave it to his grandson, Philip V, on gaining the Kingdom of Spain. There is a charming painting at Caserta, in which the youthful Ferdinand kneels to accept the jewelled weapon. His father admonished him to cherish it and, in time of need, to deliver it 'to him who shall restore the kingdom to thee'. On 13 August, the Duca di Ascoli brought this treasure, its hilt studded with diamonds, to Nelson.

The King went further in expressions of his gratitude. On the same day, Prince Luzzi, till lately the Viceroy, wrote to Nelson, asking him to accept the dukedom of Bronte, Bronte being a small estate on the slopes of Mount Etna, worth £3,000 a year. The name derived from the Greek for thunder, and was thought apposite. Nelson was at first reluctant to accept a foreign title. It is said Emma went on her knees to him. The King asked, 'Lord Nelson, do you wish that your name alone should pass with honour to posterity, and that I, Ferdinand Bourbon, should appear ungrateful?' Nelson yielded. Thenceforth he signed his letters, 'Nelson & Bronte' or 'Bronte Nelson of the Nile' – with the caveat that he would use the title only in Italian waters.

Celebrations came to a head with a magnificent fête champêtre in the gardens of the Colli Palace on 3 September. Palermo had barely recovered from the feast of S. Rosalia, 'an odd and pious ceremony . . . to which the low people is much attached'. In a temple of Fame stood three life-size effigies of the *Tria Juncta in Uno* (or Three Joined in One), as Emma liked to describe herself, Sir William and Nelson. (The Latin was the motto attached to the Order of the Bath, which both Nelson and Hamilton wore.) Maria Carolina had begged the originals' own clothes for her waxworks. 'Emma' stood in a purple full dress, embroidered with the names of the captains of the Nile. 'Sir William' wore full diplomatic dress. 'Nelson' stood between his friends, in 'full British uniform'.

Lieutenant Parsons heartily approved the enchanted appearance of the illuminated Palace and grounds. Lamps shone for miles, strung between the trees of long avenues, and ices and sweetmeats were on hand for the guests' delectation. Parsons praised the ladies' dancing, 'Italy's nut-brown daughters, their lustrous black eyes and raven tresses, their elegant and voluptuous forms gliding through the mazy dance . . .'. The whole, he breathed, was 'presided over by the genius of taste, whose attitudes were never equalled . . . I mean Emma, Lady Hamilton.'

Emma, crowned with a laurel wreath which the Queen had stripped from her effigy, watched a 'most brilliant and magnificent firework' representing the Battle of the Nile. It ended with 'the explosion of the *L'Orient* and the blowing-up of the tri-colored flag'.

After 'Rule Britannia' had been sung lustily by the entire company, trumpets sounded and Prince Leopold crowned Nelson's statue with laurel 'richly inlaid with diamonds'. With every moment, the proceedings approximated more to a French Court masque of the previous century. Inside the temple, beside an altar to Glory, an effigy of Ferdinand stood in a chariot. Then formality was swept aside. 'Tears flowed copiously down Nelson's weather-beaten cheeks.' He took Leopold on his knee, and the Prince responded by embracing him and calling him the Guardian Angel of his Papa's dominions.

Many succumbed to 'womanly weakness' on viewing this tender scene. Lieutenant Parsons, always practical, offered Nelson a handkerchief with which to stem his tears. It was, in fact, a rolled-up white stocking which he had forgotten was doing other duty. The state of the British officers' linen was so deplorable that they had celebrated the anniversary of the Nile with barely a clean shirt between them.

Presents and parties were soon forgotten in a press of new duties and anxieties. Since 20 August, when Lord Keith had quitted the Mediterranean, Nelson had been the senior officer in those waters. (St Vincent was still nominally Commander-in-Chief.) His duties included organizing the reduction of the island of Malta, protecting Minorca, and safeguarding British trade in the Mediterranean by blockading Cadiz. Besides all this, wrote the Secretary of the Admiralty, Evan Nepean, he was 'to cultivate, to the utmost of your power, the most perfect harmony and good understanding with all his [British] Majesty's allies'.

To this end Nelson devilled away at 'a more extensive correspondence than ever, perhaps, fell to the lot of any Admiral',[2] he wrote to Nepean in November. 'You must make allowances for a worn-out, blind, left-handed man.' Lord Elgin, who saw him in October, confirmed this self-portrait. 'He looks very old, has lost his upper teeth, sees ill of one eye, and has a film coming over both of them.'

Sir William was not in good shape either. He had told Greville in August that he had 'little stomach' left. Now he told Banks he was worn out. 'This thick air and sciroccos of Palermo do not agree with any of us.' Next spring, 'alive or dead', he would come home. It was 'my first wife's particular desire I am to lye by her in Slebeck [Slebech] Church when I am dead and we shall roll soon together into Milford Haven, for the sea is undermining that church very fast.'[3]

The Queen was also in melancholy mood. She now acknowledged that her mastery over her husband was a thing of the past. Her trick – smoothing long gloves over her white arms – was still effective, still won her small victories. Nonetheless, increasingly the King went his own way. Acton had likewise turned against the Queen, and was now the King's *éminence grise*. The Queen wrote agitatedly from an elegant country villa, the Bagnaria, 'Were it not for my daughters I should wish to bid adieu to the world, and retire into a convent.' Three days later, on 12 October, she had heard a rumour that the King was to go to Naples, while she remained in Palermo. Her spirits rose. 'I will positively go with him.' In fact, the King had, regrettably, no real intention of leaving Palermo. His Queen jibed at his cowardice. 'Were I King, I should have been there long since, or, indeed, should never have left, but should have risked and should certainly have conquered.' As Bonaparte said, Maria Carolina was the only man in the Kingdom of the Two Sicilies. Indeed, Sir John Moore, later of Corunna, was to write on a visit to Palermo in 1807: 'She has assumed so much of the character of a man as to make her unamiable as a woman.'

In October, Lord Elgin came to Palermo en route for Constantinople, where he was to be Minister. He had been asked by the Foreign Secretary to make a report on the situation in Sicily. While, in August, Grenville had told Charles Greville that Sir William might stay as long as he wished, now reports were reaching England of various undesirable friendships in Palermo. The British Minister seemed to be playing no very decisive part in all this. Lord Elgin was to recommend an urgent change of envoy.

Lord Elgin was accompanied by his wife of a few months, Mary Nisbet, aged twenty-one. She heard at Gibraltar that 'never was a man turned so *vain glorious* . . . in the world as Lord N. He is now completely managed by Lady Hamilton.' A sirocco wind was blowing which made the air feel 'as if it came from an oven' when the Elgins arrived in Palermo. Emma, though unwell, sent to their ship and invited them to make their home at the Palagonia. Lady Elgin was determined to do nothing of the kind.

Captain Morris, captain of the Elgins' ship, gave Mary an interesting account of his enquiry for Lord Nelson.

He went to Sir William Hamilton's house and a little old Woman with a white bed gown and black petticoat came out and said, 'What do you want Sir?' 'Lord Nelson, M'am.' (Old Woman) 'And what do you want to say to Lord Nelson?' Captain, laughing, 'Oh, M'am, you must excuse me telling you that.' Upon this a servant said to him, 'Sir, I fancy you don't know that is Lady Hamilton's Mother.' The Captain was surprized and said, 'What! does she act as Housekeeper?' 'Why yes Sir, I believe she does sometimes.'

One is reminded irresistibly of characters from nursery fiction, Mrs Tiggy-Winkle or Ninny-Nanny-Netticoat.

Curiously, though Mrs Cadogan had lived unknown so many years of her life, only a few months before Captain Morris made her acquaintance Emma had written a detailed description of her mother's position and daily doings to Greville:

> You cannot think how she is loved and respected by all. She has adopted a mode of living that is charming, she as a good apartment in our house, always lives with us, dines etc. etc. onely when she does not like it, for example, great dinners she herself refuses & as allways a freind to dine with her & La Signora Madre dell' Ambasciatrice is known all over Palermo the same as she was in Naples.

Lady Elgin's curiosity was whetted, and she consented to dine at the Hamiltons'. Of Emma she wrote,

> I must acknowledge she is pleasant, makes up amazingly . . . She looked very handsome at dinner, quite in an undress; – my Father would say, 'There is a fine Woman for you, good flesh and blood.'
> She is indeed a Whapper! and I think her manner very vulgar. It is really humiliating to see Lord Nelson, he seems quite dying and yet as if he had no other thought than her. He told Elgin privately that he had lived a year in the house with her and that her beauty was nothing in comparison to the goodness of her heart.

Captain Morris again provides us with an interesting vignette, illustrative of the retiring position Sir William, once so lively, had assumed with age.

> Captain Morris went to Sir William to deliver some despatches he had for Lord N. He read them and then called Lady Hamilton out of the room. They had a conference, and when she came back, she said 'Sir William we shall not go to the country today, you must dress yourself and go to Court after breakfast.' Poor Sir William asked 'Why?' 'Oh I will tell you presently.'

Lady Elgin's view of Maria Carolina, interestingly, was that she made 'thorough dupes' of both the Hamiltons and Nelson. Mary Elgin contented herself with: 'She flattered us beyond all credibility; to Lord N. it was the most fulsome thing possible.'

Lady Elgin could not avoid Emma's company at a spate of fêtes over the next few days. Mary dressed for one gala, with a rowing match, in 'my finest white gown, a Crazy Jane with a yellow handkerchief on it, and my fine white lace cloak'. A ball was to follow, but 'nobody would think of dressing till afterwards', Emma had said. Well pleased with her rig, Lady Elgin was handed up to the private stand where the Queen, Lady Hamilton and the Princesses were viewing the regatta. Mary found herself considerably under-dressed. The Royal ladies wore fine dresses with pearls and diamonds. Emma was decked in 'a fine gold and coloured silk worked gown and diamonds'. Apologizing to the Queen, Lady Elgin insisted on retiring, despite the King himself assuring her it was unnecessary. 'I find it is a constant trick of Lady H. to make everybody she can, go undressed,' Mary Elgin wrote angrily.

Mary Elgin found Nelson's constant attendance on Emma irritating, and the fuss the Queen made of her no less so. She was comforted by a courtier's remark that the Queen laughed at her to the Neapolitans, 'but says her influence with Lord N. makes it worth her while making up to her'. Yet Maria Carolina hardly consorted with 'the Neapolitans' and had accepted Emma's overtures of friendship long before Nelson's appearance at the Court.

On 5 October Nelson sailed for Minorca. Lord Elgin was unwise enough to propose the absent hero's health at a dinner with the Hamiltons. (Lady Elgin saw a good deal of Emma, despite her protestations of outrage.) 'My Lady actually Greeted [Scottish for "wept"]. For she loves him better than a brother.'

While Nelson was away, the Hamiltons accepted an invitation to a Royal villa at Colli, where the King made butter and kept cows. 'The house of Verdura is at your service,' wrote the Queen. With Nelson's return on 22 October, his dogged devotion to Lady Hamilton became a subject not only of scandal for gossip-mongers, but of concern to his friends. Faithful Troubridge wrote hesitantly of reports that Lady Hamilton and Nelson were to be seen nightly gaming deep. 'For an Englishwoman, gaming is the loss of her reputation.'[4] Lady Minto heard from Rushout that Nelson slept at the baize tables while Emma took undisclosed amounts from the piles of gold beside him. Lock spoke of Nelson losing fortunes at hazard.

Nelson told Miss Knight, as she reports in her autobiography, that he never gamed. As a young man, he won a small amount at the tables, when loss would have caused him distress. Rather than enjoy his win, he meditated on the dreadful fate that would have been his if he had lost, the financial embarrassment, the distress to his family, the possibility of bankruptcy, till he vowed he would never play again.[5] Emma, with Lady Spencer's approval, had been persuaded to play no more earlier in the decade. It seems all too probable, however, that in Palermo, where gaming occupied the hours which music had whiled away in Naples, Emma dabbled at the tables. She denied this to Greville. It was said that Sir William and Nelson had quarrelled and fought, that they had all lost a fortune by gaming: she listed the stories contemptuously. To Troubridge, on 8 January 1800, on the other hand, she earnestly promised she would play no more. He wrote back on the fourteenth, assuring her she would confound her enemies. She must know she had many, he had written earlier.

Emma was possible shaken by this frank remark. She had grown accustomed to popularity both at Court and even on the streets. Charles and Cecilia Lock, however, she evidently thought fair game for baiting. Though she and Sir William were not aware of the fact, a further enemy was on his way to Palermo, a worthier foe than the Locks, if Emma wished to indulge in footling shows of power. In January 1800, Sir William read the news in the *Morning Chronicle*; not until March did he hear from Lord Grenville, in a polite but curt note. His Majesty was pleased to approve his Minister's wish for retirement – last officially uttered in 1796. The Honourable Arthur Paget had embarked and would arrive in Palermo in due course. Maria Carolina heard the news with horror and dubbed the incoming Minister 'the fatal Paget'.

Sir William was candid enough to admit that he had requested leave or retirement, noted Cornelia Knight, his guest. It was no less of a blow for that. At the same time, Nelson heard that Lord Keith was returning to the Mediterranean to resume his duties as Commander-in-Chief. Nelson was requested to return to England, where it was thought he might do good service in the Channel Fleet. Nelson wrote angrily to Lord Minto that he supposed they would make him Governor of Greenwich Hospital, as he was '*evidently*' unfit to command. He felt more dudgeon at his recall than phlegmatic Sir William, who now looked to a poor life meted out in north winds and bouts of fever.

Nelson thought himself unlucky in his commander. Lord St Vincent had been kindly disposed towards the Neapolitan Royal Family, partly out of affection for Sir William (Sir William's father had persuaded St Vincent's family originally that he should make the sea his career). St Vincent wrote delightful letters to Emma. Keith now summoned Nelson to Leghorn to give an account of his command, then travelled back to Palermo with him on 3 February to inspect the position. He was not impressed. He stayed a week, which he described thus: 'I was sick of Palermo and its allurements, and much as I was made up to (their hours are beyond belief) I went to bed at ten.' Again: 'The whole was a scene of fulsome Vanity and Absurdity all the long eight days I was at Palermo.'

His stern ways were seen as old-fashioned by the younger officers. In particular, a dictum that the queue or pigtail, once every sailor's friend, should be grown, irritated all – except Nelson, who had always kept to the old-fashioned style. Lord William Stewart, on seeing Keith approach, would twist a few hairs together at the nape of his neck and execute a bow, slewing round for his commander to approve his work.

On 12 February, Keith inexorably bore Nelson off to Malta. In this, he did him a service, for on the eighteenth Nelson captured the *Généreux*. With the *Guillaume Tell*, this was one of the two ships which had eluded him at Aboukir Bay. Cornelia Knight was inspired to write some stanzas on the subject.

She soon had to revise them, for in March the *Guillaume Tell* was taken. The flag was sent to Prince Leopold. Before this, however, Nelson was allowed to return to Palermo. Lord Minto wrote from Vienna: 'It is not clear whether Nelson goes home.'[6] His devotion to Lady Hamilton was now a matter of increasing concern. Minto could well understand the fascination. 'You are both accustomed to make fools of wiser men,' he wrote to Emma of herself and the Queen; 'you . . . make Cymons of Solomons and Solomons of Cymons.'

Admiral Goodall in that winter was perhaps the first to compare Nelson and Emma to Rinaldo and Armida, a comparison now long overworked. Armida, a Saracen princess, lured Christian knights, including Rinaldo of Este, into a magic garden where they succumbed to her charms and to indolence. Thus Nelson at Palermo. To his father he wrote: 'I hope we shall one day meet, but when and where God knows.'[7]

Others wondered when Nelson would return to England, not knowing of his recall. Fanny wrote, announcing that she was advised to go to Lisbon for her health. Raised in the West Indies, she dreaded the English winter. She informed Nelson that she wore two sets of flannel under-garments, and still she felt the cold. No Armida she.

In Palermo there was something of a scandal to occupy the Hamiltons while Nelson was away. General Acton was perturbed by the thought that his two brothers, now in the Neapolitan army, were disbarred from inheriting his estate in Shropshire. They had both served in the French army. He therefore went – in full court dress – to his brother Joseph, and requested the hand of his thirteen-year-old daughter in marriage.

Miss Acton hid under a sofa during the interview. So unwilling was she to marry her uncle, fifty years her senior, that she tried to escape in boy's clothing. Apprehended in the courtyard, she was duly married in February. Emma and Sir William were witnesses in the Royal Chapel, and a second ceremony was performed in their house by Nelson's chaplain.

Emma was something of a Mrs Bennett, always promoting marriages where she could. Lady Elizabeth Foster had written to her in the autumn of 1799 asking about the marriage prospects of a friend, Eliza Ashburner; now Eliza was married by Nelson's chaplain, a busy man, to a Signor Perconte, recently appointed a *camerista* or gentleman of the bedchamber, and she was made Governess to the Royal children.

This gave Emma an idea. She wrote vaguely to Greville of settling 'the person you write of' as a *camerista* or lady of the bedchamber to one of the Neapolitan Royal Family. 'Little Emma' was now eighteen. Perhaps Emma thought that as she was returning to England shortly, the fate of her daughter could remain undecided a little longer.

'The fatal Paget' had arrived, the new broom ready to sweep clean the Augean stables of indolence, Italian manners, and the old, easy style of diplomacy. Paget had no patience with Sir William, who kept all his information in his head and in rough jottings. Besides, he mistrusted the Minister's attitude. He judged him, in Lord Malmesbury's phrasing, 'an Englishman who, after a long absence from England, returns to it with feelings and sentiments partial to other countries, and adverse to his own', ergo he had 'no real mind', was 'without the powers of discernment and comparison' and had 'no title to enjoy the superior . . . advantages to which he is born'.

By 31 December 1799, it was commonly known that Paget was to replace Hamilton. Lord Dalkeith, heir to the Duke of Buccleuch, wrote: 'I think you had better supply his place in the full sense of the Word; and occupy Lady Hamilton too, a place you are certainly much better fitted to fill than the old knight.' Paget informed his father at the end of 1799 that the post would include 'the *entire management of every thing* in the Mediterranean, Adriatic, Archipelago &c. &c'. So important was the island of Sicily judged now that Lord Wellesley himself had been offered the post. What changes since Sir William had written that he had nothing to report from the Kingdom but the odd volcanic eruption.

By 10 April 1800 Paget had gained Palermo, but a fortnight went by before Sir William presented his recall, thus enabling Paget to present his letters of credence. 'There has been a good deal of sad dirty work in all this,' Paget told his ally Keith, but he forgave Sir William. To Lord Grenville, who had 'talked confidentially about persons & things' before his departure, Paget confided the truth.

It is not to be told the pains that were taken by Lady Hamilton to set the King and Queen & the whole Court against me, even before I arrived. I was represented as a Jacobin and coxcomb, a person sent to bully and to carry them *bon gré mal gré* back to Naples [this was his commission] . . . her

Ladyship's language in general has been extremely indiscreet, representing Sir William as an ill-used man . . .

Sir William told Paget frankly that he did not wish to adopt the status of a 'private Individual' after so many years' standing. Unless Paget could show him instructions obliging him to present his letters of recall immediately, he would present them the day before he left. Paget found himself in difficulties, as his instructions contained much that he was unwilling to show Sir William. Paget surmised that the Minister would show them to Emma, who would 'have conveyed them the next moment to the Queen'. Thus he was obliged to kick his heels till Sir William decided to leave.

Paget knew he had not long to wait. Sir William and Emma were both dejected at the thought of departure. Sir William wrote tetchily to Greville that, though Emma appeared in blooming health, she swore she was at death's door. To alleviate the general gloom consequent on the imminent departure, Nelson proposed a cruise to Syracuse, on the south-west of the island, and to Malta. On return from the cruise, the Hamilton party would immediately depart for England.

If Sir William was obstructive, Paget made little allowance for the Minister's feelings at the end of a long and, till lately, distinguished career. Paget had conversations with Acton on a regular basis from shortly after his arrival. Indignant, Sir William wrote to Acton: 'Have you or have you not' seen Paget? Acton replied that he would see whom he wished, to which there was no answer. It was the first disagreement between the Ministers in a long association.

Acton made up the quarrel with an affectionate letter on Sir William's departure for Malta. In all the years they had worked together for the good of the Neapolitan Kingdom, they had been of one mind as to 'what could be of real service . . . for the two countryes'. Acton could not imagine a more successful collaboration.[8]

The evening before the cruise ship sailed, Nelson gave a ball on board the *Foudroyant* to mark General Acton's marriage and his own capture of the *Guillaume Tell*. Two spacious rooms were made on deck, with divisions of billowing silk. The masts were also clad in silk, and the guns removed. Little chocolate tables took their place. Below decks the scene was less joyful, as the Queen and Princesses, who were among the guests, were aware. Earlier in the day they had visited a casualty of the *Guillaume Tell* encounter, Lieutenant Jack West. One of the Princesses squeezed an orange and put it to his dry lips. He died during the night.

Emma was in anxious mood when the cruise began, as some verses bear witness. En route for Syracuse, she celebrated her thirty-fifth birthday on 26 April. Miss Knight, pen as ever nimble, composed some lines for the occasion: 'Come, cheer up, fair Delia / Forget all thy grief / For thy shipmates are brave, and a Hero's their chief.' Four verses of similar sentiments were sung by Miss Knight to the tune of 'Heart of Oak'.[9]

Pleasant days were spent viewing the antiquities of Syracuse. They arrived there on 30 April. Miss Knight and Sir William perhaps derived more satisfaction from the Temple of Apollo than did Emma or Nelson. Still, here was an opportunity for Emma to see the Fountain of Arethusa where Nelson had watered his ships before the Nile.

Emma had good reason to be dejected, or at least apprehensive. It seems, from a letter of 1801, that her passionate friendship with Nelson had ripened into intimacy – they had sex on a regular basis – from February of this year, 1800. 'I did remember well the 12th February', wrote Nelson in 1801, 'and also the months afterwards. I shall never be sorry for the consequences.'[10]

The outcome was a child born in January 1801. Working back on one's fingers, the date for the conception must have been round about the time of the cruise to Malta. Thus, unless Emma was possessed of extraordinary powers of foresight, she did not know on the date of her birthday that she was pregnant. The cause of her distress was, not unexpectedly, the prospect of exchanging the exalted position she had laboured to achieve in Italy for an uncertain future in England.

From the tone of Nelson's letter, one might imagine that he and Emma had exerted themselves for the precise purpose of conceiving issue. This would certainly be in keeping with the view both held of Nelson's glory, and might serve to excuse the adultery. In the lax atmosphere of the Palermo Court, anything seemed permissible.

The new Italian dukedom of Bronte, grants of £10,000 from the East India Company and other bequests – Nelson repeatedly wrote to his brother and sisters to inform them of the disposition of these honours among them after his death. His affection for Prince Leopold was on a par with his care for the midshipmen constantly wished on him by friends and relations. It would not be surprising if Nelson wished for the son and heir Fanny could never have who would inherit both dukedom and naval flair.

Emma's part is harder to fathom, if clear enough. She considered that she was entitled to behave as extravagantly with Nelson as she wished. Her extravagance, from descriptions, seems to have consisted of a good deal of caressing verbiage, some cutting-up of his meat, and very few physical attentions. Occasionally she took his good arm.

'Sir W. and Lord N. live like brothers.' Here was the crux. To please both was Emma's self-appointed task. If she could please the hero of England by bearing his child, and keep her husband from the secret, who would suffer? Sir William's and Nelson's brotherly love would continue. If Emma felt herself to be in control of this muddled situation, forging further links between the three with a child by Nelson, time away from the topsy-turvy Court of Palermo perhaps engendered more mature reflection.

While the *Foudroyant* ploughed on towards Malta, Lord Keith was in a fury at Genoa. Nelson had apparently vanished, and taken a valuable ship of the line with him. Lord Spencer, Lord of the Admiralty, wrote to remind the errant hero of his duties. In case of an enemy incursion into the Mediterranean, Spencer would be concerned to hear that Nelson learnt of it on shore at Palermo. With further masterly understatement he begged Nelson to return to England and there recuperate, rather than remain 'in an inactive situation at a foreign Court, however pleasing the . . . Gratitude shewn to you for your services'.

Nelson was beyond the call of these superiors. On 4 May the *Foudroyant* anchored in St Paul's Bay at Malta. A pleasant week was spent there, dining frequently with Emma's 'brother', Sir Alexander Ball, Governor of Malta. Emma had obtained for the starving Maltese in December 1799 several shiploads of corn from some merchant ships which opportunely docked in Palermo. The Czar of Russia, Grand Master of the Order of Malta, rewarded her with a fine enamelled cross, and made her the first English Dame of the Order. Ball had been honoured also, and from then on addressed Lady Hamilton as his sister. Emma naturally wore her Order. In her enthusiasm to see some aspect of the land she had materially aided, she hung over the shiprail. Lieutenant Parsons recalls that Nelson asked her to go below – the French were bombarding a post not far distant – and she refused. Then a bomb passed overhead and 'parted her hair'. Emma's powerful sway over members of the English navy was resented by others. Captain Thomas Masterman Hardy became incensed when she begged a pardon for a seaman he had disciplined.

A further week saw the party staying in a pretty house at Marse Sirocco, where a safe pony was among the attractions. (Nelson held horses in grave suspicion.)

On the return journey to Palermo, Emma fell ill. The entire ship's company was told to be quiet, and the ship drifted that night under the stars. It was the end of an era, Emma's dominion of the Italian Mediterranean. The 'Patroness of the Navy' was resigning her position. Keith would cease to sharpen his tongue at her expense ('Malta will fall within three months, unless Lady Hamilton takes it by siege single-handed,' was one of his jibes).

In the *Foudroyant*'s absence, Maria Carolina had determined to go to her daughter, the Empress, in Vienna. She was 'neither agreeable nor necessary' to her husband, she wrote mournfully. With her would go Leopold, her three younger daughters and a large retinue. Of necessity, Nelson offered to escort the Royal party as far as Leghorn. He would then take the Hamiltons and Miss Knight on to England.

Also in the *Foudroyant's* absence, copies of the London *Times* had come to Palermo. Charles James Fox, first cousin of Cecilia Lock, had denounced in the House of Commons the atrocities, or executions, in the Bay of Naples. It is probable that he was given Charles Lock's letter to read. Nelson fired off a stinging rebuttal of his charges, but the damage had been done. Nelson's popularity with his naval superiors was in doubt, though his ships' crews adored him. Now his popularity with the English Upper Ten Thousand was on the wane, though John Bull thought him still The Hero.

Preparations for the journey lasted a week. The Queen sent quantities of dresses, jewels and plate aboard. Finally on 8 June the *Foudroyant* sailed out of the Bay of Naples. It left under an inauspicious star. The King quarrelled with the Queen shortly before the departure, and did not come down to the shore to wish all well. Cornelia Knight, travelling with the Hamiltons, writes in her *Autobiography* that she 'left Sicily with great pain, for it was also severing myself from Italy, where I had spent so many years of happiness'.[11]

Charles Lock's comment on the departure was characteristic. '*She* is now gone, thank my stars.' If Emma and Sir William still hoped to return to their beloved kingdom, a private letter of July 1800, from the Foreign Secretary, showed those hopes to be futile. 'Sir W. is not yet arrived here . . . when he does come I shall explain to him without reserve the utter impossibility of his going back to Naples in any public situation.' Paget was the recipient of this confidence, which no doubt greatly saddened him.

(*above*) The cottage in Hawarden, North Wales, where Emma grew up 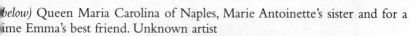 ⑨

(*below*) Queen Maria Carolina of Naples, Marie Antoinette's sister and for a time Emma's best friend. Unknown artist

⑩

The Posillipo shoreline at Naples, showing Villa Emma, the beach house where Sir William and Emma entertained. By Xavier della Gatta

Emma adopts, for
Richard Cosway, one of
her celebrated Attitudes (12)

Cartoonist Thomas
Rowlandson alludes to
rumours that Emma was
earlier a life model for
Royal Academicians

Lady H......
Attitudes

(13)

(above) James Gillray pictures Nelson destroying the French fleet – represented by crocodiles – at the Battle of the Nile

(below) Fanny Nelson, the wife that Nelson forgot when he met Emma. By Daniel Orme

Horatia Nelson, to whom Emma gave birth in secret and whom
Nelson later 'adopted'. By Thomas Baxter

16

Emma as 'Dido in Despair' by Gillray. She mourns the return of Nelson to sea,
Sir William lying neglected at her side

17

'Pray let Lady Hamilton have my hair,' said Nelson. His pigtail *(above)* became
a sacred relic – first for Emma, then for their daughter Horatia, photographed
(below)

The Death of Nelson, by Arthur Devis. 'Remember Lady Hamilton' wer
among the victorious admiral's last words

20

CHAPTER SIXTEEN

Grand Return

Wrapped in a warm cocoon of love and esteem for each other, Emma and the Queen, Nelson and Sir William entered on the last stage of their odd intimacy. A storm then blew up with some urgency, just north of the islands of Elba and Capraia, on the afternoon of 14 June. Maria Amalia, fourth of the Princesses and aged eighteen, kept a journal. Emma or 'Miladi' was no favourite with her, and she contemptuously describes her unheroic behaviour in the crisis of the gale.

'We found Miladi on her knees on a matelas in the middle of the room [below decks]. Toto [Marie Antoinette] cried out: "We are finished . . . submerged."' With practical good sense and to halt the spreading panic, the Queen ordered them to sit on the floor, and brace themselves against the beds – Castelcicala, the Neapolitan Ambassador bound for England, Alvaro Ruffo, a gentleman of the bedchamber, and the Queen on one side; Emma and the Princesses on the other. 'Miladi took me in her arms,' Amalia notes.[1] Nelson entered and attempted to encourage the Royal cargo with a prophecy that they would be at Leghorn by seven that evening. The ship, as if in defiance, plunged thrice under the waves. Nelson went 'white as a sheet' and exited hurriedly. Whereupon 'Miladi began to wail and roll about on the ground.'

Emma's unrestrained behaviour, by strong contrast with her calm in the flight from Naples, demands some explanation. As she was now some seven weeks pregnant, she had some excuse for *mal de mer*. Accounts of her mood suggest that she felt miserable. In view of her long and childless marriage and in view of her trumpeted adoration of Lord Nelson, few would believe a child born now to be Sir William's. Her long struggle for respectability, Greville's remark that the English Royal Family looked kindly on her, would be for nothing. The loss of her assured position in the Kingdom of the Two Sicilies, the uncertainty of her future life in England did nothing to encourage optimism.

The ship ploughed on and the Queen began to recite a prayer in German. Her daughters joined her in litanies of the saints and all thirteen credos. Disaster was thus warded off and the ship arrived at Leghorn at the hour Nelson had predicted. Maria Carolina celebrated the occasion by writing in English letters of thanks to Nelson and to

Captain Sir Edward Berry, the ship's captain who had enjoyed 'fraternal' quarter-deck conversations with Miss Knight during lulls in the storm. Prince Leopold and his sisters also produced elegant expressions of their thanks. After all that they had endured together, it is remarkable that Nelson's command of Italian and French was so poor that he responded with gestures and *baciamani*, or kissing of hands.

The next day, the weather not permitting a landing, a mass was held on deck with makeshift pews and altar-cloths. Maria Amalia was pleased to approve Emma's and Nelson's part. They knelt on cushions at a discreet distance from their Catholic concelebrants, between the steerage wheel and the captain's room, reading with admirable devotion, Emma with her hair flowing luxuriously over her shoulders, dressed in a plain white chemisette. Sir William was, as ever, firm in his heretic absence.

This joint observation of religious rites was to mark Emma's liaison with Nelson henceforward. Nelson, son of a devout but conservative clergyman, had come to consider God an entity more akin to the God of the Old Testament, a God to be propitiated, a God who punished. Emma had lived with Sir William, a free-thinker, for fourteen years. Rumours circulated, however, that she was accustomed to make her confession to a Catholic abbé in Naples. The devout example that both the King and Queen of Naples set their subjects had perhaps had its effect on her, but she was not so firmly wedded to the Catholic faith that Nelson would have had difficulty in persuading her to worship at the Anglican shrine with him. Nelson was to persuade himself, if not Emma, that due attention to the ritual of the Anglican faith would excuse his lapse from its dogma. In short, he grew to think the church service a rite of passage to blamelessness.

Maria Carolina had prepared farewell mementoes for her English friends. At this point it was thought that the parties would divide at Leghorn. Sir William received a gold snuffbox with the sovereigns' portraits set in diamonds. Heaven knows how many similar objects he possessed. Nelson had a medallion featuring anchors set in laurel with diamonds on green enamel. On Emma was bestowed a magnificent diamond necklace with, pendent, the Royal children's cyphers and locks of their hair set in silver.

At Leghorn the Royal party resided at the Governor's Palace, while the Hamiltons lodged with the Consul. Plans for further travel were still uncertain when the Queen was awoken on the evening of 19 June by an anxious Nelson and Emma. Lord Keith had just sent news of the Battle of Marengo, at which Bonaparte had routed the Austrians and imposed an armistice on the fourteenth. Nelson assured the Queen, as he subsequently informed Acton, that 'nothing shall make us quit [her] until their future plans are perfectly settled'. The swift march southwards of the French army over the next few days threw all into confusion.

Orders came from Keith. Nelson was to send all the ships he had to reinforce the British fleet at Genoa. Thus Nelson's plans to take the Hamiltons on to England in the *Foudroyant*, his 'darling child', were dashed. The *Foudroyant* was dispatched to Minorca for refitting, and Nelson removed his flag to the *Alexander*. When he failed to send this last ship to Genoa, Keith arrived – on the twenty-fourth – to discuss his reasons. Keith's declared opinion was: 'Lady Hamilton has ruled the fleet long enough.'

The Queen asked Keith to allow the *Foudroyant* to take her back to Sicily. The approach of the French had unnerved her. Keith 'refused positively'. There were three Neapolitan frigates at Leghorn, but the Queen trusted none of them. 'The Queen wept,' Lady Malmesbury heard from Mr Wyndham, the Consul, 'concluding that royal tears were irresistible, but he remained unmoved.' The Queen then fell into 'a sort of convulsive fit'. Nelson, Lady Malmesbury heard, 'seems entirely lost in his love and vanity . . . they all sit and flatter each other all day long'. Cornelia Knight tells us that at Leghorn Nelson looked ahead to his life in England. He and Lady Nelson and Sir William and Lady Hamilton 'would all very often dine together . . . when the latter couple went to their musical parties, he and Lady Nelson would go to bed'.

On 2 July Cornelia Knight sent Captain Sir Edward Berry an account of current plans. 'Lady Hamilton cannot bear the thought of going by sea; and, therefore, nothing but impracticability will prevent us from going to Vienna . . . Sir William appears broken, distressed and harassed.' On the sixteenth she wrote further:

> I feel all the dangers and difficulties to which we shall be exposed. Think of us embarking on board small Austrian vessels at Ancona, for Trieste, as part of a land journey! To avoid the danger of being on board an English man-of-war . . . everything commodious . . . Lady Hamilton . . . hates the sea, and wishes to visit the different Courts of Germany. Sir William says *he* shall die by the way, and . . . I should not be surprised if he did . . . If I am not detained in a French prison . . . you shall hear from me again . . .

On 8 July, Nelson was awoken early by a messenger. The people of Leghorn, alarmed by the French presence at nearby Lucca, had plundered the arsenal of its stock of arms. They had surrounded the Governor's Palace, and had vowed to keep the Queen prisoner till Nelson should agree to lead them against the French.

Nelson, with Sir William and Emma, fought his way through the crowds and up to the balcony where the Queen waited anxiously. Emma then undertook to address the menacing crowd in Nelson's name. With great verve she remonstrated on the 'impropriety of violently surrounding an amiable and illustrious queen'. She 'positively declared that his lordship would not hold the smallest communication with them', unless they immediately returned their arms to the arsenal.

The people, according to Harrison's *Life of Nelson*, 'signified their acquiescence by repeated shouts of approbation'.[2] They hurried off to the arsenal. Emma had saved the day. Maria Carolina was so unnerved by the incident that she immediately boarded the *Alexander* with thoughts of sailing to Messina. There she would await orders from Ferdinand, either to return to Palermo or to sail for Trieste. She was persuaded to disembark, and early the next morning she and the children sped off to Florence. Not till she was lodged in the massive Palazzo Pitti did her anxiety abate.

The Hamilton party followed the next day, and arrived after passing within two miles of the French advanced posts. The following day they set out for Ancona, but met with a delay. On the road the coach containing Nelson and the Hamiltons was overturned. The occupants were hurt, but not dangerously. The wheel was repaired, then broke again at Arezzo. With the French army closing rapidly, it was decided, with a singular lack of chivalry, that Miss Knight and Mrs Cadogan should remain with the broken carriage. 'It was of less consequence we should be . . . taken, than they.' Sir William suffered much at leaving them, but left they were. The two ladies had three days to wait before the repairs were effected.

At Ancona Miss Knight discovered that the Queen had dismissed the *Bellona*, an Austrian frigate, fitted out with silk hangings and eighty beds to receive the Royal ladies: there had recently been a mutiny on board. As a result, the journey to Trieste was made in some Russian frigates. Maria Amalia commented, 'Eleven beds to a room. Like a hospital.' 'Our party is very helpless,' sighed Miss Knight. Nelson, despite every effort on others' parts to turn the conversation, sighed out continually for the *Foudroyant*. 'The very precarious state of Sir William's health has convinced everybody that it is necessary he should arrange his affairs.'

The ships reached Trieste in time for grand illuminations to celebrate the second anniversary of the Battle of the Nile. The loggia, the church façade, the library were illuminated and '*Evviva Nelson!*' rang out. The *noblesse* at Trieste, Amalia noted, were rich merchants, many Greek or dressed Turkish-style. Sir William and the Queen had both caught 'violent colds' on the Russian ships. Amalia had ample time for observation of the Austrian port while they recovered.

On 14 July, the Hamilton party arrived at Laibach, now Ljubljana in Yugoslavia. The Philharmonic Society, one of the first established in Europe, rendered a symphony in celebration of the Battle of the Nile before their distinguished visitors. 'The aria, La virtù britannica, was performed with exceptional feeling and precision.'

Via Klagenfurt to Graz in Styria the party proceeded, where they stayed at Schmalzer's Gasthof. Nelson was cheered on arrival, and his room was thrown open to a large number of his admirers. Later in the evening, he walked in the streets with Emma on his arm. 'His face is pale and sunk, with the hair combed onto the forehead; the loss of an eye is less noticeable than that of the right arm as he . . . fastens the empty sleeve across his buttoned tunic.' So wrote an interested newspaper. Behind the two walked a 'counterpart in black beauty of Lady Hamilton's charms' – this was Fatima, the Nubian maid whom Nelson had brought to Emma from Egypt.

Via Bruck an der Mur, 'over the beautiful Semmering pass to Wiener-Neustadt' the coaches passed. On 18 August they left again at 4 a.m., and travelled on, via Baden, to Vienna. They were deposited at the Gasthof aller Biedermänner, or 'Inn of all honest men', a small establishment just off the Graben Square. Here they were to remain six weeks.

Contemporary prints show the inn to have been a modest affair. A shop occupies the ground floor, a broad verandah running above it, with three upper storeys ornately decorated. Under the eaves a gargoyle leered in contrast with a plaster Madonna in a niche below the verandah. The Villar family, known for the excellence of their fried beefsteaks, kept the inn and ensured that the party was lavishly supplied. Maria Carolina had munificently offered to pay all expenses.

A journal describes how the space before the inn swiftly grew congested with admirers of the Admiral. The ladies dressed in their 'Nelsons', a black cape with gay trimmings. The craze in Vienna for Nelsonian dress had begun in 1798 with bonnets which led one man to comment of his wife that she looked for all the world like a crocodile. By 1800 dresses, too, paid tribute to the hero with fringes and tassels. As H. C. Robbins Landon has said, 'Austria badly needed a war hero.' At night Nelson's admirers ceded place to the 'Nymphs' of Vienna, who posed invitingly beside the lemonade stalls erected by the fountains at either end of the Graben.

The Hamiltons and Nelson visited Lord and Lady Minto at St Veit,

a country villa once a monastery; Lady Minto wrote her impressions
of them to her sister, Lady Malmesbury.

> I don't think him [Nelson] altered in the least. He has the same shock head,
> and the same honest simple manners; but he is devoted to *Emma*; he thinks
> her quite an *angel*, and talks of her as such to her face and behind her back,
> and she leads him about like a keeper with a bear. She must sit by him at
> dinner to cut his meat; and he carries her pocket-handkerchief . . . he is
> a gig from ribands, orders and stars.

On the twenty-first, Emma was reunited with Maria Carolina at
Schönbrunn, the Imperial Palace, where the Neapolitan Royal party
was happily exchanging news with Theresa and Cristina, the two eldest
Neapolitan Princesses, now Empress of Austria and Grand Duchess of
Tuscany. 'We had the noise of five fine healthy children for an hour,'
wrote Nelson of the visit. Maria Carolina had evidently passed on her
own unfashionable liking of her children's company to her daughter,
the Empress.

The twenty-second saw Emma and Nelson at the Leopoldstadt
Theatre, enjoying the comic antics of Kasperl, a bumbling rustic with
similarities to our Punch or Pinocchio. The next day Nelson was
received alone by the Emperor, a preliminary to a grand *Cercle* or
reception on the twenty-fourth. The *Cercle* had been posponed till
the English party's arrival, so that they, together with the Neapolitan
Royal party, could be officially made welcome. A grand and formal
drawing-room was followed by a procession in open carriages down
the Prater, to loyal cheers from the Viennese lining the route. Prince
Albrecht of Sachsen-Teschen then hosted a most welcome breakfast in
the gardens of the Augarten Palace. A Count Zinzendorf noted Emma
as 'Madame Hamilton grandondon who holds his [Nelson's] hat'.

All Vienna was eager to entertain the hero and his friends. In these
entertainments Emma and Sir William had a foretaste of the relegation to
minor roles that was to be their lot in England. True, Emma's portrait by
Mme Vigée-Le Brun had been exhibited in Vienna some years earlier,
and Sir William's reputation was known to some. Nevertheless, while
in Italy the Hamiltons had been notable people in their own right, now
they were mere appendages to the hero.

There were dinners, receptions, a grand aquatic fête on the Danube,
and many fishing excursions – with increasing age, angling was becoming the Minister's favourite diversion.

Despite all this jaunting about, the party evidently spent a certain
amount of time at the inn. At one point the supplies of champagne

ran dry. Francis Oliver, educated in a Neapolitan conservatory and long employed by Sir William as a secretary and factotum,[3] had settled in Vienna and spoke fluent German. Nelson engaged him at the outset of the stay in Vienna as a secretary and aide. Oliver went off to a wine merchant in search of more champagne. It was a forbidden luxury in Austria, and the merchant at first said he had none. On hearing it was for Nelson, he pressed cases on Oliver. As the merchant would accept no payment, Oliver took only two bottles and Nelson subsequently invited the generous merchant to dinner. This was only one of several incidents where the mention of Nelson's name acted as an 'Open Sesame'.

There is proof that Emma had not been forgotten by her old enemies in Naples. In a letter from Paget to Lord Minto of 29 August, the new Minister wrote:

> I shall be curious to hear from Yr. Lp upon the subject of the Queen. I dread much from the circumstances of Lady Hamilton being with Her Majesty, whose influence is great, and whose ends are wicked . . . [The conduct of the Queen] having dragged, as it is termed, Lady Hamilton for whom Epithets are not spared with her to Vienna, is not considered here as very edifying for herself or her Royal Daughters.[4]

We have a lively account of Emma's appearance from a Swedish diplomat, Suerstolpe, in September.

> Muladi Hamilton, once considered the most beautiful woman in Europe . . . wears the Maltese Cross so that she now has all the titles that can impress people . . . She is . . . the fattest woman I've ever laid eyes on, but with the most beautiful head.

A pastel by Schmidt was commissioned by Nelson in Dresden, and bears out this description exactly. A substantial change in Emma is first seen in this portrait. She has had her flowing chestnut mane cut off and her remaining curls trimmed close to her head à la Brutus.

In September the Hamilton party paid a visit to Eisenstadt, the country estate of the Prince and Princess Esterhazy, who wished to return the hospitality Sir William had shown them on a visit to Naples many years before. (The Ambassador who threw his snuffbox overboard was a distant cousin.) The great attraction of Eisenstadt, a miniature kingdom with dairy farm, militia, theatre, vineyards and farms, was the presence of Joseph Haydn, the Court musician. He had a small house near the Palace where he lived during the summer months with a parrot whom he had taught to say, 'Come to Papa Haydn, pretty Pollykins.' From here he wrote to Vienna, requesting the score of 'my Cantata

Arianna a Naxos'. Lady Hamilton wished to sing this alto aria, a popular concert piece since 1791 when Signora Storace sang it in Oxford on the occasion of Haydn's receiving his honorary degree.

On 6 September, the Hamilton party duly arrived. At the dinner table, a hundred grenadiers, all topping six feet, stood behind the chairs at dinner. The next day there was a grand firework display in the park and a concert in the evening. James Harris, eldest son of Lord and Lady Malmesbury, attended with his cousin, Sir Gilbert Elliot. He had already told his father that he thought it was 'really disgusting to see her [Emma] with him [Nelson]. He seems to be in no hurry to sail again.' After his visit to the castle of Eisenstadt, James spoke even more plainly.

> Lady Hamilton is without exception the most coarse, ill-mannered, disagreeable woman I ever met with. The Princess . . . had got a number of musicians, and the famous Haydn . . . to play, hearing Lady Hamilton was fond of music. Instead of attending to them she sat down at the Faro table, played Nelson's cards for him, and won between 300L and 400L . . . I could not disguise my feeling, and joined in the general abuse of her.[5]

Young Harris blamed Emma for Nelson's declaration that he had no thought of serving again. His aunt Minto was no admirer of Emma's, even if his uncle felt a sneaking liking for her.

A very different picture is drawn by Haydn's friend and biographer, Griesinger, in a letter dated Vienna, 21 January 1801.

> In Mylady Hamilton Haydn found a great admirer. She paid a visit to Esterhazy's estates . . . but was little concerned with its splendours, and for two days she never left Haydn's side.

The Hungarian newspaper *Magyar Hirmondo* described Emma and her performance of the cantata, *Arianna a Naxos*:

> [She] is a 35-year-old, tall Englishwoman with a very handsome face, who knows well how to demean herself. One of her many rare qualities is her clear, strong voice with which, accompanied by the famous Haydn, she filled the audience with such enthusiasm that they almost became ecstatic. Many were reminded of the pictures of the Goddesses Dido and Calypso . . .

Suerstolpe thought he would never hear 'anything so heavenly'. 'In her are combined voice as well as method, sensitivity and musical knowledge, so as to bewitch the listener.' Contrary to James Harris's account, we gather, Emma enjoyed something of a musical feast at

Eisenstadt. 'The grey-haired Lord', as the Hungarian newspaper referred to Sir William, saw a dream come true in his favourite composer accompanying the voice he himself had trained.

In further refutation of young Harris's criticism, O.E. Deutsch has pointed out that Haydn would not have directed 'table' or 'conversation' music. Moreover, manuscripts of two English songs, one being 'The Spirit's Song', by Haydn were sold at Sotheby's in 1917. They are inscribed, in Emma's handwriting, 'Given to Lady Hamilton by the most excellent Haydn at eisenstadt at the princip Esterhazy sept. 9th 1800.' Furthermore, Haydn acceded to a request from Emma to set Cornelia Knight's lines on the Battle of the Nile to music.

With a 'very good' ball on the Princess's name day, the Feast of the Blessed Virgin, and a *chasse* where 622 partridges were shot, the visit came to an end with a further concert arranged by Haydn. The Hamilton party returned to Vienna, where a smallpox epidemic and a rainstorm served to throw into relief the pleasant excursion.

The following ten days were taken up with a series of farewell visits – to the Mintos at St Veit, to Maria Carolina at Schönbrunn. A last mark of Viennese appreciation was Herr Stower's annual firework display. This year he took as his theme the Battle of the Nile. Haydn came to dinner at the inn to present Nelson with his setting of Miss Knight's *Pindaric Ode* and accompanied Emma who sang it. There were other Viennese works of art. Nelson had commissioned Füger, the artist of the Queen's library at Caserta, to paint the Queen of Naples, Emma and himself. Only the paintings of Nelson survive, one in day dress, one in uniform. Füger imparts a haunting, spiritual air to the well-known features.

Emma's parting with Maria Carolina was a very feminine affair, with protestations of undying regard. The Queen was 'touched to tears'.[6] It is said that the Queen offered her friend a pension of £1,000 a year, but Sir William would not allow her to accept. As Maria Carolina was in financial straits – she owed money to Lady Spencer in England, for example – it is very unlikely that the money would ever have been paid. Still, given the Queen's many bountiful gestures, it is probably true that the offer was made.

On 26 September the party rolled on towards Prague. The Archduke Charles, Austria's great general, was anxious to meet Nelson, but had begged the mountain to come to him because he was indisposed. The English party was gratified to find their hotel, the Black Lion, illuminated on their arrival. They were later less gratified to find the cost of the lighting added to their bill. They remained here till the thirtieth, celebrating Nelson's birthday with a dinner at the Archduke's. After the

distinguished guests had had their fill of goose and apple sauce, Emma
sang, 'God Save the King' and some verses Miss Knight had produced
to mark the occasion.

Further travelling brought them to Dresden on 2 October. Hugh
Elliot, Minto's brother, was Envoy there, and thought it 'a very good
sofa to repose on'. With the Elliots this autumn was often present a
young widow, Melesina St George Trench. She was touring the courts
of Germany and found, like the Elliots, that Dresden was a comfortable
billet. Her comments on the Hamilton party make interesting, if sad,
reading. On 3 October they all dined at the Elliots'.

> It is plain that Lord Nelson thinks of nothing but Lady Hamilton, who is
> totally occupied by the same object. She is bold, forward, coarse, assuming,
> and vain. Her figure is colossal, but, excepting her feet, which are hideous,
> well shaped. Her bones are large, and she is exceedingly *embonpoint*. She
> resembles the bust of Ariadne; the shape of all her features is fine, as is the
> form of her head, and particularly her ears; her teeth are a little irregular,
> but tolerably white; her eyes light blue, with a brown spot in one, which,
> though a defect, takes nothing away from her beauty of expression. Her
> eyebrows and hair are dark, and her complexion coarse. Her expression
> is strongly marked, variable, and interesting; her movements in common
> life ungraceful; her voice loud, yet not disagreeable. Lord Nelson is a little
> man, without any dignity . . . Lady Hamilton takes possession of him, and
> he is a willing captive, the most submissive and devoted I have seen. Sir
> William is old, infirm, all admiration of his wife, and never spoke to-day
> but to applaud her . . . Mrs Cadogan, Lady Hamilton's mother, is – what
> one might expect. After dinner we had several songs in honour of Lord
> Nelson, written by Miss Knight, and sung by Lady Hamilton. She puffs
> the incense full in his face; but he receives it with pleasure, and snuffs it
> up very cordially. The songs all ended in the sailor's way, with 'Hip, hip,
> hip, hurra,' and a bumper with the last drop on the nail, a ceremony I
> had never heard of or seen before.

The next week was spent agreeably enough. There were evenings at
the theatre in Mr Elliot's box, where Emma and Nelson were wrapped
in conversation. Nelson went off to Court, 'a perfect constellation of
stars and Orders', in Mrs Trench's opinion. He wore the diamond
aigrette, the Order of the Bath, the King of Naples' medallion, the
Order of St Januarius and three medals from naval battles. On the sixth,
Mrs Trench dined with Lord Nelson, went to a concert in honour
of the Admiral and his companions, later to a party: 'Lady Hamilton
loading me with all marks of friendship at first sight, which I always
think more extraordinary than love of the same kind.'

On 7 October, Mrs Trench breakfasted with Lady Hamilton and:

saw her represent in succession the best statues and paintings extant . . .
Several Indian shawls, a chair, some antique vases, a wreath of roses, a
tambourine, and a few children are her whole apparatus. She stands at one
end of the room with a strong light to her left, and every other window
closed. Her hair (which by-the-bye is never clean) is short, dressed like
an antique, and her gown a simple calico chemise, very easy, with loose
sleeves to the wrist. She disposes the shawls so as to form Grecian, Turkish,
and other drapery, as well as a variety of turbans. Her arrangement of the
turbans is absolute sleight-of-hand, she does it so quickly, so easily, and so
well . . . Each representation lasts about ten minutes. It is remarkable that,
though coarse and ungraceful in common life, she becomes highly graceful,
and even beautiful, during this performance. It is also singular that, in spite
of the accuracy of her imitation of the finest ancient draperies, her usual
dress is tasteless, vulgar, loaded and unbecoming.

A problem arose. Emma wished to go to Court. Unfortunately, the
Electress would not receive her, 'on account of her former dissolute
life'. Memories were long at the Court of Saxony. Lord Nelson said,
'If there is any difficulty of that sort, Lady Hamilton will knock the
Elector down.' A solution was attempted. There was to be no Court
while Lady Hamilton was in Dresden.

Mrs Trench and Mr Elliot dined together to their mutual enjoyment,
Mrs Elliot making a nominal third, while their tongues rattled merrily
on. To Mrs Elliot, over the teacups, Mrs Trench perhaps made her
criticisms of Emma's dress sense. 'She has borrowed several of my
gowns, and much admires my dress; which cannot flatter, as her own
is so frightful. Her waist is absolutely between her shoulders.'

For Mr Elliot was reserved the burden of Mrs Trench's critique of
Lady Hamilton. 'She acts her songs, which I think the last degree of
bad taste . . . To represent passion with the eyes fixed on a book . . .
must always be a poor piece of acting *manqué*.' Besides which, Mrs
Trench judged, Emma was frequently out of tune and her voice lacked
sweetness. In short, she thought her:

bold, daring, vain even to folly, and stamped with the manners of her
first situation much more strongly than one would suppose, after having
represented Majesty, and lived in good company fifteen years. Her ruling
passions seem to me vanity, avarice, and love for the pleasures of the table.
She shows a great avidity for presents, and has actually obtained some at
Dresden by the common artifice of admiring and longing.

Mr Elliot's opinion of Lady Hamilton was no kinder. He could
not regard the Electress's snub as likely to be repeated in England.

Gloomily, he prophesied, 'She will captivate the Prince of Wales, whose mind is as vulgar as her own, and play a great part in England.'

On 9 October a breakfast was held at the Elliots', and Emma repeated her Attitudes 'with great effect'. Other guests took their departure before dinner, leaving the Hamilton party, Mrs Trench and the Elliots. Emma then 'declared she was passionately fond of champagne', and 'took such a portion of it' as to astonish Mrs Trench. Nelson was not far behind. He 'called more vociferously than usual for songs in his own praise', and ended, after many bumpers, by proposing the Queen of Naples. 'She is my Queen; she is Queen to the backbone.'

> Poor Mr Elliot, who was anxious the party should not expose themselves more than they had done already, and wished to get over the last day as well as he had done the rest, endeavoured to stop the effusion of champagne, and effected it with some difficulty; but not till the Lord and Lady, or, as he calls them, Antony and *Moll* Cleopatra, were pretty far gone.

Mrs Trench then retired.

> After I went, Mr Elliot told me she acted Nina intolerably ill, and danced the *Tarantola*. During her acting Lord Nelson expressed his admiration by the Irish sound of astonished applause, which no written character can imitate. Lady Hamilton expressed great anxiety to go to Court, and Mrs Elliot assured her it would not amuse her, and that the Elector never gave dinners or suppers – 'What?' cried she, 'no guttling!' Sir William also this evening performed feats of activity, hopping round the room on his backbone, his arms, legs, star and ribbon all flying about in the air.

So ended the Grand Tour of the German courts on a note of high comedy. It would seem, from Emma's deliberate vulgarism and from Sir William's extravagant exercise, that the Hamilton party thought the Elliots as dreary as they themselves were thought brash. The next day Mr Elliot hurried them on board a barge. He had heard that a frigate awaited them at Hamburg. He recounted to Mrs Trench the embarkation.

> The moment they were on board, there was an end of the fine arts, of the attitudes, of the acting, the dancing, and the singing. Lady Hamilton's maid began to scold in French about some provisions which had been forgot, in language quite impossible to repeat, using certain French words, which were never spoken but by *men* of the lowest class, and roaring them out from one boat to another. Lady Hamilton began bawling for an Irish stew, and her old mother set about washing the potatoes, which she did as cleverly as possible. They were exactly like Hogarth's actresses dressing in the barn.

Mrs Trench went to congratulate the Elliots that evening on their 'deliverance'.

Mr Elliot would not allow his wife to speak above her breath, and said every now and then, 'Now don't let us laugh to-night; let us all speak in our turn; and be very, very quiet.'

One would enjoy hearing Emma's view of this odious trio.

The journey to Hamburg in gondolas along the River Elbe took eleven days, the last few marred by a lack of provisions. The 'jackal' or caterer was not always able to scrounge sufficient provisions for the party.

Among distinguished residents of Hamburg eager to see Nelson was General Dumouriez, the diplomat Baron de Breteuil, and the famous German poet Klopstock. Miss Knight and Mrs Cadogan dined with him one evening and he read some passages from his *Messiah*. His room was hung with engravings by Füger from the epic. Miss Knight found the odes he was writing currently 'very sublime . . . but too metaphysical to be easily understood'. Mrs Cadogan no doubt agreed.

On 31 October the party embarked on the *King George* mail packet. At the last moment, Nelson bought a 'magnificent lace trimming' for a court dress for his wife. They crossed the bar just in time to avoid a tremendous gale and landed at Great Yarmouth in Nelson's home county on 6 November. The horses were removed from Nelson's carriage and it was drawn by willing human agency to the Wrestlers' Arms.

The Grand Return was accomplished, after five months. Throughout, Emma's pregnancy, now seven months advanced, had escaped detection.

CHAPTER SEVENTEEN

In the Face of Heaven

On Sunday 9 November the party from Italy finally reached London. Amid the wearisome displays of enthusiasm for the hero on the road from Yarmouth, there had been a disappointing interlude. Lady Nelson had sent an invitation to await Nelson at Yarmouth, asking him to bring his friends, the Hamiltons, to Roundwood. Accordingly, the party rolled up at the house near Ipswich which Nelson had bought but never inhabited. A neat, well-built house with six bedrooms and two parlours, it lacked only a hostess. Lady Nelson had gone to London, having heard nothing from her husband, and was awaiting him there.

In London, which seemed curiously dark and cold to the travellers after their long sojourn abroad, Mrs Cadogan and Miss Knight went to a hotel in Albemarle Street. Hot on their heels, Sir Thomas Troubridge arrived and earnestly recommended Miss Knight to leave her companions forthwith. She took his advice with some qualms over its seeming ingratitude, and went to an old friend, Mrs Evan Nepean, wife of the Secretary of the Admiralty. She found that all her friends in London concurred in their advice to break her connection with the Hamilton party.[1]

Meanwhile, Nelson and the Hamiltons dined with Fanny Lady Nelson and the Reverend Edmund Nelson, Horatio's father. It is said that, at the coldness of Lady Nelson's reception, 'the warmth of his [Nelson's] heart felt a petrifying thrill'. Poor Lady Nelson was, no doubt, stiff with nerves. The Ladies Hamilton and Nelson having made each other's acquaintance, the dinner ended and Nelson went off to pay his respects to Lord Spencer, First Lord of the Admiralty.

William Beckford lent Sir William and Emma his house in Grosvenor Square till they should find a home of their own. Miss Knight came to dinner here to find present Lord and Lady Nelson, Prince Augustus and Lady Augusta Murray, his wife (according to the Catholic Church). Charles Greville was another of the company. Perhaps aware of the peculiar relations between various members of the distinguished company, Miss Knight did not again visit her friends from Italy. Nelson was to refer to her ungraciously in later years as 'that b— Miss Knight'.

Charles Greville's frequent attendance at Grosvenor Square, and the visits of another of Sir William's nephews, Lord Cathcart, were the subject of some criticism, both among the clannish ranks of the family and on the part of outsiders. Before the Italian party's arrival in England, there had been a flurry of correspondence on the propriety or otherwise of meeting Lady Hamilton. Greville attempted honourably to persuade the family that 'the reports concerning Lady H. are false . . . report strongly says otherwise.' Lady Frances Harpur, Greville's sister, summed up the family consensus in a letter to Mary Dickenson: 'It was settled . . . that it could not be avoided noticing *Ly H.*, without offence to *Sr Wm* or at least *affecting his feelings*; & as He has met with much *Vexation* & *disappointment*, as to *His Recall*, & is in Weak Health . . .' the family graciously assented to visit. Lady Frances went to see the Hamiltons on 10 November. She thought Emma grown fat, Sir William thin – like Jack Sprat and his wife. 'I believe She *constitutes* His *Happiness*; I cannot but *lament* this *Idolatry*,' Lady Frances grieved.

Following the dinner party at Grosvenor Square, the Nelsons and Hamiltons made several joint expeditions to the theatre. On 18 November, Lady Nelson wore white with a violet satin headdress, Emma wore blue satin and feathers and was considered rather *embonpoint*, Nelson was applauded. The play on the twenty-fourth was *Pizarro*, with Emma's old friend Jane Powell playing Elvira. In the third act there was a disturbance in the box Beckford had lent to the Hamiltons. A lady had fainted. Lady Nelson was distressed by the passage:

> How a woman can love, Pizarro, thou hast known . . . how she can hate, thou hast yet to learn . . . thou, who on Panama's brow . . . wave thy glittering sword, meet and survive – an injured woman's fury.

Lady Nelson was 'carried out of her box', the *Morning Herald* noted next day, but later returned – 'to the great satisfaction of all present'.

Both Lord and Lady Nelson were exhibiting every indication of a strained relationship. Since 15 November they had been living at 17 Dover Street. Nelson had taken the house for a year. His father noted that the house, 'tho' not small, is really filled with servants . . . The Suite of nobility is long.' Nelson, he added, was 'constantly on the wing'.

Wishing to distinguish Lady Nelson by her attentions, Lady Spencer had invited both Fanny and her lord to dinner at Spencer House on 12 November. The evening presented the strongest contrast possible to a similar dinner at Spencer House at the beginning of 1798. Lord Nelson scowled throughout dinner in the elegant dining-room. Lady Nelson, perhaps inadvisedly, peeled a walnut for her husband and offered it to him across the table. With an oath he pushed it roughly away. It struck the edge of a glass, which then shattered. Lady Nelson rose and escaped from the room to hide her tears. Later, in the drawing-room, she told a shocked and sympathetic Lady Spencer 'how she was situated'.[2]

Lady Nelson underwent further trials in this most dreadful winter. Nelson did nothing to hide the antipathy he felt towards her. He insisted they invite the Hamiltons to dinner at Dover Street. During the course of the meal, Emma left the table, saying she felt unwell. Nelson openly reproached his wife for not following her guest to offer aid. Lady Nelson rose and went to do his bidding. She found Emma being sick into a basin. Whether she suspected the cause or not, Lady Nelson held the basin for her guest. No hostess could do more. Then Nelson himself arrived, to make the incident still more remarkable to guests left below.

Nelson, when not at receptions such as the Lord Mayor's banquet held in his honour – at which he insisted Sir William be present – spent an increasing amount of time at Grosvenor Square. Lady Frances told Mary: 'They have continual Company; but I don't know their set. Prince Augustus is one, & Foreigners. Few Ladies visit Ly. H. except those have been at Naples.' There were plenty of those.

It is said that on the night of the dinner at Dover Street Nelson made his decision to linger no more unhappily with his wife. He roamed the streets of London and ended by ringing the door of the Hamiltons' house. Gaining admittance, he threw himself on the bed of his astonished hosts, and begged that they would take him in. Sir William consulted Emma. 'What say you?' Emma demurred, mentioning the odd appearance it would present to the world. Sir William replied that he 'cared not a fig for the world'. The last sentiment certainly accords with views Sir William expressed at other times.

The matter was not decided and Nelson returned home in the morning. He entered his wife's bedroom and stood silent. She understood what was in his mind, and asked him, stretching out an arm from the bed, had she ever given him cause for complaint in their married life? He answered her that she had not, and strode from the room. That same morning he offered his services to the Admiralty.

How much of the foregoing rumours and reports we should believe is not clear. It was a period of cruel unhappiness and humiliation for Lady Nelson. Nelson's unfeeling behaviour was compounded when he accepted an invitation from William Beckford to accompany the Hamiltons to Fonthill for Christmas. Lady Nelson was not included in the invitation, and she remained in London, with only the prosy William, Nelson's reverend brother, and his wife Sarah for company. William, a burly, rough-looking character, had come from Norfolk ostensibly to greet his brother. None was deceived. He was after pickings from his brother's hoard of fame.

The *Tria Juncta in Uno* sped off in merry mood towards Salisbury on 21 December. Mrs Cadogan was also included in the invitation to Emma, whom Beckford now dubbed 'Madonna of the lovely eyes'. At Salisbury, the Yeomen Cavalry came out to escort Nelson and present him with the Freedom of the City. Touching scenes followed his reunion with men once under his command. Then, at the lodge to Fonthill, Beckford's volunteers stood ready to escort the carriage, a thirty-man band going ahead playing 'Rule Britannia'. Sir William and Emma had had a standing invitation to return to Fonthill Splendens, the mansion Beckford's father had built, since their last visit in 1791. Now, Christmas 1800, Beckford, long a recluse, decided to throw a magnificent party to celebrate new abbey and new century together.

Among the Hamiltons' and Nelson's fellow guests were Peter Pindar, or Dr Wolcot, the satirical poet who had written amusing lines on Sir William's marriage to Emma; Benjamin West, the American-born President of the Royal Academy; William Hamilton the painter – no relation – and many others. The festive week was to be spent at the mansion, a monastic soirée at the abbey to crown and end the party.

Three days were spent quietly enjoying the pictures and library of the house, while the weather failed; when the sun came out, there were extensive grounds in which to stroll. Thirty servants, headed by Perro, Beckford's Portuguese dwarf, attended to every comfort. There was only one incident of any note. Beckford took Nelson out for a drive in his phaeton one afternoon. They were touring the high walls which the owner had erected in an attempt to keep out sportsmen: 'They will take no denial when they go hunting in their red jackets to excruciate a poor hare.'

Nelson became increasingly nervous as the drive proceeded through the entrancing wilderness. 'The birds, the plantations of Fonthill seemed to know me – they continued their songs as I rode close to them,' Beckford would say in later years. The horses gathered speed, Nelson protested, and ended by jumping from the box.[3]

On 23 December the moment came to view the famous abbey. Carriages took the party from the mansion at five o'clock on a long, winding drive through planted avenues. At dusk, the light ebbing from the sky, they saw the spire of the abbey soar above them through the trees now illuminated about them. A vice-admiral's flag waved in honour of Nelson's presence, above the flying buttresses and other fragile constructions with which James Wyatt, Beckford's architect, had temporarily gratified his patron.

Through a groined gothic hall, between long lines of soldiers, the party passed solemnly to the Cardinal's Parlour. Long curtains of rich purple fell behind ebony chairs set at a long refectory table. Fir and pine cones burnt redolent in a cavernous fireplace. With the monastic setting now firm in their minds, the party took their places and a dazzling array of silver dishes was uncovered to reveal a repast fit for the most sumptuous pre-Reformation abbey.

After dinner the party proceeded upstairs, past mysterious hooded figures who held smoking torches, and entered a charming room, hung with yellow damask and set off by japanned chests. Chairs were placed here and the guests were invited to seat themselves. Lady Hamilton, meanwhile, had discreetly slipped away. On her now hung the success of the entire festivities, and she did not mean to disappoint the company. She gave her most celebrated performance of her Attitudes, superbly overcoming the encumbrance which was the eight-month-old child in her womb.

The subject of Emma's peformance was perhaps chosen by Beckford. The virtues of a Roman matron seemed more suitable to a gothic abbey than scenes from Greek drama. Agrippina, however, had been a familiar Attitude since the origin of the entertainment. If Beckford requested Emma to play this part, it was Sir William who coached her. Never before had she acted only one Attitude and it was far more developed than her performances before now. At Fonthill Emma told in mime the entire sad story of Agrippina. For those moments she was perhaps transported to the world of the antique that Sir William had made over to her. Her performance was for Sir William, her keenest critic. Ten to one, Nelson had no idea who Agrippina was and did not comprehend the force of her acting. Benjamin West was so struck by Emma's performance that he painted the scene she created. Emma's wonderfully modelled mouth, the elegant sweep of the eyebrow, make the identification certain. (The painting was sold with Beckford's other effects from Bath on his death, though he never hung it – later in life, he was to turn against Emma.) For an encore to this highlight of the evening, Emma most inappropriately imitated an abbess welcoming novices to her convent.[4]

January 1801 saw the dispersal of the party. Nelson returned briefly to Dover Street, where he received the news that he was a Vice-Admiral of the Blue. The Hamiltons took possession of 23 Piccadilly, a small but charming house which Sir William rented at £150 a year, opposite Green Park. (Like so many Piccadilly houses, it has now been demolished.) To furnish the house, Emma had sold her diamonds. In return, Sir William made over the contents of the house to her.

A year earlier, Lady Minto had estimated Lady Hamilton's collection of Royal gifts of jewellery at £30,000. Emma was later to say that she did very badly from her sale. There was the chain of diamonds and cyphers; there was the Queen's 'picture and hair set in bracelets with an aigrette of diamonds and earrings of pearls and diamonds' – all commemorated Emma's services to her dear, dear Queen. She was left with a pretty mosaic necklace from Rome and other trifles. Sir William replaced her diamonds with more pretty trifles from the Strand jeweller, John Salter. A hundred and twenty items totalled £169 11s 7d by 1803. Pearl bandeaux bound her polished forehead; she had a variety of gilt combs and 'an antique ornament for the head' – perhaps these were of use in her Attitudes. Pendant earrings of gold are listed in Salter's account, of mother of pearl, of cornelian. Strings of pearls, of coral, of cornelian and snake bracelets jostle in the account with lockets shaped like lyres and crescent moons, pearl sautoirs and long gold chains from Venice. Diana Scarisbrick tells us: 'This fascinating account . . . presents a picture of fashionable taste at the turn of the century with its mixture of classical and sentimental motifs, decorative and useful ornaments.'[5]

A boisterous inhabitant came to swell the ranks in the New Year, when Nelson bought Emma a mongrel puppy. Named Nilus, he was a present to amuse Emma in Nelson's absence. On 13 January Nelson heard that he was to command the *San Josef* in the Channel fleet. He was to proceed to Torbay that day, which he did with his brother William in attendance. Two weeks later he sent her news of his health. The ship's doctor had ordered him not to write, his eye was very bad. He must have 'green shades' for his eyes – 'Will you, my dear friend, make me one or two? Nobody else shall.'

Emma had little time to lament his departure. She was occupied in deceiving the world as to the parentage of the child she was about to bear. In this last month of her pregnancy she was remarkably social. Nelson's sister-in-law, Sarah Nelson, became a firm friend. 'Our souls were congenial,' Emma was to write when Mrs Nelson had gone back to Norfolk. 'How dull my bedroom looks without you. I miss our friendly chats.'[6] Sarah was a foolish woman, dazzled by this new intimacy with the celebrated Lady Hamilton. The burden of her 'friendly chats' with Emma was the great antipathy they felt to 'Tom tit and the Cub', as Emma dubbed Lady Nelson and her son, Josiah Nisbet. Considering that Lady Nelson had behaved with the utmost kindness to Sarah Nelson's children, Horace and Charlotte, this was hardly admirable.

If Emma spent a deal of time with William and Sarah Nelson, it was perhaps not entirely from choice. The letter Maria Carolina had

written in praise of Lady Hamilton had been delivered to the Queen
of England. Then no more was heard. Sir William had, perforce, gone
to the Queen's drawing-room alone on his return from Italy. Nelson
was characteristically affronted. 'You know I would not in Sir William's
case have gone to Court without my wife, and such a wife . . .'

By January no answer from the Court had come. Emma resigned herself to creating a social circle outside the confines of Court. Nevertheless,
the speculation in the press was humiliating. With the passing of every
drawing-room the papers commented gleefully on Lady Hamilton's
absence. Lord St Vincent's prophecy that Nelson would 'get into much
brouillerie about . . . getting Lady Hamilton received at St James's, and
everywhere' proved unfounded. Nelson himself was in no good odour
at Court. The King had only asked him if he were well again, then
turned away to talk for a full half-hour to a general. It could not have
been about his successes, Nelson wrote furiously to Troubridge. This
Royal treatment confirmed all his prejudices against those he termed
the 'great people'. He harangued a dinner party on the subject that
night, despite Emma's attempts to hush him. Nelson, if he felt strongly
on some subject, did not hide it, which, if honest, was often impolitic.
Sir William and Lady Hamilton were both natural politicians. This was
only one difference which made the three awkward now they were back
in England. Emma's manners and habit of thought were now those, as
were Sir William's, inalienably of the 'great people'. Nelson was of a
different turn of mind.

Throughout January 1801 he bombarded poor Lady Nelson with
reproaches. He had to break into his chests, as only one key could be
found. 'I have no one thing for comfort come.' 'Half my wardrobe is left
behind.' 'If I want a piece of pickle it must be put in saucer.' Nails had
been driven through the mahogany table. Lady Nelson had retired to
Brighton, and defended herself, but Nelson was set on quarrelling.[7]

Nelson certainly displayed a provincial turn of mind when he objected
to a proposal that the Prince of Wales come to dinner at Piccadilly.
Nelson had heard that the Prince had said Emma 'hit his fancy'. The
Prince had heard reports of Emma singing a duet with the Banti at
Fonthill and wished them to recreate the ensemble for his pleasure.
Fearfully, Nelson wrote: 'You cannot be seduced by any prince in
Europe.'

The Prince's meditated visit was not forgotten, but Emma's time
was drawing near. From Plymouth Nelson wrote the first of a series
of letters dubbed 'the Thompson letters'. Mindful of navy censors and
other curious eyes, Nelson wrote in the character of a sailor on Nelson's
ship. The supposed sailor, Thompson, had a supposed wife under Lady

Hamilton's protection. To Lady Hamilton, then, 'Thompson' addressed his letters, with messages for 'his wife'. These concern the sailor's fears for his wife and the infant she is about to bear. They make curious reading, not least because Nelson is often confused about whose voice he is speaking in and whom he is addressing.

The confusion is compounded, as Nelson kept up simultaneously an official correspondence with Lady Hamilton. Conversely, Lord St Vincent told Lady Betty Foster that Lady Hamilton wrote to Lord Nelson sometimes four times a day. St Vincent suppressed her letters when he could.

We can be thankful that this confusion does not entirely mask the quality of Nelson's prose, the intensity of longing which the man absent at sea felt for his woman. 'It is your sex that makes us go forth [to battle],' he wrote, '. . . and you, my dear, honoured friend, are, believe me, the *first*, the best, of your sex. I have been the world around, and in every corner of it, and never yet saw your equal . . .' he wrote on 8 February. Mrs Trench thought, when they were published in 1814, that they expressed very much what any man would feel, separated from a pair of fine eyes. The letters, rather, bring to mind the poems of the Latin love poets: Tibullus and his *militia amoris*, Propertius and his fears for his mistress's chastity, above all Ovid with his facility for imagining in tormenting detail his mistress's little infidelities. Indeed, the epithet which springs to mind when considering this batch of letters is *insanus*, stock epithet of the lovers in Latin poetry. After which proem, let us read them.

Nelson solemnly destroyed all Emma's billets. She preserved his, though what he wrote contrived to lose her finally her slipping reputation. From January to May 1801, Nelson wrote all he felt, paying only lip-service to the censors. The following extracts are all from letters written after the birth of Horatia at the end of January, the 'dear pledge of love' Emma gave him.

On 3 February he wrote: 'He swears before heaven that he will marry you as soon as it is possible, which he fervently prays may be soon.' On the sixth he wrote:

> Your letters are to me gazettes . . . Mr Davison . . . says you are grown thinner but . . . look handsomer than ever . . . He says you told him to tell me not to send you any more advice about seeing compny [*sic*], therefore I will not say a word . . . I was sure you would not go to Mrs Walpole's, it is no better than a bawdy house.

On the eighth he confided:

I own I sometimes fear that you will not be so true to me as I am to you,
yet I cannot, will not believe you can be false. No, I judge you by myself;
I hope to be dead before that will happen, but it will not.

In an undated letter Nelson was again miserable:

He wishes there was peace, or that if your uncle [Sir Wm.] would die,
he would instantly then come and marry you, for he doats on nothing but
you and your child.

On the seventeenth Nelson was so agitated by thoughts of the Prince
of Wales's impending visit, he could write about nothing else.

Do not have him *en famille*, the more [guests] the better. Do not sit long
at table . . . he will be next you, and telling you soft things. If he does,
tell it out at table, and turn him out of the house . . . at dinner he will
hob glasses with you . . . Oh God, that I was dead . . . I shall that day
have no one to dinner; it shall be a fast day to me. He will put his foot
near you.

There is much more of the same. Ovid's instructions to his mistress,
who is to be present, with her husband, at a dinner party, come to
mind: '*Nec femori committe femur nec crure cohaere . . . Multa miser timeo,
quia feci multa proterve*' (Do not press thigh to thigh or touch his leg.
Alas, I fear all, having done all shamelessly myself).

To return to Horatia's birth, on 25 January Nelson wrote that
Thompson 'is very anxious . . . he appears to me to feel very much
her situation . . . he is so agitated and will be so for 2 or 3 days, that
he says he cannot write . . .' Later he wrote: 'Mrs Thompson's friend
appears almost as miserable as myself . . .' On 1 February there was a
change in his mood.

I believe Mrs Thompson's friend will go mad with joy. He swears he will
drink your health this day in a bumper. I cannot write, I am so agitated
by this young man at my elbow. I believe he is foolish; he does nothing
but rave about you and her.

In the interval the child known as Horatia Thompson had been born
in great secrecy at 23 Piccadilly. Piccadilly was not a large house. How
was the birth, the commotion consequent upon it, kept secret from
Sir William? Undoubtedly he chose not to hear or comment. Emma's
increased weight, her faints and sickness, would hardly have escaped
him. Following the birth, he commented on her headaches and 'foul

stomach'. The marvel is, how he preserved the appearance of dignified oblivion while his wife gave birth to his declared best friend's child.

Early in February, a Mrs Gibson in Little Titchfield Street, just off the modern Oxford Circus, received a visit from a lady wrapped in furs and bearing a child born, in Mrs Gibson's experienced opinion, less than a week before. Lady Hamilton made no secret of her name, asking Mrs Gibson to look after the infant in return for a tempting amount of money. Mrs Gibson, a lady without a husband but with a young daughter, Mary, agreed, and Lady Hamilton climbed into her waiting hackney carriage and was driven away again. Mrs Gibson promised to report frequently on the child's health.[8] The only puzzle was Lady Hamilton's insistence that the child had been born the preceding October. Mrs Gibson could see that the child was a few days old. This was, of course, a precautionary lie. Emma had been in Dresden in October. Thus she could not be the mother.

On 3 February Emma was reported in attendance at a grand concert given by the Duke of Norfolk in St James's Square. In fact, this report was contradicted in a later edition of the paper, and anxiety expressed for Lady Hamilton's indisposition. Though some have tried to convince themselves that these reports in the press hid suspicions that Emma had had a child, no such rumours appear in any diaries of the time. Emma had triumphantly kept her secret.

She was understandably worried when Nelson made some indiscreet alterations to his will, leaving property to any child born in or out of wedlock, whom Lady Hamilton should propose. He was mad with joy. Emma was very worried, and persuaded him to change the codicils.

The gap between Nelson's excited plans for his daughter and Emma's wish to pursue her own life widened. Nelson wrote as Mr Thompson on 4 February about christening the child. He suggested St George's, Hanover Square, and proposed that he and Lady Hamilton should stand sponsors. 'Its name will be Horatia, daughter of Johem and Morata Etnorb! If you read the surname backwards and take the letters of the other names, it will make, very extraordinarily, the names of your real and affectionate friends, Lady Hamilton and myself.' Emma wrote to point out the difficulties and he changed his mind. The clergyman might want to verify the parents' names – 'which would put poor Mrs T. in trouble', Nelson agreed. Horatia was in the event not christened for two years.

Nelson longed to see his child, but had to be content with a lock of hair Emma sent him from the infant head. 'Poor fellow,' he wrote of himself, 'he would give anything to have seen the child, especially in your charming company.' His thoughts were centred upon Horatia's existence. Emma had other matters to which she was forced to pay attention, mainly monetary.

The sale of Emma's diamonds had barely relieved the crippling debt under which Sir William and she struggled. Sir William had to sell his collection of pictures and antique busts, etc. He owed, for rent of the Palazzo Sessa – now finally given up – and servants' wages and pensions, etc., nearly £2,000 to a Mr Ragland in Naples. He arranged the sale at Christie's auction-room in March, and was meanwhile busy cataloguing them. Besides this, he was making every effort to secure £8,000 for 'extraordinary expenses' at Naples and the pension of £2,000 generally, but not invariably, afforded to retired ministers. He wrote a memorial to Lord Grenville, setting out his claim. A new Government was formed, he had no answer; and he took the step, unwillingly, of waiting on Lord Hawkesbury, the new Foreign secretary, at the Foreign Office. When he had waited some hours without the Minister deigning to receive him, he returned home and wrote a mortified letter. It was hardly courteous, considering the length of his service and, indeed, his friendship with Hawkesbury's family, to keep him kicking his heels in public like a lackey and to no purpose. Eventually, a pension was granted, after Sir William had appealed to the King himself. 'My mother looked after us both, the same nurse suckled us.' The pension was not to revert to Emma on his death.

The unwholesome spectre of the Prince of Wales manifested its interest in the Hamilton household once more. Nelson wrote in an ecstasy of jealous outrage. 'He is permitted to visit only houses of notorious ill fame. For heaven's sake let Sir William pause before he demeans your good name.' On 19 February Sir William wrote a curious letter to Nelson:

> I am well aware of the danger that would attend the Prince's frequenting our house, not that I fear that Emma could ever be induced to act contrary to the prudent conduct she has hitherto pursued . . . this dinner must be, or the Prince would be offended . . . I have been thus explicit as I know well your Lordship's way of thinking . . .

Nelson wrote to Emma the next day: 'By the bye, Sir Wm must be mad to attempt giving his wife the reputation of w—e to the P.'

The much-vaunted visit never, in fact, took place. Emma was indisposed on the Sunday agreed. For several weeks after Horatia's birth, as we have heard, she suffered from a 'foul stomach'. No doubt Horatia suffered too, according to modern views on the importance of early maternal contact. Emma's notes to Mrs Gibson regarding the child's welfare could not replace this. Two further plans came to nothing, and the Prince of Wales passed from the Hamiltons' lives. It has been said that Emma tormented Nelson with reports of the Prince's attentions, the better to ensnare him and wean him from his wife, but the question only arose following Nelson's coldness to his wife and his departure for the fleet.

At the end of February Nelson was granted three days' leave and proceeded immediately to London. Lady Nelson wrote from Brighton that she would join him, and he begged that she would not.

So Nelson's brief reunion with his Santa Emma, his 'pattern of perfection', at the end of February was unmarred by his wife's presence. He took the opportunity to visit his daughter at Mrs Gibson's, and was gratified to find that she resembled Emma in the upper part of the face. Portraits of Horatia as a child confirm that she had inherited her mother's wide eyes and strong eyebrows.

A less pleasant duty took him to Alexander Davison's office, so his friend could help him finalize the settlement he had drawn up in favour of his wife. (Davison acted as man of business, as well as confidential friend, to Nelson). Lord Nelson's mind was 'fixed as fate'. Rather than live with Fanny again, he would 'reside abroad'. He allotted his wife £1,800 per annum, half his income. There was, however, no question of divorce. A special Act of Parliament was needed for this. Though the divorce rate crept up slowly throughout the eighteenth century, divorce was still an exceptional measure. Cruelty had to be proved, and Nelson had only shown mental cruelty to Fanny. She was 'astonished' by the letter her husband now wrote her, confirming their separation.

All too soon Nelson departed. He had only been granted this leave because he was now to join Sir Hyde Parker on a special expedition in the Baltic. 'My heart is fit to burst with Greef. Oh what pain, only God knows,' Emma informed his sister-in-law Sarah, while Nelson wrote to her of Horatia: 'A finer child was never produced by any two persons. It was in truth a love-begotten child.' On the eve of sailing for the Baltic, a surprise visit from Francis Oliver at Portsmouth furnished him with the means to send a most private letter to Emma, a fine and frank avowal of his love for her.

Now, my own dear wife, for such you are in my eyes and in the face of heaven, I can give full scope to my feelings ... You know, my dearest Emma, that there is nothing in this world I would not do for us to live together, and to have our dear little child with us. I firmly believe that this campaign will give us peace, and then we will sett off for Bronte ... I love, I never did love anyone else. I never had a dear pledge of love till you gave me one, and you, thank my God, never gave one to any body else.

Emma had kept the existence of 'little Emma' a secret even from Nelson. When she came briefly to visit Emma later this year, Nelson thought she was just another of Emma's innumerable relatives. Ironically, Mrs Cadogan was even now on her way to visit Emma Carew in Manchester, en route for Hawarden. She wrote on 16 April to ask Emma to send her 'every particular how I am to proceed about the little girl'.

Nelson went on:

> You, my beloved Emma, and my country, are the two dearest objects of my fond heart . . . My longing for you, both person and conversation, you can readily imagine. What must be my sensations at the idea of sleeping with you! it setts me on fire, even the thoughts . . . if any woman naked were to come to me, even as I am this moment from thinking of you, I hope it might rot off if I would touch her even with my hand.

Nelson was jealous of every aspect of Emma's life into which he did not enter. Sir William's cousin, the Duke of Abercorn, the elderly Duke of Queensberry, and a variety of singers like the Banti, Madame Bianchi and Mrs Denis came frequently to Piccadilly and prompted him to write on 10 March:

> What can Sir William mean by wanting you to launch out into expense and extravagance? He that used to think that a little candle-light and iced water would ruin him, to want to set off at £10,000 a year . . . concerts and the style of living equal to it.[9]

Despite these anxieties and fears which tormented Nelson, a soft word from Emma could calm him and induce in him a lyrical tranquillity. He wrote, on one occasion, that he had scored through all the scolds in her letters and burnt one fulminating epistle – she was furious with his comment that the West Country women wore black stockings. Thus expurgated, her letters were so much prettier, he told her.

Meanwhile, Sir William was making progress with his financial affairs. On 28 and 29 March he sold the bulk of his pictures for over £5,000. Among them was a St Cecilia by Romney which Nelson was keen to acquire. He sold Emma's portraits by Vigée-Le Brun and Gavin Hamilton and Reynolds also.

Even the very perilous state of the Baltic could not deflect Nelson from thought of Horatia. Shortly after the Battle of Copenhagen he was disturbed by news that Horatia's wet nurse had been ill, and had infected the child. 'He has cried on account of the child,' he wrote of 'Thompson'. Nelson had himself spent six days on open boats in the

Baltic, crossing from ship to ship. The surgeon of the *Elephant*, his command ship, marvelled at his relentless vigour.

The news of the British victory at Copenhagen reached London in the middle of a dinner party at 23 Piccadilly. The Reverend William Nelson was odd man out in a party which could have taken place in Naples. There was the Duca di Noja, son of the celebrated map-maker of the Neapolitan Kingdom; there were Prince Augustus and Lady Augusta; Lord William Gordon, Charles Greville; and an old friend of Sir William's, Sir Nathaniel Wraxall. This last described the scene in his *Memoirs*. Emma danced a tarantella, first with her husband, then with the Duca di Noja, finally with Fatima, her black maid. The performance was remarkable for its 'screams, attitudes, starts, and embraces'.[10]

Sir William, congratulating Nelson, wrote that Emma did not know if she were on her head or her heels. The Reverend William's behaviour was characteristically hideous. He sat still for a time, then leapt up to 'cut a caper' and rub his hands in glee at the thought of his brother's increased bankability. Then he would be still, then repeat his pantomime.[11] Nelson's victory brought congratulations from his wife. His father, however, was less enthusiastic: 'All things have their alloy.' Lady Nelson's distress at hearing no word from her husband, despite a letter which she had written to him, outweighed his son's achievement, in his eyes. Nelson wrote to Emma on 9 April: 'He never wrote to his aunt since he sailed; he believes she has a most unfeeling heart.' The Battle of Copenhagen was celebrated again at a christening at the Foundling Hospital on 19 April. Emma stood godmother to a child named Emma Hamilton. Another was named Baltic Nelson. There was further wholesale joy in May when the hero was created Viscount Nelson of the Nile and of Burnham Thorpe.

The first of July brought Nelson home on leave. Naturally, his first concern was to see his daughter. It was agreed, however, that what he stood most in need of was rest and country air. Emma organized a visit to an inn at Burford Bridge near Dorking, then a further sojourn at the Bush at Staines. Here Sir William fished peacefully, while William Nelson, who joined the party with his wife and children, pressed his brother for recommendations to prebendaries and cathedral stalls.

A protégé of Nelson's, young Captain Parker, joined the holiday-makers at Staines, so was present when a barbel Sir William caught was found to be quite inedible. On his return to the Channel with Nelson, Parker teased Emma about Horatia. 'You do not mean to mention her for sixteen years, I suppose.' No doubt he met the child at Piccadilly when delivering letters from Nelson. Emma often had the child over from Little Titchfield Street, when Sir William was out at a meeting of one of his societies. On one occasion, it is thought, he and Horatia came face to face, due to Mrs Gibson's early arrival and his delayed departure. No doubt he turned the incident off lightly.

Captain Thomas Hardy was another who unknowingly made the acquaintance of his friend's child, when she was only an infant. He called on Emma after the Battle of Copenhagen. She left him for a moment, then returned with a child in her arms. 'Look what a pretty baby I have got,' she said simply. This was a rare moment of maternal pride, though Hardy had no more idea than Parker that the child was Nelson's or Emma's.

Parker took good care of Nelson when they were forced to return to duty on 27 July. He wrote to Emma, asking her to send cream cheese and other delicacies; Parker engaged to cut them up for his commander. Nelson was not in spirits at this time. He found the special operation, or defence of the Channel, irksome, chafing at being so near and yet far from those he held dear. His brother William and sister-in-law Sarah came to visit him in September, in company with the Hamiltons. They all lodged at the Three Kings in Deal, then a 'grimy seaport'.

If Deal was hardly the ideal holiday spot, Nelson's delight in their company reconciled all to their situation. Sir William was just back from a tour of his Welsh property with Greville, and in cheerful mood. His finances seemed in better order. A surprise in the shape of some better vases being included by mistake in the cargo from Palermo – they were supposed to have been sent on board the ill-fated *Colossus* – had brought him £4,000 from the collector, Thomas Hope. He thought all Greville's improvements at Milford Haven excellent. Sir William fished, the Reverend William went to church, and a variety of houses in the district contend for the honour of having been Emma's and Nelson's love-nest in this autumn. They certainly stole away occasionally to Laleham, where 'Mrs Nelson', or 'Blindy', the lady friend of Nelson's dead brother Maurice, lived.

The cheerful breakfast parties with Nelson gave way to more useful work on the ladies' part in the wake of the English fleet's attack on Boulogne. It had been a mismanaged business, and left the English with forty-four dead, twenty more wounded. Among these last was 'brave little Parker', his thigh broken in three places. Emma and Sarah Nelson worked hard to bring him what comfort they could but his condition worsened. Amputation, long disputed, followed, but could not save him. Emma was not there to the end; she and Sir William returned to London on 27 September. Nelson felt more than ever bereft. 'I came on board, but no Emma. No, no, my heart will break. The four pictures of Lady Hn. are hung up, but, alas, I have lost the original . . . better times will come, *shall* come, if it pleases God.' Parker's death followed at the end of September, to set Nelson back further.

Nelson attempted to raise his spirits with thoughts of settling. Earlier in the year he had had a plan to quit England and the fleet and settle at Bronte. In December of this year young William Hoste was to be dispatched to the Sicilian estate with hoes and other gardening implements, overcoming protests from bemused superiors. Nelson's plans for the Italian pastoral idyll with Emma were to bear no more fruit than this. If he had no conception of the wilderness which was Sicily, Emma could form an accurate picture from her tour of Puglia with Sir William. Bronte was a dream to calm a lonely, sickly seaman in the blasting Channel winds. Graefer, appointed steward to the estate, wrote dispirited letters, speaking of the dearth of any form of amusement beyond tilling the poor soil.

In the summer of 1801, Nelson formed a more practical plan, though he was still to hanker sometimes after the estate's shady chestnut trees. He would buy a 'little farm' outside London where he could live when not on active service. Emma was deputed to find the farm. She set to assiduously, and by July had discovered a suitable property in Turnham Green. It had faults and she looked elsewhere, in Chiswick. In September she had lighted on another property – in Merton, in Surrey. Nelson was enthusiastic and sent a surveyor to make his report.

Nothing could have been more damning than Mr Cockerell's findings. It was quite unsuitable to be a gentleman's residence. Through the grounds ran 'a dirty, black-looking canal . . . which keeps the whole place damp'. The house was 'paltry', the furniture inferior, and public roads surrounded the property.

Nelson was not deterred, specifically requesting that the inferior furniture remain. He wrote to Emma: 'You are to be lady paramount of Paradise Merton, all its territories and waters.' Her picture was to hang there, also his picture of the Battle of the Nile. He enquired whether there was a nice church – he intended that they should set a good example to the parishioners. He left all to Emma's management, firm on only one point: not a book or a cook belonging to Sir William should be allowed in the house, though Sir William was to be made most welcome. Mr Cockerell's 'canal', a tributary of the Wandle, was to be stocked with fish for the old knight. The stream, which widened into a lake and was crossed by a pretty ironwork bridge, was soon christened the Nile.

Sadly, Nilus, the dog Nelson gave Emma in January, had been lost only days after his presentation, and an advertisement in the *Morning Herald*, offering a guinea reward, failed to produce him. Sir William placed instead an antique statue of the River Nile by the stream. Approving of the stream and lake, Nelson was fearful of its attractions for Horatia. He envisaged the child as being a permanent inhabitant of the house, and Emma made no demur. He begged Emma repeatedly to have some netting put round the edge of the water. Again and again, Emma delayed.

By October the house was Nelson's. The previous owner, Widow Greaves, showed some reluctance to move out, to Emma's annoyance. Emma wrote to tell her that Lord Nelson was shortly returning from sea and would want to come direct to Merton. Mrs Greaves replied that she would be delighted to look after him. She was given short shrift, and when, on 24 October, Nelson came to Merton, Emma and Sir William were in occupation.

Nelson had had a lively description of Paradise Merton's charms from Sir William some days earlier.

We have now inhabited your Lordship's premises some days, and I can now speak with some certainty. I have lived with our dear Emma several years. I know her merit, have a great opinion of the head and heart that God Almighty has been pleased to give her; but a seaman alone could have given a fine woman full power to chuse and fit up a residence for him without seeing it himself. You are in luck, for in my conscience I verily believe that a place so suitable to your views could not have been found, and at so cheap a rate, for if you stay away three days longer I do not think you can have any wish but you will find it compleated here, and then the bargain was fortunately struck three days before an idea of peace got abroad. Now every estate in this neighbourhood has increased in value, and you might get a thousand pounds tomorrow for your bargain. The proximity to the capital, and the perfect retirement of this place, are, for your Lordship, two points beyond estimation; but the house is so comfortable, the furniture clean and good, and I never saw so many conveniences united in so small a compass. You have nothing but to come and enjoy immediately; you have a good mile of pleasant dry walk around your own farm. It would make you laugh to see Emma and her mother fitting up pig-sties and hen-coops, and already the Canal is enlivened with ducks, and the cock is strutting with his hens about the walks. Your Lordship's plan as to stocking the Canal with fish is exactly mine. I will answer for it, that in a few months you may command a good dish of fish at a moment's warning.

Emma was as happy as Sir William. Owing to Sir William's own interest in decoration, she had never had the opportunity to fit up a house previously. Her taste in interior decoration, if not in dress, seems to have been charming. Not for nothing had she made Greville and Sir

William, in turn, exceptionally comfortable in their homes. Drawing on her experience, she installed a large number of water closets, fitted the bedrooms with their own bathrooms, and rigged out the kitchens with modern stoves. The essentials covered, she next attended to the receiving rooms. A carpenter once employed in the house reminisced: glass mirrors and plate glass dazzled wherever you looked. Thus an airy impression of light was created in a house not naturally so favoured. There was sunshine within and without, Emma wrote gaily. For the ladies, she had miradors or verandahs built outside the parlours on the south side, where they could shelter from the sun while taking a modicum of air. Nelson, arriving through drifts of fallen leaves on the October morning, was entranced by Emma's work.

He was in need of rest as ever after the ardours of sea life. 'He has frequent sickness . . . and he throws himself on the sofa tired and says I am worn out,' Emma informed Sarah, her 'jewell'.[11] He was slowly recovering, she considered.

Fourteen-year-old Charlotte Nelson was on hand, on leave from her boarding school, to entertain the invalid. Nelson's sisters felt at this time upset by the preference he appeared to feel for his brother's children. It was, in fact, a question of propinquity. Horace and Charlotte Nelson were at school near London, while the Bolton children lived in Norfolk and the Matchams in Sussex. His sisters had too much pride to foist themselves and their progeny on his attention, besides. So Charlotte turned the leaves of his prayerbook in church.

Nelson now enjoyed the longest period of rest he was to experience at Merton. The preliminaries of a peace signed at Paris had released him from active service. War was not to break out again till the following May. His first act was to take his seat in the House of Lords. Lord Hood, the respected naval commander, was one of his sponsors. Nelson wrote anxiously to Mrs Cadogan regarding the lordly robes he had ordered. Though he made no great stir in the chamber, Emma was proud of him. She wrote dotingly to Mrs Bolton that Lord Nelson spoke like an angel.

Pleased with his new demesne, Nelson wished all his family to share in his delight. He persuaded his father to come on a visit in November. The Reverend Edmund, long the recipient of every attention from Lady Nelson, accepted only after a most noble missive from Fanny, urging him not to cut his ties with his son. Though a Norfolk rector might have his own reservations about the ménage at Merton Place, Mr Nelson's visit passed off happily enough. The Reverend Edmund found his son's good spirits and returned health recompense for all the trials his behaviour had brought him. Quite rightly, he placed this turn for the better at Emma's door. Nelson's sisters thought the more kindly of Emma, and, though neither Kitty nor Susannah came themselves, some young Boltons and Matchams were dispatched to spend the Christmas season with their uncle.

Nelson found the parish, under the supervision of the Reverend Mr Lancaster, all he could have wished. Lancaster's daughter was to recall the many donations Nelson made to the needy, always anonymously. He and Emma appeared regularly at church, while Sir William maintained his heretic position at home. The winter was passed agreeably enough, though Sir William sometimes hankered for London and the British Museum. January 1802 came and went, bringing 'a white robe, bespangled with ice' to clothe Merton's parterres in snowdrops.

It had been arranged that Fatima, Emma's maid, would be christened on Emma's birthday, 26 April 1802. Then news came that Nelson's father had died and the funeral was to take place that day. Nelson, however, shirked the customary scene of mourning at Bath, where his father had died, and the christening of Fatima Hamilton went ahead – black armbands being worn by all. Sir William wrote Nelson a formal letter of condolence from London, informing him that Emma had instructed him to do so. Sir William judged the Reverend Edmund's death was a not unexpected relief. There had been no painful lingering. Nelson thanked him for his note, agreeing that he felt he had nothing for which to reproach himself in his relations with his late father.

The condolence notes that flew between Emma and Mrs Bolton and Mrs Matcham pushed open gates of friendship hitherto only ajar. Both ladies committed themselves to visiting Merton. The death of their father caused them to hanker after other family ties. Emma would not now have liked to have been reminded of phrases she had employed regarding Boltons and Matchams, when she thought them still friendly to Lady Nelson. 'Those filthy Boltons,' she had written to Sarah Nelson, and much more. Nelson's happiness was to be surrounded by his sisters, she told her new friends, pouring honey on treacle.

Lady Frances Harpur, responding to an enquiry about Sir William's whereabouts in early 1802, declared that she had not seen him for a twelvemonth. 'They live chiefly at *Merton*, with Ld *Nelson*.' She could not bring herself to 'continue to visit *Ly Hamilton*; Her conduct is so censurable.'

Lord Minto had resigned from his post in Vienna in 1801, his 'anti-Gallican zeal' rendering it impossible for him to remain. He visited Merton in March 1802 and reported:

The whole establishment and way of life is such as to make me angry as well as melancholy . . .

She looks ultimately to the chance of marriage, as Sir William will not be long in her way, and she probably indulges a hope that she may survive Lady Nelson; in the meanwhile she and Sir William and the whole set of them are living with him at his expence. She is in high looks, but more immense than ever. She goes on cramming Nelson with trowelfuls of flattery, which he goes on taking as quietly as a child does pap. The love she makes to him is not only ridiculous, but disgusting; not only the rooms, but the whole house, staircase and all, are covered with nothing but pictures of her and him, of all sizes and sorts, and representations of his naval actions, coats of arms, pieces of plate in his honour, the flagstaff of *L'Orient* &c. – an excess of vanity, which counteracts its own purpose. If it was Lady Hamilton's house there night be a pretence for it; to make his own a mere looking-glass to view himself all day is bad taste.[12]

Emma wrote unconcernedly to Sarah Nelson that Charlotte's school-friend Miss Furse ate so much at dinner she was sick 'before us all'. A guest, Mrs Tyson, was drunk. Incidentally, she hoped 'Tom tit' would 'burst, but there is no such good luck'.

Sir William was not content. If he had given up Piccadilly and lived entirely at Merton, he might have made ends meet. As it was, he paid for the upkeep of Piccadilly and also a third of the household bills at Merton. He wrote to Greville on 24 January 1802:

Nothing at present disturbs me but my debt and the nonsence I am obliged to submit to here, to avoid coming to an explosion, which would be attended with many disagreeable effects, and would totally destroy the comfort of the best man and the best Friend I have in the World. However, I am determined that my quiet shall not be disturbed, let the nonsensicall World go as it will.[13]

Emma wrote to a friend in February: 'We are very busy planting, and I am as much amused with pigs and hens as I was as the Court of Naples' Ambassadress.'

In July Sir William taxed Emma with neglect:

My Dear Emma, It gave me much uneasiness to leave you as I did in a most uncomfortable state but consider you had not had your breakfast and the communication I made you of what passed *amicably* between Oliver and me did not quite coincide with your Ideas – then came *passion humour* and *nonsence*, which it is impossible to combat with reasoning whilst the passion lasts. There is no being on earth that has a better understanding or better heart than yourself, if you would but give them *fair play* and keep down the passions that make you see every thing thro' an improper and false medium. I am an old sinner I confess – but I am not the hard hearted man you do not scruple to make me. Your Ladyship is exactly what your old aunt told you, *so noble, so generous, so beautifull*, that you would give away your A— and H— thro' your ribs – it is all well and so would I if I could afford it, and our dear Ld. N. is noble, generous, open and liberal to all and I wish to God he could afford it. In this state you must excuse me if my having lived so long has given me Experience enough that the greatest fortunes will not stand the total want of attention to what are called trifling *Expences*. La Bruyère says *Qu'on se mine plus en faux frais qu'en grandes articles de dépence*, that is that any great sum strikes you, but you do not think of Shillings and Sixpences that in time make up a great sum . . . It is not my fault if by living with a great *Queen* in *intimacy* for so many years that your *ideas* should so far outrun what my means can furnish. Believe me, happiness is in a much *narrower* compass than most people think. But my Dear Emma let us cut this matter short. I am the old Oak and by God I can not give way to nonsense. Do not then strain the bow too tight, as the Duke of Grafton said to Ld. Ossory, least the string should break. I love Ld. Nelson. I know *the purity of your connection with him*. I will do every thing in my power not to disturb the quiet of my best Friend, and his heart God knows is so sensible that a sudden change from his present peace and tranquility might prove fatal to him . . .

I dined at home on *pickled salmon, pidgeon and peas, cold lamb, and Tart –* GOOD PORT which after every delicacy is most necessary. Would to God I could enjoy all that is mine and which I know to be superior to what any other person on Earth possesses, but one can not have eaten one's Cake and have one's cake. Ponder well my Dear Emma these lines, let your good sense come forward – as to me it is perfectly indifferent what may happen! I shall be Patience in Purity. Ever yr. W. Hamilton.

Harmony was in part restored. Sir William and Nelson had both been awarded honorary doctorates in civil law by Oxford University. They meant to attend the ceremony and then proceed to Wales, there to tour Sir William's estate. Nelson was to propose to the Government a scheme for a mail packet from Milford. Numerous cities in the West Country, besides, wished to bestow freedom on Nelson.

The Matchams joined the party at Oxford in August 1802, young George, the eldest son, forming part of the group. Then, with Greville, the *Tria Juncta in Uno* went west, but not before a slight offered at Blenheim Palace, home of the descendants of another Hero of England. The party with Nelson was not admitted to the house, though an offer was made that they could be brought into the garden. Emma declared that if she were King, she would grant Nelson a house to which Blenheim would be as a kitchen garden.

In Wales, Greville's friend, Lady Cawdor, now premier peeress of Pembrokeshire, prevailed on her husband to organize a regatta at Haverfordwest. The party was also hospitably received at Stackpole Court, Lord Cawdor's seat. Nelson declared Milford Haven as stout a port as Portsmouth or Yarmouth, news pleasant to Sir William's ears. All in all, a good deal of celebrating this and that was endured – more readily, one gathers, by Emma and Nelson than by others. Greville had a caustic note from Sir Joseph Banks, hoping he had enjoyed his tour of mayoral feasts and rotten boroughs.

On the party's return to Merton, Emma made plans to go sea-bathing at Margate and instructed Mrs Gibson to take Horatia to nearby Ramsgate. Unfortunately she mislaid Mrs Gibson's address at the resort, as appears from a distraught note. Nelson would hardly think very highly of her maternal regard, if she had no clue where her daughter was. The address was discovered, but meanwhile Emma had had sharp words, or rather correspondence, with Sir William. She began:

> As I see it is a pain to you to remain here, let me beg of you to fix your time for going. Weather I dye in Piccadilly or any other spot in England 'tis the same to me, but I remember the time when you wished for tranquility, but now all visiting and bustle is your liking. However, I will do what you please, being ever your affectionate and obedient E H.

Sir William wrote on the back:

> I neither love bustle nor great company, but I like some employment and diversion. I have but a very short time to live, and every moment is precious to me. I am in no hurry, and am exceedingly glad to give every satisfaction to our best friend, our dear Lord Nelson. The question, then, is what we can best do that all may be perfectly satisfied. Sea bathing is usefull to your health; I see it is, and wish you to continue it a little longer; but I must confess, that I regret, whilst the season is favourable, that I cannot enjoy my favourite amusement of quiet fishing. I care not a pin for the great world, and am attached to no one so much as to you.

Letter and answer were briefer now. She wrote: 'I go when you tell me the coach is ready.' Sir William replied: 'This is not a fair answer to a fair confession of mine.'

The matter was not left there. On return to Merton, costs and entertainment redoubled themselves. Sir William addressed Emma in November 1802:

> I have passed the last 40 years of my life in the hurry and bustle that must necessarily be attendant on a publick character. I am arrived at the

age when some repose is realy necessary, and I promised myself a quiet home, and although I was sensible, and said so when I married, that I should be superannuated when my wife would be in her full beauty and vigour of youth. That time is arrived, and we must make the best of it for the comfort of both parties. Unfortunately our tastes as to the manner of living are very different. I by no means wish to live in solitary retreat, but to have seldom less than 12 or 14 at table, and those varying continually, is coming back to what was become so irksome to me in Italy during the latter years of my residence in that Country. I have no connections out of my own family. I have no complaint to make, but I feel that the whole attention of my wife is given to Lord Nelson and his interest at Merton. I well know the purity of Lord Nelson's friendship for Emma and me, and I know how very uncomfortable it would make his Lordship, our best friend, if a separation should take place, and am therefore determined to do all in my power to prevent such an extremity, which would be *essentially detrimental* to all parties, but would be more sensibly felt by our dear friend than by us. Provided that our expences in housekeeping do not encrease beyond measure (of which I must own I see some danger) I am willing to go on upon our present footing; but as I cannot expect to live many years, every moment to me is precious, and I hope I may be allowed sometimes to be my own master, and pass my time according to my own inclination, either by going [on] my fishing parties to the Thames, or by going to London to attend the Museum, R. Society, the Tuesday Club and Auctions of pictures. I mean to have a light Chariot or post Chaise by the month, that I may make use of it in London and run backwards and forwards to Merton or to Shepperton &c. This is my plan, and we might go on very well, but I am fully determined not to have more of the very silly altercations that happen but too often between us and embitter the present moment exceedingly. If realy we cannot live comfortable together, a *wise* and *well concerted* separation is preferable; but I think, considering the probability of my not troubling any party long in this world, the best for us all would be to bear those ills we have rather than flie to those we know not of. I have fairly stated what I have on my mind. There is no time for nonsence or trifling. I know and admire your talents and many excellent qualities, but I am not blind to your defects, and confess having many myself; therefore let us bear and forbear for God's sake.

The *Morning Herald* noted his 'elegant new chariot' shortly after this.

A shock in the form of a letter from Coutts Bank, informing Emma that her balance was twelve shillings and elevenpence was left by her for Sir William on 'her Toilet'. Wearily he paid the £700 she owed. In January 1803, after a sociable Christmas with the little Boltons, Emma went skating on the Serpentine. She was in plain white, 'with a white satin cloak, trimmed with ermine, and lined with amber'. Reports spoke admiringly of her appearance.

A month later trouble came to Piccadilly. Sir William became seriously ill, soon after a grand concert which he and Emma had hosted. He was devotedly nursed by Emma and her mother. Among the most endearing images of his last years is a picture he drew of himself and Mrs Cadogan stepping out, under the shelter of a large umbrella, on return from the Royal Society. He caught no cold, he informed Emma, 'as the bed by her care is comfortable'.[14] On 6 April Sir William died, Emma holding him in her arms, Nelson at his side. He was seventy-two. Emma penned a note to herself: 'Unhappy day for the forlorn Emma ten minutes past ten Dear Blessed Sir William left me.'[15]

CHAPTER EIGHTEEN

Towards Trafalgar

Sir William had computed correctly in 1786 when he meted out for himself seventeen more years of life. Francis Oliver, strange, flawed creature, wrote: 'I lose a friend who has spoke well of me for thirty-seven years.' By his own declaration, Sir William had been attached to no one as much as to Emma for the last fifteen-odd of those years. It was hard for all of them to live without that generous love that characterized Sir William. In his will he named Nelson as 'my dearest friend . . . the most virtuous, loyal, and truly brave man I ever met with'.

The hatchment, public declaration of mourning, was affixed to the front of 23 Piccadilly, and on 12 April Sir William was buried quietly, beside his first wife in the Barlow family vault in Slebech, Pembrokeshire, as she had wished. Mourning jewellery – a necklace, earrings and bracelet – was ordered by Emma, and she wrote to ask Greville, 'how long Mr Greville can permit her to remain in the house in Piccadilly. She also begs to know if he will pay her debts, and what she may depend on.'

Greville had come into the inheritance he had so long husbanded. The will was read at the Piccadilly house in May, as was the 1801 deed of settlement of the contents of the house on Emma, by Nelson's direction. He was concerned that, otherwise, it might be thought Greville had given the same to Lady Hamilton.

The will was simple. Emma was left an annuity of £800, chargeable on the Welsh estates and payable quarterly. By a codicil, the debts which she had amassed and a note of which she had left on her dressing table at Christmas for Sir William were to be paid. She received also a lump sum of £800, £100 for her mother, to be paid immediately. Nelson received two sporting guns and a miniature in enamel by Henry Bone of Vigée-Le Brun's painting of Emma as a Bacchante. After delivering his encomium of his dearest friend, Sir William closed with the stirring phrase: 'And shame fall on those who do not say amen.'

The obsequies concluded, Emma moved to a smaller house in nearby Clarges Street. Nelson had removed to lodgings in Dover Street on the day of Sir William's death. As a footnote to earlier accounts of Greville's character, it may be noted that he deducted income tax from Emma's jointure in disobedience to his uncle's stipulation that the jointure be paid 'clear of all deductions'. In Sir William's codicil, besides, dated 31 March of this year, Sir William had left Greville an additional £7,000, for some specific but undisclosed purpose. If this, as seems likely, was destined to benefit Emma and her mother, it went astray.

After his own half-hearted fashion, Greville tried to make amends. When he returned his uncle's Red Ribbon to the Foreign Office, he mentioned a 'dying conversation' in which his uncle hoped a part of his hard-won pension might revert to his wife on his death. Greville noted in his letter that the Foreign Office must be fully aware of the distinguished part Lady Hamilton had played in her years in Naples, and mentioned that there were encomia to this effect from the sovereigns of that Kingdom in the Foreign Office's possession.[1]

Emma's jointure was considered by all to be inadequate to the lady's needs. Lord Minto commented, after a visit to the widow, that she was 'worse off' than he had imagined. While he did not, as she asked, take up the cudgels to secure her a Government pension to supplement her income, others, immediately on Sir William's death, began the battle.

On 9 March, George Rose, an influential friend of Nelson's at the Treasury, sent to Emma a draft of a letter setting out her claims that he proposed she should copy, sign, and send to Addington, the Prime Minister. By 17 April, Emma knew, via Lord Melville, that Addington was favourably inclined to her. Emma's claims were to grow more extravagant. At this date, her petitioners – Nelson also wrote in May – begged only recognition of her services to her country in Naples, and her assistance to the British fleet in securing them entry to the port of Syracuse before the Battle of the Nile.

Pursuance of Emma's claims lapsed as greater matters occupied the Government and Nelson. The Peace of Amiens of 1802 came to an end, with France and Spain combining to declare war on England. On 6 May, Nelson was ordered to prepare for sea. Thus in one month Emma was dealt a double blow, losing both husband and 'husband of my heart'.

Before Nelson left, he arranged an event that had long been on his mind. On 13 May Horatia was christened at St Marylebone Church, where Emma and Sir William had been married. Alone among the children presented, she had no parents inscribed on her baptismal certificate. There were last visits to Little Titchfield Street – Mrs Gibson's daughter Mary recalled Lord Nelson playing on the floor with Horatia. On the sixteenth he left for Portsmouth to take up the Mediterranean command. That same day he wrote to Emma in the first of a long series of letters, 'Cheer up, my dearest Emma,' admitting, however, two days later, 'the being afloat makes me now feel that we do not tread the same element . . . My heart is full to bursting.' These letters were the beginning of a copious correspondence between Lord Nelson and Lady Hamilton while he was at sea over the next two years. We have only his letters to Emma, as he carefully destroyed hers to him. He wrote freely when his letter could be privately dispatched; he was guarded when the navy censors would read it.

A wedding celebration at Clarges Street consolidated Emma's links with Nelson's Bolton relations that same day. His niece Kitty Bolton married her cousin William and, thanks to Nelson's absence, they began their married life with a flourish as Sir William and Lady Bolton. This elevation occurred because, on the next day, the first investiture since 1788 of the Order of the Bath, a ceremony only inferior in pomp to a coronation, was to take place with full flurry of feathers and cloaks. Protocol demanded that proxies be knights, at the least, so William, standing in for Nelson, had been hastily knighted.

The party dispersed and Emma began her widowhood in earnest. Mme Vigée-Le Brun received a visit from her and was as shocked by the girth, which mourning could not disguise, as by the widow's shorn locks à la Brutus. She records that Emma spoke of herself as desolate, and the next moment picked up some sheet music and sang a lively air. These alternations of mood Vigée-Le Brun thought indicative of the insincerity of Emma's grief.[2] Rather, they attest to the fact that Emma was, if not distraught, distracted by grief and worry. She knew now that she was expecting another child.

She could not settle anywhere, drifting between Merton and Clarges Street. Nelson had settled on her £100 a month with which to pay for living expenses at Merton. While household bills in the past at Merton had totalled between £150 and £200, with only Emma, Charlotte Nelson and Mrs Cadogan in residence this should have been ample. Not surprisingly, Emma found Paradise Merton melancholy and left her mother to supervise Marianna, the cook, Dame Francis, the housekeeper, and Mr Cribb, the gardener. Emma did put in hand some improvements, a task which was to occupy her increasingly in later years, but at this date they were half-hearted measures. She turned for diversion from her troubles to friends in London.

Singers from the Italian opera – Mrs Billington, the Grassini, Mrs Bianchi, the Banti – were frequent visitors to Clarges Street. The Devonshire House set was friendly. The Countess of Mansfield and some few others of Sir William's relations visited. At once the most lively and most disreputable of Emma's circle in London, however, was the elderly Duke of Queensberry.

'Old Q' had been a Pink of the Turf in his younger days as the Earl of March. He had also, till late in life, had so many ladies under his protection in different parts of the town that he was likened to the Grand Turk with his seraglio. Now, the 'antiquated beau' had resigned himself to being a mere observer. To this end, after a refreshing milk bath, he would sit in a cane chair on the balcony of his house overlooking Green Park. A shady chip hat lined with green velvet tipped over one eye, he ogled every petticoat that tipped along Piccadilly. In summer, to vary the routine, he went every afternoon to his villa on the Thames at Richmond – not to admire the view (his view of the Thames was 'There it goes – flow, flow, flow, always the same'). Instead, it was whispered, the old Duke dressed up as the Greek shepherd Paris, while three ladies 'in a perfect state of nature' danced for his entertainment.

The Duke, old and rheumy and quite deaf, dined with Emma most evenings when she was in London. When she was out of town, she wrote to him daily. She was among hundreds of ladies whom the Duke kept in a constant state of agitation about the disposition of his immense fortune. Still, to make of Emma's friendship with the old roué mere legacy-hunting would be to overlook their shared liking for outrageous and extravagant conversation.

When at Merton, there were good friends in two neighbouring families against whose charms Nelson's assertions that he wished for no visiting had not been proof. James Perry, editor of the *Morning Chronicle*, was known among his friends as 'the miller of Merton'. He had set up a corn mill and, decked out in a white hat, he fed his hens and fattened porkers devotedly, undeterred by mockery. There was a steady stream of businessmen and journalists to interrupt this rural tranquillity, and Nelson often joined them, eager to know the latest reports and rumours.[3]

Perhaps more to Emma's taste was the interesting household of Mr Abraham Goldsmid at Morden Hall, a few miles away. Abraham and his brother Benjamin, who lived at Roehampton, had an international reputation as bullion brokers and bankers. They had been much involved in the financing of the Napoleonic Wars and were said to have the ear of Pitt. Even before Nelson came to live at Merton, Benjamin Goldsmid had hosted a grand fête at Roehampton in honour of the Battle of the Nile. It lasted twenty-four hours, and was thought worthy of some mighty foreign potentate. In fact, the Goldsmids came from no further away than Amsterdam, and both brothers had been born in London.

Abraham and Emma had a bond in their love of music. Haydn had been a frequent visitor to Abraham's house when in London, and the Goldsmid young ladies were pupils of Attwood, organist of St Paul's and himself a pupil of Mozart. Abraham's wife, Anna, was 'a Dutch lady and very outspoken'. A special set of Worcester china was commissioned for a dinner to which the Prince of Wales was invited. The Goldsmids had raised money for the Prince in Holland. When he duly admired the dinner service, Mrs Goldsmid said, 'Yes, Your Royal Highness, and it's all paid for.'[4]

Despite the attentions of her friends, these were unhappy months for Emma. It was long since there had been no man in the house to make comfortable with the attentions at which Emma was so adept. She cried herself sick when Frederick Hamilton visited her, he was so like Sir William, his brother. A letter from Nelson, written from Naples, did nothing to cheer her. With a lamentable lack of feeling, Nelson told her her old home was now a hotel, her servants all leading dissolute lives. Nelson found solace in the paintings of Emma and of Horatia which he had hung in his cabin, but he was busy with victualling arrangements for the fleet and other duties. Emma had little to do but keep secret her pregnancy, and wait for the birth.

Charlotte Nelson's presence in Clarges Street and at Merton was welcome. Emma forgot her own woes in her aspirations for the girl's education. Sir Alexander Ball, now Governor of Malta, hoped Charlotte was 'sensible of the great and very rare advantages in the tuition of so accomplished a patroness'. Thomas Bowen was another who approved of Emma's gubernatorial role. Out of her own money, it seems, Emma lavished languages tutors, singing masters, dancing mistresses on Charlotte. One is reminded of Emma's excitement when Sir William began her own education, and her laments that it began so late. Charlotte proved a painstaking pupil, and was growing into a pretty if dull young woman. Society took a kindly interest in Lord Nelson's niece, and began to look on Lady Hamilton more kindly, also. Oddly, the girl's presence, though proof of a tie Society did not condone, lent propriety to the household. Perhaps because Nelson was held in such affection, even reverence when at sea, many believed Emma's protestations that her relations with the hero were entirely innocent. Now that Sir William was dead and Nelson was at sea, slowly Emma gained admittance to many houses where before she had not been received.

Nelson was happiest when Emma was visiting his people, rather than the great and grand whom he mistrusted. In July of 1803 Emma took up a long-standing invitation to visit Mrs Bolton at Cranwich in Norfolk. Some fifteen miles from Swaffham, the Boltons' Manor Farm was a most attractive family house. Elegant rooms on the ground floor gave way, up a choice of three staircases, to a jumble of bedrooms on the first and attic floors. Outside the french windows on the eastern side, there was an orchard. It was 'meek, mild' Tom Bolton's pleasure to send baskets of dried apples each autumn to Merton.

Nelson's niece Lady Bolton was at home, expecting her first baby. The children were home from school and helping their father in the fields. Their life compared favourably with Emma's own childhood, but the countryside, flat and with high hedges thick with cow-parsley and the occasional errant poppy, was not dissimilar to the Hawarden surroundings. Emma appeared an exalted being to the Boltons. Mrs Bolton consulted her on her daughters' deportment. Eliza and Anne wrote to her from school. The days when Emma had written to the William Nelsons of the 'lousy Boltons' and of 'her and her filthy spawn' – Nelson's sisters then still loyal to Fanny Nelson – were long past. Mrs Bolton, quiet and capable, was a good friend.

Emma went on to Canterbury to visit William and Sarah Nelson, and they accompanied her on to Southend, a sea-bathing resort. Here Emma heard from Nelson that Sir William's old contemporary at Westminster School, the Earl-Bishop, had died at Naples. His body was packed up in a crate for dispatch to England, and the sailors were told it was an antique statue they carried.

The old order was passing. At Southend Emma was in low spirits on 6 September:

> This sad sad widdowed anniversary what must my feeling be this day that Sir William used to keep as the happiest of his Life because it gave him Emma . . . this day am I at South End forlorn & alone my husband gone to a better world and Nelson our friend gone out to serve his Country I was kept with pomp & splendour, every Honner done to me as tho' born an Empress . . .

Nelson was cheerful about prospects of 'golden ships' or prize money, less so about his health. His sight was dimming in his one good eye. 'Blind people are supposed to be cheerful,' he wrote, but he feared he would bear it ill. He also wrote – sadly but perhaps a little late in the day – that he was now alive to the follies of the King of Naples. He had come to his senses about that unhappy Kingdom. The Queen was proving very deaf to Nelson's plea that she would write and recommend Emma for a pension. (Maria Carolina did eventually write to condole with Emma, on her pecuniary distress rather than the loss of Sir William. She made no offer to help Emma.) Yet Emma must not worry about her pension. 'From Ambassatrice to the duties of domestic life, I never saw your equal.' He reinforced his admiration in October. 'My soul is God's, my body Emma's.'

Nelson was busily making plans for Horatia's future. In September he sent to his solicitor, Haslewood, a codicil to his will, bequeathing her £4,000. In October he wrote his first letter to his daughter, assuring her of his fond love and trusting that she would be obedient to her noble guardian, Lady Hamilton. Emma was more occupied with the question of her pension than with her daughter, making infrequent visits to Little Titchfield Street. In November she addressed George Rose, ostensibly on the subject of a Customs post for Mr Bolton. She took the opportunity to press her claims again. 'I did more than any *ambassador* ever did, though their pockets were filled with secret-service money . . . poor Sir William and myself never got even a pat on the back. But, indeed, the *cold-hearted* Grenville was in then [as Foreign Secretary].'5

Christmas neared and Nelson was arranging for earrings and gold chains to be sent to Emma from Naples, also a watch which Horatia was convinced he had promised her. He wrote that he hoped next Christmas to be with his dear ones himself. With typical daring Emma crammed the house at Merton with guests, knowing full well that her pregnancy was about to come to its term. Charlotte and Horace, the latter home from Eton, were joined by the Boltons, and drawings by Thomas Baxter, the artist, record the pastimes of the holiday. Like ladies from the pages of Miss Austen, the Merton females sit complacently on verandahs or play a hand of cards, their plain dresses falling in elegant folds. Horatia stands, composed, in a riding hat, clutching a whip to her smock. Her wide eyes remind one of her mother.

Some time between Christmas and the New Year's beginnings, Emma had her second child by Nelson. She was close on thirty-nine now, and not in the high animal spirits which had characterized her youth. The child did not survive long, though the circumstances of its birth and short life are uncertain. It was a girl, and when Nelson heard Emma's cautious announcement of its birth he asked that it be named Emma. The delays in letters reaching the fleet at sea were such that he received this announcement in May. By the next postbag he heard that the child was dead. The news induced in him a 'raging fever'. Only the fact that Horatia had recovered from the smallpox – he had not known of her illness till it was over – raised his spirits. It is possible that the baby Emma survived till the date of Horatia's illness and was too weak to survive the dire disease. Oliver was put in charge of rented lodgings in Lower Sloane Street, where Horatia stayed till the disease had passed its course. Possibly the new baby was lodged there too.

Instead of the new baby, a young girl called Mary Gibbs joined Emma's wandering tribe. She was the daughter of Mr Gibbs the banker, who with his family had lived with the Hamiltons at Palermo. Gibbs now sent her to England for schooling, and Emma urged him to let her house the child. Though Emma took a sincere interest in Mary and found her a suitable school, she was perhaps alive to the confusion she was arousing in others' minds with this bevy of young girls to whom she stood guardian. Horatia's presence would cause little comment, if Nelson were to force her to have the child constantly with her. So far, Nelson only hinted and Emma chose not to hear the hints.

Emma did not wish to be saddled with a three-year-old in her wanderings. Her old friend William Hayley made efforts to find her at the beginning of this year, 1804. He and the poet William Blake were meditating an illustrated *Life* of Romney – the artist had, at the end of his life, retired to his wife in Kendal and had died there in 1802. Hayley and Blake wanted Emma's own account of her modelling sessions with the artist, but she was nowhere to be found.

Emma was perhaps wary of such a project, which was likely to mention her illegitimate union with Greville. In fact, when Hayley came to write his memoirs, he carefully avoided that subject. Another biographer applied to Emma in May. This time it was a gentleman wishing to record Sir William's distinguished life. Emma refused him access to Sir William's papers, that higgledy-piggledy mass at which Paget had sneered. Again, one may suppose that she did not wish her unmarried years with her husband to be recalled.

Still there were doubts about Emma's pension. Rose wrote again to Addington, telling Emma that it was worth making the attempt though warning her not to hope overmuch. Emma refused to be cast down, and lent Mr Bolton the large sum of £200. Nelson had just written to her, counselling economy – 'no loaded tables'. A cottage in a barn at Merton would do very well as a lodge at the gates of the property. The gate itself should be plain white wood; no need to emulate the imposing wrought-iron structure at Morden Hall. He was amazed by Emma's loan, which represented a quarter of her annuity. Nevertheless, he gave instructions to Davison to repay her that amount. In anticipation of her birthday on 26 April, he sent her some curious gloves from Taranto made of mussel beards or, properly, from the golden threads by which the mussel adheres to rocks. Even more welcome was a banknote. If she spent some of it, the remaining notes would look very pretty in her pocket-book, he wrote sweetly.[6]

Emma had the satisfaction in May 1804 of seeing her portrait hung at the Royal Academy Exhibition. The artist was one Masquerier, an immensely successful and exceedingly indifferent artist. For all that, his portrait of Emma was generally acknowledged to be the *clou* of the exhibition, beating Sir William's old friend, Mrs Damer's bust of Nelson in modern dress into second place. The Masquerier portrait is interesting as it is the last portrait of Emma executed in her lifetime. She sits pensive in a simple white dress – with short sleeves, as requested in a letter by the artist[7] – against a background of Vesuvius and the Bay of Naples. Her hair is cropped as Vigée-Le Brun described, but, allowing for Masquerier's heavy line, her face is little changed from earlier portraits. She is said to have much enjoyed her sittings.

As the London season wore on, Emma with Charlotte attended a number of parties, including a Rout at the Goldsmids. 'We are respected and could be out all day,' Emma wrote proudly to Mrs Bolton. That lady probably never entertained any other idea. There were charming days at Lady Stafford's, and evenings at Lady Dashwood's. Lord Ashburton, a popular young man, was quite taken with Charlotte. Mrs Billington gave tickets for an evening at the opera. The days when Lady Hamilton had her own box at the San Carlo were long gone. In her catalogues of triumphs Emma remarked that she had received several proposals of marriage – from the second son of a viscount, from another 'quite mad', and 'allso from a relation & an Earl'. Emma thought it amusing to tell Nelson of these proposals. He wrote back that he cared nothing for her 'titled offers'. In fact, she told Mrs Bolton that, despite all this attention, 'Oh my heart is in the mediterranean without him all is a blank.'

Poor Charlotte tried gamely to keep up with her energetic sponsor, and to fulfil her exacting demands. Emma told Sarah Nelson that her daughter wore to one party 'a new dress of blue & white spangled & look'd divine'. Nevertheless, Emma wrote severely, she did not as yet think Charlotte 'fit to come out presentable at Court till next winter . . . she must practise every day for 3 months coming in and going out with a Hoop . . .' A month or two later, Emma confirmed that this rigorous practice had begun. Emma made Charlotte practise 'setting down & getting up & all the elegances that is necessary Beauty will not do without Grace & Elegance'.

Nelson's mind was still occupied by his Horatia's future. He was in hopes that the decisive battle with the French might be fought in June. On his return he hoped to see Horatia at Merton. 'Why not?' he said tentatively. Meanwhile Emma was filling Clarges Street, almost as a defence against her own child, with others' children. Eliza and Anne

Bolton came on a visit, Mrs Bolton hoping that they would have the rough edges, of which indeed Lady Nelson had once complained, honed by town life. Poor Anne fell ill and was sent by Emma to convalesce at Stanmore Priory, home of the Marquess of Abercorn. Lord Abercorn had been a good friend to Emma ever since he had stood witness to her wedding. Anne found his wife – his third – alarmingly eccentric, and in her isolation thanked Emma with pathetic fervour for remembrances like 'the little darling pincushion'.

In July Emma paid another visit to Canterbury, taking with her the celebrated singer, Mrs Billington, as well as Charlotte. A canon of the cathedral recorded the impression these two lively ladies made on the Close. Mr Nelson hosted a dinner party in their honour, and provided an amount of champagne, a rare luxury in his circles. Emma, accustomed to drink it like water, toasted the company deep, then called for more. They would have a drinking contest. The Nelsons' guests were astonished. William Nelson was mortified, both by Emma's free manners and by the necessary revelation that there was no more champagne in the house. It is said in the 1815 *Memoirs of Lady Hamilton* that, during the whole of Emma's visit to Canterbury, clerical invitations to the Nelsons were superscribed 'But not Lady Hamilton'.[8]

Each Sunday of her visit Emma accompanied her 'Jewell', Mrs Nelson, to church. One morning in the cathedral, after Emma and Mrs Billington had lifted their fine voices in hymn, vergers took round boxes. It was a special collection for the navy. Emma, perhaps with thoughts that she was still 'Patroness of the Navy', is said to have called out to the organist that she would gladly sing an anthem to accompany the collection. The organist politely affected deafness.

All in all, the Nelsons were probably as thankful as the Elliots had once been when their boisterous visitor left. Nelson had written from the Mediterranean to say he feared for her safety in the event of an invasion. Canterbury would be filled with soldiers. One imagines that Emma, like an elderly Lydia Bennett, would have been thrilled by such an event.

No invasion occurring, Emma went off to Ramsgate, to visit an old friend, as she informed Nelson. This was Lady Dunmore, mother of Prince Augustus' consort, Lady Augusta Murray. Lady Dunmore had crowned a 'String of Peccadilloes' by turning in her old age to religion. Whether this made her a more agreeable companion is not recorded. Both her daughters, whose 'free' manners Lady Knight had attributed to their 'mixture of Scotch and American education', were with her. Emma did a little sea-bathing and then returned to Merton.

Soon after her return, she had a distressing letter from Nelson. It was an open communication, and was intended to give the official version of Horatia's parentage to any who might wish to know it. Enquiries would now be numerous, when Horatia was seen to live, as Nelson determined she should, permanently at Merton.

Dated 13 August 1804, the letter begins:

> I am now going to state a thing to you, and to request your kind assistance, which, from my dear Emma's goodness of heart, I am sure of her acquiescence in. Before we left Italy, I told you of the extraordinary circumstances of a child being left to my care and protection. On your first coming to England, I presented you the child, dear Horatia. You became, to my comfort, attached to it, as did Sir William, thinking her the finest child he had ever seen. She is become of that age when it is necessary to remove her from a mere nurse, and to think of educating her. Horatia is by no means destitute of a fortune. My earnest wish is that you would take her to Merton, and if Miss Connor will become her tutoress under your eye, I shall be made happy. I will allow Miss Connor any salary you may think proper.

Of course the story of Horatia being entrusted to Nelson in Italy is a mere fabrication, intended, like Horatia's false birthdate, 29 October 1800, to lull suspicions that Emma was her mother. The story probably originated in the banker Gibbs's entrusting of his daughter to Emma's guardianship. (By this same post Emma heard that Gibbs had sent her some fine Palermo silk as a token of thanks for her care of Mary.) 'Miss Connor' was a cousin of Emma's who had materialized from Wales. Mrs Cadogan's sister Sarah had married a Mr Connor from Ferry, near Hawarden, and 'Miss Connor' was one of a gaggle of children who now came to their aunt and distinguished cousin for support – there were Mary and Cecilia and Ann and Sarah and Charles. Nelson had already found Charles a midshipman's post. Sir William, it seems from a letter of Nelson's, had been reluctant to have Emma's relations to stay in London. Greville, in days long past, had stated that he did not wish Emma's relations visiting her. In fact, the Connor girls were surprisingly well educated, and Nelson made a good choice in them as governesses for Horatia. Mary and Cecilia and Ann Connor seem to have alternated in the position.

Nelson went on: 'I know Charlotte loves the child, and therefore at Merton she will imbibe nothing but virtue, goodness, and elegance of manners with a good education to fit her to move in the sphere of life which she is destined to move in.' Emma, however, made no efforts to remove Horatia from Mrs Gibson's affectionate charge. She went off to Cranwich in October on a much delayed visit to stand godmother

to Lady Bolton's baby Emma. The occasion was a happy one, and
Emma performed as Lady Bountiful to the satisfaction of all.

Nevertheless, she was not happy. Following Sir William's death, she
had wished to go abroad. From a letter Nelson addressed to her in the
autumn, it seems, astonishingly, that she had now begged him to allow
her – and Horatia and Charlotte – to join him at sea.

> I know my own dear Emma [he wrote], if she will let her reason have
> fair play, will say I am right: but she is, like Horatio, very angry, if she
> cannot have her own way . . . Absence to us is equally painful: but if I
> had either stayed at home, or neglected my duty abroad, would not my
> Emma have blushed for me? . . . I am writing, my dear Emma, to reason
> the point with you; and I am sure you will see it in its true light.

She stayed with the Boltons for about ten days, attending concerts in
Swaffham and a lord mayor's banquet where she toasted His Worship
'in three times three'. Mrs Bolton wrote nostalgically after Emma's
departure that she and her daughter Susannah sat by the fireside and
wondered what their dear Lady Hamilton might be busy with now.
Even the imagining made them feel closer to their friend.

Emma was organizing a birthday party for Anne Bolton and Horatia,
whose birthdays supposedly fell on the same date. She was writing
to Nelson. So vivid was her scrawl, Nelson thought she wrote 'so
naturally', he could almost think himself in her company. He hoped
Horatia was now fixed at Merton. Letters from Mrs Gibson, acknowledging late payment of a part of Horatia's bills and requesting the arrears
of £24 4s that remained, show that Horatia was still very much fixed at
Little Titchfield Street.

Emma was laying out funds in every direction. Thinking herself
neglectful of Mrs Bolton, she sent her a magnificent tippet. She invited
all Nelson's relations to come to Merton for Christmas. Mrs Bolton
wrote a letter of thanks for her tippet, making it clear she valued Emma's
friendship for its own sake: further lavish presents must be declined. That
said, she accepted the invitation to Merton, with thanks.

The William Nelsons remained in Canterbury for the holiday, but
allowed Horace to join his sister at Merton. (Sarah wrote anxiously
that Lady Hamilton must be sure and send Horace to bed at eleven.)
Mrs Matcham judged that they were too many to invade all at once,
they would stay in Bath. As a Christmas present, she informed Emma
that she had lately seen Lady Nelson, but the lady and she had not
exchanged greetings. Despite these absences, a very jolly time was had
by all at Merton. Of course, the £100 a month Nelson allowed Emma

for expenses at Merton would have gone a very short way to cover the cost, but Emma was not inclined to worry about such trifles.

The New Year of 1805 brought no Nelson, and Emma whiled away the time with improvements at Merton. New kitchens were being constructed, with covered ways. The entrance was being altered and the grounds brought to a pitch of perfection. When in London, she was 'teased with invitations'. Mme Vigée-Le Brun asked her to perform her famous Attitudes before a select audience. 'As to the garden Cribb and myself are planners and gardeners and if you can allow him eight men for three months he will be content,' she wrote to Davison. But this would cost Lord Nelson £4,000, Davison remonstrated. Emma argued that Lord Nelson desired it, and she estimated it would only cost £1,500. The matter lapsed.

Although by now Emma might reasonably have been thought to have eliminated Lady Nelson from the picture, Fanny was still Nelson's wife. With her widowhood of a year and more's date, Emma began to brood on the prospect of a second marriage. To Davison she wrote, in the autumn of 1804, with bilious spite:

> What a sad thing it is to think such a man as him should be entrapped with such an infamous woman as that apothicary's widow . . . Whilst I am free – with talents he likes, adoring him, that never a woman adored a man as I do my Nelson, loving him beyond this world, and yet we are both miserable . . . patience.

She wrote at greater length, a veritable soliloquy: 'Ours is not a common dull love. My mind was taken with Glory, my heart beat high with His great deeds, and I never can nor ever will try to get the better of my true and virtuous passion that I feel for him.' Here we have, in the absence of her letters to Nelson which he destroyed, Emma's frank admission of her struggles with conscience and convention. Again she insisted that the strength of her passion was such as to sanctify it.

> My love is no common love. It may be a sin to love – I say it might have been a sin when I was another's, but I had then more merit in trying to suppress it. I am now Free and I must sin on and love Him more than ever, it is a Crime worth going to Hell for. For should I not be an ungrateful unfeeling wretch [she went on, in curious imitation of a speech she once made about Sir William] not to pay two fold with love the man that so idolises me . . .

She ended by saying sorrowfully of Lady Nelson, 'She will never burst.' According to Euripides, to a woman frustrated in marriage there is no equal in bloodthirstiness. Emma would gladly have presented Lady Nelson with a poisoned robe and diadem.

Mrs Matcham and her family fed Emma's hatred of Lady Nelson with snippets of the poor woman's insipid goings-on at Bath. Mrs Matcham was later to refer to her brother's desertion of his wife: 'He had many excuses. She was so very cold.' She told Emma that there was 'a strong party against Nelson . . . whom we know to be all goodness and liberality'. At a chance encounter, Lady Nelson looked, as Mrs Matcham passed her, 'in that scornful way'. Lady Bolton, staying with the Matchams in March, was to describe a visit from Lady Nelson to Lady Charlotte Drummond, who lived next door to the Matchams: 'She called in her carriage . . .' Lady Charlotte was not at home, so Lady Nelson 'walked as stiff as a poker about half a dozen steps, turned round, got in again . . . She need not have taken so much pains, if nobody wanted to see her more than I do.'

In a less sordid area, Emma had grounds for hope. Only a year before she had enthusiastically remarked, on Pitt's return to power, 'He is the Nelson of Ministers.' Now, Davison told her, Lord Melville had spoken to Pitt, on Nelson's urging. Melville suggested a pension for Emma of £500 a year and, when Davison asked if he might say as much to Lady Hamilton, Melville said immediately, 'Yes, certainly.' 'He spoke very handsomely of you and of your services in favour of this country when in Naples,' Davison added. The matter of her pension, which so occupied Emma, was already becoming one of principle rather than real alleviation of distress. Emma was spending in excess of her jointure, and of Nelson's £1,200. Five hundred pounds a year would do very little to stem her debts. In 1802 Sir William had written to her: 'the greatest fortunes will not stand the total want of attention to what are called trifling *Expences*.' She had not listened. With his death and the insecurity that followed, her determination to woo with gifts had only increased.

The new hopes of a pension persuaded Emma to embark on a riot of party-going with Charlotte. She was overwhelmed with invitations: 'That devil Tom Tit' had not succeeded in turning Society against her. We hear of her dancing at Lady Cholmondeley's till 4 a.m. The Cholmondeleys owned Houghton, a magnificent estate close by Burnham Thorpe, so were probably more interested to receive Miss Charlotte Nelson than Lady Hamilton. However, the very fact that Emma was received by Lady Cholmondeley shows that the ostracizing she had dreaded, on Sir William's death, was not taking place. When the Prince of Wales first 'formed a connexion' with Mrs Fitzherbert, it was Lady Cholmondeley whom he asked to receive his mistress. 'As

Her Ladyship's character stood high, her countenancing Mrs F. would cause others to do it.' So, it would appear, it proved with Emma.

At the house of Lady Cawdor, Greville's great friend, Emma conversed long with the Duchess of Roxburghe. Then Emma hosted her own party at Clarges Street, with seven tables. Resplendent in white and gold, Charlotte a foil in pure white, her vivacity outweighed her 'fat shoulders and breast manifestly having the appearance of one of the bacchantes of Rubens',[9] which Joseph Farington had noted the year before at Ramsgate.

Emma's greatest triumph of the season was at Lady Abercorn's concert on 5 March. Lady Bessborough described the scene to Lord Granville Leveson-Gower, her lover: 'Lady Hamilton did her Attitudes beautifully, notwithstanding her enormous size – at least, the grave ones; she is too large for the Bacchante.' Among the guests was a child actor called Young Roscius, or Master Betty. His popularity in this year was extraordinary. Ladies from Edinburgh to London wept and conceived romantic passions for him after seeing him play once. The proceedings of the House of Commons were adjourned one evening to allow the Members to attend one of his performances. Lady Abercorn scored a great hit by his presence at her party.

Lady Bessborough recorded that the child was 'very shy, but amus'd with the attitudes'. In turn, Emma was wonderfully struck by the boy's cleverness when he acted, and she kissed him. Young Roscius, 'colouring up like scarlet, said, "I'm too old to be kiss'd, Ma'am," as if he was resenting the greatest insult.'

After all this gaiety, Emma was brought back to earth by worrying news from Plymouth. Her cousin, Charles Connor, had gone unexpectedly mad. His commanding officer, on the advice of the ship's surgeon, had been obliged to confine him and bind his hands. On 2 March, he was taken to hospital. Emma footed the bill for all his medical expenses, another drain on her purse. Curiously, Charles recovered so swiftly from his derangement that, only ten days later, he was writing quite sanely to one of the Boltons. The unstable streak he had exhibited, however, proved to be a family trait which was later to have some uncomfortable consequences for the Connors' benefactor, Lady Hamilton.

Removed from all this, Nelson was putting his effects in order in early May. On the eleventh, the French fleet escaped the English ships blockading Toulon, under veil of heavy fog, and made for the West Indies. Before Nelson followed, he wrote to inform Emma that he was putting Horatia's money, her £4,000, out of Emma's reach, by an arrangement with Haslewood. Whether this decision was prompted by pure caution or whether Nelson had suspicions that Emma was keeping the extent of her spending secret from him, it is not possible to say. In this very month Emma applied to Mr Tyson, Nelson's old secretary, for a loan of £150. She said that it was merely to bridge a gap between her expenditure on improvements at Merton and Nelson's repayment of these funds. As we know, Nelson had specifically requested that Emma always send bills for improvements to Davison. If she applied to Nelson's friends for loans, it seems likely that she had borrowed from other sources too at this date.

Before he left for the West Indies, Nelson drafted two very important letters, an attempt to reconcile his and Emma's differing views on Horatia's upbringing. He told Haslewood he intended to settle an annuity on Horatia's keeper, Mrs Gibson:

> When that she gives up my adopted daughter, Horatia Nelson Thompson, to the guardianship of my dear friend Lady Emma Hamilton, and promises not to have anything more to do with the child either directly or indirectly.

To Emma he wrote that he wished her to take his 'adopted daughter from under the care of Mrs Gibson, and to place her under her guardianship, in order that she may be properly educated and brought up'.

Write what he might, Horatia remained at Mrs Gibson's throughout the summer of 1805. Nelson pursued the French to the West Indies, where he went briefly on shore for the first time since May 1803, and then chased them back again to Cadiz. Throughout the summer of 1805 he was in hopes of returning to England and Merton, where he fondly imagined Horatia to be ensconced.

In fact, Emma seems to have seen less than usual of Horatia. She did take her, with Charlotte and a friend, to Eton on the Fourth of June, the King's birthday and a happy occasion. Horace delighted them by his appearance on the river in a tunic of white and gold, pulling with companions at the oars of a rowing boat dressed up as a Roman galley. Otherwise, Horatia stayed in Titchfield Street, playing with the watch and the 'books of Spanish dresses' her father sent her.

In late July Emma was off again on a trip. This time it was to Southend, the sea-bathing resort, where she hoped to cure 'nettle rash' – so Charlotte, who went with her, described the ailment to her mother. It was probably a recurrence of the old nervous complaint, some sort of eczema, that had plagued Emma since her days at Edgware Row and that tended to manifest itself when she felt under stress. She had now been managing her own life for a period of two years and more. A letter from the resilient Mrs Cadogan at Merton indicates that Emma's debts were escalating. The general praise for her improvements at Merton was very well, but there was no money to pay for them.

> My dear Emma, Cribb is quite distrest for money, would be glad if you could bring him the £13 that he paid for the taxes, to pay the mowers. I have got the baker's and butcher's bills cast up; they come to one hundred pounds seventeen shillings. God Almighty bless you, my dear Emma, and grant us good news from our dear Lord. My dear Emma, bring me a bottle of ink and a box of wafers. Sarah Reynolds thanks you for your goodness to invite her to Sadlers Wells.

Sarah was another niece of Mrs Cadogan, daughter of her sister Ann who married Richard Reynolds, a Hawarden man.

Emma remained at Southend. She was having Clarges Street repainted, just to add to her expenses, and Charlotte sniffed daintily at the smell. So it was here, in lodgings, that Emma received a letter from Nelson on 18 August to say that he was at Spithead and travelling immediately to Merton. An unexpected victory at Cape Finisterre on the part of Sir Robert Calder had released him from duty. Emma went swiftly to work, sending to every part of the country to bid Nelson's family join her at Merton. Sarah Connor wrote in agreeable ecstasy from Clarges Street: 'Cold water has been trickling down my back ever since I heard he was arrived. Oh! say how he looks, and talks, and eats, and sleeps. Never was there a man come back so enthusiastically revered.'[10]

We may see in Emma's desire to cram Merton full of guests the intention, perhaps subconscious, to reduce the opportunities for awkward questions – about her failure to establish Horatia at Merton, her own frequent absences from the house, and her mounting debts.

On the morning of 20 August, Nelson arrived at Merton. Horatia was there, summoned from Little Titchfield Street. Her father was delighted with her. At four and a half, she was learning to read and was quick in every way – a fellow pupil at the Reverend Mr Lancaster's afternoon service for children, which Horatia attended on the twenty-sixth, attested to this in later years. Emma had finally arranged for netting to be fixed to the bridges over the stream in the grounds, which relieved Nelson. Surrounded by his near and dear ones, Nelson saw the domestic idyll of which he had dreamed at sea amply realized.

Contrary to the general view that Nelson spent his last leave in isolation from the world, there was a steady stream of visitors to the house, and several dinner engagements in town. Sir Peter Parker and Lord Minto were among the first to come. Minto recorded his impressions of the scene:

> I went to Merton on Saturday [he wrote to his wife] and found Nelson just sitting down to dinner, surrounded by a family party, of his brother the Dean, Mrs Nelson, their children, and the children of a sister [Mrs Bolton]. Lady Hamilton at the head of the table and Mother Cadogan at the bottom. I had a hearty welcome. He looks remarkably well and full of spirits. His conversation is a cordial in these low times . . . Lady Hamilton has improved and added to the house and the place extremely well without his knowing she was about it. He found it all ready done. She is a clever being after all: the passion is as hot as ever.

The Duke of Clarence came to see his old seamate. Nelson put his good arm round one nephew and, nodding to the other two, told the Duke that Horace, Tom Bolton and George Matcham were his three props. George, though pleased by these attentions, reveals in a diary he kept of his visit that it was a dull time for him. When he arrived in the small hours, he was directed by Emma, half asleep and *en chemise*, to share a room with Tom, a cousin he hardly knew. He found that rough shooting and fishing hardly occupied the days. Everyone was worried about his mother, who had lost a baby in Bath on 27 August. Mrs Bolton had earlier told Emma that she feared her sister, like their mother, would die from over-breeding. Mr and Mrs Matcham were persuaded to leave their house of mourning for the more cheering company at Merton in early September. With their arrival, the family party was complete.

Nelson's mind was at rest about his daughter's future. She had now been formally removed from Mrs Gibson's care. Conversations with Minto, with Sir Sidney Smith, and with James Perry and the Goldsmids, however, were bolstering his suspicions that Government intelligence concerning the French fleet's movements was incorrect. Increasingly restless, on 1 September he went to see Pitt to deliver his own theory that the French would be found off the Spanish coast, and not off the West Indies.

Pitt and Nelson had the highest opinion of each other's talents. After this exchange, in which the Admiral fully persuaded the Minister, Pitt's 'opinion of his merit and great conception was higher than it had ever been'. So Lady Bessborough informed Leveson-Gower.

In confirmation of Nelson's suspicions, at 5 a.m. the next morning, 2 September, Captain Blackwood came hotfoot to Merton with the news that the French fleet had indeed been sighted off Cadiz. He had announced the news to the Admiralty three hours previously, and had been ordered to inform Nelson immediately. The Captain found Nelson already up, and eager for such details as were known. It was evident, from the Admiralty's order that he should be informed immediately, that he was to be offered command. At present, Cuthbert Collingwood was Admiral.

There was no doubt in the public mind who should command the fleet. Minto reported a chance meeting with the hero in Piccadilly in late August. Nelson was being mobbed, and Minto, holding on to his arm, found himself mobbed too.

> It is really quite affecting to see the wonder and admiration, and love and respect, of the whole world; and the genuine expression of all these sentiments at once, from gentle and simple, the moment he is seen. It is beyond anything represented in a play or a poem of fame.

Emma was later to relate that, when Blackwood left Merton, she walked with Nelson on 'the quarterdeck'. She says that Nelson was reluctant to leave her and his home. 'Even this last fatal victory, it was I bid him go forth. Did he not pat me on the back, call me brave Emma, and said, "If there were more Emmas there would be more Nelsons."' However, Nelson had told Minto on 31 August that, though the *Victory* had gone to the Channel fleet without him, 'if there is anything material in the Mediterranean he will go.' By 4 September Minto had seen Nelson again: 'There seems no doubt of his going immediately to take Calder's fleet.' That same day Emma wrote to Mrs Bolton in Bath to tell her it was settled. Nelson's only reluctance in the matter was his fear of offending Collingwood by being appointed over his head. He was persuaded by Pitt that it was in the nation's interests, and wrote to his friend on the sixth, 'My dear Coll', hoping he would remain as second-in-command.

There were still visits to be made before Nelson left. The Prince of Wales's secretary wrote to say the Prince would be 'miserable' if his friend left without visiting him. So, in duty bound, Nelson went up to London to see the man he had so constantly traduced in his letters to Emma. Emma went with him, and they did not return till the evening, to find Minto waiting for them, and the Perrys, whom Nelson had previously asked to dinner. Last time Perry and Minto had met, the peer had committed the editor to three months' 'durance vile' in Newgate gaol for an article linking bishops and opera singers.

The *Victory* was ready and waiting Nelson at Portsmouth. He was to set off the next day from Merton. Once at sea, he would be commanding forty sail of the line, 'and a proportional number of frigates, sloops and small vessels', Minto told his wife. 'This is the largest command that any admiral has had for a long time.' Minto stayed till ten at night, talking it over with Perry and Nelson.

Judge of Emma's feelings. It was her last evening with her lover, his family had mostly faded tactfully away, and now there were two gentlemen visitors to entertain. 'Lady Hamilton was in tears,' Minto noted, 'could not eat, and hardly drink, and near swooning, and all at table . . . He is in many points a really great man, in others a baby. His friendship and mine is little short of the other attachment [to Emma] and is quite sincere.' Minto was always jealous of Nelson's reliance on Emma.

While the *Victory* was being made ready, Nelson and Emma had fulfilled some few other engagements. They dined at 'Fish' Crawfurd's, where Lady Betty Foster and the Duke of Devonshire were present, on the tenth. Nelson was 'so far from appearing vain and full of himself', Lady Bessborough reported, 'as one had always heard, he was perfectly unassuming and natural.' Emma wanted him to give an account of his having been 'Mobb'd and Huzza'd' in the streets. He stopped her. 'Why, you like to be applauded – you cannot deny it,' said Emma. Nelson owned that popular applause was acceptable to him – 'but no Man ought to be too much elated by it . . . it may be my turn to feel the tide set as strong against me as ever it did for me.' In this as in other remarks, he was probably thinking of Sir Robert Calder, though the company thought he meant Lord Melville, who had also fallen from favour. As ever, when the prospect of decisive action approached, Nelson became an altered being. A shipmate truly said of him that he was little in little matters, but great in great affairs. Only when his career was in the doldrums or at a standstill did he pursue the cult of his glory.

While Nelson undertook to take a letter and a kiss from Lady Betty to her son Clifford serving under him, Emma had a frank conversation with the Fish. This intimate of the Devonshire House set lost no time in repeating her confidence. Emma said, 'If she could be Ld. Nelson's wife for one hour she should die contented, and that he always invokes her in his prayers before action, and during the battle cries out very often, "For Emma and England."' Lord Holland, when told of this, remarked that 'Nelson was always as much cried up for his devotion as his bravery, but that if this mode of invocation was commonly known it would ruin him with the Saints.'

Emma had intended her remark to Crawfurd about marriage quite seriously. Hopes that Lady Nelson would not recover from an illness in July of this year had come to nothing. To all, with the exception of Davison and her mother, she had long impressed the innocence of her relationship with Lord Nelson. Now the Dowager Lady Spencer assisted at an odd little church ceremony, 'a private Sacrament which Nelson has taken before he embarks . . . After the service was over, Nelson took Emma's hand and facing the priest, said: "Emma, I Have taken the Sacrament with you this day, to prove to the world that our friendship is most pure and innocent, and of this I call God to witness."'[11]

It was presumably at this ceremony that, unnoticed by Lady Spencer, Nelson and Emma exchanged the gold bands that are now in the National Maritime Museum. Thus the ceremony served a double purpose, affirming the innocence of the relationship while regularizing it with marriage. The Dowager Countess went direct, as she was perhaps intended, to her daughter-in-law, Lavinia Countess Spencer, and said: 'Lavinia, I think you will now agree that you have been to blame in your opinion of Lady Hamilton.'

Among the final visits before departure, the Goldsmids were not forgotten. The younger boys and girls at Merton were sent over to Morden Hall, Abraham's house, to spend the day with their Goldsmid contemporaries.

According to young Lionel Goldsmid, fifth son of Benjamin, Nelson spent his last night before leaving for Portsmouth at Benjamin Goldsmid's villa at Roehampton. This was a packed schedule indeed, considering that Nelson had been up to London to see the Prince of Wales and entertained the Perrys and Minto to dinner already that day. Possibly Nelson had financial matters to discuss with Benjamin. There is no reference in Lionel's account to Lady Hamilton, and it must remain a mystery whether or no Nelson chose to spend his last night on shore apart from her.

Lionel recalled a scene the next morning. Nelson was walking with Mrs Goldsmid up and down the drawing-room –

> a large room with two immense glasses – then a rarity – from the top to the floor of the room at the upper end, and my youngest sister and myself on the side of his armless body and each time he told us two to look at that old fellow Lord Nelson and see what a funny-looking fellow he was, he was dressed in a naval coat, white naval breeches with naval buttons at knees, silk stockings, invariably hanging on as if not pulled up, too large and shoes rather high in the quarters large with buckles. He was kind in the extreme and we all loved him.[12]

Nelson promised both Lionel and his twelve-year-old cousin, John Leviene, that he would take them to sea next time he went.

The day of the thirteenth brought Nelson briefly back to Merton.

At ten that night he kissed Horatia's sleeping form, left Emma, and rattled away to Portsmouth. There he wrote in his diary:

> Friday night
> at half-past ten drove from dear dear Merton where I left all which I hold dear in this World to go and serve my King & Country. May the Great God whom I adore enable me to fulfil the expectations of my Country and if it is His good pleasure that I should return my thanks will never cease being offered up to the throne of His mercy. If it is His good providence to cut short my days upon Earth I bow with the greatest submission relying that He will protect those so dear to me that I may leave behind. His will be done amen, amen, amen.[13]

Nelson's mind, as so often before an engagement, was half-occupied with the prospect of his death. He had heard in Naples a dirge which he admired; he obtained the music, and placed it in the coffin Captain Hallowell had had made for him from the mast of *L'Orient*. He now spoke about this to Emma and told her that he wished she should sing his dirge. 'But how could that be?' she asked. 'For unless I sung it in madness, if I lost [you] I should be unable to sing.' 'Yes, yes, I suppose you would,' he replied.[14]

Southey has left a moving account of Nelson embarking the next day at Southsea by the bathing machines in order

> to elude the populace . . . but a crowd collected in his train, pressing forward to obtain sight of his face; – many were in tears, and many knelt down before him, and blessed him as he passed. England has had many heroes, but never one who so entirely possessed the love of his fellow-countrymen as Nelson . . . They pressed upon the parapet to gaze after him when his barge pushed off . . .

Nelson waved to them with his hat. 'I had their huzzas before,' he said to Hardy. 'I have their hearts now.'

His last act before quitting England was to entertain George Rose and Canning, Treasurer of the Navy, to dinner on board the *Victory*. He made Rose swear to interest Pitt in Emma's claims to a pension. Meanwhile at Merton Emma wrote: 'My face is an honest picture of the sufferings of my heart.'[15]

CHAPTER NINETEEN

Broken Hearted and going into Norfolk

Emma very sensibly accepted an invitation from Sarah Nelson to visit at Canterbury. To stay on at Merton with Nelson gone would have been to wish additional pain on herself. Even before Nelson left, she told his niece Lady Bolton: 'It seems as though I have had a fortnight's dream.' She was brought a letter from her dream's companion, now charged with energy as he prepared for sea. He looked forward, he told his dear Emma, to 'many, many happy years . . . surrounded by our children's children'. Emma had written to a friend recently that she wished she could sign her letter Emma Nelson – 'How pretty it sounds.' Now Nelson finished his letter, 'God Almighty can, when he pleases, remove the impediment.'

Canterbury was dull, Charlotte complained, and Emma agreed. 'So it is . . . Today we dine alone, to eat up the scraps, & drink tea with old Mrs Percy.' So we learn from a letter of 8 October which, together with an earlier one of 4 October, are the only letters of this period from Emma to Nelson which have survived. All he received, he destroyed.

Emma was in good spirits, notwithstanding the tedium of her hosts' routine. 'My dearest life,' she addressed Nelson, 'we are just come from church, for I am so fond of the Church Service and the cannons [*sic*] are so civil; we have every day a fine anthem for me.' She told of a fine dinner the Doctor, or the Reverend William Nelson, hosted, with the Marquess of Douglas among the guests. Marianna, Emma's cook from Merton, had come to Canterbury and 'dressed the macaroni and curry, so all went off well'.

Emma knew that what interested Nelson was not letters she was writing to Old Q or visits to old Lady Dunmore, which she was planning. Horatia was uppermost in his mind. If Nelson's brief residence in England had been only an interlude for Emma from money worries and loneliness, for Horatia it had been decisive. The child was now firmly lodged at Merton Place and, it seems, hugely enjoying herself. Mary Connor, Horatia's current governess, wrote daily to Emma of the child's doings. When Emma passed on the information to Nelson there is, for the first time, a note of pride and interest in Horatia's quickness. Mrs Cadogan, wise old owl, had written to Emma in very positive terms, that she doted on Horatia, she could not live without her. 'What a blessing for her parents', Emma wrote with real enthusiasm, 'to have such a child, so sweet, altho' so young, so amiable.'

Emma dispatched to Nelson a letter Miss Connor had sent her. '[Horatia] is to me a most delightful companion. We read about twenty times a day, as I do not wish to confine her long at a time, & she is now learning the names of the keys on the pianoforte.' Horatia at this age was evidently curious about Lady Hamilton's absorption in the instrument. 'I am quite busy dressing her doll. I've just completed a mattress & pillows for the bed; it is a continual source of amusement.' Miss Connor took the child to London, on an expedition to buy Tom Bolton some clothes. They bought some shoes and stockings and a hat for the doll.

Miss Connor, an excellent governess, thought Horatia 'uncommonly quick, & I dare say will read tolerably well' by the time Emma saw her next. As Horatia was only four and three-quarters, this does seem promising. Horatia herself finished off the letter. 'My dear my lady, I thank you for the books. I drink out of my lord's cup every day [Nelson had had a silver cup engraved for her at his sword-cutler, Mr Salter's] give my love to him every day when you write, and a kiss. Miss Connor gave me some kisses when I read my book well. O, here three kisses. My love to Mis Nelson. My dear my lady, I love you very much.'

Small wonder that Emma was charmed by her growing daughter. The dangerous enquiries as to her parentage had subsided. It was tacitly acknowledged that Nelson was the child's father, but Emma was not thought to be her mother; thus she felt free to enthuse about the child and all her doings. Emma was particularly tickled by a remark Horatia made about one Julia, one of the maids at Merton. Julia had got married at an advanced stage of pregnancy. Horatia commented to her grandmother, 'Mrs Candogging, I wonder Julia did not run out of the church, for I should, seeing my squinting husband come in, for my God, how ugly he is and how cross-eyed; why, as my lady says, he looks 2 ways for Sunday.' 'She is clever, is she not Nelson?' wrote her mother.

Emma told Nelson that her heart was broke away from Horatia:

but I have now had her so long at Merton [only a month!] that my heart cannot bear to be without her . . . She says, 'I love my dear, dear, godpapa, but Mrs Gibson told me he killed all the people, and I was afraid.' Dearest angel she is. Oh, Nelson, how I do love her . . .

Then Emma moved on to surer ground:

but how do I idolize you – the dearest husband of my heart, you are all

in this world to your Emma ... Write often; tell me how you are &
how the sea agrees with you, weather it is a bad port to blockade, in
short, the smallest trifle that concerns you is so very interesting to your
own, faithful, &c.

After her visit to the reprobate Lady Dunmore at her house on the
cliffs at Ramsgate, Emma returned to Merton. Mrs Bolton was begged
from her sister at Bath as a companion for the dull hours, and was with
Emma by 22 October. As Mrs Bolton had hoped, a letter from her
brother had arrived to 'drive away all the blue devils' of which Emma
complained.

Nelson had written on 1 October to say he would have only
twenty-three ships of the line soon, as Admiral Louis and a squadron
had to be dispatched elsewhere. 'But we shall do very well. I am sensible
that Ministry are sending me all the force they can, and I hope to use it.'
The rest of the letter, written in haste the next day, consisted mainly of
remembrances from his brother officers, Hoste, Hallowell and Louis,
to Emma, and from himself to all in England. He comforted Emma:
'You must not complain of my short letters for all that I could write,
was it a ream of paper, might be comprised in one short sentence, that
I love you dearly, tenderly, and affectionately.'[1]

Nelson's letters exercised a sort of magical power over Emma, lulling
her fears and worries. His sisters constantly refer in their letters to Emma
to the healing effect Nelson's had on her. Even when she was unhappy,
as in the wake of Sir William's death, a letter from Nelson would
revive her spirits. Mme Vigée-Le Brun, who had never been in love,
was shocked when Emma put a rose in her hair to celebrate one such
letter.[2] Powerful as the letters seem two centuries later, they are now
objects of curiosity. Nelson's passionate language takes us by surprise,
we raise eyebrows at his anxieties, express wonder at the modernity
of his sentiments. We view his feeling for Lady Hamilton through
a mirror, darkly. These letters were meant for Emma, not for casual
observers. In his absence after Sir William's death, they had become as
much part of Nelson for Emma as his flopping hair.

On the morning of 6 November, Emma was lying in bed at Merton,
Mrs Bolton sitting beside her. Her nervous rash was bothering her. At
one point Emma raised herself on one elbow. She thought she heard the
Tower guns. 'Some victory in Germany,' she commented. Mrs Bolton
suggested it might be some victory of her brother's. Emma dismissed
the suggestion. Five minutes later a carriage drove up to the door.

I sent to enquire who was arrived. They brought me word, Mr Whitby, from the Admiralty. 'Show him in directly,' I said. He came in, and with a pale countenance and faint voice said, 'We have gained a great Victory.' – 'Never mind your victory,' I said, 'My letters – give me my letters' – Capt. Whitby was unable to speak – tears in his eyes and a deathly paleness over his face made me comprehend him. I believe I gave a scream and fell back, and for ten hours after I could neither speak nor shed a tear . . .

So Emma later described to her friend, Lady Betty Foster, the day when she learnt that Nelson was dead.

The great victory had taken place on 21 October in the shoals of Trafalgar off Cadiz. Nelson wrote his last letter to Emma two days before. Though she was not to receive it till December, it is quoted here as a worthy proem to what went after.

Victory Octr 19th: 1805 Noon

My Dearest, beloved Emma the dear friend of my bosom the Signal has been made that the Enemy's Combined fleet are coming out of Port. We have very little Wind so that I have no hopes of seeing them before tomorrow May the God of Battles crown my endeavours with success at all events I will take care that my name shall ever be most dear to you and Horatia, both of whom I love as much as my own life and as my last writing before the battle will be to you, so I hope in God that I shall live to finish my letter after the Battle. May Heaven bless you prays your Nelson & Bronte. Octr. 20th, in the morning we were close to the mouth of the Streights, but the Wind had not come far enough to the Westward to allow the combined fleets to weather the shoals off Trafallgar, but they were counted as far as forty Ships of War, which I suppose to be 34 of the Line and six frigates, a Group of them was seen off the Lighthouse of Cadiz this Morng, but it blows so very fresh & thick weather that I rather believe they will go into the Harbour before night. May God Almighty give us success over these fellows and enable us to get a peace.

On the twenty-first, the fleet was sighted, and Nelson hoisted his famous signal, 'England expects every man to do his duty.' As the furniture in his cabin was hauled out to make room for the guns, Nelson asked a midshipman carrying Schmidt's pastel of Emma to take care of his Guardian Angel. A few minutes earlier he had gazed at Emma's picture and told Captain Blackwood, 'This is what inspires me; she loves glory and will either triumph in my fame or weep over my Grave.' Then the famous action began.

As Nelson went about directing the arrangements, he was conspicuous in his admiral's frock-coat, glorious with orders and stars. It is alleged that his officers asked him to change his dress or at least cover his stars. The *Victory*'s surgeon, Dr William Beatty, denied this in his narrative of the battle. It was mediated, but it was felt that his lordship would be highly displeased with whomever suggested the precaution. Beatty himself intended to mention the matter, but the opportunity did not offer.

The action was progressing well at a quarter past one in the afternoon, though many had fallen, among them Mr Scott, Nelson's secretary. Nelson was walking the quarterdeck with Hardy, and was 'in the act of turning near the hatchway' when a musketeer on the mizzen top of the French ship, the *Redoutable*, fired. The 'fatal ball' travelled fifteen yards to strike the epaulette on Nelson's left shoulder and penetrate his chest. Nelson fell to the deck. Hardy had walked on a few steps, unconscious of these events, and turned to see Nelson being raised from the deck by sailors. Scott had fallen on the identical spot earlier, and Nelson's clothes were soiled with blood. 'They have done for me at last, Hardy,' he whispered. 'I hope not,' replied his friend. 'Yes, my backbone is shot through.' Even as he was helped down the companionway, Nelson noticed that the tiller ropes which had likewise been shot through had still not been replaced, and ordered that it should be done. He then took a handkerchief and spread it over his face and coat, so as few as possible would know the commander had fallen.

Down below, Dr Beatty hurried to attend the Admiral, though Nelson protested he would take his turn with the others. Dr Scott, Nelson's chaplain, described the sick bay as a 'butcher's shambles'. The surgeon examined the wound, while Nelson said in a low voice, 'I have to leave Lady Hamilton, and my adopted daughter Horatia, as a legacy to my Country.'

After a pause for breath, he stated that he felt a gush of blood rise every minute within his breast; he had felt the ball break his back. Beatty realized the case was hopeless. There was little anyone could do. 'Fan, fan,' Nelson muttered, and 'Drink, drink.' Lemonade and wine and water were brought, paper fans were constructed, and Dr Scott rubbed his friend's stomach, which seemed to ease him.

Nelson continually called for Hardy. Till the captain of the *Victory* came, Nelson would not believe he was not killed. At length Hardy appeared and announced that fourteen or fifteen of the French ships were now theirs. 'Come nearer to me,' Nelson told him. 'Pray let my dear Lady Hamilton have my hair, and all other things belonging to me.'

In this he included the miniature of Emma by Vigée-Le Brun which he wore round his neck. Hardy shook hands with his dying commander, and returned to the deck.

'He often exclaimed, "God be praised, I have done my duty,"' Beatty records. Beatty asked him about two hours after the injury was sustained if the pain was still great. It continued so severe, Nelson replied, that he wished he were dead. 'Yet one would like to live a little longer, too,' he added in his quaint way. 'What would become of poor Lady Hamilton, if she knew my situation.'

Hardy now visited for the second time, and congratulated Nelson on a brilliant victory. 'Anchor, Hardy, anchor,' Nelson replied emphatically. Hardy supposed Lord Collingwood would now direct affairs. 'Not while I live, I hope,' Nelson swore, and tried to raise himself from his bed. 'If I live, I'll anchor,' he said energetically. 'Don't throw me overboard,' he next requested, and then, 'Take care of my dear Lady Hamilton, Hardy; take care of poor Lady Hamilton.' He ended, 'Kiss me, Hardy.'

Captain Thomas Masterman Hardy, a burly and undemonstrative seaman, knelt and kissed his commander on his cheek. 'Now I am satisfied. Thank God I have done my duty,' Nelson said. There was a moment's silence. Then Hardy knelt and kissed Nelson again, this time on the forehead. 'Who is that?' 'It is Hardy.' 'God bless you, Hardy!' Hardy then immediately returned to duty.

Now Nelson's confidant was his chaplain, Scott. 'Doctor, I have *not* been a *great* sinner,' he said. Scott later told a lady that he had been unable to answer this. '*Remember*, that I leave Lady Hamilton and my Daughter Horatia as a legacy to my Country; and never forget Horatia.' Then, 'Drink, drink,' and 'Fan, fan,' and 'Rub, rub,' were all he could utter. He roused himself several times to repeat the pronouncement, 'Thank God I have done my duty.' Scott rubbed Nelson's stomach till Beatty stopped him. Nelson was dead.

With the battle won according to Nelson's brilliant design, accounts of the day were hurried to England. Pitt had only just gone to bed on the morning of 6 November when he was woken with the news of the victory and of Nelson's death. He had been up till late, writing a long dispatch to the Admiral. He was shattered. The Admiralty was, meanwhile, dispatching messengers, Captain Whitby among them, to break the sad news to Nelson's family.

All over Europe, English men and women felt quite stupid with grief. Nelson had captured the popular imagination as no commander of army or navy had done or was to do. Lady Bessborough could 'think of nothing else, and hardly imagined it possible to feel so much grief for a man I did not know . . . Do you know, G., it makes me feel almost as much envy as compassion – I think I should like to die so . . .' So she wrote to Lord Granville Leveson-Gower. The next day she could write of nothing else but Nelson. On 10 November she must 'still rave . . . of Nelson; it has taken possession of every one's Mind . . . Almost every body wears a black crape scarf or cockade with Nelson written on it – this is general high and low . . .'[3] Abraham Goldsmid perhaps expressed best the sentiments of Nelson's friends and admirers on land when he said: 'I rejoice with my country, but I mourn for my friend.'

After the victory, Nelson's hair was cut off and his clothes, all but a shirt, stripped off. His body was placed in a 'leaguer' cask of brandy mixed with camphor and myrrh to preserve it till, according to Nelson's wish, he should be buried in England. The crew of the *Victory* had stoutly refused to allow the body to be taken home directly on the *Euryalus*. Instead, the body was carried to Gibraltar, where, at the end of October, repairs were made to the limping ship. The brandy was topped up with spirit of wine, and then the flagship began its sad journey home on 2 November. A sailor on the *Royal Sovereign* recorded the sense of desolation the entire navy felt: 'All the men in our ship who have seen him are such soft toads they have done nothing but Blast their eyes and cry ever since he was killed.'

To Hardy fell the task of sorting Nelson's effects. The letter he had written to Emma on the nineteenth lay open on his desk, and Hardy put it, with the hair Nelson had requested Emma be given, and Emma's portraits, away in a box, safe from the Admiralty's grasp. This was the beginning of a sort of conspiracy on the part of Nelson's companions at sea to ensure that what they judged to have been Nelson's wishes should be honoured. Sir William Hoste's letter to his parents in Norfolk bears witness to this conspiracy. Half-defiantly, he tells them that he has written to Lady Hamilton, as the least he could do for so great a friend as Lord Nelson.[4] In his letter Hoste hoped Emma would forgive 'the gloomy disposition of my mind'. Sir Richard Keats, who sent back the gay letters Emma had written to Nelson in October – he never received them – was equally sombre. Admiral Louis wrote too. He begged that Emma would give him some memento of Lord Nelson, something that was really his. He had never made a request of this kind before, he wrote with dignity, and did not envisage ever doing so again.

Emma lay in her bed at Clarges Street, where she had come on the fatal sixth. Now all Nelson's relations were with her, surrounding her bed weeping and wailing, as Mrs Cadogan informed George Rose in late November. Lady Betty Foster went to see Emma on the thirteenth and found her in bed, with Sarah Nelson acting as a kind of lady's maid. Emma's bed was covered with Nelson's letters. 'She had the appearance of a person stunned and scarcely as yet able to comprehend the certainty of her loss. "What shall I do?" and "How can I exist?" were her first words.' Emma ended her account of 6 November: 'Days have passed on, and I know not how they end or begin – nor how I am to bear my future existence.'

In December Emma found she had some hopes to sustain her. With Nelson's personal possessions, Hardy was bringing back to England in the *Victory* 'a will' Nelson had made, greatly in Emma's favour. Captain Henry Blackwood's wife wrote to Emma in December, announcing this, and Captain Blackwood himself added a postscript, begging Emma to let past quarrels with Hardy be forgotten. They were long ago now, in Palermo, when Emma had tried to beg sailors off punishments. Hardy was now determined to do by her as well as Nelson would have wished.

With the arrival of the *Victory* at Spithead on 6 December 1805 there began to be a resolution to Emma's grief. She wished to see Nelson's body, she wished to kiss his lips before he was interred. It had now been decided that he should be buried in St Paul's. Hardy tried to dissuade her, and it seems that when the *Victory* came to Greenwich, Emma was not among 'Lord Nelson's friends' who silently viewed the body. But for a faint discoloration of the lips, the corpse was little affected by its preservation. Emma was not to be at the State Funeral, to be held in January 1806 with the Prince of Wales as Chief Mourner. This was an occasion for authorized persons – relations and brother officers of the dead man.

With the *Victory* came witnesses to Nelson's death and, most importantly, there came Hardy. He went directly to George Rose at his country residence, Cuffnells, as Rose informed Emma on 9 December. 'I learn from him that Lord Nelson, almost with his last breath, manifested a confidence that I would do all in my power to make effectual the wish he had more than once stated to me respecting you.'

Rose, painstaking in his wish to have the clearest possible picture of Nelson's directive to him, wrote to Scott the next day for his account of Nelson's mention of his name. Scott had not left Nelson's body since it was committed to the cask. He replied from his post by Lord Nelson's side, which he did not intend to leave till the Admiral's body was in the ground:

When I first saw him, he was apprehensive he should not live many minutes, and told me so, adding with a hurried, agitated manner, though with pauses,

'Remember me to Lady Hamilton – remember me to Horatia – remember me to all my friends. Doctor, remember me to Mr Rose; tell him I have made a will, and left Lady Hamilton and Horatia to my country.'

At the end, Scott wrote, Nelson had said, 'George Rose has not yet got my letter – tell him' – he was interrupted by pain here; after an interval he said, 'Mr Rose will remember – don't forget, doctor, mind what I say.'

Only Nelson could have left his mistress and his illegitimate daughter as a legacy to his country. The 'will' was, in fact, a last *codicil* to his will. There is something sublime about the request, which Nelson wrote down in his pocket book, 'then in sight of the Combined fleets of France and Spain distant about Ten miles'. With his mind on the ensuing action, he yet had the coolness of mind to try and make provision for others in the event of his death.

He prefaced his codicil with a prayer:

May the Great God whom I worship Grant to my Country and for the benefit of Europe in general a great and Glorious Victory, and may no misconduct in any one tarnish it, and May humanity after Victory be the predominant feature in the British fleet. For myself individually I commit my Life to Him who made me, and may his blessing light upon my endeavours for serving my Country faithfully, to Him I resign myself and the Just cause which is entrusted to me to Defend – Amen, Amen, Amen, Amen, Amen.

He then went on:

Whereas the Eminent Services of Emma Hamilton Widow of the Right Honourable Sir William Hamilton have been of the very greatest Service to our King & Country to my knowledge without her receiving any reward from either our King or Country, first that she obtained the King of Spains letter in 1796 to His Brother the King of Naples acquainting him of his intention to Declare War against England from which letter the Ministry sent out orders to then Sir John Jervis to Strike a Stroke if opportunity offered against either the arsenals of Spain or her fleets – that neither of these was done is not the fault of Lady Hamilton the opportunity might have been offered, secondly the British fleet under my Command could never have returned the second time to Egypt had not Lady Hamilton's influence with the Queen of Naples caused Letters to be wrote to the Governor of Syracuse that he was to encourage the fleet being supplied with everything should they put into any Port in Sicily. We put into Syracuse, and received every supply went to Egypt, & destroyed the French fleet. Could I have rewarded these services I would not now call upon my Country but as that has not been in my power I leave Emma Lady Hamilton therefore a Legacy to my King and Country that they will give her an ample provision to maintain her Rank in Life. I also leave to the beneficence of my Country my adopted daughter, Horatia Nelson Thompson and I desire She Will Use in future the name of Nelson only, these are the only favours I ask of my King and Country at this moment when I am going to fight their Battle May God Bless my King & Country and all those who I hold dear My Relations it is needless to mention they will of course be amply provided for.

Nelson & Bronte[5]

Nelson had Captains Hardy and Blackwood sign this just before the battle began.

Rose informed Emma that he would 'take the very earliest opportunity of a personal communication with Mr Pitt to enforce that solemn request upon him'. However, Rose reminded Emma, the reward '(to which I think you entitled both on principle and policy) must . . . be from the foreign Secretary of State, on account of the nature of the service'. Rose could promise nothing but zeal.

If Emma was cheered by Rose's promises of zeal, his judgement that it was properly the Foreign Secretary's business was less welcome. She had hoped that Pitt would make the matter his own affair. She waited uneasily to hear more. Meanwhile, Hardy sent to her by Nelson's servant Chevalier, Nelson's hair and ring, her pictures, and the coat he wore on 21 October.

An interesting account of Emma's desolation at this time is supplied by young Lionel Goldsmid, Benjamin's son. He could never forget the moment when he heard of Trafalgar. The family was at Roehampton on the morning of 6 November, and Lionel was performing the daily ritual of hanging by his nose from the library table. He hoped that this exercise would promote his growth so that, when Nelson next returned, he would judge the boy tall enough to accompany him back to sea. 'Children, Lord Nelson is killed!' his mother 'screamed out'. Lionel let go of the table and 'was caught by his nose which slipt off the table, bleeding' as he fell.

Recovered, he went with his mother to call at Emma's bedside in London. In his journal, he recalls:

I was eight years old and was allowed to accompany my mother and those of the family who made up the party from our House. I was a great favourite of Lady Hamilton's and bathed in tears at times as she talked over his virtues and exhibited the various gifts he had made her on different occasions. I was on the bed to aid in passing the rings, shawls, bracelets, etc shewn to the company of about 15 persons seated in a semicircle at the foot of the bed – and as she thought perhaps at moments of her truly lamented Hero and friend, I came in for numerous kisses and her usual remark – thank you my funny boy – or child you must come every day. The very coat in which the dear old Admiral was dressed in the fatal battle and received his death wound was on the outside of the bed – the hole where the bullet passed through stiffened with congealed blood. There was most certainly a very serio-comic performance throughout the visit.[6]

When all were urging Emma to take up the reins of her life again, she seems to have derived most comfort from a correspondence with her old friend Hayley. He wrote to her in January 1806:

Believe me, my dear Emma, the most valuable of all victories are those we obtain over ourselves! Self-conquest is the summit of real heroism . . . you tell me you are most unhappy. No! *you must not be so.* You must allow your friendly Hermit to lead you to discover, and to enjoy, perhaps, the very sweetest of human gratifications. In a pilgrimage of threescore years on earth, I have learnt that the most soothing and satisfactory of all human pleasures may be found in discharging our affectionate duties to the dead; and particularly in acting, upon all occasions, as the pure Spirits of the Just made perfect must wish their surviving friends to act. Now, dear Emma, you have abundance of such delightful duties . . . to furnish you with the most animating occupation. I conjure you, therefore, to let *no sort of trouble depress the native energy of your mind.*

Emma replied sadly later in the year:

I was very happy at Naples, but all seems gone like a dream. I am plagued by Lawyers, ill-used by the Government, and distracted by that variety and perplexity of subjects which as you may suppose press upon me. I pass as much of my time at dear Merton as possible – and I always feel particularly low when I leave it. Mr Clarke [possibly Nelson's biographer] has read me well, for I was leaning my cheek upon my hand, and very unhappy, but I did try and get a victory over myself and seem to be happy altho' miserable.

Preparations for Nelson's funeral proceeded in the New Year. By then 'the Doctor' and Sarah had become Earl and Countess Nelson, Horace Viscount Merton, of Trafalgar, and Charlotte Lady Charlotte. The Earl behaved in character, and was heard to say Trafalgar was a great day as it had made him an earl. Emma wrote sharply to Rose: 'A man must have great courage to *accept* the honour of – calling himself by *that* name.' The Matchams, who left Emma in late November, seem to have been reluctant to attend the funeral. Lady Charlotte wrote that they must do so, the College of Heralds insisted, so duly on 6 January both Boltons and Matchams descended on Emma in Clarges Street.

George Matcham noted that Emma was 'in bed and very low', but in fact Emma was now to some degree recovered. She spent some time at Brompton, a village now part of London, where Mrs Lind, an operatic friend, had a house, or walking in the park with the Bolton ladies. The day of the funeral she spent at Clarges Street, providing breakfast and then dinner for the official mourners. While the rest of London lined the streets to pay homage to the hero, Emma depended on the accounts of others for her information.

With the awesome business effected, Emma resumed her attempts to order her life. On 23 January England suffered another momentous loss. Pitt the Younger died unexpectedly. With his death Emma lost a supporter who might well have worked on Parliament to honour Nelson's legacy of Emma and Horatia to the nation. Of course this is a might-have-been of history. There were difficulties in the way, most obviously the insult this would have been to Fanny, now the Dowager Lady Nelson. Yet Pitt had found in Nelson's last visit to England that the tenor of Nelson's mind accorded remarkably with his own. He had expressed himself to George Rose sympathetic to Nelson's wish. With the appointment of Lord Grenville as Prime Minister, Emma must have known that her hopes of recognition were slim. Rose wrote to her that he now intended to resign, thus could no longer assist her. He counselled her to rely on Nelson's will. This he wrote on 27 January.

So now the last codicil was with Lord Grenville, faithfully delivered by Hardy. It was to remain with him till May, when he sent it to William, the Earl, with the note that nothing could be done. The Earl came to dinner at Clarges Street and, with a satirical grin peculiar to him, threw it into Emma's lap, so she claimed.[7]

This is invention, as the dinner was to celebrate the grants made by Parliament to the Nelson family. The sisters got £10,000 apiece, and the Earl £100,000 with which to buy a family seat. The grants were made in mid-May. Grenville did not return the pocket book till the end of the month.

The point, however, was that, though Earl Nelson certainly did nothing to prevent the document being shown about, he equally did nothing to advance or support Emma's claims. The pensions to Nelson's family had been granted. The matter was now closed, yet Emma's claims had stood most chance of recognition if presented at the same time as the claims of Nelson's blood relations. Grenville was undoubtedly responsible for the delay.

From this date the friendship between the Earl and Lady Hamilton sensibly declined. Lady Charlotte had been removed from Emma's care in January. The break, however, was not abrupt. Sarah invited Emma to accompany the lordly family to Cromer for a seaside holiday in the summer. There was a succession of irksome correspondence over relics, such as will occur in any family after a death. Nelson's coat, Nelson's diamond aigrette were fought over with barbed politeness. Emma kept the coat, the Earl bore off the aigrette. The Earl, despite the vast sum he had been granted to buy a seat for the Nelson family, was as mean-spirited as ever. He also made himself quite ridiculous with his search for a suitable residence. Lord Cholmondeley, owner of Houghton, the mansion next to Burnham Thorpe, was amazed to hear that Earl Nelson had designs on it. He had no intention of selling, he said firmly.

Mrs Cadogan, with Horatia and Miss Connor at Merton, now assumed a dominant role in attempting to govern Emma's uncertain finances. Under the terms of Nelson's will, his executors were to pay all expenses at Merton for six months after his death. Mrs Cadogan wrote to Emma in February 1806 that the Earl and Mr Haslewood were coming down to Merton. 'I will not show them one bill or receipt,' wrote this redoubtable mother. 'I will tell them that you have them locked up . . . I have receipts for thirteen hundred pounds, besides the last forty-two. Mrs Cribbe [the gardener's wife] advises me not to show them till you have seen them . . . I had a very canting letter from Haslewood.'

Mrs Cadogan was fierce in her protection of her daughter. In March she wrote to Emma: did she have a copy of the will, regarding the executors' duties? Had she employed a lawyer against Haslewood? If not, Mrs Cadogan would. 'I am well informed of the measure the land your house stands on, and will not allow the pleasure ground that is taken in.' The Earl was left Nelson's farm lands. Why did Emma not write to Mr Goldsmid?

Emma did write 'a few lines' to Abraham Goldsmid. He was sorry that her spirits were not yet recovered. 'On mature reflection', he was persuaded, Emma would be convinced that 'it' was done for the good of those Nelson esteemed. 'His time was to die, and if not by a shot you might have lost him by sickness.'

Emma was staying with the Boltons at Cranwich in April. 'What a blank you have made in our party,' Mrs Bolton wrote to her on 22 April, when Emma had left. Emma, Mrs Bolton's granddaughter, was calling for Horatia to go to her bed every morning, and all were in fear to see the vacant places at dinner. On the twenty-sixth of the month it was Emma's birthday. Her mother wrote a characteristic letter on the occasion. It seems Emma was hosting a dinner party, as Mrs Cadogan sent her Marianna. 'I wish I had ten thousand pounds to send you,' she said warmly. As it was, she sent a gown of Sarah Reynolds' making, and promised her an appetizing Italian repast on Sunday – 'a mennestra verde and one thing roasted'. Mrs Cadogan had to end her letter with some disagreeable requests for money. Sarah Connor needed money to pay her washing, and Marianna needed shoes and stockings.

Despite these difficulties, Emma continued to entertain Nelson's relations as faithfully as she had done in his lifetime. In the early summer of 1806 Merton accommodated, besides Horatia, Mrs Cadogan and at least one Connor, Lady Bolton and Emma's goddaughter, Mary Anne Peirson, and her daughter Caroline, Anne Bolton, and probably Mr Bolton as well.

Before Emma set out on a second visit to Norfolk – Mrs Bolton asked for only one or two days' notice, so she could have something in the pot – she resumed an acquaintance with a gentleman she had not seen for twenty-five years. This was Sir Harry Fetherstonhaugh, now fifty-odd and still a bachelor. After some heady years as the Prince of Wales's bosom friend, he had fallen from grace and spent much of his time at Uppark. He was far from being the womanizer of his youth; his closest friend now was his footman; and, when very old, he would marry a young dairymaid.

Emma now wrote to Sir Harry, in large part to beg a loan of £500. The Earl owed her £2,000, she said, from Nelson's will, but the matter was still in Chancery. Lord St Vincent had promised to speak to Mr Fox (Charles James Fox), and had 'profest great friendship'. Emma wrote that begging made her feel dreadful, but she hoped never to do it again. The surprise lay in the coda to the letter. Emma wrote, 'Burn this . . . E goes tonight but she is taken care of in case of any accident.'

Where had Emma Carew, Emma's daughter by Sir Harry, appeared from? When last heard of, in 1801, she had been begged from Merton, where she was a guest, by Captain Tyson's wife for a ball at Woolwich. She was now twenty-four, and what she had been doing since she left the Blackburns' establishment in Manchester, with the exception of that visit to Merton, is a mystery.

Emma wrote to Sir Harry the next day. He had promptly answered her letter.

Your letter my dear Sir Harry has made me very happy I write from bed very unwell having had a little fever all night I was agitated yesterday with Ld St Vincent's kindness allso last evening with parting for a time from a very *amiable naive good good* Hearted person whose Health requires air

& exercise. her tears and real sorrow on parting unmand me for I do not
know that I felt more in parting with any friend than I did with her – I
shall be in town tomorrow by one will you call on me that I may give
you my thanks . . . I shall be rich enough one of these days when they
do something for me.[8]

Emma said that Sir Harry had made her mind easy 'to me that never
owed nor probably shall again'. Here Emma discounted a whole host
of shopkeepers and tradesmen. 'It made me compleatly uneasy and I
wish to do all that could be comfortable to *our* friend to be of use
in Case of accident is provided for & she is gone in to the country
happy.' Emma ended, scrawled up one side of the letter, 'Excuse this
written from bed,' and well he might. It is the most difficult scrawl.
Ever honourable in spirit, she enclosed a note for Coutts Bank, asking
them to pay to the order of Sir H. F. £500 in nine months' time.

Armed with the money – or did she really lay it out on her daughter
Emma? – she prepared to go to Norfolk. She wrote to Alexander
Davison:

I am very unwell, Broken Hearted and going into Norfolk with Lady
Bolton. I shall beg of my mother to send you the gun and cantine that
our departed angel left you. I have now a wide world before me, nor any
friends, though although when I was in power many basked in my sunshine.
I have done the state no little service . . . All is now over, all forgotten,
and the poor unhappy forlorn Emma's services allso forgotten but never
mind . . . I am giving up my home and establishment in Clarges Street and
I fear I must give up Merton if Government do not do anything for me.

Emma could not forget her past. She wrote to Hayley and her
vivid prose, which often contains echoes from others' letters to her,
reminded her friend unceasingly and often angrily of what had been
and what should be now. She was inventing freely now, for instance
when she said she thought of going to the Queen of Naples. She had
promised she would do so, 'in case of accidents'. Emma knew very
well that Nelson had failed to get Maria Carolina to do anything for
her but protest affection after Sir William's death. It was hardly likely
she would now have a change of heart. Fortunately, for Emma's pride
if not for the Queen, this summer the Royal Family of Naples had to
flee to Sicily once again, so could provide no refuge.

On their second visit of the year to Norfolk, Emma took Horatia to
Brancaster to see the child's cousins at the vicarage there. Some time,
too, was naturally passed at Cranwich with Mrs Bolton. The Earl and
Sarah, with their children, were visitors at the same time, profiting by

their stay at Cromer to see their relations. The Earl was perhaps put out to see one particular relation, Horatia. The Cranwich party soon dispersed, all going to Swaffham but the Hamilton and Nelson party staying there separately.

The *Norwich Mercury* in August reported that Emma gave a dinner at the Crown Inn – where she was staying with the younger Bolton ladies – for the most considerable families of the locality. These necessarily included the Taylors, the Langfords, the Rolfes and other Nelson connections. Horatia scored a great hit with them all.

As a matter of record, though she was named in the *Norwich Mercury* as Miss Horatia Nelson Thompson, Horatia was now officially Horatia Nelson Nelson. The Earl had carried out that part of Nelson's 1803 codicil concerning Horatia, and had the child's new name lodged in Doctor's Commons in May.

In the first week of September Emma was planning her return to the south, to Merton. A letter she wrote to Dr Scott gives some account of the nervous fears and grandiloquent thoughts that now harassed her. Her dinners in the Crown at Swaffham, her junketings about Norfolk with a bevy of children and young girls, the stream of gifts she dispensed had done nothing to increase funds.

My dear Friend – I did not get your letter till the other day, for I have been with Mrs Bolton to visit an old respectable aunt of my dear Nelson's [Mrs Rolfe].

I shall be in town, that is, at Merton, the end of the week . . . I want much to see you; consult with you about my affairs. How hard it is, how cruel their treatment to me and Horatia. That angel's last wishes all neglected, but to speak of the fraud that was acted to keep back the Codicil; but enough! when we meet we will speak about it . . . It seems those that truly loved him are to be victims to hatred, jealousy, and spite. I know well how he valued you, and what he would have done for you had he lived. You know the great and virtuous affection he had for me, the love he bore my husband, and, if I had any influence over him, I used it for the good of my country. Did I ever keep him at home? Did I not share in his glory? Even this last fatal victory, it was I bid him go forth . . . Did he not in his last moments do me justice, and request at the moment of his glorious death, that the King and Nation will do me justice? And I have got all his letters, and near eight hundred of the Queen of Naples's letters to show what I did for my King and Country, and prettily I am rewarded. Psha! I am above them, I despise them – for, thank God, I feel that having lived with honour and glory, glory they cannot take from me. I despise them, my soul is above them, and I can yet make some of them tremble, by showing them how he despised them; for in his letters to me he thought aloud . . .

This was Emma in her worst, black-doggish mood. During her two months' sojourn in Norfolk, she was under pressure, part self-imposed, to entertain, to play the Lady Bountiful, to provide the 'gala days' in the dull family round of which a Matcham child was to speak with such fondness to her son. They were always gala days when Lady Hamilton came to stay.

Emma returned to Merton to find that a young woman calling herself Ann Carew was causing trouble, swearing that she was her daughter. Emma wrote hurriedly to Mrs Bolton and to Mrs Matcham to assure them that, whatever viperish and malicious tongues might say, this was not the case. They both wrote in surprise, assuring their dear Lady Hamilton that they would never believe idle gossip against her. Emma was placated, but now made her will.

The truth of this new imbroglio is unclear. What seems most likely is that Ann Connor, one of the several sisters who looked after Horatia by turn, was with Lady Hamilton earlier in the summer when Emma Carew visited. Profiting by the disappearance of Emma's daughter to the country, it would seem she decided to impersonate her. Emma Carew, of whom we next hear six years later, was by Emma's own admission a most good-hearted young woman, determined to bear the cross of her uncertain parentage with grace. A letter she wrote to Emma in 1810 shows that she had a very rational cast of mind. The letter is written without the constraint that would have existed had Emma Carew bruited abroad her relationship to Emma. As perhaps the only steps she could take to discredit the gossip, she excised the Connors from her will and drew attention to the insanity which ran in their family.

The story of mad Ann Connor's tricks thankfully never went beyond Emma's closest circles at this time. Meanwhile, Emma had embarked on a project which was to bring her no happiness. Early in 1806, Emma had sent George Rose a lock of Nelson's hair with the remark: 'I have near 1500 of his letters. Some of them you shall see but my project is one of these days to have his life written by someone who will do him justice.' In a hack journalist called James Harrison, Emma now thought she had a worthy scribe. Oliver had recommended Harrison and his large family to Emma's mercy in August, when the writer was desperate for money. So Emma, in financial straits herself, took on a further half dozen dependants. She would also appear to have paid for publication of Harrison's two-volume *Life*, printed for C. Chapple of Pall Mall.

Emma had taken heed of the reluctance of Nelson's friends to see his private letters to her in print. The book is concerned with Nelson's public life; she furnished only the odd 'matchless words' – as on the rude reception at Blenheim Park in 1802.

The splendid reward of Marlborough's services, was because a woman reigned, and women had great souls; if I had been a Queen, after the battle of Aboukir Bay, he should have had a principality, so that Blenheim Park should have been only as a kitchen garden to it.[9]

There was another biography of Nelson in preparation, from the Prince of Wales's librarian, the Reverend James Stanier Clarke, but this was not to appear for some years. The Harrison book, appearing so soon after Nelson's death, was perhaps Emma's most subtle attempt to impress the public with the justice of her case for a pension. Only at the end of the two volumes, so vividly rehearsing Nelson's heroism, does Harrison touch on the question of Nelson's last codicil.

First, he stresses that Nelson's and Lady Hamilton's affection was 'a pure and virtuous attachment, founded entirely on mental esteem . . . the result of a most enthusiastic admiration of each other's heroic and magnanimous qualities'. Then, quoting Nelson's last codicil, Harrison writes: 'Woe to the nation, which could dare to neglect such strong claims on it's justice and beneficence.' Writing of Horatia, Harrison says: 'What real affinity, if any, that charming child may bear to his lordship, is a secret at present known by few . . . though the family in general appear disinclined to believe her his daughter, it seems highly probable that she is so . . .' Harrison then disingenuously adds, following a dissertation on seduction and profanity as vicious habits of British seamen: 'Could the biographer believe, that Lord Nelson had ever indulged even an idea of dishonouring the wife of his bosom friend . . . he would that moment indignantly throw up his brief . . .'

The only reason Nelson confided Horatia to Lady Hamilton's care, Harrison asserts, was because she was so eminently well qualified, witness Lady Charlotte and Ann Bolton, as a preceptress. 'With what incomparable skill, indefatigable zeal, and ardent affections, Lady Hamilton discharges the difficult and important duty of cultivating such comprehensive minds to the full extent of their faculties.' Pretty praises. Harrison completes his work with the hope:

> May every virtuous individual, in whom the blood of the Nelsons shall flow, to the last drop which can be traced, for ever find friendly patronage among the rulers of a nation which has certainly at an eventful crisis, been powerfully exalted, and perhaps preserved, by the example of the immortal hero who so freely and fatally shed his own last drop in the faithful service of his King and Country.

In other words, honour the last codicil.

Harrison's *Life* had no more effect on Lord Grenville than Emma's

other petitioners had had. Nelson's naval friends disliked the book.
Lord St Vincent threw it aside after the first volume. It stands now
as a monument to Lady Hamilton's extraordinary determination that
she would have justice. She took on all corners in her efforts to
secure it. Government held no terrors for Emma, and she continued
to address ministers with much the same familiarity as she had once
written to Acton or Lord St Vincent in Naples. Her boldness matched
the temerity, as one might put it, of Nelson's request to the nation.
Still, nothing came of it. Earl Nelson, to whom she wrote this winter
of 1806, was only one of many who gave no more than vague promises
of help.

The year went on. Nelson's birthday came and went. Horatia's
supposed birthday was celebrated with *Birthday Verses* from Harrison,
set to music by Signor Bianchi. A dreary Christmas was spent in
London. In March 1807 a large party of Boltons came there. A friend
of Dr Scott's was hailed by Lady Hamilton from a carriage window one
day in London, perhaps about this time. She asked him to return home
with her for dinner to Merton but he came instead the next day. In
no expectations of meeting company, he was astonished to find 'Signor
Rovedino, and Madame Bianchi, and other birds of the same feather'.
They were regaled with a sumptuous dinner and, after the ladies retired,
'the superb wines of the Merton cellars, gifts of crowned heads, &c.,
were liberally dispensed by Rovedino, as master of the ceremonies.'
Carlo Rovedino was a member of the Italian Opera and a friend of
Charlotte Nelson's old music master, Viganoni.

Scott's friend waited for Emma in the gardens of Merton the next
morning. When she joined him, he remonstrated on her mode of
life and her companions. She answered that 'it was a less expensive
plan than taking Horatia to town for singing and Italian lessons'.
Eventually she confessed that 'her affairs were already in a state of
grievous embarrassment'. With Emma's agreement, a retired financier
undertook to remedy Lady Hamilton's difficulties. He found that two
or three years' retirement into Wales, on a small annuity, would release
her from her difficulties. This was certainly not what had happened by
1808. According to the *Life* of Scott, Emma did retire into Wales, but
only for a short season. The harp and viol were soon resounding from
her lighted apartments in Bond Street, wilder extravagances than ever
were committed, and she was once again a suppliant for relief. There
is no other record of a spell in Wales, but Emma may conceivably have
visited Hawarden in early 1807. A letter from her old employer, Mrs
Thomas, in 1808 is concerned with payments Emma may have left at,
rather than sent to, Hawarden for relief of indigent relations, among

them Sarah Reynolds's father. Certainly, Emma's movements in the early part of the year are ill documented.

In August of 1807 a most happy plan, that Emma should bring her mother and Horatia to the Matchams' new home in Sussex, was realized. The Matchams had bought their agreeable property, Ashfold Lodge in Slaugham, with the £10,000 grant from Parliament. This is the last recorded occasion on which Mrs Cadogan went visiting. She had been ill, and it was hoped that a planned trip to the seaside at Worthing would benefit her health. Horatia had had chickenpox in the spring, and there were worries that she had grown thin and tall following the illness.

Mrs Bianchi accompanied the three ladies, and the Bolton sisters, to Ashfold. She and Emma entertained the company with 'some favourite airs' of an evening. There was a visit to the house of Lady Di Beauclerk's son Topham, set in a forest nearby. Emma exclaimed it was a scene in the Apennines and the house a convent. A few weeks were spent at Ashfold, then it was on to a 'good house' in Worthing which Emma had found.

George Matcham has left a pretty picture of the occupations of Emma's party at the resort. 'On the shore . . . the younger half ie. Miss A B, Miss H N, and Miss M M were driving themselves in little vehicles drawn by asses. In the evening we were favoured by some duets by Lady H. and Mrs Bianchi.' A chaplain present at the Battle of the Nile was in duty bound entertained, though he was most dreadfully talkative. 'Nothing could stop his tongue, not even a reproof from his wife.'

Emma wrote to Sarah Nelson in August:

> Here we are in this delightful place and my dearest Horatia is got well and strong. She Bathes and now Eats and drinks and sleeps well and creates universal enterest alltho' Princes Charlotte is here. She is left and all come to look at Nelson's angel.

This was plain speaking. The Earl did not quite take Fanny Nelson's line that she did not know who this adopted child of Nelson's might be. He had, after all, seen Horatia often enough at Merton two years before and in Norfolk the preceding year, and had registered her as Horatia Nelson Nelson. Nevertheless, he did nothing to acknowledge his niece, let alone promote the match between Horace Viscount Trafalgar and Horatia that his brother had dreamt of.

Emma continued:

> She improves in languages musick and accomplishments but my heart Bleeds to think how proud her glorious Father would have been He that

lived only for her . . . Tis dreadfull to me however she is my Comfort
and solace and I act as alltho' he could look down and approve and bless
Emma for following up His every wish . . .

Here we see that Emma had taken Hayley's mystical sermon to heart.

Emma stayed with Horatia and her mother at Worthing till the end
of September, cheerily enduring the wet weather. Young George was
summoned as an extra man for a farewell ball which Emma was bent
on attending. Despite his protests, he danced till half past three in the
morning. Then, with a long weekend at Ashfold, the Merton ladies
finally called the summer a day, and returned home.

Hardly were they settled before gala days loomed again. George
Matcham and Tom Bolton were summoned to celebrate Horatia's
and Anne Bolton's joint birthday in October. Emma had had a silver
hot-water plate and cover, decorated with little cherubs and scrolls,
inscribed: 'Horatia, 29th October 1807'. Among the guests, some of
them more regular lodgers than guests, were Mrs Graefer and James
Harrison. A large company attended a birthday dinner on the twenty-
eighth, and then, to George Matcham's disappointment, country dances
only formed the evening's entertainment. He opened the festivities with
'the little Horatia', and the Reverend Mr Lancaster closed them with a
song which George affected to mistake for a funeral oration.

Increasingly, we hear only of the high days and holidays. At the
end of November 1807 Merton was honoured with a visit from three
Princes of the Blood. The Duke of Sussex, staunch friend, was joined
by his elder brothers, the Duke of Clarence and the Prince of Wales.
Here was an opportunity for Emma to make some advances in her
pension schemes and, sure enough, in a will she made in 1808, we
find Horatia committed to the care of the Prince of Wales, in the
event of Emma's death. In March 1808, George Matcham, stopping
in at Clarges Street, still Emma's London residence, found the Duke
of Sussex, '(a Gentleman of enormous stature) in his Highland dress.
He had been to dine with the Scotch society, and had sung a tender
Vaudeville, which was of Course rapturously received.'

George Matcham was less amused by a caller he found with Emma
on another occasion in March, 'that devil in ye shape of a man, Font-l
Beck-rd'. It is possible that Emma was attempting to do a little business
with 'England's Wealthiest Son'. Her affairs had now reached a desperate
point, and she had determined to put Merton up for sale. In June George
Matcham met her as he was driving over Westminster Bridge in his
landau and four. She was 'low on account of ye house at Merton not
being sold when put up to auction the day before'.

Emma still pursued her elusive pension with vigour. She wrote to St Vincent:

The widow of Mr Fox, whose services to his country are, at best, very problematical, had instantly a grant of £1,200 per annum ... Even the widow of Mr Lock, only about two years Consul at Palermo, a man not remarkable either for great loyalty or the most correct attention to his official duties, had a pension assigned her, almost immediately on his death, of £800 a year.

But then, Lord Grenville had liked Charles Lock (Lock had died of the plague in the *lazaretto* on Malta in 1804). Nothing came of this. Lord St Vincent had ambiguous feelings about Emma. On the one hand, he disapproved of the shabby way she had been treated, 'stripped of every feather', and thought Nelson's brother's and sisters' squabbles over Nelson's will showed they were 'all vile reptiles'. On the other hand, St Vincent felt strongly that Emma had come between him and Nelson.

In September 1808, Emma begged the Duke of Queensberry to buy Merton. She was now in fear of being gaoled for debt. 'If I could but be free from Merton ... you will live to see me blessing you, my mother blessing you, Horatia blessing you ... only let me pass my winter without the idea of a prison.' The Duke declined to add another house to his collection of properties at a price of £15,000. This was the sum Emma needed to clear her debts. A valuation of the property put the figure at £12,000.

In November an extraordinary meeting took place at Sir John Perring's house in the City. Emma wrote exuberantly of the result to Charles Greville: 'Goldsmid and my City friends came forward and they have rescued me from destruction.' Abraham Goldsmid, Alexander Davison and six other distinguished financiers had gathered to attack Lady Hamilton's financial difficulties. They raised £3,700 immediately to pay off her most pressing debts, and assigned themselves trustees of Merton and of Emma's valuables, such as her collection of china and wine at Merton. With a sigh of relief, Emma left the Perrings' house in the City, where she had spent a week answering questions.

Emma had sold Clarges Street earlier in the year, and was now based at a charming house called Heron Court in Richmond. The Duke of Queensberry, its owner, had been distressed by the accommodation in Bond Street to which Emma was reduced after selling Clarges Street. She had had to share a sitting-room and eat her meals with her landlady. So Heron Court, originally Herring Cort, was placed at her disposal.

Two stone herons flanked the front porch of the neat house on the riverbank beside newly built Richmond Bridge. The Castle Inn stood next door, and Emma's love of a waterfront was amply satisfied by the view of the Thames, with an island thick in willows opposite, and swans sailing haughtily by for Horatia to feed.

Emma and her mother and Horatia lived here quietly throughout 1809. Mr Matcham noted that Emma had reduced her establishment to two maids and a footman, and was determined to recoup. To her great relief, in April Asher Goldsmid, diamond-broking brother of Abraham and Benjamin, bought Merton. Mrs Bolton wrote happily that Emma must be relieved that a Goldsmid had it. Sadly, Asher, whom Emma knew least of the brothers, was soon to be the only one of them alive. Benjamin Goldsmid, prone to melancholy, had committed suicide at Roehampton the year before. Abraham, who was devoted to his brother, was stricken. Benjamin's children, young Lionel and all, took their mother's name, Prager, in an attempt to forget the family misfortune. Abraham soldiered on alone in the family firm.

Meanwhile, Emma had further troubles. She had quarrelled with Francis Oliver, Sir William's and then Nelson's secretary. Oliver knew a great deal about her – he had carried Nelson's letters to her, he had taken care of Horatia. He now threatened to publish. He was dissuaded from this scheme, and only after Emma's death did he make use of his remarkable fund of information concerning her private life in the 1815 *Memoirs of Lady Hamilton*. In this year, also, Emma fell very ill at Richmond with jaundice, Horatia was consistently unwell, and Mrs Cadogan's health was anxiously enquired after.

Charles Greville died this year, too, at his bachelor house in Paddington. He was only fifty. Perhaps a life of penny-pinching had taken its toll. There had been no need for his economies. His collection of minerals was valued after his death at over £13,000. Sir William's estates in Wales passed to his brother, Robert Fulke Greville.

On 14 January 1810, the worst occurred. After a short illness, Mrs Cadogan died, to the sorrow of all. 'Was she not a mother to us all,' Mrs Bolton wrote to Emma. To Emma she had been more than a mother. Mrs Cadogan had been a constant source of strength, a last link with Emma's chequered and sometimes glorious days when 'many basked in my sunshine'. The sunshine of Italy had suited Mrs Cadogan, where the November fogs of London did not. Emma buried her mother in the church on Paddington Green, erected in 1788, two years after Emma and her mother had set out on that long journey to Naples. Now Emma and Horatia had to face 'a wide world' alone.

CHAPTER TWENTY

Toujours belle

'I have lost the best of mothers, my wounded heart, my comfort, all buried with her,' Emma wrote to a Nelson relation, Mrs Girdlestone. With the letter, she sent a box which the Duke of Sussex had given to Mrs Cadogan years before in Naples. Mrs Cadogan herself would have condemned the lachrymose note, written eighteen months after her death. Was the vigorous Emma Hamilton destined to spend declining years regretting dead friends till Victorian old age?

Sir Harry Fetherstonhaugh had resumed his correspondence with Lady Hamilton during her mother's brief illness. The old-fashioned beau with his French phrases and his delicate compliments seems to come dancing forward like a marionette caught out of time. He regretted the financial considerations which had necessitated Emma's move from Richmond to Albemarle Street. He sent her some baskets of game. Of her sufferings on behalf of her mother's pain he wrote: 'As I am alive to all nervous sensations, be assured I understand your language. They are . . . *de trop*, sometimes, yet I would not wish to . . . wrap myself in cold indifference.'

The death of Mrs Cadogan was reported in the newspapers. Sir Harry wrote on 28 January 1810: 'Time alone can heal the wound which such a loss naturally inflicts, with the assistance of excellent sense, great fortitude, and the most amiable disposition, all of which you possess in an eminent . . . degree.' He was agreeably surprised to learn on 19 February that Lady Hamilton, together with Horatia and Miss Connor, had moved to a better address at 76 Piccadilly. He hoped to visit her, but must remain at Uppark as guests were coming '*chez moi* . . . then, *chemin faisant*', he must pay a visit elsewhere. Did she have music often? he enquired. 'Do you go out, or how do you pass your time? No one better deserves to be happy. You have resources within yourself which no one can deprive you of.' He ended with a note that he would send her some game *sub rosa* – the pheasant season was over.

On this friendly correspondence followed some time this year a reminder of days when Emma's relations with Sir Harry had not been so tranquil. Emma Carew wrote a dignified letter to Lady Hamilton, perhaps prompted by the news of Mrs Cadogan's death. Miss Carew had been incommunicado since her visit to Emma in 1806. An encounter with Mrs Denis, one of the singing Lind sisters, had encouraged her to hope that Lady Hamilton would welcome her.

'Mrs Denis's mention of your name and the conversation she had with you have revived ideas in my mind which an absence of four years have not been able to efface.' If Miss Carew was not employing a letterwriter, then her Manchester education had been excellent.

It might have been happy for me to have forgotten the past, and to have begun a new life with new ideas; but for my misfortune, my memory traces back circumstances which have taught me too much, yet not quite all I could have wished to have known.

Here Emma Carew refers to childhood memories.

With you that resides, and ample reasons, no doubt, you have for not imparting them to me. Had you felt yourself at liberty so to do, I might have become reconciled to my former situation and have been relieved from the painful employment I now pursue.

Both old and new situation are mysterious.

It was necessary as I then stood, for I had nothing to support me but the affection I bore you; on the other hand, doubts and fears by turns oppressed me, and I determined to rely on my own efforts rather than submit to abject dependance, without a permanent name or acknowledged parents. That I should have taken such a step shews, at least, that I have a mind misfortune has not subdued.

Here is a clear echo of Emma's own fighting talk.

That I should persevere in it is what I owe to myself and to you, for it shall never be said that I avail myself of your partiality or my own inclination, unless I learn my claim on you is greater than you have hitherto acknowledged.

Here Emma Carew drew on her memories of that one seaside holiday with Emma, then her acknowledged mother.

Miss Carew finished by hoping that 'the same reasons may cease to operate, and then, with a heart filled with tenderness and affection, will I shew you both my duty and attachment.' If Mrs Denis had not overestimated Emma's expressions of kindness respecting her, Miss Carew 'may be believed in saying that such a meeting would be one of

the happiest moments of my life . . . It may also be the last, as I leave
England in a few days, and may, perhaps, never return to it again.'

We must hope that Miss Carew's wish was granted. Emma Hamilton
would appear to have felt a great bond with this, her elder daughter.
The fraught circumstances of that pregnancy had been as nothing to
the trauma of carrying Horatia eighteen years later. In the wake of her
mother's death, that stable influence removed, Emma perhaps toyed
with the idea of taking her daughter Emma into her household. The
young woman would have made a splendid and sensible adjunct. This
did not occur, and Emma Carew is not known to have corresponded
with her mother again. Many years later she was to settle in a convent
in the East End of London as a useful member of the community.

With the less beloved Horatia, Emma lived quite quietly at 76
Piccadilly, above a confectioner's, for some months. She then moved
to nearby Dover Street, and went out quite regularly. From Richmond
she had told the Countess Nelson that she had done with the 'wretches'
who 'robed and plundered' her house. Then she dined at Strawberry
Hill, visited the Mansfields and other of 'my husband's relations . . . in
short, I live now with that rank of friends I had been used to live with.'
This was a masterly, if unconscious, snub to the Nelsons. Unfortunately,
young George Matcham tells us that her company at table there was
very vulgar.

In Piccadilly, we find Emma sallying forth for musical evenings at
Peterborough House in Parson's Green. She sang some Irish melodies
at Lady Cork's, a lady who combined kleptomania with lion-hunting
to great effect. Alderman Boydell, Hawarden's famous son, had guests
to dinner to meet Lady Hamilton. And then there were the singers from
the Opera, Michael Kelly, Carlo Rovedino, Viganoni, Signora Storace,
Mrs Billington – both ladies now retired – and old friends from Naples
like the loyal Abbé Henry Campbell, an English Catholic. It was a mixed
bag of society that Emma kept.

When at home she lived very simply, as letters from Sarah Connor
show. Miss Connor was manning the fort while Emma and Horatia
paid a visit to Ashfold in the summer of 1810. She wrote, worried,
that Mrs Damier, the London landlady, was rooking Lady Hamilton.
One hundred pounds in a few weeks seemed excessive, and Mrs
Damier was charging full board while all but Sarah and the servants
of the household were away. Considering that Lady Hamilton lived
so simply, on 'good plain joints', Sarah wrote, the 'plan of cheapness'
they had concerted did not seem so cheap now. Sarah had set herself to
replacing Mrs Cadogan as Emma's woman of business, in addition to the
task of educating Horatia. It was to prove fraught and thankless work.

In a charming aside, Sarah noted that Dame Francis, the housekeeper at Merton, had come from there to remove the parrots. A naval captain had sent these from Africa long ago to Emma. The artist Thomas Baxter sketched one bird taking the air on a verandah at Merton. Presumably kindly Asher Goldsmid, who had bought Merton, had kept Emma's dearest Dame as caretaker. He never lived there.

Emma had been empowered to go to Ashfold with a relatively easy heart. The Duke of Queensberry had agreed to pay debts to the value of £2,500 which she had incurred. In his letter to Coutts Bank he stated that Lady Hamilton was not to touch the money; the transaction would be in Abraham Goldsmid's hands.

Goldsmid was, unfortunately, hard to find at this juncture. Sarah Connor went to Finsbury Square in search of him in September, and was told by a gossipy clerk that Goldsmid was in serious difficulties. As it transpired, Goldsmid owed £350,000 to the East India Company in respect of a claim. Owing to a sudden fall in stocks, Abraham found himself unable to meet the demand. Since his brother Benjamin's suicide in 1808, Abraham Goldsmid's large, benevolent figure had curiously diminished. On 28 October 1810 he shot himself in the grounds of Morden Park, which he had so loved. 'He is a good man; it's a pity he should suffer,' Sarah Connor had written when she heard of his trouble. In his desk were found IOUs to the value of £100,000 from the great and the grand, never presented.

That the Queensberry debts were not the whole of Lady Hamilton's commitments is shown by the fact that she was directing Sarah Connor in September to find 'the codicils' and take them to Lord Eardley. Eardley was the son of a financier, Sampson Gideon, who had stood to Walpole rather as the Goldsmids stood to Pitt. Just what he was to do with the documents – copies of Nelson's codicils in favour of Emma and Horatia – is not clear. Emma enlisted supporters wherever she could find them out. She needed them. 'Cunning' Mrs Damier was busy adding charges to her bill to 'make up for the pound a day not being enough when all is at home'.

Financial difficulties did not abate one whit Emma's habit of distributing largesse. In October Anne Bolton received a gown and a brooch for her birthday. She wrote that Lady Hamilton should 'coin words to thank you in, for you, who give so many, and, of course, receive so many thanks, must be tired of hearing the same thing so many times over'.

Soon enough Emma and Horatia were expected at Cranwich for Christmas with the Boltons. The Duke of Queensberry's condition suddenly declined, and Emma would not leave London. She added her mite to the forty-odd *billets doux* which littered the antiquated rake's bed – all from ladies hoping to have some tangible remembrance of Old Q. On Christmas Eve he died, and Mrs Bolton wrote to say she hoped Lady Hamilton would be a 'great gainer'. Her husband was betting on the sum; 'Anne dances', and Susannah was 'low' for fear it was not as much as all wished.

Emma's long courtship of the Duke was destined to be without profit. He bequeathed her £500, half the amount he had first set. Sir Harry, unaware of the Duke's generosity earlier in the year, commiserated – the Duke had always been 'a little capricious'. Even the £500 legacy was to be denied Emma. A tradesman contested the will, and the affair languished in Chancery for a decade. Sir Harry ended his letter by hoping that Lady Hamilton would come to 'old Up Park in the *belle saison*'. At present, the bad weather made the invitation unacceptable.

Disappointed in her legacy, Emma turned every way she could to meet her outstanding debts. She applied in May 1811 to Matcham for a hundred pounds. If he was surprised by the request, he readily allowed her the sum, but begged she would not mention it to anyone. It was part of a sum sent him by the trustees for investment on behalf of his wife and children. Emma also borrowed two sums of £150 from the singer Carlo Rovedino in this month.

It would seem that Emma had by now begun a most dangerous game. She was mortgaging her annuities. Colonel 'Wellbred' Robert Fulke Greville had inherited his brother Charles's estates and responsibilities in 1809. Lord Mansfield, the Colonel's trustee, wrote to Emma in the spring of 1811 that he had given 'positive direction' that Emma's quarterly allowance of £200 be paid regularly. In the hiatus after Charles's death, the payments had lapsed. It is all too probable that in the interval Emma had borrowed, and borrowed several times over, against the sums due her. Lord Mansfield, suspecting this, wrote gravely: 'Allow me to add that I hope you never anticipate the quarter you expect to come due ... You should be cautious not to increase your expenditure ... or your creditors will become very troublesome' – fearing she was spending her legacy before paying them. Lord Mansfield was not to know that Emma had not received her legacy.

Lord St Vincent's words, 'Care must be taken lest she be reduced to indigence,' were proving true. Not all Emma's financial problems were of her own making. The rental of £500 on the Bronte estate, so mismanaged by Graefer, had never materialized. The delayed payment of her annuity from Sir William had not helped matters. Still, those who wished to help her came constantly up against Emma's conviction that she was entitled to command the best in life. This conviction was not conducive to economy.

This is apparent in an encounter she had with the odious Pryse Lockhart Gordon. They met in the park at Greenwich. 'It was St George's Day, the anniversary of her birth as well as of my own.' (Here Gordon was mistaken; Emma kept her birthday on 26 April not the 23rd.) Lady Hamilton told Gordon that she had come down with 'her dear little Horatia Thompson Nelson'. Gordon thought Horatia 'a pretty, lively child'. She intended to give Horatia and a half-dozen other children a fete at the Ship Inn. 'An elderly, vulgar-looking dame, and a solitary footman, the carriage a shabby remise', were the other components of the expedition.

Pryse Lockhart Gordon described Lady Hamilton's altered appearance.

> Age and circumstances had made sad ravages in her formerly splendid countenance; but the eye, though less brilliant, was still beautiful and that fascinating mouth from which sculptors had modelled yet retained its expression. The lovely hair which was wont to hang over her polished forehead was now tucked under a huge cap, or perhaps it had become gray – be that as it may, it no longer served as an ornament.

Gordon noted that Lady Hamilton's dress was now sombre and shabby. 'The only part of it that denoted a person above the middle rank was a Cashmere shawl.' Nelson had given it to her, and with it she had wrapped the Queen's feet on the passage from Naples.

Gordon was sure that Lady Hamilton considered the meeting 'very *mal à propos* and to her humiliating'.

> She was humiliated to find that I, who had beheld her in all her glory, surrounded by royalty, and grandees kissing her hand, should now see an old woman, divested of all her charms, and reduced to comparative poverty . . . She dropped her veil and I observed her eyes filled with tears. Alas, those were happy days, never to return.

A moment later, Emma was having 'a lively conversation' with Lord Montgomerie's uncle, who came up.[1]

Emma could find the money for a celebration, but Cecilia Connor, once Horatia's governess, appealed to her in vain for thirty guineas salary owed to her. In Emma's rage against the Connor family – Sarah excepted – she had refused to give the able Cecilia a reference. The young woman had thus no means of obtaining further employment as a preparatory governess. 'I think your Ladyship will find you have been misinformed in many circumstances concerning me,' Cecilia pleaded. But Lady Hamilton's ire was implacable, and her purse unopened.

Sarah Connor was not to remain long in the Hamilton household. In June 1811 Lady Hamilton went with a party of friends to see a historical play, *The Royal Oak*, at the Haymarket. Its subject was the adventures of Charles II. Emma fastened on a 'plaintive ballad' composed by Michael Kelly for a fine contralto singer, a Miss Wheatley, in the second act. She saw in the ballad's description of a warrior fallen in battle references to Lord Nelson. Overcome, she begged her friends to remove her from the box. 'I cannot bear it.' She was conveyed home 'in a fainting condition'.

Miss Wheatley, whose singing had unwittingly alarmed Lady Hamilton, was surprised to receive a note from the lady the next day, begging her to come to her house. 'You overwhelmed me at the moment, but now I feel as if I could listen to you in that air for ever.'[2] Miss Wheatley obliged with the song, was asked to repeat it four times – 'as if increase of appetite grew by what it fed upon'.

She ended by becoming Horatia's musical governess, and Lady Hamilton's amanuensis. 'Not a day afterwards elapsed but Emma called for "Rest, warrior, rest".' Messages from the Boltons and Matchams were regularly included for 'Miss Wheatley' – a pupil of Attwood, incidentally – from this date on, which corroborates the story to be found in Michael Kelly's *Reminiscences*. This account of Emma's irrational emotionalism is only topped by a story J. T. Smith, of the British Museum, tells. Some few years after Lord Nelson's death, he showed Lady Hamilton an etching of the Battle of Trafalgar – and she fainted dead away.

Lady Hamilton's movements become increasingly difficult to trace, but fortunately from Horatia Nelson-Ward, as she was to become, we have a detailed account. After staying in the Piccadilly house a few months, she says, Lady Hamilton 'went to board and lodge in a house in Dover Street – Mrs Damier's establishment – where she remained and after that took a house in Bond Street, where she remained till she became too involved to remain at large and then went to Fulham to Mrs Billington'.

Matters had not reached their nadir yet. It would be misleading to paint too bleak a picture – Emma's house in Bond Street was well appointed. When an inventory of the contents was made, each room had what might reasonably be expected in a fashionable lady's modest town house. There were dinner services to accommodate sixty, silver and plate in quantity. If the parcels of good, plain foodstuffs from Nelson relations and presents of game from Sir Harry palled, Emma could always borrow a sum from her opera singer friends like Mrs Billington. If 'the English Catalani' had not made quite the fortune her Italian counterpart amassed, her friendship with the Duke of Sussex and her own talents had made her rich in retirement.

In July 1811 Lady Hamilton made her last journey up to Cranwich. The lease on the pleasant and roomy farmhouse was ending, and the Boltons had found more imposing quarters an hour's drive away in West Bradenham Hall. As 'little Tom' Bolton was now the heir to the earldom, following the death of the Earl's cherished son Horace in 1810, the Hall would be a more suitable residence. Emma seems to have held Cranwich in great affection. In part it was the character of Mrs Bolton, serene and dependable, which made visits there so enjoyable. Emma was made to feel comfortable just sitting by the fire, or playing with the family pet, young Emma Bolton.

There was an interesting sighting of Emma in November 1811. Mrs Dollond, the optician's wife, was invited to attend the Lord Mayor's banquet at the Guildhall. In 1810 Louis Simond, a French visitor to England with a critical eye, had noted the 'huge barbarous' figures of Gog and Magog which flanked the entrance. A statue of Lord Nelson stood nearby. Emma managed to pass the monument without swooning, for Mrs Dollond noted her presence at the banquet. 'There were more women of fashion than usual,' she wrote in her journal, but she was 'sorry to see Lady Hamilton and Signora Storace [the singer Anna or Nancy Storace] there'. Mrs Dollond thought it very poor form that 'women of that character should . . . be introduced to dazzle the citizens' wives and daughters'.[3]

At Christmas Emma and Horatia duly returned to Norfolk, and Emma was guest of honour at Eliza Bolton's wedding to a cousin in West Bradenham Church. The Reverend William Bolton, uncle to bride and groom, officiated. With Thomas Bolton Emma Hamilton witnessed the ceremony, and her signature is to be seen in the registry book. It marked her last visit to Norfolk.

Emma and Horatia returned to Bond Street, and to pressing demands from creditors. Still, Emma was eager to assist others in distress, and to use her much vaunted influence. A Dr Lawrence, previous owner of Ashfold, was sent to her by Matcham; it was thought that Lady Hamilton might use her influence with George Rose to aid the doctor in a financial scheme. Dr Lawrence gave this opinion of his proposed benefactor after spending some unprofitable minutes with Lady Hamilton: 'She is one of those characters that promise everything and do nothing, nevertheless she is possessed of great good nature and has great abilities with much benevolence.'

This year, 1812, Emma went neither to Ashfold nor to Norfolk. Callers found her not at home. In June Samuel Rogers saw her again singing Moore's Irish melodies in the company of the Prince Regent, and breaking into a eulogy on Irish songs. In October James Perry came to celebrate Horatia's pseudo-birthday. Shortly after this, it would appear, Emma made her flight to Mrs Billington's villa. She had sent many of her papers and other treasures on before her.

One of the few friends – though he later declared himself no admirer of Lady Hamilton – who found her at home was William Beckford. He franked a letter for Lady Hamilton on 25 December 1812. Emma was writing to a Mrs Russell on the Isle of Wight, to tell her that her husband was doing wonders on her, Emma's, account. He was drafting two memorials of Emma's claims on the Government: one document, four pages in length, was addressed to His Majesty George III; the other, twenty-three pages in length, was destined for the Prince Regent.

For ten years now Lady Hamilton had been petitioning for reimbursement of the funds she had spent in her country's service in Naples, and for some pecuniary recognition of her services. Her address to Addington in 1803 had been pithy. She wished her claims 'to be heard only as they can be proved; and being proved, may I hope for what I have now desired'. Now she rambled on.

She reminded the King of her services to Malta, the recognition of same by the Emperor Paul. She referred to that old chestnut, the King of Spain's letter, and of course recalled her procurement of the secret order enabling Nelson to water his ships in Sicily. All this had been rehearsed before. In her longer document, Emma effectively wrote her autobiography from marriage to the current year. Both memorials were constructed by Russell but in this we see much more of Emma.

The King and Queen of Naples, she announced, 'would often say I had de-Bourboniz'd them and made them all English'. She prayed and implored the Queen on her knees to grant the watering order. 'I brought her pen, ink, and paper to the bed, I *dictated*, and she *wrote*.' Emma asserted that she had suggested the ill-fated invasion of Rome. Her main point, however, had to be that in assisting the Royal Family to take their treasures with them to Sicily – '36 barrels of gold . . . these I marked as Stores for Nelson' – she and Sir William 'were compel'd to abandon our houses and all our valuables as they stood . . .'. Her private property thus left she valued at £9,000, Sir William's at £30,000.

On and on the memorial went, full of good points, if time had dimmed their urgency. On parting with Emma in Vienna, the Queen had wished to bestow on her a pension. 'I destroyed the instrument, saying, "England was ever just, and to her faithful servants generous."'

Emma wound up with a statement she would regret. She appealed to 'Messrs Canning and Rose, to state if, on behalf of Government, they had not reassured his Lordship [Nelson] on their taking leave of him on board the *Victory* . . . on his last sailing, "that the promises made by Mr Pitt in my favour should be fully realized".'

It was no accident that Emma was busy on these petitions when creditors were becoming pressing in their demands for repayment. She had fended off foreclosure by letting it be known that she was expecting a substantial sum on the old Duke of Queensberry's death. Now she let it be understood that she had high hopes from other august personages.

A year earlier Emma had written to a Col. Sir Richard Puleston in Shropshire, an admirer who felt 'as among millions, your bequeathed Guardian and Protector'. She envied him the clear, salubrious air of the Welsh mountains. In another letter she wished she could 'ramble over [her] almost native mountains'. Puleston urged her to visit. The air 'bites, it invigorates, and there is no demon in its tooth'.[4] Emma's appetite for country life was ever strong, but it could never provide her with the titillation town life offered. It is a charming thought that Emma Hamilton might have lived a happy old age in her native Welsh borders, town turned country mouse, perhaps marrying her military admirer.

In fact she was arrested early in 1813. She was taken from Fulham to the King's Bench Prison, on the south side of Blackfriars Bridge. She was not committed to live within the dreadful walls of the prison itself, but lived Within the Rules of the prison – that is, in accommodation, or a 'spunging-house', in a prescribed area, roughly two and a half miles in circumference round the prison. The practice of granting this parole to debtors 'had its origin in a Temporary Arrangement whilst the Prisons . . . were rebuilding, and has long continued'. Emma was fortunate not to live within the forbidding building illustrated in *The Microcosm of London*, the famous picture book of the capital. Exceedingly high walls excluded all prospect from the windows of the rooms within, few more than nine feet square.[5]

In 1815 there were 220 debtors living Within the Rules. Though the Surrey Theatre, famous for its circus riders, faced Emma's lodgings at 12 Temple Place, places of entertainment and taverns were out of bounds to 'rulers'. If found in the prohibited places, they were deemed to have 'escaped'.

The Marshal of the Prison, who lived in very handsome apartments, was William Jones. He drew no salary, but made a large income by granting prisoners, like Lady Hamilton, the liberty of the Rules. He 'sent round' regularly to check that the 'rulers' had not fled.

In contrast to Lady Hamilton's well-appointed house in Bond Street,

Temple Place was meanly furnished and ill served even in cutlery, as will be seen. This was evidently a very unsuitable dwelling for a child. Horatia, besides, had just had whooping cough, and the dusty conditions may have contributed to lengthen her convalescence. Mrs Matcham, on hearing of Emma's new address, wrote to beg her to send Horatia to them in Sussex. 'While we have a loaf for them [the Matcham children] she shall share it and our best affections.' They had a 'fine snow scene, and not able to stir out of the house, either in carriage or on foot', she added. Emma, of course, was constrained by other considerations than the weather to remain where she was. She did not allow Horatia to go to the Matchams.

It has been suggested that Lady Hamilton wished to keep Nelson's acknowledged daughter with her, as a lever on the Government. Certainly, in her memorial to the Prince Regent, she laid some stress on Nelson's last codicil, bequeathing her and Horatia to the nation. Still, at all times Emma asserted her services to England, not her attachment to Lord Nelson, as the reason he had left her to the nation. It was these services, not the legacy of the codicil, that she was fighting to see recognized, and in these services Horatia, then unborn, necessarily had no part. Emma was willing that something should be done for the child as well, but her presence or absence from Lady Hamilton's side made little difference to Emma's case. If the Matchams had taken Horatia to live with them, as Mrs Matcham evidently wished to do, then the Government might, in fact, feel less inclined to do anything for Nelson's child, comfortably ensconced with Nelson relations, whose very house had been paid for by a Government grant.

Emma Hamilton had always a goal. It had once been marriage to Sir William; it had been Lord Nelson's comfort; she had expressed herself quite clearly to Sir William Scott, the Admiralty judge, in 1809 concerning what she then saw as her goal: 'My only ambition now is that I shall fulfill Nelson's last request, take care of his Horatia, make my mother comfortable, pay everyone what is their due . . .' She could not pay her dues, her mother was now beyond her care, but Emma took the sacred trust of Horatia very seriously. She had left her pianos in Bond Street. A piano was therefore hired at fifteen shillings a month, so that Horatia could practise. For company, the child was provided with the daughters of Alderman Joshua Smith, a kindly president of the borough council of Southwark.

Eighteen hundred and thirteen was to be a year of 'glorious news' for England. Napoleon had been beaten into retreat from Moscow; Wellington was at the head of a magnificent army in the Spanish Peninsula. The Prince of Wales was now officially Regent, as his father slipped again from sanity – a resolution at last to the monarchy question.

Lady Hamilton had little reason for rejoicing. In February the news that she had written another memorial came to Rose's attention. It was printed in the *Morning Herald*. Rose took grave exception to Emma's record of Nelson's last evening at Portsmouth before he sailed, ultimately, for Trafalgar. Canning, seeing the report of the memorial in the paper, wrote indignantly to Rose on 17 February: Rose must know he had no part in the exchanges on the *Victory*. Rose intimated as much to Emma the next day.

Emma delayed answering Rose till March. Meanwhile she addressed a second letter to the Prince Regent. She had no doubt that his ministers were considering her appeal, but she was 'harassed by extreme embarrassments'. Tradesmen were 'clamorous and cruil'. She begged the Prince to allow her to explain how her embarrassments had multiplied. She outlined her grievances. Sir William 'left me but little to what he otherwise would have done'. Merton she had to sell, because of the debt incurred on it. The Bronte rental had not materialized. This was stale news, but now Emma made a new claim.

> The slender provision left by Lord Nelson for the bringing up of his daughter Horatia comes short of which I deem necessary for the Education of one of her descent the only Living Blood of that glorious man who Loved and adored your Royal Highness.

Here Emma entered into fantasy.

While she waited for His Royal Highness to reply, Emma addressed Rose on 4 March. If she had not been so ill, she explained, she would have sent a copy of her claim to him. She had been told that her claims had not been well received, because of a slur on Lord Nelson and herself. Quite unfounded. Surely the country would not let one who had acted with such zeal on its behalf linger in prison!

Her release from the King's Bench was secured by the friendly Alderman Joshua Smith on 6 March. On the same day she was informed by Rose that he was sending back the copies of her memorials that she had sent to him. He wished she had 'stuck to' what he wrote in February to be the truth of his conversation with Lord Nelson. He could do nothing for her.

Lord Sidmouth, now Home Secretary, wrote on the same day to tell Lady Hamilton that he had had a full talk with Lord Liverpool, the Prime Minister, on the subject of her memorial to the Prince Regent. While he regretted her embarrassments, it was an impossible object. Many other deserving cases existed and could not be aided. The money was urgently needed for matters of national importance.

So Lady Hamilton's assault on the powers of the land foundered. Her creditors came to know of her disappointed hopes, and closed in. Emma wrote to Horatia on Easter Sunday:

> Listen to a kind good mother, who has ever been to you affectionate, truly kind, and who has neither spared pains nor expense to make you the most amiable and most accomplish'd of your sex. Ah, Horatia! if you had grown up as I wish'd you, what a joy, what a comfort might you have been to me! for I have been constant to you, and willingly pleased for every manifestation you shew'd to learn and profitt of my lessons, and I have ever been most willing to overlook injuries. But now 'tis for myself I speak & write. Look into yourself well, correct yourself of your errors, your caprices, your nonsensical follies, for by your inattention you have forfeited all claims to my future kindness. I have weathered many a storm for your sake, but these frequent blows have kill'd me. Listen, then, from a mother who speaks from the dead! Reform your conduct, or you will be detested by all the world, & when you shall no longer have my fostering arm to sheild you, whoe betide you! you will sink to nothing. Be good, be honourable, tell not falsehoods, be not capricious, follow the advice of the mother whom I shall place you in at school, for a governess must act as mother. I grieve and lament to see the increasing strength of your turbulent passions; I weep & pray you may not be totally lost; my fervent prayers are offered up to God for you; I hope you will yet become sensible of your eternal wellfare. I shall go join your father and my blessed mother, & may you on your death-bed have as little to reproach yourself as your once affectionate mother has, for I can glorify, & say I was a good child. *Can Horatia Nelson say so? I am unhappy to say you CANNOT.* No answer to this – I shall tomorrow look out for a school, for your sake & *to save you*, that you may bless the memory of an injured mother.
>
> P.S. Look on me now as gone from this world.[6]

In May Lady Hamilton's collection of silver and plate was sold. Among the items was a silver dinner service engraved with Nelson's arms. She kept only some gold cups and other trinkets.

The sum collected did not meet all her obligations. By the end of June 1813 she was committed to live Within the Rules once more. Once more she took 12 Temple Place, and now the contents of her house in Bond Street were sold by order of the Sheriff of Middlesex. The inventory of the house contents lists a magnificent seven-foot bed with rich chintz hangings, pianos, a mahogany Canterbury (or music holder), yards of lace, the Worcester tea-set Baxter had painted. Emma was much attached to her possessions. She had built up a considerable collection of china – all of it was to be auctioned. Bidet frames, ewers, even board games like draughts and Pope Joan were up for auction.

Emma was as ever fortunate. Alderman Smith stepped in before the auction and bought and stored at the borough warehouses in Southwark a proportion of Emma's belongings. He held them against a sum of money he advanced to her.

We know of at least one creditor, a coach-builder, who was still awaiting payment in 1814. He headed a long list of annuitants Emma had amassed. Since Emma had 'put down' her carriage in 1809, it is probable that others of her creditors had been unpaid for longer still. Lady Hamilton was wise to remain free from their grasp, at least, in Temple Place. While she lived Within the Rules, no further creditors could assault her.

There was no particular stigma attached to a spell Within the Rules. Extravagant habits, usurious rates of interest and the uncertainties of the time had consigned many another to the confines where Emma now settled again. At this date Emma was in good spirits, as a letter to Sir Richard Puleston of 24 July shows. She asked him to drive out and see her. 'You will not see me an ambassadress nor in splendour but you will ever find me firm and my mind uncorrupted. Shame on those who will let me and Nelson's daughter pass the first of August in anguish.'

In fact, she seems to have passed the anniversary of the Nile quite pleasantly – with a group of 'sincere and valued friends all hearts of Gold, not Pinchbeck', as she wrote to Sir Thomas Lewis of the Treasury, inviting him to join in. 'Do come, it is a day to me glorious, for I largely contributed to its success . . . we will drink to his Immortal Memory.' Lewis was not to be found at the address Lady Hamilton had indicated. Emma had her other invitees, her doctor Mr Tegart, and Abbé Henry Campbell to console her.

Emma was finding Alderman Smith her most dependable friend. On 29 September her lawyer, Mr Trickey, wrote to Smith concerning a payment the latter was making to a creditor on Emma's behalf. Emma was much distressed by the trouble this caused; 'poor thing she commits errors often without the intention.'

Summer turned to autumn, and on Horatia's supposed birthday Lady Hamilton made another attempt to enliven her confinement. On 30 October she wrote to the financier John Lambert's widow regarding Mrs Lambert's proposed visit to Temple Place. Emma had some devoted friends. Mrs Lambert meant to stay several days in the grim shadow of the prison.

Yesterday my dear Horatia's birthday, His Royal Highness [the Duke of

Sussex] dined with me, Mrs B, Mr Perry of the *Morning Chronicle*, Col O'Kelly & in the evening Col Smith – we were very merry. [Signora] Storace called today for the first time . . .

This letter refers to the presence of Dame Francis, Emma's old housekeeper from Merton. A reference to Laura may denote Miss Wheatley, Horatia's governess. Clearly Lady Hamilton was not in actual want at this time. In a letter to Sir Richard Puleston of November, Emma draws a little picture of her 'two Welch women' drinking the baronet's health each time they tasted the cheese he had sent from Shropshire. Emma was full of spirit and boasted that she felt better than she had for three years. However, she had been confined to her bed for some time before with 'the remains of the jaundice' she had contracted in Richmond. This jaundice never left her properly, despite the attentive care of first Mr Heavihide and now Dr Tegart. Her conspicuous consumption of alcohol exacerbated the problem. The worst effect of jaundice, in many ways, is the depressed frame of mind it engenders in the sufferer. Emma's letter to Puleston is so cheerful that, granted Emma's wish to prove an entertaining correspondent, we may assume she was over the worst of her last attack. She did not hestitate to tell Puleston that she had been 'at Deaths door', of course.

She told Puleston that she had had Sir William Scott and Rose with her – 'so we are getting on'. Both Scott and Rose were now, one has the impression, resigned to a lifetime of imaginative directions from Lady Hamilton. They performed their parts with great good humour and probably some enjoyment. Sir William, though responsible for the famous phrase, 'the elegance of the three per cents [consuls]', had his more human side, and was described by Boswell as a 'two-bottle man'.

Emma passed easily to national and international affairs. 'What glorious news how fortunate the Regent has been and with what eclat he oposed the porliment,' she effused. 'They may load us with taxes but good generous John Bull will bleed freely.' She mentioned a rumour that Bonaparte had arrived in Paris back from Moscow, and had ordered five thousand men to be mustered. 'But will they come when he calls?' Emma doubted it.

She gives a vivid picture of the ordinary man's reaction to the news. At a dinner at Alderman Smith's, 'all the Citizens seem for Commerce reviving again, all triste faces turned merry. A man that meets another says well we have got little Boney in a scrape the dog is ours . . . But this Boney is a devil He finds resources etc no one else will,' Emma reflected.

Now the ambassadress spoke.

> Can anything be more rediculous than the Russian and Spanish ambassadors
> not meeting, nor did Russia go to Guildhall because Little Spanish insists
> on token place for their ancient monarchy whi Russia is a new born thing
> Their has been more battels lost and kingdoms gone for a Trifling form
> of Two little . . . fellows wishing to walk before the other than for any
> just cause.

Here was a political commentary Sir William would have enjoyed.
Emma ended that her 'paper would not let her write more and my
nonsense is not worth a double letter nor even a single one'. She was
not to be in such good form again for some time.

Though Lady Hamilton herself was in fine fettle, she was proving
no pattern of a mother to Horatia. A week or so before she wrote to
Puleston, two days after Horatia's birthday fête, Horatia had committed some misdemeanour. Lady Hamilton addressed this letter to her
daughter:

> Horatia, – Your conduct is so bad, your falsehoods so dreadfull, your cruel
> treatment to me such that I cannot live under these afflicting circumstances;
> my poor heart is broken. If my poor mother was living to take my part,
> broken as I am with greif and ill-health, I should be happy to breathe my
> last in her arms. I thank you for what you have done today. You have
> helped me on nearer to God, and may God forgive you. In two days all
> will be arranged for your future establishment, and on Tuesday at 12, Col
> & Mrs Smith, Trickey, Mr & Mrs Denis, Dr Norton will be here to hear
> all. Every servant shall be put on their oath, for I shall send for Nany at
> Richmond – Mr Slop, Mrs Sice, Anne Deane – and get letters from the
> Boltons and Matchams to confront you, & tell the truth if I have used you
> ill; but the all-seeing eye of God knows my innocence. It is therefore my
> command that you do not speak to me till Tuesday, & if to-day you do
> speak to me, I will that moment let Col & Mrs Clive into all your barbarous
> scenes on my person, life and honnor.

What occasioned this terrifying letter we cannot know. Later in
Horatia's life, her aunt Matcham was to say there was no fault in
Horatia, only 'a few childish foibles'. The barbarous scenes, the dreadful
falsehoods of which Emma complained were surely to be excused in a
child in such circumstances. Emma's relationship with her daughter was
built on shifting sands. In her letter to Mrs Lambert the day before this,
Emma had said Horatia was 'attentive to her Studies & behaves very
affectionately'. Emma told Mrs Lambert that Horatia would accompany

them to the Magdalen or reformatory, an institution close by in which Horatia tells us Lady Hamilton took a great interest. Never a fortnight passed but Emma assuaged her charitable zeal by a visit there or to the Blind School.

Christmas Day, 1813, was a pleasant affair. The Matchams sent a fine turkey from Ashfold, and Sir William Dillon, Admiral, was among the guests invited to share it. The Duke of Sussex and Mrs Billington, firm friends, were the others at the table. Dillon has left an account:

> I noticed a splendid display of plate on the table, and covers laid for four, but made no enquiries who the guests were . . .
>
> While we were thus occupied, I was surprised by the entrance into the room of HRH the Duke of Sussex. Soon afterwards Mrs B made her appearance. The Prince was all kindness, and wondered I had not been to see him . . .
>
> The dinner being served, the conversation turned in another direction. I had to do the honours – carve, etc – The first course went off in complete order, and I could not help thinking that rather too much luxury had been produced. HRH did not expect such an entertainment from the lady who received him. However, there was a sad falling off in the second course, and a great deficiency in attendance, as also of knives and forks. I had to carve a good-sized bird, but had not been supplied with the necessary implements. Time passed on, but no servant made his appearance. At last Lady Hamilton said: 'Why don't you cut up that bird?' I told her I was in want of a knife and fork. 'Oh!' she said, 'you must not be particular here.' 'Very well my lady' I rejoined. 'I did not like to commit myself in the presence of HRH but since you desire it, I will soon divide the object before me. Besides, you are aware that, as a Midshipman, I learnt how to use my fingers!' Then, looking round, I found what I wanted, and soon had the bird in pieces. My reply produced some hearty laughter, and the repast terminated very merrily. After a sociable and agreeable entertainment, I took my leave of the company.[7]

The New Year found Lady Hamilton abed and very ill. She remained in bed, according to her own account, for the first three months of 1814. The symptoms she manifested agree with those of advanced alcohol poisoning. Emma believed this was another jaundice attack, but it may be that her weakness was caused by a cirrhotic liver. In June she was to write to Puleston that she was recovered, 'but still orangey'. One pointer that her illnesses really constituted a progressive deterioration of the liver is her great size. Horatia spoke of 'dropsy' and 'water on the chest'. Liver failure causes edema, this swelling.

While she was still 'orangey', Emma was alerted by an advertisement in the *Morning Herald* to the news that a book entitled *The Letters of*

Lord Nelson to Lady Hamilton was about to be published. She wrote immediately to James Perry, asking him to publish her refutation.

> I have not seen the book, but I give you my honour that I know nothing of these letters. I have now been nine months in Temple Place & allmost all the time I have been very ill with a bilious complaint, brought on by fretting & anxiety, & lately I have kept my bed for near twelve weeks, nor have I seen any person except Dr Watson & Mr Tegart, who have attended me with kindness & attention, & to whoes care I owe my life. About four years ago my house in Dover Street was on fire, & I was going into Sussex for 3 months, & I left part of my papers in a case with a person to whom I thought I cou'd depend on. Weather this person has made use of any of these papers, or weather they are the invention of a vile, mercenary wretch, I know not, but you will oblige me much by contradicting these falsehoods . . .

The person she had thought she could depend on was of course James Harrison, the scribe she had employed in 1806. The mercenary wretch was probably Francis Oliver, with whom she had quarrelled in 1809. Perry did not print her denial, and the two volumes were duly published in May. Emma should properly have asked the Earl Nelson, as heir to his brother's copyright, to apply to the court for a common law order restaining publication on grounds of copyright breach. The letters which Nelson had enjoined Lady Hamilton to burn, which had been her comfort after Nelson's death, were now available for all to read. The book was a fine illustration of the old saying: 'Do right to men; do not write to women.' Emma's despair at seeing Nelson's letters to her made public seems to have manifested itself in an outbreak of rage of stupendous proportions. How else to account for a bill for 'Breakages', mostly china, for £13 4s 11d, which Alderman Smith paid her landlord in July?

Curiously, a great many people believed the letters to be forgeries. In the wake of Napoleon's abdication, there was a renewed surge of patriotic fervour. Many did not wish to believe Lord Nelson had slandered the Prince Regent and abused his officers (Admiral Hallowell was one of the few who escaped, Lady Shelley noted). Still, after the publication of these letters, forgeries or no, the Prince Regent was not going to feel well disposed to Lady Hamilton. Lord St Vincent was among many who believed Emma had sold her letters for profit. 'What a diabolical bitch,' he wrote.

Shortly before the publication of the letters, Matcham had written to Emma informing her that the family intended to take advantage of the peace and realize Matcham's cherished plan of settling abroad. 'I offer a joint wish that we may all settle abroad in some city, town or village,' he wrote.

In fact, Emma was making her own plans for leaving England. The publication of the letters as well as the peace may have been responsible. On 6 June she wrote to Puleston, 'It is your kind advice at this momentous epoch of my life I wish for.' She hoped he could help her to secure an unconditional discharge from the debtor's court. She wrote again that she had not foreseen the difficulty he mentioned. Perhaps Lord Eardley could help. If not, 'then I am lost, Life Liberty and all is gone.'

Alderman Smith, as so often, came to the rescue. Possibly on his advice, Emma had applied to Earl Nelson for half of her Bronte pension, which had never been paid to her.

> As every sixpence is of the utmost consequence to me, on account of Horatia Nelson's education . . . I do not in the midst of poverty neglect her education, which is such as will suit the rank in life which she will yet hold in society & which her great father wished her to move in.[8]

The Earl duly handed over the £250 owed. With this money to pay out to some of her 'clamorous' creditors, Emma received her discharge. There were, of course, others to avoid, the coach-builder among them. If she could reach the Continent, she would be safe.

On 2 July 1814 Emma Lady Hamilton, with Horatia, slipped away on a small boat named the *Little Tom*. Its advantage lay in that it embarked from the Tower of London, rather than Dover, where a watch might have been kept. The disadvantage was that the journey took three days, and mother and daughter were very seasick.

When she landed at Calais, Lady Hamilton went, as by right, to the best hotel in the town – Dessin's, immortalized in countless travellers' tales. The hotel, and Quillac's, a comparable hostelry, stood in the Rue Royale, near the old lighthouse, now a ruin. Although she had left England with only £50 in her pocket – and out of this she paid the boat fares – Emma felt for the first time in years free of care.

The water-sellers with their monotonous cry, '*Eau, eau, bonne eau!*' the scrum of beggars in the narrow streets, the Calais women in their picturesque dress, with short, coloured petticoat, white *bonnet rond* and sabots, brought memories of the street scenes Emma had loved in Naples.

'I feel so much better,' she wrote to her friend George Rose on 4 July. The change of climate, food, air, large rooms and liberty had effected such wonders, 'There is a chance I may live to see Horatia

brought up.' She had found a French maid; 'my old dame', Dame
Francis, was coming out, and an excellent day school had been found
for Horatia, run by an English lady. This was probably Mrs Cavendish,
a schoolteacher who had been arrested at the outbreak of the war with
England in 1793. She had now resumed her classes. Emma detailed her
daily routine. At eight in the morning she took Horatia to school, and
fetched her at one. 'At three we dine, and then in the evening we walk
out . . . Horatia learns French and Italian, the harp, the piano, grammar,
at her school. Not any girls but of the first families go there.'

There was a general and 'his good old wife' who were very attentive,
but 'our little world of happiness is in ourselves.' One hopes Emma was
now kinder to Horatia. She declared she would be even happier if Lord
Sidmouth could do something for Horatia's education and also her dress.
By and large, however, the bracing air, and sea-bathing, always a delight
to Emma, were clearing her mind of too extravagant wishes in that
direction.

Many English now passed through Calais in search of a Continent
little visited since the outbreak of war in 1793. Emma recorded that
Lord Cathcart was one visitor who called. Lady Charlotte Campbell,
daughter of Emma's patron the Duchess of Argyll, was briefly in Calais
in August. She received a note from Lady Hamilton begging her to call.
Lady Charlotte thought it a prostitution of the term that Lady Hamilton
should say that she had 'dearly loved those I loved', but obliged.

> I was sorry for her, and a mixture of curiosity and sadness made me desire
> to see her once more. I went to her apartment – time had marred her
> beauty, but not effaced it – and when I said 'toujours belle', a smile of
> pleasure reanimated her fine eyes. My compliment was not altogether
> untrue . . . Her eyes were filled with tears; she said the remembrance of
> the past crowded upon her, and excited them. She talked agreeably, and
> spoke of her own fate

– incidentally assuring Lady Charlotte that the child she brought up
was 'not her own, nor could be'.[9]

In August Emma moved from her fashionable hotel to a farmhouse
about two miles out of Calais, in the Commune of St Pierre. She wrote
to Sir William Scott a description of the economical rural life she led
there, with Horatia and Dame Francis. There was no suitable school
for Horatia, so Emma taught her herself. Fascinatingly, we learn that
Emma was instructing her daughter in German and Spanish. Neither of
these languages is mentioned hitherto as being part of Lady Hamilton's
repertory, but she would have heard them both at the Bourbon Court

of Naples. 'We read English, Roman and Grecian history, but it is a great fatigue to me as I have been eight months ill and am now in a state of convalescence.'

She described the farmhouse as very quiet – 'a fine garden, common, large rooms ... I have an ass for Horatia, as she wants, now she is fourteen, exercise.' Emma herself went in a cart for her health. This was improving on a diet of fresh and plentiful food. 'The Jaundice is leaving me, but my Broken Heart does not leave me.' She had seen enough of grandeur not to regret it, but she did wish for 'what would make Horatia and myself live like gentlewomen'.

She was proud of her economy: 'We have excellent beef, mutton, and veal at five pence a pound, chickens a shilling for two, and turbot per pair half a crown. Bread very cheap, milk from the cows on the Common like cream ...' There was also good cheap wine. Their mornings were given up to study. They walked and dined at two, then went out again, Emma in her cart, Horatia on her donkey. For amusement, every Wednesday there was a dance for 'persons of Rank and their daughters'. 'We pay three pence for going in.'

Of Horatia Emma wrote: 'She is good, virtuous and religious. We go to the Church of St Peter's, and read our prayers in French, for they are exactly like our own.'[10] This was not a Protestant but a Catholic church, the Église de St Pierre, to which Emma referred. Horatia testified that, ever since Lady Hamilton's arrival in France, she had professed the Catholic faith. Whether the Abbé Campbell had had a part in fostering this faith, Emma's long sojourn in Catholic Naples made her transition to Rome easy.

Even good plain foodstuffs cost money. Emma applied to Robert Fulke Greville for relief. Would he send her her quarterly allowance? Greville wrote back to say that he had received several applications from persons who appeared to think that Emma had pledged this and future sums to them. He could do nothing.

There was sad news for Emma in the autumn. Maria Carolina had died on 20 September of this year at Hertzendorf in Austria. Her body was laid out in the Court chapel, fat candles lighting her features, still imperious in death.

Winter approached, and a move back into Calais seemed advisable. It seems that Dame Francis returned to England at this point. Finances were critical. Robert Fulke Greville forwarded demands from more creditors in December 1814. Two sums of money from England, of £20 from an unknown friend and £10 from the Earl, were obtained by Horatia. They helped to establish Emma and Horatia in rooms in a house near Dessin's Hotel. An ex-Minim monk, Sieur Damas, was the landlord. The lodgings were bleak. Mr Hartshorn, British Consul to Calais in 1944, was shown the two north-facing upper rooms where Emma and Horatia lived. A grimy wallpaper and a narrow, uncomfortable bed were said to have been part of the fittings in Emma's day. This was very different from the Hotel Dessin's 'chateau-like hostelrie, embosomed in flowers, foliage and tranquillity'. Portraits of Sir William and of Nelson were hung in the alcove where Emma's bed stood. She became seriously ill.

Horatia gave two accounts of the winter in Calais in the Rue Française, first in 1846, then in 1874. She said that Lady Hamilton was in great financial distress, and she, Horatia, used the £30 from England to provide 'the necessaries of the house'. 'After the first week of [Lady Hamilton's] removal to the lodgings she hired in Calais of Monsieur Damas but once she left her bed.' Horatia herself never went out, 'and I hardly ever during the day left her room, my own almost opened into it . . . Latterly she was scarcely sensible.' It would seem from this that Emma was now weakening fast, but Horatia does not mention that a doctor was called. There was, of course, little money to spare.

As Emma drifted in and out of consciousness Horatia became increasingly desperate to discover the truth of her parentage. Emma would not tell her, 'influenced then I think by the fear that I might leave her'. Emma relented so far as to tell her that she had left a written account of the facts to be given to her later. Horatia states that 'for a very long time before her death [Lady Hamilton] took little interest in anything but the indulgence of her unfortunate habit'. Emma was able to afford the comfort of 'Wine and Spirits', thanks to the kindness of Henry Cadogan, Lloyd's agent in Calais. He paid her wine merchant's bill of £77. Unfortunately, Horatia attests, Emma's mind was made 'extremely irritable by drinking', and 'for some time before she died, she was not kind to me'. In desperation, Horatia wrote to Matcham, who urged her to proceed immediately to England. This Horatia could not do. There was nobody but she to care for Emma.

Emma continued to support life by sending Horatia with small items to the Monte-di-Pietà – dresses, a gold pin, a watch. She gave to Cadogan as some return for his kindness a letter of Nelson's, and some hair combs, presents from the Queen of Naples, and an onyx necklace for his wife. Lady Bountiful continued to the end.

The only other visitor to Lady Hamilton this winter was the priest of the Église Notre Dame close by. Later Horatia, as the wife of a Church of England vicar, remarked: 'Had I lived so long with such a decided free thinker as Sir W. H. professed to be, it is not surprising that she should not have had any very fixed principles of religion.' This was uncharitable. A dying woman must find comfort where she can.

Horatia added: 'With all her faults – and she had many, she had many fine qualities, which, had she been placed early in better hands, would have made her a very superior woman.' From another viewpoint, Emma Hamilton had passed through some of the more interesting hands to be found in the eighteenth century. Horatia finished:

> It is but justice . . . to say that through all her difficulties she invariably till the last few months expended on my education etc, the whole of the interest of the sum left me by Lord Nelson and which was left entirely in her control.

Time passed slowly in the dreary sickroom. Horatia was, not unreasonably, asked in 1874 how she could remember in such detail events of sixty years before. 'Circumstances form an almost child's character into that of a woman,' she replied. 'Alas my dear Sire the time I spent in Calais is too indelibly stamped on my memory ever [to] forget. More recent things pass perhaps, those never.'[11] Emma lay in her bed in the alcove. She is not mentioned as having been in pain. On 15 January 1815, at one in the afternoon, she drifted into death.

She had wished to be buried in England, and an item in the undertaker's account for 'dressing the body, spirits, etc.' shows that her body was embalmed, perhaps with a view to transporting it across the Channel. In the event, she was buried in Calais a week after her death. The *Gentleman's Magazine* noted that Henry Cadogan volunteered to pay for the funeral. She was laid to rest 'with all the ceremonies prescribed by the Holy Church', in the graveyard of the Église Notre Dame. 'Burial ground men' kept watch over her oak coffin, casked, through the Friday night. There are items in the undertaker's account for 'church expenses, priests, candles', and the Funeral Mass was read over her body by the priest who had attended her during the winter, Cadogan and 'all the English gentlemen in Calais and its vicinity to the number of fifty attended as mourners'.[12] There was nothing to complain of in the manner of her rites of passage.

The graveyard where Emma was buried, once the Duchess of Kingston's Garden, is supposed to have been marked at first by a wooden sign, 'like a battledore, handle downwards', and to have borne the inscription, 'Emma Hamilton, England's friend'. By 1833 a headstone had been long erected, for the legend in Latin it bore was only partly decipherable: '. . . Quae/ . . . Calesiae / Via in Gallica vocata/ Et in domo C. VI obiit / Die XV. Mensis januarii / A.D. MDCCCXV /

Aetatis suae LI' (Who . . . at Calais in the Rue Française died in No. 106 on the 15th day of January AD 1815. In her fifty-first year).[13] During rebuilding of Calais, the graves in this cemetery were transported, and Emma's grave vanished.* In the First World War, English officers fixed a plaque to the house where Emma had died. German bombing during the Second World War destroyed house and plaque. A second plaque has been placed in the street now standing on the approximate location of the old Rue Française. But Calais is greatly altered since Emma Hamilton briefly lived there. Only the shingled seashore where she walked with Horatia is unchanging, recalling the seascapes of the Wirral Peninsula, of Naples, of Southend, where she spent her energy.

* On 23 April 1994 an American benefactor, Mrs Jean Kislak, unveiled a monument to Emma Hamilton in the Parc Richelieu, on the approximate site of Emma's original grave, which she had donated to the city of Calais.

England's No. 1 Enemy

Emma Hamilton lay buried in the Duchess of Kingston's Garden, when the news of her death was inserted in the English newspapers. James Perry's newspaper, the *Morning Chronicle*, followed the *Gazette de France* in reporting that 'pursuant to her request her body was to be conveyed to England'. *The Times* was laconic the next day: 'Death of Lady Hamilton – A letter from Calais published in the Paris papers says that LADY HAMILTON died in that town the 16th instant.'

The reports in the papers stimulated Lady Hamilton's creditors to apply to Robert Fulke Greville, trustee of her Hamilton annuity. One creditor had had the wit to insure Lady Hamilton's life with the Pelican Insurance Office. Greville obtained a copy of the death certificate from the Calais Mairie, so that the creditor could claim his reward. And there Colonel 'Wellbred' closed his ledger on his erstwhile aunt.[1] The plague she had constituted to the family of Greville and Hamilton for over thirty years was ended.

Napoleon's escape from Elba on 2 February and his resumption of government in France cast all other topics into shadow. All those most closely bound to Emma Hamilton were already dead. She had been 'out of circulation' since her first spell Within the Rules. The French authorities had stopped much of the correspondence with which she was accustomed to beguile her own and others' time so vividly. Still, it seems odd that there are no references to Lady Hamilton's death in private diaries and letters of the time. When her every movement had been of consuming interest to the British public for the past twenty years, why this blank?

The British public still felt revolted that Emma, as they believed, had sold her letters from Lord Nelson for publication in 1814. The *Morning Post* was the only newspaper to publish a full obituary. It dwelt at length on this betrayal. 'It is much to be regretted that she was induced to give those letters to the world. But she perhaps might urge the plea of Shakespeare's Apothecary, "My poverty, but not my will, consents."'[2] So the old business was raked up again, and now there was no Emma to write indignant denials to the editor.

The *Post* concluded: 'in private life she was a humane and generous woman, intoxicated with the flattery and admiration which attended her in a rank of life so different from the obscure condition of her early days.' Here we have a further clue to the blank which followed her death. Through her efforts to become somebody, Emma had ended as kin to nobody. The upper classes thought her an interloper; despite her efforts, she had ended by breaking with her Connor and Reynolds cousins. Few felt tied to her after death. To fend off disgrace, she had disavowed both her daughters. As we have seen, the elder, Emma Carew, bore no grudge and was probably her mother's most sincere mourner. Horatia was in her turn to refuse to recognize Emma as her mother, though presented with the strongest evidence that this was the case.

The Matchams were, rightly, chiefly concerned with Horatia's welfare, following Lady Hamilton's death. Henry Cadogan, the Lloyd's agent, brought her across the Channel on 28 January, and delivered her to Mr Matcham at Dover. Horatia brought little with her. An inventory of Lady Hamilton's possessions at death, lodged with the Juge de Paix, listed a box of clothes to the value of two hundred odd francs, and fifteen francs in coin.[3] The rest was at the pawnbrokers, and Mrs Cadogan was to redeem for Horatia a few months later some gold cups, a pin, a shawl and a dress.

Mr Haslewood, the Matchams' solicitor, thought that the past two years had dealt a shock to Horatia's constitution, but hoped that the invigorating breezes of Sussex at Ashfold would 'restore her bloom'. It took a long time for the memories of Calais to fade. Perhaps as an antidote, Horatia cherished the memory of Lord Nelson with obsessive zeal. She lived first with the Matchams, then in 1817 went to live with the William Boltons in Burnham Market in Norfolk. Here she had a romantic meeting with a curate over a garden wall. Horatia and Philip Ward were married in 1822, had nine children, and lived a sedate and happy life in livings in Norfolk and then in Kent.

On Horatia's return to England in 1815, Haslewood had attempted to help her recover the possessions which Lady Hamilton had stored with her own on leaving England. Mrs Billington had some items; the bulk lay in Alderman Smith's sugar warehouses in Southwark. Haslewood wrote to ask Smith 'to separate every letter and paper which belonged to Miss Nelson or to any member of the family of the late Lord Nelson or to myself' from his 'sacred deposits'.[4] (These were the letters from Lord Nelson to Lady Hamilton which he also held.) Alderman Smith did not oblige. While he produced the will of September 1811 which Emma had lodged with him, he kept silent about the identity of the items that he had in his care.

He had stood a very good friend to Lady Hamilton since 1813, and he had reimbursed Cadogan for her funeral expenses. Emma died insolvent, so her legacies were not binding. There was no reason why Alderman Smith should not keep her possessions. He did so, but he confused matters by ever being on the point of munificently handing them over to Horatia.

In 1816 Horatia discovered that Mrs Smith had some miniatures belonging to Lady Hamilton. Mrs Cadogan had just forwarded a bundle of letters to Horatia at Ashfold, which had been held by the French Government. In the letters, as Horatia reminded Alderman Smith, his wife had offered to send to 'my poor lady' some miniatures in her possession. Horatia confided that she had felt 'much anxiety with regard to these pictures tho' of little value'. Would the Alderman please forward them to Mr Salter, once Nelson's sword-cutler and silversmith, who would dispatch them to Horatia?[5] Again, nothing resulted. As time passed, Horatia discovered that Alderman Smith had in his keeping Lady Hamilton's china – once a magnificent collection now boasting a few items of many services. Horatia particularly wanted the Nelson and Nile service. She also discovered that Smith held Lady Hamilton's plate. Lady Hamilton had given over to Horatia several items of this on the anniversaries of her supposed birthday and they were engraved to this effect. There were also some knives and the silver-gilt cup which Nelson had given to the infant Horatia. She attempted to recover these items on her eighteenth birthday, telling Alderman Smith that she had always understood from Lady Hamilton that she was to receive these on her coming of age. Now Smith agreed, then decided that he needed security for his transfers, which Horatia could not afford. She pursued him after marriage. Now he thought of putting Lady Hamilton's deposits for sale. On and on the business dragged. Alderman Smith died in 1835, and then there was his widow to deal with.

No more successful were the efforts of Horatia and of others to secure for her the Government aid which Lord Nelson had requested. Immediately on her return to England in 1815, the Prime Minister, Lord Liverpool, told George Rose that £200 might be got for her. While she had lived under Lady Hamilton's roof, nothing could be done for her. Lord Liverpool wrote to the French Government to secure Lady Hamilton's papers. It seems that none existed. In the event, it made little difference whether Horatia was under Lady Hamilton's roof-tree or not. Lord Liverpool's 'reservoir' of funds ran dry. In 1827, Horatia appealed for support, this time to Canning, just become Prime Minister. She was hopeful, but his unexpected death dashed her chance of success.

In March 1815 Coutts Bank informed Haslewood that the Duchess of Devonshire had deposited with them a package which Lady Hamilton had entrusted to her the previous year. Perhaps these were the documents of which Emma had spoken to Smith and to Haslewood, the documents which would reveal the identity of Horatia's mother. The package was opened. Horatia was very glad to have the letters within. They were Lord Nelson's first and last letters to her, of 1803 and 1805. In the last, he called himself her father. The letters shed no light, however, on her mother. Haslewood declared he knew nothing; no one else knew any better.

Time passed, Horatia collected more relics of her father. In 1828 a Mary Johnson wrote to Horatia. This was Mrs Gibson's hunchbacked daughter, Horatia's early playmate in Little Titchfield Street. Horatia made contact, via her brother-in-law. He secured for Horatia the thirty-eight notes making appointments to see Horatia and so on from Lady Hamilton to Mrs Gibson. There was also a lock of Horatia's hair, and Mary related the circumstances under which the infant Horatia was brought to her mother. She recalled Lord Nelson sitting on the floor and playing with Horatia. Surely Horatia must now have suspected that Emma was her mother. She did not.

In 1843 an historian, Sir Nicholas Harris Nicolas, was inspired by the publication of Wellington's dispatches to compile Nelson's *Dispatches and Letters*. The project took four years, in the course of which he had several meetings with Horatia Ward. Nicolas became interested in the subject of her birth and went to visit Haslewood, now an old man. Haslewood would give no details, but professed to know the truth of Horatia's birth. He solemnly authorized Nicolas to inform Horatia and his public that Lady Hamilton was not the mother of Horatia.

Just as Nicolas had completed his seventh and final volume of *The Dispatches and Letters*, a Mr John Wilson Croker approached him. He had bought from Thomas Lovewell in 1817 the originals of the letters from Lord Nelson to Lady Hamilton which were published in 1814. Lovewell sold them when he went bankrupt, and Croker had bought them by private treaty. Nicolas informed Horatia that the letters were authentic, and proved Lady Hamilton to be her mother. Horatia replied that she could not help rejoicing that the letters had not come under Nicolas's notice till after the seventh volume was published. 'Now they cannot sully his fame . . .'[6]

She did not alter her opinion when a doctor, Pettigrew, bought Croker's letters and published them in his *Memoirs of the Life of Lord Nelson* in 1849. Fifty years after Horatia's birth, she was publicly proved to be the daughter of Lord Nelson and Lady Hamilton. Horatia thought Pettigrew's text was so inaccurate that few would believe it. She remained obdurate in her refusal to accept that Lady Hamilton was her mother till the end of her life. Her children favoured prim Cornelia Knight as a grandmother. Philip Ward died in 1859. Thanks to Nicolas, they had lived in better spirits lately. A Nelson Memorial Fund was launched in 1849. In seven years it successfully won grants and advancement first for Horatia's sons, and then for her daughters. Horatia lived after her husband's death with her son Nelson in Pinner on the outskirts of London. She was physically more akin to her father than to Emma Hamilton. Huge deep-set eyes under blackish brows were set close above a long nose and hanging jaw. She made her rooms a veritable Nelson museum, as her mother had before her. Nelson's twist of bleached hair and ribbon, his pistols, were displayed, but she never made reference to her relationship with him. Only once did she show violent emotion. Her son Horace received his call-up papers for the navy. Horatia had hysterics, and the papers were consigned to the fire. Horace became a clergyman, by her wish. Curiously, when Horatia died in her eightieth year, the generation of Matchams then living at Newhouse, the home for which Ashfold was sold, had no idea that a daughter of Lord Nelson existed, much less had spent her childhood and adolescence intermittently with earlier Matchams.

Horatia was not interested in collecting items that had belonged to Lady Hamilton, apart from her china and plate. Nelson had drunk and eaten from these. Emma's possessions are scattered far and wide. A superb satinwood book case, one of a Chippendale pair, is believed to have belonged to Lady Hamilton, and is currently in the Victoria Art Gallery, in Australia. A table, painted with garlands, is at Faringdon Park. The bed in which she is said to have slept with Nelson at Fonthill is at Charlecote Park. Her piano, richly painted, has been to Kenya and back. A large corset is in the Victoria and Albert Museum, and a wreath of flowers which she made and tied with her own and Nelson's hair has recently been bequeathed to the National Maritime Museum. A moonstone in a box inscribed 'E. H. Her luck' was sold in 1985 at Christie's. The list is endless, the authenticity often doubtful.

Of the many houses associated with Emma Hamilton, the one best preserved is the reputed house of her birth, Swan Cottage in Neston. Edgware Row has vanished, Paddington Green is overshadowed by the mighty Westway. In Naples, the Palazzo Sessa is little altered within, but the hill on which it stands is now choked with buildings which obscure its view of the Bay. The Villa Emma still looks on the romantic palace of Donn'Anna. It has been neatly divided into a doctor's surgery and apartment. Both 23 Piccadilly and Emma's house in Clarges Street are gone. On the site of Merton Place stands a housing estate. In 1985 Heron Court in Richmond, long dilapidated, was demolished.

So every tangible souvenir of Emma Hamilton is eradicated – except that galaxy of portraits entitled *Lady Hamilton*. Some are authentic, some quite impossible. Many were brought together in an exhibition at Kenwood House in Hampstead in 1972, entitled 'Lady Hamilton in relation to the art of her time'. The aim of the exhibition was to set off the neo-classical splendour of Kenwood House with Lady Hamilton's portraits and vice versa. The excellent catalogue to the show by Patricia Jaffé stimulated interest in Emma's role in the neo-classical movement. With every succeeding publication or exhibition concerning the neo-classical, Sir William's and his wife's part in spreading the gospel of the antique is more firmly acknowledged.

The first biography of Sir William was published in 1969, while a steady stream of Nelson biographies has been published since 1805. In 1905 with the centenary of Trafalgar, these celebrations threatened to reach such a pitch that F. M. Jane (of *Jane's Ships* fame) remarked that there was 'Too Much Nelson'. He elaborated: 'I deplore the cult of Nelson.' It was 'pure and unadulterated moonshine'.[7] No English sailor would do his work more efficiently because he had 'England expects every man to do his duty' emblazoned all over his ship.

Nelson enthusiasts were not noticeably deterred by Jane's disparagement. In 1905, Emma Hamilton was awarded a mighty and scholarly biography some five hundred pages long by Walter Sichel. Since then there have been many. Why she should so fascinate is difficult to answer. There are those who are not fascinated, of course. Their view is that she drank and was fat, and that she ruined Nelson's life. The National Maritime Museum issued a poster to the London Underground in 1984, bearing a portrait of Emma and the legend, 'England's No. 1 Enemy'. Still, Emma has always had admirers. Sir Moses Montefiore, when asked for his impressions of Lord Nelson whom he met when young, said, 'Ah, my boy, I only had eyes for Lady Hamilton.' Winston Churchill watched Alexander Korda's 1941 film, *Lady Hamilton*, over a hundred times. The answer is perhaps that she was an original. 'I love to surprise people,' she said, and, on the whole, she did just that.

Bibliography

I MANUSCRIPTS

British Library:	Additional MSS
	Egerton MSS
	Spencer Papers
National Maritime Museum:	Bridport Papers
	Phillipps Papers/Croker Collection
	Phillipps Papers/Girdlestone Collection
	Nelson-Ward Collection
	Trafalgar House Collection
National Trust:	Uppark Papers
Mrs James Teacher:	d'Avigdor Goldsmid Papers

2 PRINTED BOOKS AND ARTICLES

Acton, Harold, *The Bourbons of Naples* (London, 1959)

Acton, Harold, 'Three Extraordinary Ambassadors', Walter Neurath Memorial Lecture 1983 (London, 1983)

Alisio, Gian Carlo, *Architettura napoletana del Settecento* (Bari, 1979)

Angelo, Henry, *Reminiscences of Henry Angelo* (London, 1828), 2 vols

Anon., *Memoirs of Lady Hamilton* (London, 1815) [with much info from Francis Oliver 330]

Anson, Elizabeth and Florence (eds), *Mary Hamilton* (London, 1925)

Anspach, Margravine of, *Memoirs* (London, 1826), 2 vols

Argyll, Duke of (ed.), *Intimate Society Letters of the Eighteenth Century* (London, 1910), 2 vols

Baily, J. T., *Life of Emma Hamilton* (London, 1905)

Beatty, W., *Authentic narrative of the death of Lord Nelson* (London, 1807)

Beckford, William, *Dreams, Waking Thoughts and Incidents* (London, 1783)

Beckford, William, *Italy, with sketches of Spain and Portugal* (London, 1834), 2 vols

Biddulph, Violet, *The Three Ladies Waldegrave* (London, 1938)

Bladon, F. M. (ed.), *The Diaries of Colonel The Hon. Robert Fulke Greville* (London, 1930)

Bor, M., and Clelland, L., *Still the Lark: A Biography of Elizabeth Linley* (London, 1962)

Burney, Dr Charles, *Music, Men and Manners in France and Italy*, ed. H. E. Poole (London, 1974)

Bury, Lady Charlotte, *Diary illustrative of the Times of George the Fourth* (London, 1838–9), 4 vols

Caldora, Umberto, *Diario di Ferdinando IV di Borbone*, 1796–99 (Naples, 1965)

Calton, R. B., *Annals and Legends of Calais* (London, 1852)

Carafa, Giovanni, Duca di Noja, *Mappa topografica della città di Napoli e de suoi contorni* (1775) ed. Mario Rotili (Naples, n.d.)

Casanova di Seingalt, J., *Memoirs*, transl. A. Machen (Edinburgh, 1940), 8 vols

Catalogue of Foreign Paintings, Drawings, etc., Lady Lever Art Gallery, Merseyside City Council (Liverpool, 1983)

Catalogue of the Sale of the Calvin Bullock Collection, Christie's, 8 May 1985

Catalogue of a Select Part of the Capital, Valuable and Genuine Collection of Pictures, The Property of The Rt. Hon. Sir W. Hamilton KT, Christie's, 27 March 1801

Civiltà del '700 a Napoli, 1734–1799, Catalogue of the Exhibition mounted in Naples, 1979–80 (Florence, 1980), 2 vols

Clarke, J.S., and Macarthur, J., *The Life of Admiral Lord Nelson, KB, from his Lordship's Manuscripts* (London, 1809)

Connell, Brian, *Portrait of a Whig Peer* (London, 1957)

Croce, B., Ceci, G., D'Ayala, M. and di Giacomo, S., *La rivoluzione napoletana del* 1799 (*illustrata*) (Naples, 1899)

Croce, Benedetto, *Aneddoti e Profili Settecenteschi* (Naples, 1922)

Damas d'Antigny, R., *Memoirs*, ed. J. Rambaud (Paris, 1913).

Dawson, Warren R. (ed.), *The Nelson Collection at Lloyd's* (London, 1932)

De Nicola, Carlo, *Diario napoletano*, 1798–1825 (Naples, 1906)

De Seta, Cesare, *Napoli nel Settecento: Nelle vedute de Etienne Giraud* (Naples, 1977)

Deutsch, O. E., 'Nelson and the Hamiltons in Austria and Hungary' (1935), unpublished translation of German original

Di Giacomo, S. (ed.), *Aneddoti di Giacomo Gotifredo Ferrari* (Naples, 1910)

Doria, Gino, *Le Strade di Napoli* (Naples, 1943)

Duncan, Isadora, *My Life* (London, 1928)

Düntzer, H., and Herder, F. G. (eds.), *Herders Reise nach Italien* (Giessen, 1859)

Dupaty, C. M. J. B. M., *Lettres sur L'Italie, en* 1785 (Rome, 1788)

Edgcumbe, Richard (ed.), *Diary of Frances, Lady Shelley* (London, 1912), 2 vols

Eliott-Drake, Lady (ed.), *Lady Knight's Letters to Mrs Drake from France and Italy* 1776–95 (London, 1905)

Emden, Paul H., 'The Brothers Goldsmid and the Financing of the Napoleonic Wars', *Transactions of the Jewish Historical Society*, 4 (London, 1939), pp. 225–45

d'Espinchal, Comte J.T., *Journal d' Émigration*, ed. Ernest D'Hauterire (Paris, 1912)

Eyre-Matcham, Mary, *The Nelsons of Burnham Thorpe* (London, 1911)

Fothergill, Brian, *Sir William Hamilton* (London, 1969)

Fremantle, Anne (ed.), *The Wynne Diaries* (Oxford, 1935–40), 3 vols

G. E. C. (ed. George Edward Cokayne), *The Complete Peerage* (London, 1910–1959), 12 vols

Galante, G. A., *Guida Sacra della città di Napoli* (Naples, 1872)

Galanti, Giuseppe Maria, *Napoli e Contorni* (Naples, 1828)

Gamlin, Hilda, *Emma, Lady Hamilton* (Liverpool, 1891).

Garden, Francis Lord Gardenstone, *Travelling Memorandums* (Edinburgh 1791–5), 3 vols

Gatty, M. and A., *Recollections of the Life of the Rev. A. J. Scott, DD* (n.p., 1842)

Gérin, Winifred, *Horatia Nelson* (Oxford, 1970)

Gerning, Isaac, *Reise durch Oesterreich und Italien* (Frankfurt, 1802), 2 vols

Goethe, J. W., *Italian Journey*, transl. W. H. Auden and E. Mayer (London, 1970)

Gordon, Major Pryse Lockhart, *Personal Memoirs* (London, 1830), 2 vols

Graham, M. E. Maxtone, *The Beautiful Mrs Graham and the Cathcart Circle* (London, 1927)

Grant, Lt.-Col. Nisbet Hamilton, *The Letters of Mary Nisbet of Dirleton Countess of Elgin* (London, 1926)

Granville, Castilia Countess (ed.), *Lord Granville Leveson-Gower, Private Correspondence from* 1781 *to* 1821 (London, 1916), 2 vols

Greig, J., *The Farington Diary* (London, 1922–8), 8 vols

Gutteridge, H. C., *Nelson and the Neapolitan Jacobins*, Navy Records Society XXV (London, 1903)

Harcourt, Rev. Leveson Vernon (ed.), *The Diaries and Correspondence of the Rt. Hon. George Rose* (London, 1860), 2 vols

Hardwick, Mollie, *Emma Lady Hamilton* (London, 1969)

Harrison, James, *The Life of the Right Honourable Horatio Lord Viscount Nelson* (London, 1806), 2 vols

Hayley, William, *Life of George Romney* (Chichester, 1809)

Holmstrom, K. G., *Monodrama, Attitudes, Tableaux Vivants etc.* (Stockholm, 1967)

Home, J. A. (ed.), *The letters and journals of Lady Mary Coke* (Edinburgh, 1889–96), 4 vols

Hoste, Sir William, *Memoirs and Letters of Capt. Sir William Hoste* (London, 1833), 2 vols

Hurstone, J. P., *The Piccadilly Ambulator or Old Q* (London, 1808), 2 vols

Ilchester, Earl of (ed.), *The Journal of Elizabeth Lady Holland* (London, 1908), 2 vols

Jaffé, Patricia, *Catalogue of Lady Hamilton in relation to the art of her time* (London, 1972)

Jeaffreson, John Cordy, *Lady Hamilton and Lord Nelson* (London, 1888)

Jowett, Evelyn M., *A History of Merton and Morden*, Merton and Morden Festival of Britain Local Committee (London, 1951)

Kelly, Michael, *Reminiscences* (1826), ed. A. Hyatt King (New York, 1968), 2 vols

Knight, Carlo, 'I Luoghi di Delizie di Sir William Hamilton', *Napoli Nobilissima*, 20, Sept – Dec., 2nd series (Naples, 1981)

Knight, Cornelia, ed. Sir J. W. Kaye, *Autobiography of Miss Cornelia Knight*, 3rd ed. (London, 1861), 2 vols

Landon, H. C. Robbins, *Haydn: Chronicle and Works* (London, 1976–80), 5 vols; vol. iv (1977), *The Years of 'The Creation'*

Layard, G.S., *Sir Thomas Lawrence's Letter-Bag* (London, 1906)

The Letters of Lord Nelson to Lady Hamilton with a Supplement (London, 1814), 2 vols

Leveson-Gower, Iris, *The Face without a Frown: Georgiana Duchess of Devonshire* (London, 1944)

Llanover, Rt. Hon. Lady, *The Autobiography and Correspondence of Mary Granville, Mrs Delany* (London, 1862), 2nd series, 3 vols

Mahan, Capt. A. T., *The Life of Nelson* (London, 1897), 2 vols

Malmesbury, 3rd Earl (ed.), *Diaries and Correspondence of James Harris, First Earl of Malmesbury* (London, 1844), 4 vols

Manners, V., and Williamson, Dr G. C., *Angelica Kauffmann RA: Her Life and Works* (London, 1924)

Marinoin, G. E., *Letters of John B. S. Morritt of Rokeby* (London, 1914)

Maurice, Sir J. F. (ed.), *The Diary of Sir John Moore* (1904)

Meade-Fetherstonhaugh, M., and Warner, O., *Uppark and its People* (London, 1964)

Miller, Lady Anne, *Letters from Italy . . . in the years* 1770 *and* 1771 (London, 1776), 3 vols

Minto, Countess of (ed.), *Life and Letters of Sir Gilbert Elliot, First Earl of Minto, from 1751 to 1806* (London, 1874), 3 vols

Moore, Dr John, *A view of Society and Manners in Italy* (London, 1783), 2 vols

Morris, Roland, *HMS Colossus: The Story of the Salvage of the Hamilton Treasures* (London, 1979)

Morrison, Alfred, *Autograph Letters and Historical Documents: The Hamilton and Nelson Papers*, privately printed (1893–1894), 2nd series, 2 vols

Naish, G. P. B., *Nelson's Letters to his Wife and Other Documents, 1795–1831* (London, 1958)

Napoli Nobilissima, 1st series (Naples, 1892–1906), vols 1–15; 2nd series (Naples, 1979–), vols 16—

Nicolas, Sir Nicholas Harris, *Dispatches and Letters of Vice-Admiral Lord Viscount Nelson* (London, 1844–6), 7 vols

Nicoullaud, M. C., *Memoirs of the Comtesse de Boigne, 1781–1814* (Paris, 1907), 3 vols

Oman, Carola, *Nelson* (London, 1947)

Paget, Rt. Hon. Sir Augustus (ed.), *The Paget Papers* (London, 1896), 2 vols

Paget, John, *Paradoxes and Puzzles* (Edinburgh, 1874)

Paget-Toynbee, Mrs, *The Letters of Horace Walpole,* 4th Earl of Orford (Oxford, 1905), 16 vols

Palumbo, Raffaele (ed.), *Maria Carolina, Regina delle due Sicile, suo carteggio con Lady Hamilton* (Naples, 1877)

Parsons, Lieut. G. S., *Nelsonian Reminiscences* (London, 1843)

Pettigrew, Thomas J., *Memoirs of the Life of Lord Nelson* (London, 1849), 2 vols

Rathbone, Philip, *Paradise Merton: The Story of Nelson and the Hamiltons at Merton Place* (London, 1973)

Redding, Cyrus, *Fifty Years' Recollections* (London, 1858), 3 vols

Rehberg, Frederick, *Drawings Faithfully Copied from Nature at Naples* (Rome, 1794)

Romney, John, *Memoirs of the Life and Works of George Romney* (London, 1830)

Russell, Jack, *Nelson and the Hamiltons* (London, 1969)

Sacchinelli, Domenico, *Memorie Storiche sulla Vita del Cardinale Fabrizio Ruffo* (Naples, 1836)

Scarisbrick, Diana, 'Emma Hamilton and her Jewellery', in the handbook to the International Silver and Jewellery Fair and Seminar (London, February 1985), pp. 19–25

Sermoneta, Duchess of (Caetani, Vittoria), *The Locks of Norbury* (London, 1940)

Seroff, Victor, *The Real Isadora* (London, 1972)

Sharp, Samuel, *Letters from Italy in the years 1765 and 1766* (London, 1767)

Sichel, Walter, *Emma, Lady Hamilton* (London, 1905)

Sichel, Walter (ed.), *The Glenbervie Journals* (London, 1910)

Simond, Louis, *An American in Regency England*, ed. Christopher Hibbert (London, 1968)

Smith, J. T., *A Book for a Rainy Day* (London, 1861)

Solari, Catherine Govion Broglio, *Venice under the Yoke of France and Austria* (London, 1824), 2 vols

Solmi, Angelo, *Lady Hamilton* (Naples, 1982)

Southey, Robert, *The Life of Nelson* (London, 1813)

Storia di Napoli, Edizione Scientifiche Italiane (Naples, 1975–80), 10 vols

Stuart, Dorothy M., *Dearest Bess* (London, 1955)

Swinburne, Henry, *Travels in the Two Sicilies* (London, 1783), 2 vols

Tischbein, W., *Aus Meinem Leben* (Berlin, 1861)

Toso Rodinis, Giuliana, *La commedia degli intrighi e degli amori: Le più belle lettere da Napoli di Dominique Vivant Denon* (Florence, 1977)

Tours, Hugh, *Life and Letters of Emma Hamilton* (London, 1963)

Trench, R. Chevenix, *Remains of the late Mrs Richard Trench* (London, 1862)

Vendôme, La Duchesse de, *La Jeunesse de Marie-Amélie, Reine des Français, d'après son journal* (Paris, 1935), 2 vols

Vigée-Le Brun, M. L., *Souvenirs* (Paris, 1867), 2 vols

Ward, H., and Roberts, W., *Romney, a biographical and critical essay with a catalogue raisonné of his works* (London, 1904), 2 vols

Warner, O., *Nelson's Last Diary. A Facsimile* (London, 1971)

Weil, M. H., and Somma Circello, Marquis de (eds), *Corréspondance inédite de Marie-Caroline avec le Marquis de Gallo* (Paris, 1911), 2 vols

White, Arnold, and Moorhouse, E. Hallam, *Nelson and the Twentieth Century* (London, 1905)

Williams, D. E., *The Life and correspondence of Sir Thomas Lawrence* (London, 1831)

Wraxall, Sir Nathaniel, *Historical Memoirs of my own Time* (London, 1815), 2 vols

Notes

These notes are designed to elucidate passages in the text where the source is unclear, or where hitherto unused sources are employed. Alfred Morrison's *Hamilton and Nelson Papers*, and Walter Sichel's *Emma, Lady Hamilton* pervade the text, and so are acknowledged here, and not generally in the notes. A list of sources used widely in each chapter heads each list of specific notes. To discover full bibliographical details of sources not quoted in full in the notes, the first name cited in the notes tallies with the first name cited in the bibliography.

BL = British Library, London
HMC = Historical Manuscripts Commission, London
NMM = National Maritime Museum, Greenwich

CHAPTER ONE

Hilda Gamlin's *Emma, Lady Hamilton* gives useful details of her early life. Henry Angelo's *Reminiscences*, vol. ii, pp. 236ff., shed light on her teenage career. The anonymous *Memoirs of Lady Hamilton* (1815) were the work of Francis Oliver, who was personally acquainted with Emma's doings from 1786 to 1806. Outside of this period, the *Memoirs* rely on hearsay.

1 Pettigrew, vol. ii, p. 593
2 Bor and Clelland, p. 103
3 William Hickey, *Memoirs*, ed. Peter Quennell (London, 1960), p. 322
4 *A Sketch of Dr Graham's Medical Apparatus &c. erected about the beginning of the year* 1780 in his house on the Royal Terrace, Adelphi, anon. (London, 1780)
5 *Life and Times of Frederick Reynolds*, (London, 1826), 2 vols: vol. ii, pp. 153, 154
6 Meade-Fetherstonhaugh and Warner, p. 48
7 Argyll (ed.), vol. ii, pp. 415, 416

CHAPTER TWO

Alfred Morrison's *Autograph Letters . . . The Hamilton and Nelson Papers*, vol. i, are of particular importance here. John Romney's *Memoirs* of his father, George Romney, pp. 172–210, and William Hayley's *Life of George Romney* have been liberally consulted.

1 G.E.C., *The Complete Peerage* (1912), vol. ii, p. 336, note b
2 *Gentleman's Magazine* (June, 1810), p. 584
3 Ward and Roberts, vol. ii, p. 107
4 Anon., *Memoirs*, pp. 63 ff.; Romney, p. 183
5 Paget-Toynbee (ed.), vol. xii, p. 338

CHAPTER THREE

Alfred Morrison's *Autograph Letters . . . The Hamilton and Nelson Papers*, vol. i, are the chief source for Sir William's and Catherine Lady Hamilton's married life. Elizabeth and Florence Anson's *Mary Hamilton*, pp. 150 ff., and Rt. Hon. Lady Llanover's *The Autobiography . . . of . . . Mrs Delany*, vol. iii, pp. 184–225, provide details of Sir William Hamilton's visit to London. John Romney's *Memoirs* supplement these sources.

1 Home (ed.), vol. iv, p. 260
2 Beckford (1783), p. 215
3 Wraxall, vol. i, p. 226
4 Paget-Toynbee (ed.), vol. xiii, p. 308
5 Anspach, vol. ii, pp. 188–9
6 Morrison, vol. i, pp. 85–90, M 124–9, 12/6/84–10/8/84

CHAPTER FOUR

Alfred Morrison's *Autograph Letters . . . The Hamilton and Nelson Papers*, vol. i, pp. 96–147, and Elizabeth and Florence Anson's *Mary Hamilton*, pp. 244–53, are the chief sources.

1 Ward and Roberts, vol. ii, pp. 97–107
2 Morrison, vol. ii, pp. 375–81
3 BL Add. MS 42071, fo. 6, 1/6/85
4 HMC 78: Hastings MSS, vol. 3, p. 86

5 Casanova, vol. viii, p. 145
6 BL Add. MS 42071, fo. 2, 22/2/85
7 BL Add. MS 34, 048, fo. 24
8 BL Add. MS 42071, fos. 3–6

CHAPTER FIVE

For the description of Naples in 1786, Cornelia Knight's *Autobiography*, vol. i, C. M. Dupaty's *Lettres sur l'Italie* and J. W. Goethe's *Italian Journey* are of value. Samuel Sharp's *Letters from Italy*, and Henry Swinburne's *Travels in the Two Sicilies* are lively reading. W. Tischbein's *Aus Meinem Leben*, p. 100 f., Dr Burney's *Music, Men and Manners*, and Francis Garden's *Travelling Memorandums*, vol. iii, p. 97 give details of Sir William's residence.

1 Moore, vol. ii, p. 111
2 Galante, p. 383
3 *Catalogue of . . . Sir W. Hamilton KT*, Christie's
4 Anson (eds), pp. 305–6, 30/5/86
5 HMC 24: Rutland MSS, vol. 3, p. 311
6 BL Add. MS 34048, fo. 30, 4/7/86
7 BL Add. MS 41, 198, fo. 134 ff., 20/11/86

CHAPTER SIX

For Emma's correspondence with Sir William in the winter of 1786–7, see Alfred Morrison's *Autograph Letters . . . The Hamilton and Nelson Papers*, vol. i, pp. 122 ff. For the Coltellini sisters' musical circle, see S. Di Giacomo's *Aneddoti di . . . Ferrari*.

1 BL Add. MS 40, 714, fo. 195, 19/4/81
2 Ilchester (ed.), vol. i, p. 219
3 Kelly, vol. i, p. 54
4 Anon., *Memoirs*, p. 395
5 Toso Rodinis, p. 76

CHAPTER SEVEN

Goethe's encounters with Emma appear in *Italian Journey*, pp. 315 ff., and see the entire section on Naples, pp. 179–329.

1 Biddulph, pp. 53, 59
2 Gerning, vol. i, p. 291
3 Seroff, p. 42, citing André Levinson in *Dance Magazine*, June 1919
4 BL Add. MS 34048, fo. 42, 30/10/87
5 Anson (eds), pp. 307–8, 7/2/88
6 Graham, p. 231
7 BL Add. MS 34048, fos 50–2, 2/6/89

CHAPTER EIGHT

For a description of the Hamilton ménage at this date, we have Mme Vigée-Le Brun's *Souvenirs*, vol. i, pp. 193 ff. Present in Naples also was Lady Craven, later Margravine of Anspach: her plagiaristic memoirs are to be found in the bibliography.

1 BL Egerton MS 2641, fo. 140, 12/11/87
2 BL Add. MS 34048, fo. 59, 20/10/89
3 Düntzer and Herder (eds), pp. 259 ff.
4 BL Add. MS 34048, fo. 61, 6/4/90
5 Anson (eds), pp. 306–7
6 Angelo, vol. ii, p. 243
7 d'Espinchal, pp. 88–9
8 Burney, p. 103
9 *Catalogue of . . . Sir W. Hamilton KT*, Christie's
10 Morrison, vol. i, p. 151, M 189, 1/91
11 BL Spencer Papers, file 105, 17/8/91

CHAPTER NINE

Elizabeth and Florence Anson's *Mary Hamilton*, pp. 308 ff., William Hayley's *Life of George Romney*, pp. 158 ff., and Dorothy M. Stuart's *Dearest Bess*, p. 59, are the chief sources for Sir William's and Emma's junketings in England.

1 Solari, vol. i, p. 50
2 BL Spencer Papers, file 113, 27/7/91 and 23, 24/8/91
3 Paget-Toynbee (ed.), vol. xv, pp. 40–41, 17/8/91; vol. xv, p. 46, 23/8/91
4 Williams, p. 103; Layard, p. 29
5 BL Add. MS 30805, fo. 51

CHAPTER TEN

Lord Palmerston's account of the Hamiltons' Parisian honeymoon and his wife's subsequent remarks on Emma occur in Brian Connell's *Portrait of a Whig Peer*, pp. 248–56, 276–8. Sir William's letters to Emma Lady Hamilton occur in *The Letters of Lord Nelson to Lady Hamilton*, vol. ii, pp. 132–79. For English observers of the Neapolitan scene we have Lady Elliot in the Countess of Minto, *Life and Letters*, vol. ii, pp. 400 ff; Lady Elizabeth Foster in Dorothy M. Stuart, *Dearest Bess*, pp. 32 ff; the Duchess of Devonshire in Iris Leveson-Gower, *The Face Without a Frown*, pp. 190 ff; and Lady Webster in the Earl of Ilchester, *The Journal of Elizabeth Lady Holland*, vol. i, pp. 16 ff.

1 Manners and Williamson, pp. 161, 197
2 Anson (eds), pp. 316–18
3 M. C. Nicoullaud, Comtesse de Boigne, vol. i, pp. 83–6
4 Palumbo (ed.), p. 147

CHAPTER ELEVEN

Sir Nicholas Harris Nicolas' *Dispatches . . . of Lord Viscount Nelson*, vol. i, now comes into play. Raffaele Palumbo's *Maria Carolina*, pp. 148 ff., is the chief source for Emma's developing friendship with the Queen.

1 Harrison, vol. i, pp. 108–9
2 Connell, pp. 398 ff.
3 Minto, vol. ii, p. 191, 24/11/93 and ii, p. 206, 20/12/93
4 BL Spencer Papers, file 113, 6/11/94

CHAPTER TWELVE

Two English girls chronicle events at Naples in Anne Fremantle's *The Wynne Diaries*, vol. ii, pp. 148 ff. Umberto Caldora's *Diario di Ferdinando IV*, pp. 247 ff., offers the King of Naples' private view of the English. Cornelia Knight's *Autobiography*, vol. i, pp. 106–10, details the dramatic turn of events in 1798. With this chapter, on 1 January 1798, we broach Alfred Morrison's *Autograph Letters . . . The Hamilton and Nelson Papers*, vol. ii.

1 Marinoin (ed.), pp. 268–9, 18/12/95 and p. 281, 14/2/96

2 Minto, vol. ii, pp. 364 and 366, 12/96
3 Gerning, vol. i, pp. 290–5
4 Ilchester (ed.), vol. i, pp. 242 ff.
5 Anon., *Memoirs*, p. 166
6 Eliott-Drake (ed.), p. 180
7 HMC 30: Fortescue (Grenville) MSS, vol. 4, pp. 237–9

CHAPTER THIRTEEN

Sir Nicholas Harris Nicolas' *Dispatches . . . of Lord Viscount Nelson*, vol. iii, with G. B. P. Naish's *Nelson's Letters to his Wife*, offer a wealth of information. Umberto Caldora's *Diario di Ferdinando IV*, pp. 382 ff. and Raffaele Palumbo's *Maria Carolina*, pp. 176 ff., give insight into the royal machinations.

1 Hoste, vol. i, pp. 105 ff.
2 Hoste, vol. i, pp. 96 ff.; account by E. Poussielgue, 3/9/98
3 Cornelia Knight, vol. i, pp. 112–13
4 BL Add. MS 34989, fo. 4, 8/9/98
5 *Catalogue of the . . . Calvin Bullock Collection*, Christie's, p. 95
6 Eyre-Matcham, p. 144
7 BL Add. MS 34989, fo. 8 (falsely dated 2/10/98 for 2/12/98)
8 BL Egerton MS 1616, fo. 92

CHAPTER FOURTEEN

H. C. Gutteridge's *Nelson and the Neapolitan Jacobins* provides relevant documents for the events of 1799. Harold Acton's *The Bourbons of Naples* weaves the disparate strands into a coherent narrative. Umberto Caldora's *Diario di Ferdinando IV*, with Carlo de Nicola's *Diario napoletano*, and Sir Nicholas Harris Nicolas' *Dispatches . . . of Lord Viscount Nelson*, vol. iii, are important sources. For the English enmities in Palermo, we have the Duchess of Sermoneta's *The Locks of Norbury*, pp. 164 ff., and Major Pryse Lockhart Gordon's *Personal Memoirs*, vol. i, pp. 208 ff.

1 Weil and Somma Circello (eds), vol. ii, p. 19, letter 308, 27/12/98
2 Cornelia Knight, vol. i, p. 132
3 Weil and Somma Circello (eds), vol. ii, p. 19, letter 312, 12/1/99
4 Pettigrew, vol. i, p. 220, 10/4/99
5 Harcourt (ed.), vol. i, pp. 229–30

6 Palumbo (ed.), p. 198, 2/7/99
7 NMM, Girdlestone Collection 3a
8 Naish, p. 487, 4/8/99

CHAPTER FIFTEEN

Hostility to Emma in the Duchess of Sermoneta's *The Locks of Norbury*,
pp. 190 ff., is supplemented by Lt.-Col. N.H. Grant's *The Letters of
Mary . . . Countess of Elgin*, pp. 17–25 and Sir Augustus Paget's *The Paget
Papers*, vol. i, pp. 169–269. Sir Nicholas Harris Nicolas' *Dispatches . . .
of Lord Viscount Nelson*, vol. iv, is now the relevant source for Nelson's
correspondence.

 1 BL Add. MS 34048, fo. 95, 13/9/99
 2 Pettigrew, vol. i, p. 198
 3 BL Add. MS 34048, fo. 95
 4 Mahan, vol. i, p. 398
 5 Cornelia Knight, vol. ii, p. 286
 6 Minto, vol. iii, p. 114, 23/3/1800
 7 Eyre-Matcham, p. 174
 8 BL Egerton MS 2640, fo. 386, fo. 398, 15/4/1800, 8/6/1800
 9 Cornelia Knight, vol. i, p. 147
10 *The Letters of Lord Nelson to Lady Hamilton*, vol. i, pp. 270–1,
    25/2/01
11 Cornelia Knight, vol. i, p. 148

CHAPTER SIXTEEN

Cornelia Knight's *Autobiography*, vol. i, pp. 153 ff., gives us details of the
Grand Return to England. O. E. Deutsch's 'Nelson and the Hamiltons
in Austria and Hungary', unpublished in England, has been of great
use. H.C. Robbins Landon's *Haydn*, vol. iv, pp. 560–2, 'The Years
of "The Creation"', is illuminating. Sir Gilbert and Lady Elliot's, and
Hugh Elliot's, reactions to the Hamilton party are to be found in Minto,
Life and Letters, vol. iii, pp. 139 ff., and R. Chevenix Trench's *Remains*,
pp. 105–112.

 1 Vendôme, vol. i, pp. 18–47
 2 Harrison, vol. ii, pp. 245–66
 3 Burney, p. 184
 4 Sir Augustus Paget (ed.), vol. i, p. 269, 29/8/1800

5 Malmesbury (ed.), vol. ii, pp. 222 ff.
6 Palumbo (ed.), p. 214, 23/9/1800

CHAPTER SEVENTEEN

For this complicated period, the chief sources are *The Letters of Lord Nelson to Lady Hamilton*, G. P. B. Naish's *Nelson's Letters to his Wife*, pp. 572–87, and Mary Eyre-Matcham's *The Nelsons of Burnham Thorpe*. Also relevant are James Harrison's *The Life of . . . Nelson*, vol. ii, pp. 270 ff., and Elizabeth and Florence Anson's *Mary Hamilton*, pp. 325 ff.

1 Cornelia Knight, vol. i, p. 158
2 Edgcumbe, vol. i, pp. 78–9
3 Redding, vol. iii, p. 99
4 *Gentleman's Magazine*, April 1801
5 Scarisbrick, pp. 19–25
6 BL Add. MS 34989, fo. 37, 20/2/01
7 Naish, pp. 618–19
8 NMM, Nelson-Ward Collection 29
9 *Catalogue of the . . . Calvin Bullock Collection*, Christie's, p. 97, 10/3/01
10 Wraxall, vol. i, pp. 229–31
11 BL Add. MS 34989, fo. 51
12 Minto, vol. iii, p. 242, 22/3/02
13 Morrison, vol. ii, p. 182, M 651, 24/1/02
14 Henry E. Huntingdon Library, San Marino, California, HM 21718, HM 21719, 2/2/02, 29/4/02
15 *Catalogue of the . . . Calvin Bullock Collection*, Christie's, p. 104, 6/4/03

CHAPTER EIGHTEEN

The chief sources are generally as cited for Chapter Seventeen, with the Countess of Minto's *Life*, vol. iii, and Lady Bessborough's letters in Castilia Countess Granville's *Lord Granville Leveson-Gower*, vol. ii, replacing Elizabeth and Florence Anson's *Mary Hamilton* as commentary. The *Catalogue of the Sale of the Calvin Bullock Collection* at Christie's contains fascinating letters of the Nelson circle.

1 Sichel (1905), p. 524, 12/4/03
2 Vigée-Le Brun, vol. i, p. 198

3 Gordon, vol. i, p. 247
4 d'Avigdor Goldsmid Papers
5 Harcourt (ed.), 4/11/??, pp. 240–1
6 Pettigrew, vol. ii, pp. 596–7
7 NMM, Phillipps/Croker Collection 22, fo. 78
8 Anon., *Memoirs*, p. 335
9 Greig, vol. ii, p. 275
10 Dawson, p. 211, 20/8/05
11 Edgcumbe, vol. i, p. 79
12 Emden, p. 236
13 Warner, p. 23
14 Stuart, p. 129
15 Letter of 14/9/1805 to J. D. Thomson; quoted in Sichel (1905), p. 507

CHAPTER NINETEEN

W. Beatty's *Authentic narrative*, pp. 22–52, is the source for the account of Nelson's death. For Emma's distress we have Lady Elizabeth Foster's account in Dorothy M. Stuart's *Dearest Bess*, pp. 127 ff. Rev. Leveson Vernon Harcourt's *The Diaries . . . of George Rose*, vol. i, pp. 246 ff. and M. and A. Gatty's *Recollections of . . . A.J. Scott*, pp. 209 ff., detail the fate of the Last Codicil; Mary Eyre-Matcham's *The Nelsons of Burnham Thorpe*, pp. 244 ff., is relevant to the years after Nelson's death.

1 *The Letters of Lord Nelson to Lady Hamilton*, vol. ii, p. 96, 17/9/05
2 Vigée-Le Brun, vol. i, p. 198
3 Granville (ed.), vol. ii, pp. 131–3
4 Hoste, vol. i, p. 257, 27/11/05
5 Warner, pp. 28–9
6 Gérin, p. 111
7 Anon., *Memoirs*, p. 382
8 National Trust Uppark Papers, 1806
9 Harrison, vol. ii, p. 382

CHAPTER TWENTY

Alfred Morrison's *Autograph Letters . . . The Hamilton and Nelson Papers*, vol. ii, feature here as ever. The American tourist Louis Simond describes the London scene, pp. 136 ff. Rev. Leveson Vernon Harcourt's *The*

Diaries . . . of George Rose, vol. ii, pp. 265–73, tell of Emma's fruitless petitions to the Government. The Parliamentary Select Committee's *Report On the King's Bench, Fleet, and Marshalsea Prisons* (1814–15), vol. iv, pp. 533 ff., makes sober reading.

1 Gordon, vol. ii, pp. 388–90
2 Kelly, vol. ii, p. 318
3 Hardwick, p. 257, n. 1
4 Transcripts in the possession of Mollie Hardwick
5 W. H. Pyne and W. Combe (eds), *The Microcosm of London* (London, 1808–11), 3 vols, vol. ii, p. 161
6 Morrison, vol. ii, p. 365, M 1047
7 Tours, p. 253
8 NMM, Bridport Papers 4A
9 Bury, vol. i, pp. 31–2
10 Sotheby's Catalogue for 8/7/1905. Letter of 12/9/14.
11 NMM, Nelson-Ward Collection 34, referring to Mr Paget's letter of 11/11/74
12 *Gentleman's Magazine*, March 1815
13 Calton, p. 88

POSTSCRIPT

Winifred Gérin's *Horatia Nelson* is illuminating regarding the fortunes of Nelson's and Lady Hamilton's fame and reputations.

1 Morrison, vol. ii, pp. 372–3, M 1066, 8/2/15
2 *Morning Post*, 26 January 1815
3 Pettigrew, vol. ii, p. 636
4 Eyre-Matcham, pp. 278 ff.
5 NMM, Trafalgar House Collection 22, 1/5/16
6 NMM, Nelson-Ward Collection 34, 21/8/46
7 White and Moorhouse, p. 295

Index